THE
FRENCH CHEF
COOKBOOK

THE

FRENCH CHEF

COOKBOOK

30th Anniversary Edition

Julia Child

Drawings and photographs by Paul Child

Ballantine Books . New York

A Ballantine Book
Published by The Ballantine Publishing Group

Many of the recipes were taken form or were based on *Mastering the Art of French Cooking,* Volume One, and are printed with the permission of Alfred A. Knopf, Inc., and of my colleagues, Simone Beck and Louisette Bertholle. Many other recipes, techniques, and culinary ideas have been inspired by Simone Beck, and are freely used with her permission. —J.C.

http://www.randomhouse.com

Library of Congress Catalog Card Number: 98-96078

ISBN: 0-345-42542-1

This edition published by arrangement with Alfred A. Knopf, Inc.

Manufactured in the United States of America

Cover photo by James Scherer
Cover design by Kathleen Lynch

First Ballantine Books Mass Market Edition: August 1994
First Ballantine Books Trade Paperback Edition: May 1998
10 9 8 7 6 5 4 3 2 1

TO

WGBH-TV-Channel-2-Boston

AND TO

The Twenty-four Members
of "The French Chef" Television Team

Introduction

I am delighted that we are reissuing this little book, which accompanied our first "The French Chef" television series. Program Number One aired here in Boston on February 11, 1963, in the days of black-and-white TV.

The Kennedys were in the White House then with their fine French chef, René Verdon, and since their every move was news, so were their splendid French meals. The Kennedy factor plus the ability to reach Europe in a few hours by air (rather than almost a week by sea) combined to awaken American palates to the pleasures of the table. However, European cuisine, especially French, was considered so complicated and refined that it was quite beyond the capabilities of ordinary American cooks.

Yet Americans returning from abroad were anxious to eat the French way, and during 1960s there was more time to cook at home since usually only one family member worked. This was the culinary climate when "The French Chef" appeared on television. My first book, *Mastering the Art of French Cooking*, had been published in 1961, and the TV series, which borrowed from it, was designed to be a primer teaching the basics of French classical cuisine through a series of recipes, such as Coq au Vin, Beef Bourguignon, French Onion Soup, and so forth.

During those halcyon years of the sixties the solemn subject of nutrition had not raised its head, and the recipes in this book represent that happy guilt-free era. I have not changed them at all. I leave it up to you to edit them yourself as you go along. When a particular preparation calls for a big dollop of hollandaise sauce, for instance, you might use just a spoonful, or when you are directed to beat 1 cup of heavy cream into a fish mouse, use less. However, you don't want to destroy the beauty of the dish. Far better to make it as directed at first, then eat just a spoonful, so that you will know how it is supposed to taste. Certainly one of the best ways to good health is to follow a well-balanced diet and the motto of the American Institute of Wine and Food:

Moderation
Small helpings
A great variety of food
No snacking
Weight watching and sensible exercise
Above all—HAVE A GOOD TIME

Good'French cooking is careful cooking, and a question of techniques. This book endeavors to give you the essentials, from learning how to fry an egg or making salad dressing to poaching a whole salmon and constructing a Christmas bûche decorated with meringue mushrooms. Besides giving you a full index at the back of the book, the front pages give a list of the shows by title, and of recipes in categories such as *chicken, sauces and soups, desserts,* and so forth. I think you will find it a fine introduction to French cooking and hope you will make many satisfying meals from it.

Bon appétit!

Julia Child
Cambridge, Massachusetts

About This Book

This book grew out of the educational television series "The French Chef," which was designed to cover as much as possible of French cooking in several seasons of weekly half-hour programs. It ranges from sauces, stews, and meats to appetizers, vegetables, desserts, cakes and pastries, and from the very simple to the fairly complicated. The book represents 119 programs, the complete television series as it then existed, and the recipes are printed in the order that the shows were produced. Although about one half were taken from *Mastering the Art of French Cooking*, some of the television recipes differ slightly from the book recipes: there is more than one good way of skinning a duck or cooking a *ragoût*, and occasionally our TV time-limitations forced me to eliminate a frill or two. The rest of the recipes have evolved from studies for Volume II of *Mastering the Art of French Cooking*, and as I had to cook each dish six, eight, ten, or more times to test or to precook it for my half-hour program, television has provided an invaluable opportunity for me to prove them out to my satisfaction.

You will wonder why this book begins with the fourteenth show. This is because the first thirteen shows no longer exist. When we started, "The French Chef" was purely a local New England program, and before WGBH-TV realized duplicates were needed to serve other educational stations throughout the country the first thirteen tapes had worn out, and I am glad of it. Although they did possess some of the unpredictable quality of a contemporary happening, their demise allowed us to do over all but one of those recipes later on when we were more expert. Number 36 is missing, an unsatisfactory *bûche* later redone as Number 73; Number 37 was a local New Year's show which has disappeared from view, and for some technical television reason Number 82 has become Number 134.

Although the book is arranged according to the sequence of

the television programs, it can be used like any book. In addition to the alphabetical index at the back, you can consult the subject guide at the front, where recipes are broken down into those familiar categories of soups, sauces, meats, and on to desserts.

About the Television Series

"How in the world did you ever manage to get on television?" is a question frequently asked me. It was purely by accident. My husband, Paul, had resigned from the diplomatic service in 1961, after almost twenty years. We had settled in our great gray pre-Victorian house in Cambridge with its comfortable kitchen, and *Mastering the Art of French Cooking* had just been published. He was planning to write, paint, and photograph; I was to cook, write, and teach. We had even bought ourselves a budget television set, which was so ugly we hid it in an unused fireplace.

One evening a friend we had known in Paris, Beatrice Braude, who was then working at Boston's educational television station, WGBH-TV, suggested it would be a useful push for *Mastering* if I could appear on one of the station's book-review programs. Always happy to do anything for the book, I agreed that it might well be worth thinking about. She persuaded the station and the interview took place with a bit of conversation about food and France, and at one point I beat some egg whites in a large French copper bowl to enliven the talk. The program brought numerous requests for some kind of a cooking program, and WGBH-TV asked me if I would be willing to try three pilots, or experimental half-hour shows, to see whether there might be a real cooking audience out there over the air waves. Paul and I accepted the challenge, although we knew nothing at all about television and had hardly watched a program.

The studio assigned Russell Morash, producer of "Science Reporter," as Producer-Director. Assistant Producer was Ruth Lockwood, who had been working on the Eleanor Roosevelt shows. Because Channel 2's studio had burned almost to the ground a few months before, The Boston Gas Company loaned us its display kitchen. The budget was minute.

Ruth, Paul, and I blocked out a rough sequence of events for three programs: French omelettes, *coq au vin*, and a noncollapsible soufflé, which provided a varied and not-too-complicated sampling of French cooking. After thinking up dozens of titles for the show, we could find nothing better than "The French Chef"; it was short and told a story. Ruth dug around somewhere and came up with the anonymous but spritely musical theme song we are still using. As our own kitchen had enough equipment to furnish a small restaurant, there were no problems in that quarter.

It was out of the question for us to film a live show since we had only two cameras attached by long cables to a mobile bus. Besides, with an absolutely amateur performer, it would have been far too risky. We decided, however, that it would be taped as though it were live. Unless the sky fell in, the cameras failed, or the lights went off, there would be no stops, and no corrections—just a straight thirty minutes from start to finish. This was a good fundamental decision, I think. I hate to stop. I lose that sense of drama and excitement which the uninterrupted thirty-minute limitation imposes. Besides, I would far prefer to have things happen as they naturally do, such as the mousse refusing to leave the mold, the potatoes sticking to the skillet, the apple charlotte slowly collapsing. One of the secrets of cooking is to learn to correct something if you can, and bear with it if you cannot.

The day in June for our first taping, "The French Omelette," Paul and I packed our station wagon with pots, pans, eggs, and trimmings and were off to the Gas Company. Parking was difficult in downtown Boston, so he off-loaded inside the main entrance, and I stood over our mound until he returned. How were the two of us to get everything down to the basement of that imposing office building? There was nobody to help, as we were hours ahead of our WGBH camera crew. Office girls and business-suited executives looked disapprovingly at our household pile as they rushed in and out. A uniformed elevator operator said, "Hey, get that stuff out of this lobby!" Eventually Paul located a janitor with a rolling cart and we clanked down to the basement where we unpacked, setting up our wares according to the master plan we had worked out.

Ruth arrived shortly to arrange a dining room setup for the final scene, and to go over our sequence of events. Then came Russ and our camera crew. After a short rehearsal to check lighting and camera angles, Russ said, "Let's shoot it!" And we did. Within the next week, following the same informal system, we taped the other two shows. I still have my notes. There is the map of the free-standing stove and work counter: "Simmering water in large alum. pan, upper R. burner." "Wet sponge left top drawer." "6 eggs in nest of 3 alum. plates w. ramekin." Paul, who was acting as invisible helper, had made himself a sheet of instructions: "When J. starts buttering, remove stack molds." "When soufflé is cheesed, take black saucepan."

On July 26, 1962, after we all had eaten a big steak dinner at our house, we pulled the television set out of hiding and turned it on at 8:30. There was this woman tossing French omelettes, splashing eggs about the place, brandishing big knives, panting heavily as she careened around the stove, and WGBH-TV lurched into educational television's first cooking program. Response to the three shows indicated that there was indeed an audience in New England, Channel 2 suggested we try a series of twenty-six programs, and "The French Chef" was underway. We were to start taping in January, and the first show would be on the air February 11, 1963.

What to pack into each of those thirty minutes? If we showed dishes that were too complicated, we would scare off all but a handful of people. Yet if we remained in the kindergarten, we would soon be a bore. Ruth, Paul, and I decided to start out with a few audience catchers, dishes that were famous, like *boeuf bourguignon*, but easy to make, and then gradually work into the subject. We also wanted to vary the weekly menu and take time to show French techniques, such as how to wield the knife, bone the lamb, clean the leek, whip and fold the egg whites. The idea was to take the bugaboo out of French cooking, to demonstrate that it is not merely good cooking but that it follows definite rules. The simplicity of a *velouté* sauce, for instance, is butter, flour, and seasoned liquid, but the rule is that the flour is cooked in the butter before the liquid is added. Why? (I, myself, will not do anything unless I know why.) "If you don't cook the flour in the butter, your sauce will have the horrid pasty taste of uncooked flour"—I have certainly given tongue to that one a hundred times. Finally we agreed on our program of twenty-six shows, starting with *"Boeuf Bourguignon"* and "French Onion Soup," ending with "Lobster *à l'Américaine"* and *"Crêpes Suzette."*

In January when we started taping four shows a week, WGBH-TV still had no studio. The shows, like the three pilots, would have to be done where the mobile bus could park and string out cables to its two cameras. Fortunately for us, the Cambridge Electric Company offered their display kitchen located in a large loft room, with ample parking space nearby. We could reach it by a front stairway, by a freight elevator from two floors below, or by an outside iron fire escape that descended into the parking lot. Though our lighting arrangements were makeshift and the sound track was likely to mingle with the roar of the freight elevator, the cooking facilities were fine. The ceiling was high enough for us to hang a mirror over the stove that the camera could peer into when it needed the inside view of a pot. Best of all, we had the whole place to ourselves.

Although we were now an actual and official enterprise, our budget remained small. Paul and I did all the shopping and pre-cooking, and he continued to act as porter and unpacker, as well as chief dishwasher, until we got some volunteer cleaner-uppers for the taping days. Tuesdays and Thursdays were the long cooking rehearsals for the two shows scheduled the following days. Nobody at WGBH had the slightest idea what we were cooking in our loft until the cameras were lugged up the outside fire escape at 10 o'clock on Wednesdays and Fridays, to begin the tapings. We depended on Paul for advice when we were doubtful, and Russ for great openings and closings as well as all the techniques of camera and direction. Otherwise, Ruth Lockwood and I had complete freedom to work up anything we wished and to present it in any manner we chose.

The general pattern of the first three pilot shows seemed to fit my style, so we continued it, perfecting details as we went along. I found I had no sense of timing whatsoever, 1 minute or 5 minutes meant nothing to me as sadly illustrated by our second show and first try at "Onion Soup." I had to show the proper professional way to slice onions fast, the first cooking to soften them, the second cooking to brown them, the several ways to serve the soup; then there was *croûton*-making and gratinéing. I rushed through that program like a madwoman but I got everything in, only to find that when I carried the onion soup to the dining room I had gone so fast we still had 8 minutes left. Agony. I had to sit there and talk for all that time. Russ erased the tape back to about the 15-minute point, but after it happened again, Ruth devised the plan of breaking up the recipe into blocks of time. I could go as fast or slow as I wanted in the allotted time block, but I could not go into the next step until I got the signal.

Signals to the performer are written on placards known as "idiot cards." They are handed to the floor manager, who, by earphones, is plugged into one of the television cameras so he can hear and talk to the director who is shut away in the control room. The floor manager holds the idiot card just under the camera lens, and the performer appears to be gazing right into your eyes but is really reading that message: "Turn on burner number three!" In our case, the floor manager has a big loose-leaf book, and flips the pages according to a time schedule carefully worked out on a stop watch by Ruth. For the onion soup we were very simple: "The Knife & 1st Cook 5 min," "Browning and Simmering 4 min," "Soup in Bowls 2 min," and so forth. Later we became more elaborate, and put key words onto the idiot cards so I would not forget important points. I remember when we did *brioches*, we opened with a shot of three of them: the great big grandfather *brioche*, the middle-sized mother *brioche*, and the little baby *brioche*; we had obviously fallen into the story of Goldilocks and the Three Brioches. The idiot cards read like an Indian massacre—"This Baby; Remove head," "Punch Grandpa," "Slash Mother," "30 sec. Before Wash Hands." Often I am faced with Ruth's helpful reminders: "Stop gasping," "Wipe face," "Don't gallop."

The nonstop taping we have always continued, and in only a few instances, after the disaster of the first onion soup show, have we had to break off, erase, and pick up again. I can remember only half a dozen occasions, some of which were due to electrical failures, others due to me. Once, doing the "Lobster à l'Américaine," every time I touched the cooktop I got a short-circuit in the microphone against my chest, and kept clutching my breast in a very odd fashion. It felt like a bee sting. We wiped out back to the worst clutch, and were able to continue in midstream. Another time, "The Flaming Soufflé" collapsed in its dish on the way to the dining room; I had forgotten to put in the cornstarch. We merely waited for the standby soufflé to come out of the oven and used that. Otherwise we let the gaffes lie where they fell, and on the whole it is just as well.

About halfway through, at the "Beef Gets Stewed Two Ways" show, WGBH-TV moved into its fine new building and we had a beautiful set with the most modern lighting, sound, and equipment. Wonderful as it is, we miss our old loft. It had an intimate atmosphere. We were a happy and independent family of twenty-four, we could eat up all the food ourselves, and even throw a party on occasion. But we could never have done color television there. In the new series, there are no more gray strawberries, pale and sickly veal, livid lettuce or pallid pickles. Even the tongue is utterly lifelike as it licks the *mousse au chocolat* off the spoon, and "The French Chef" has a new dimension.

Acknowledgments

To those unscreened wonders who kept the pots boiling:

The WGBH-TV Crew, whose cheerful appetites for hard work and French food never wavered.

Our Volunteer Cleaner-uppers, Bess Begien, Liz Bishop, Catherine Copeland, Bess Hopkins, and Mary O'Brien, and to our Volunteer Office Managers, Gladys Christopherson, Pat Crawford, Amey De Friez, Helen Richmond, and Edith Seltzer, steady, capable, and invaluable partners.

Design Research Associates of Cambridge, who loaned us furniture, dishes, linens, and all manner of decorative pots and baubles for our first sixty-six programs.

The Cambridge Electric Company, whose friendly loft gave birth to those first programs, whose skilled mechanics repeatedly unplugged the bouillabaisse remains from three floors of drainpipe, and all of whose people were kindly and helpful, from the cozy telephonists to the executives.

Francis Mahard, who designed and built our beautiful new kitchen.

The Boston Edison Company, who, with the Boyd Corporation, Frigidaire Sales Corporation, and Gray Sales, equipped our new studio with every conceivable electrical kitchen marvel.

S&H Green Stamps, whose initial donation enabled WGBH-TV to produce our first thirteen shows, and Sentry Stores, whose contribution brought us to Milwaukee.

Safeway Stores, Hills Brothers Coffee, Inc., and the Polaroid Corporation, whose generous public service grants to WGBH-TV made it possible for us to continue.

Russell Morash, our original producer-director, who gave "The French Chef" its visual techniques and so much of its inspiration, and David Griffiths, who ably continued as director.

Ruth Lockwood, my alter ego and producer, who worked

tirelessly in the designing and staging of the programs, whose talent for turning a recipe into a drama is unique, and whose diplomatic and steady friendship have been basic to the whole enterprise.

Paul Child, the man who is always there: porter, dishwasher, official photographer, mushroom dicer and onion chopper, editor, fish illustrator, manager, taster, idea man, resident poet, and husband.

My love and thanks to you all, and

TOUJOURS BON APPÉTIT!

J. C.

Contents

Subject Guide

The numbers following each entry indicate the
television shows, followed (in parentheses)
by page references.

I

SAUCES AND SOUPS

II
ENTRÉES, APPETIZERS, EGGS,
ALL SOUFFLÉS

III
LES PÂTES
(DOUGHS AND PASTRIES)

IV

FISH

AND SHELLFISH

V

POULTRY AND GAME

VIII

VEGETABLES

XI

DESSERTS AND SWEET SAUCES

XII
CAKES, FROSTINGS AND FILLINGS, COOKIES

XIII
DINNERS IN HALF AN HOUR

XIV
MISCELLANEOUS INFORMATION

Notes on Wine

WINES TO USE IN COOKING

The only reason for using wine in cooking is because of its natural flavor. The alcohol in the wine is supposed to evaporate, and does, almost the moment the wine goes into a hot dish. If the wine is thin, or sour, or sweet, or sickly, these unpleasant qualities will only be exaggerated as its flavor concentrates during the cooking process. Therefore any wine you use for cooking should be a good one. This does not mean it has to be an expensive vintage bottle; it simply means that it must be healthy, full of natural flavor, usually young, and tastes the way a proper wine should. You will have to search around and experiment yourself to find the right cooking wines at the right price; here are some suggestions for the types to look for.

RED WINES. Red wine for cooking should be dry, full-bodied, and young. French Mâcon is ideal in France but expensive when imported. Domestic alternatives are California Mountain Red, Pinot Noir, Cabernet, and many of the Chiantis.

WHITE WINES. White wine for cooking should be dry but full-bodied; it presents more of a problem than red wine because those white wines that are reasonably priced are often too thin or too sour. Again, French white Mâcon is ideal but expensive. Domestic choices are among the White Pinots and Sauvignons. An excellent substitute is very dry white vermouth; because it is always available and is always far better than the wrong white wine, I usually specify it.

BRANDIES, LIQUEURS, PORT, MADEIRA, AND SHERRY. As with red and white wines, these must be of top quality, and although they are always expensive, most recipes call for only a few tablespoons. Ports and Madeiras should be dry. There is no standardized nomenclature for dry port, but the label will usually give some printed indication. Dry Madeira is always labeled "Sercial." Sherry is not used to any extent in French cooking, but you can use the dry sherry, "Fino," if you have run out of port or Madeira.

COOKING WITHOUT WINE

There is no substitute for the flavor of wine, but if you prefer wineless cooking, simply omit it whenever it appears in a recipe. If you need added liquid to replace the wine, use beef or chicken bouillon or fish stock for main dishes, and usually orange juice or cider for desserts.

WINES TO ACCOMPANY A MEAL

When you are just starting to think about wine as a part of the menu, what to serve with what often looms as a problem. Simple, inexpensive wines and informal foods present no difficulties: red wine with meat, white with fish, *rosé* with anything. But in the two-dollar-a-bottle class a disappointment really hurts; you hate to spend your money, and then find that the wine you bought and the food you cooked just don't hit it off together.

As an example, you might have decided to celebrate and have wine with your luscious, creamy, sugary masterpiece of a dessert. So you buy a rather expensive, highly recommended, fashionably dry champagne. What happens? The dessert is so sweet that the champagne tastes thin, sour, and you decide you don't like champagne very much after all. But had anyone helped you out by telling you to buy the *demi-sec* or semisweet champagne, or an Asti Spumanti or a sparkling Vouvray, or a Sauternes or a Barsac, you would have been absolutely delighted with the results. The sweetness of the wine would have matched the dessert.

In much the same way, with a beautiful dish of fillets of sole in a rich, white-wine sauce, a light, dry Riesling tastes thin and sour; wine with more body, such as a white Burgundy, a Graves, or a Rhône is needed. Or you may choose such a strong-flavored

red wine for a chicken in tarragon sauce that all the art you put into the dish is blotted out by that big red.

On the other hand, what delight there is in the perfect combination: the cold lobster and the chilled *rosé*; the strong cheese and the full-bodied Burgundy; the roast chicken and the mellow red Bordeaux.

The simplest way to start in on this pleasant hobby is to buy wines, start sampling, discussing, keeping notes, reading about wines, thinking about them, and enjoying them. Most good wine shops have brochures giving general rules, descriptions, and vintage charts, and there are loads of books on the subject. Always keep in mind, though, the simple concept that the food must bring out the taste of the wine, and the wine should accentuate all the subtle flavors of the food.

Here are a few pointers, if you need them, on what goes with what. When you are serving one wine only, it goes with the main course; when you have two or more at a feast, you start with the lightest wine and end with the heaviest or most full-flavored.

LIGHT, DRY WHITE WINES (serve chilled): Riesling, Sylvaner, many of the less expensive Moselles and Rhines, Muscadet, Sancerre, Pouilly Fumé, Chablis, Pouilly Fuissé. *Serve with:* egg dishes, lean boiled or broiled fish, shellfish, hors d'oeuvre, light cheese dishes.

MEDIUM TO FULL-BODIED DRY WHITE WINES (serve chilled): Pinot, Sauvignon, Traminer, many of the Moselles and Rhines labeled *auslese* and *spätlese*, many of the Graves, and especially the Burgundies. *Serve with:* fish, shellfish, poultry, and veal in cream sauces; *foie gras* and liver *pâtés*; strong cheeses.

LIGHT TO MEDIUM RED WINES (serve at room temperature): Cabernet, Gamay, Beaujolais, Bordeaux, Merlot. *Serve with:* poultry, veal, ham, cold meats, mushrooms, soft cheeses, meat *pâtés*.

FULL-BODIED RED WINES (serve at room temperature): Pinot, Chianti, Burgundy, Châteauneuf-du-Pape, Hermitage. *Serve with:* red meat, red-wine stews, wild game, strong cheeses.

A Note on the Importance
of Flour Measuring

For all the cakes and pastries in this book, be sure to measure your flour exactly as indicated in each recipe. The weight of flour one cup can hold will vary more than an ounce depending on how you get the flour into the cup, whether you sift it in or scoop it in. As the measurements for all the other ingredients in each recipe are based on the weight of the flour, you can throw off the proportions entirely if you do not follow the measuring system indicated for each particular case.

THE
FRENCH CHEF
COOKBOOK

The Fourteenth Show *

CHICKEN BREASTS AND RISOTTO
⋘ · ⋙

The skinless and boneless meat from one side of a chicken breast is called a *suprême*. Never cooked in liquid because that would toughen it, the *suprême* is broiled, sautéed, or simply poached in butter and seasonings in a covered casserole. As *suprêmes* cook in only 6 to 8 minutes and may be served very simply, they make an exquisite quick meal.

PREPARING SUPRÊMES FOR COOKING. Choose whole or half breasts from a 2½- to 3-pound frying chicken. Slip your fingers between skin and flesh, and pull off the skin. Then cut against the ridge of the breastbone or the top of the rib cage to loosen flesh from bone. Cut through the ball joint of the wing where it joins the carcass, and continue down along the rib cage, pulling flesh from bone as you cut until you have freed the meat in one piece. Remove the wing and reserve it for something else. Underneath the *suprême* you will see a small white tendon that runs about two thirds of its length; cut along it for an inch or so, grab the end in a towel, and pull out the tendon against the dull edge of your knife. Trim off any jagged edges and flatten the meat lightly with the side of a heavy knife. The *suprême* is now prepared for cooking; wrap in waxed paper and refrigerate until you are ready. You will need one per serving.

* For the explanation of why this book begins with the Fourteenth Show, see Mrs. Child's introductory note, "About This Book," page vii.

SUPRÊMES DE VOLAILLE A BLANC

(*Chicken Breasts Poached in Butter; with Wine and Cream Sauce*)
For 4 people

COOKING THE CHICKEN BREASTS

4 *suprêmes*	A heavy, covered flameproof
½ tsp lemon juice	casserole about 10 inches
¼ tsp salt	in diameter
Big pinch white pepper	A round of waxed paper cut
4 Tb butter	to fit casserole
	A hot serving dish

(Preheat oven to 400 degrees.)

Rub the *suprêmes* with drops of lemon juice and sprinkle lightly with salt and pepper. Heat butter in casserole until foaming. Quickly roll the *suprêmes* in the butter, lay the paper over them, cover casserole and place in hot oven. After 6 minutes, press tops of *suprêmes* with your finger; if still soft and squashy, return to oven for a minute or two more. They are done when they feel lightly springy and resilient; do not overcook them. Remove the *suprêmes* to hot serving dish; cover and keep warm while making the sauce, which will take 2 to 3 minutes.

WINE AND CREAM SAUCE, AND SERVING

¼ cup white or brown stock	1 cup heavy cream
or canned beef bouillon	Salt, white pepper, and
¼ cup port, Madeira, or dry	lemon juice
white vermouth	2 Tb fresh minced parsley

Pour the stock or bouillon and the wine into the casserole with the cooking butter and boil down rapidly over high heat until liquid is syrupy. Then pour in the cream and boil rapidly until lightly thickened. Season carefully with salt, pepper, and drops of lemon juice. Pour the sauce over the *suprêmes*, sprinkle with parsley, and serve immediately.

VARIATIONS ঽ▸

Suprêmes de Volaille à l'Écossaise
(*Chicken Breasts with Aromatic Vegetables*)

Ingredients for preceding
recipe
1 medium carrot, peeled
1 medium onion, peeled

1 or 2 tender celery stalks
⅛ tsp salt
1 additional Tb butter

Cut the vegetables into neat ¹⁄₁₆-inch dice, making ⅔ to ¾ cup in all. Cook them with the butter and salt for about 10 minutes in the casserole over very low heat until very tender. Then proceed with the recipe for the *suprêmes*, leaving the vegetables in the casserole when you cook the *suprêmes* and when you make the sauce; then pour sauce and vegetables over the *suprêmes*. (*Note*: You can use the same system with sliced or diced mushrooms, cooking them briefly in the casserole with a tablespoon of minced shallots or scallions before adding the *suprêmes*.)

WINE AND VEGETABLE SUGGESTIONS

Serve the *suprêmes* with a chilled white Burgundy, Graves, or Traminer. Vegetable accompaniments could be buttered asparagus tips, peas, artichoke hearts, or spinach, and steamed rice or *risotto*. Here is a recipe for *risotto*.

Risotto
(*Rice Braised in Chicken Stock*)
For 4 people

⅓ cup finely minced onions
2 Tb butter
A heavy 6-cup saucepan or
flameproof casserole
1 cup unwashed raw white
rice

2 cups chicken stock or
broth, heated to boiling
Salt and pepper
A small herb bouquet: 2
parsley sprigs, ⅓ bay
leaf, and ⅛ tsp thyme
tied in washed cheesecloth

Cook the onions slowly in the butter for several minutes until soft and translucent. Add the rice and stir over moderate heat for 3 to 4 minutes until the rice grains, which first turn translucent, become a milky-white. This step cooks the floury rice coating and prevents the grains from sticking together. Then stir in the chicken stock, season lightly with salt and pepper, and add the herb bouquet. Stir briefly until the simmer is reached, then cover tightly and cook at a moderate simmer on the stove or in a preheated 350-degree oven. Regulate heat so that rice has absorbed the liquid in about 18 minutes, but do not stir the rice at all during the cooking. When done, fluff lightly with a fork, adding more salt and pepper if needed. (The *risotto* may be cooked in advance and set aside, uncovered; to reheat, place in a pan of simmering water, cover the rice, and fluff with a fork occasionally until rice is hot through. Do not overcook.)

The Fifteenth Show

VEGETABLES THE FRENCH WAY
⋐ · ⋑
(*Beans, Spinach, Carrots, Mushrooms*)

Anyone who has been fortunate enough to eat fresh home-cooked vegetables in France remembers them with pleasure, with trembling nostalgia: "Those delicious little green beans! They even serve them as a separate course!" There are those who are convinced that it is only in France that one can enjoy such experiences because French vegetables are somehow different. Fortunately this is not the case. Any fine, fresh vegetable in season will taste just as good in America or anywhere else when you use the French vegetable-cooking techniques.

It is in the realm of green-vegetable cookery that these methods differ so radically from traditional American techniques. When you cook green vegetables the French way, you plunge them into a very large kettle full of rapidly boiling water; as soon as they are barely tender, you plunge them into cold water to stop the cooking and to set the fresh green color and texture. Just before serving, you toss them briefly in hot butter and seasonings. If you have never tried cooking green vegetables this way, you will be amazed at how beautiful they look, how fresh and full of flavor they taste, and you will begin to feel like the French, who look upon vegetables not merely as necessary nutrients but as the gastronomical delights they are meant to be.

HARICOTS VERTS AU MAÎTRE D'HÔTEL

(Fresh Green Beans Tossed with Butter, Lemon Juice, and Parsley)
For 6 to 8 people

PRELIMINARY COOKING OR BLANCHING

3 lbs. fresh green beans	3½ Tb salt
A large kettle containing 7 to 8 quarts of rapidly boiling water	

Snap ends off beans. Just before cooking, wash rapidly under hot water. Drop beans into kettle, add salt, and bring rapidly back to the boil. Boil uncovered for 8 minutes, then test a bean by eating it. Beans are done when they are tender but still retain a suggestion of crunchiness. As soon as they are done, place a colander over the kettle and drain the water off the beans. Then run cold water into kettle for several minutes to cool the beans and to set the color and texture. Drain. Set aside until ready to use.

SERVING

A heavy 8- to 10-inch enameled or no-stick saucepan or skillet	3 to 4 Tb butter
	1 tsp lemon juice
Salt and pepper	2 to 3 Tb minced fresh parsley

To serve, toss beans in the saucepan or skillet over moderately high heat to evaporate all their moisture. Then toss with salt, pepper, and the butter until well heated—2 minutes or so. Toss again with a teaspoon of lemon juice and the minced parsley. Serve immediately.

ÉPINARDS AU JUS; ÉPINARDS A LA CRÈME

(*Spinach Braised in Stock or Cream*)
For 6 people

PRELIMINARY COOKING OR BLANCHING

3 lbs. fresh spinach	3½ Tb salt
A large kettle containing 7 to 8 quarts of rapidly boiling water	A stainless-steel chopping knife

Trim and wash the spinach. Drop it into the boiling water a handful at a time, add salt, and boil slowly, uncovered, for 2 to 3 minutes, or until spinach is limp. Drain, run cold water into kettle for a minute or two, drain again. By handfuls, squeeze out as much water from the spinach as possible. Chop. Set aside until ready to use. (Makes about 3 cups.)

SERVING

2 Tb butter	1 cup beef stock, canned beef bouillon, or heavy cream
A heavy-bottomed 8-inch enameled saucepan or skillet	Salt and pepper
1½ Tb sifted flour	1 to 2 Tb softened butter

Melt the butter in the saucepan. When bubbling, add the chopped spinach and stir over moderately high heat for 2 to 3 minutes to evaporate moisture. When the spinach just begins to adhere to bottom of pan, lower heat to moderate and stir in the flour. Cook, stirring, for 2 minutes. Remove from heat and blend in the stock, bouillon, or cream. Season lightly, bring to the simmer, cover, and cook very slowly for 10 to 15 minutes.

Stir frequently to prevent scorching. Correct seasoning, stir in softened butter, and serve.

CAROTTES ÉTUVÉES AU BEURRE

(Carrots Braised in Butter)
For 6 people

5 to 6 cups peeled and sliced or quartered carrots (about 1½ lbs.)	1½ cups water
	1½ Tb butter
	½ tsp salt
A heavy-bottomed 2-quart enameled saucepan	Pinch of pepper
	2 Tb fresh minced parsley
1 Tb granulated sugar	1 to 2 Tb additional butter

Place the carrots in the saucepan with the sugar, water, butter, salt, and pepper. Cover and boil slowly for about 30 minutes, or until the carrots are tender and the liquid has evaporated. Correct seasoning. Just before serving, reheat by tossing with the parsley and additional butter.

CHAMPIGNONS FARCIS

(Stuffed Mushrooms)
For hot hors d'oeuvre or as garnish for meat platter

STUFFING THE MUSHROOMS

12 large mushrooms	½ Tb flour
2 to 3 Tb melted butter	½ cup heavy cream
A shallow baking dish	3 Tb fresh minced parsley
Salt and pepper	Additional salt and pepper
2 Tb minced shallots or scallions	¼ cup grated Swiss cheese
	1 to 2 Tb melted butter
2 Tb butter	

Remove mushroom stems and reserve. Wash and dry the caps, brush with melted butter, and arrange, hollow-side up, in the baking dish. Season lightly with salt and pepper.

Wash and dry the stems and mince. By handfuls, twist in the corner of a towel to extract as much juice as possible. Sauté with the shallots or scallions in butter for 4 or 5 minutes until the pieces begin to separate. Lower heat, add flour, and stir for 1 minute. Stir in cream and simmer for a minute or two, until thickened. Stir in parsley and seasonings. Fill the mushroom caps with this mixture; top each with 1 teaspoon of cheese and dribble on droplets of melted butter. Set aside until ready to finish the cooking.

FINAL COOKING

Fifteen minutes or so before serving, bake in upper third of a preheated 375-degree oven until caps are tender and stuffing has browned lightly on top.

The Sixteenth Show

VEAL SCALLOPS

French veal scallops are boneless slices of meat cut ⅜ inch thick and then flattened to ¼ inch. So that each scallop will constitute a neat, flat serving piece, the meat is cut across the grain from a solid piece of veal which contains no muscle separations. Because scallops cook in less than 10 minutes, you should choose the tenderest veal of the best possible quality or they will be tough.

QUALITY. Train your eye when you are picking out veal. Best prime-quality veal is milk-fed with firm, smooth, fine-grained flesh of a very pale pink color, no deeper than the dark meat of raw broiling chicken. Veal that is dark pink or reddish does not have the flavor or tenderness of pale-colored milk-fed veal. As it is often difficult to find good veal when you want it, pick up any you see in the market and store it in the freezer; veal takes well to freezing.

CUTS TO CHOOSE. In France, because of the French method of cutting the hind leg into lengthwise muscles, scallops are usually taken from the top round or *noix*. This cut gives solid slices of meat with no separations, which cook without curling. You may obtain the same effect if you buy slices of round roast (leg) ⅜ inch thick and then separate each slice into its natural muscle divisions. The largest piece is the top round, which you may wish to cut in half. The bottom round with its eye insert will furnish one or more scallops. Usually another of reasonable size can be found among the muscle divisions which make up the sirloin tip or knuckle at the side of the meat nearest the bone. Save small pieces for second helpings or reserve them for something else, like stew or ground meat. A more expensive scallop comes from the rib section or rack, boned and cut into ⅜-inch slices across the grain.

PREPARATION FOR COOKING. Remove the transparent membranes or skin, and any fat surrounding the scallops. If left on, the meat will curl up as it cooks. Place each scallop between sheets of waxed paper and pound briefly with a mallet, the flat of a cleaver, or a rolling pin to reduce the scallop to a thickness of ¼ inch. Wrap in waxed paper and refrigerate until you are ready to cook them. You will need 1 to 2 scallops, depending on size, per person.

ESCALOPES DE VEAU
SAUTÉES A L'ESTRAGON
(*Sautéed Veal Scallops with Tarragon*)
For 4 people

SAUTÉING THE SCALLOPS

4 or more veal scallops	A 10-inch enameled or no-
1½ Tb butter	stick skillet
½ Tb cooking oil	

Dry scallops thoroughly on paper towels. Heat butter and oil in the skillet over high heat. When butter foam has almost subsided but is not browning, add scallops. Do not crowd them to-gether; cook them a few at a time if necessary. Sauté on one side for about 4 minutes, regulating heat so fat is always very hot but not browning; then turn and sauté meat on the other side. Scallops are done when they are just resistant to the pres-sure of your fingers, and the juices run clear yellow when meat is pricked. Remove scallops to a side dish and make the sauce as follows:

SAUCE AND SERVING

1 Tb minced shallots or scallions

Optional: ¼ cup Sercial Madeira or dry white vermouth

½ Tb dried tarragon leaves

1 cup brown stock or canned beef bouillon; or ¼ cup stock and 1 cup heavy cream

Optional: 1 cup mushrooms, previously sautéed in butter for about 5 minutes

½ Tb cornstarch blended to a paste with 1 Tb water

Salt and pepper

1 Tb soft butter

A hot serving dish

Parsley sprigs

Pour all but a tablespoon of fat from the skillet. Add shallots or scallions and stir over moderate heat for ½ minute. Then add the optional wine, the tarragon, and the stock or the bouillon. Scrape up all coagulated sauté juices with a wooden spoon, and simmer for a moment. (If using cream, add it now.) Boil rapidly to reduce liquid to about ⅔ cup. Remove from heat, beat in cornstarch mixture and optional mushrooms. Simmer, stirring, for 2 minutes. Season scallops lightly with salt and pepper, re-turn them to the pan, and baste with the sauce. Correct season-ing. Set aside uncovered until a few minutes before serving.

Just before serving, reheat to the simmer, basting scallops with sauce for a minute or two until heated through. Remove from heat, place scallops on a hot serving dish, and add butter to sauce in pan. Swirl pan until butter has been absorbed, then pour sauce over scallops. Decorate with parsley, and serve im-mediately.

VEGETABLE AND WINE SUGGESTIONS

Serve with buttered rice or *risotto*, and green beans, peas, or braised endive, and either a chilled white Burgundy wine or a light red Bordeaux.

ESCALOPES DE VEAU GRATINÉES
(Casserole of Veal Scallops with Ham and Cheese)
For 4 people

3 Tb butter
A heavy-bottomed 2-quart saucepan
4 Tb flour
2 cups hot veal or chicken stock or bouillon
A wire whip
½ cup finely minced onions, previously cooked in butter until translucent
1 cup sliced mushrooms, previously sautéed in butter for about 5 minutes

⅓ cup heavy cream
½ cup grated Swiss cheese
A baking-serving dish, 2 inches deep
Salt, pepper, and lemon juice
4 to 8 previously sautéed veal scallops or sliced leftover roast veal
Optional: 4 to 8 slices lean boiled ham
1 Tb softened butter

(Preheat oven to 375 degrees.)

Melt butter in saucepan, then blend in flour and cook slowly, stirring, for 2 minutes without browning. Remove from heat. Pour in all the hot stock or bouillon at once and beat vigorously with a wire whip to blend. Boil, stirring, for 1 minute. Stir in cooked onions and simmer for 5 minutes. Stir in mushrooms and simmer for 5 minutes more. Thin out with spoonfuls of cream, but the sauce should be quite thick. Correct seasoning; add two thirds of the cheese. Lightly butter the baking-serving dish. Spread a spoonful or two of sauce on bottom of dish. Salt and pepper veal and lay in overlapping slices in dish, with a spoonful of sauce and a slice of optional ham between each. Cover with remaining sauce, sprinkle on remaining cheese, and dot with butter. Set aside or refrigerate until about ½ hour before serving.

To finish cooking, place in upper third of a preheated 375-degree oven until it bubbles and the top has browned lightly. Do not overcook.

The Seventeenth Show

SALADS

৽৽ৣ · ৡ৽

(Green, Potato, and Niçoise, Plus Sauce Vinaigrette and Mayonnaise)

Crisp mixed greens, potato salad done the French way, or that tantalizing Mediterranean combination of greens, vegetables, tuna, olives, eggs, and anchovies known as *salade niçoise*—it's the dressing that makes the dish. And it's the excellence of the oil and the vinegar that make the dressing. You will probably have to try out several brands of each to find what suits you best. For real French dressing, you want a wine vinegar, either red or white, which is not overly strong and biting. The best imported French wine vinegars come from Orléans; there are good domestic brands also available. Finest-quality olive oil is labeled "virgin," meaning it is a first pressing of the olives using no heat; some French people prefer a tasteless salad oil, or a combination of oils. Lettuce leaves must be dry when they are tossed for a salad, so you should wash them several hours before use. Shake off the water, spread the leaves on a towel, roll up loosely, and refrigerate; the towel will absorb the moisture.

Sauce Vinaigrette

(French Dressing for Green Salads and Salad Combinations)
For about ½ cup, enough for salad for 6

1 to 2 Tb excellent wine vinegar, or a combination of vinegar and lemon juice
⅛ tsp salt
¼ tsp dry mustard

6 to 8 Tb best-quality olive oil or salad oil, or a combination of both
Big pinch of freshly ground pepper

Optional: ½ Tb minced   or ¼ tsp dried herbs, such
    shallots or scallions and/   as tarragon or basil

Either beat the vinegar, salt, and mustard in a bowl until dissolved, then beat in the oil and season with the pepper and herbs, *or* place all ingredients in a screw-top jar and shake vigorously for 30 seconds to blend thoroughly. Taste carefully for seasoning.

Mayonnaise
For about 2½ cups

A heavy 2½-quart round-
    bottomed mixing bowl
    and a large wire whip (or
    an electric mixer)
3 egg yolks
½ tsp wine vinegar or
    lemon juice
½ tsp salt

¼ tsp dry mustard
1½ to 2¼ cups excellent
    olive oil or salad oil, or a
    combination of both
Drops of wine vinegar or
    lemon juice as needed
Salt, white pepper, and
    mustard

Warm the bowl in hot water, dry it, and add the egg yolks. (If you are beating by hand, set a wet potholder under the bowl to keep it from jumping about.) Beat the egg yolks for a minute or two until thick and sticky, then add the vinegar or lemon juice, the salt and mustard, and beat vigorously for 1 minute more. Beating the yolks at moderately fast speed, start adding the oil by droplets until about ½ cup has gone in and the mixture has thickened into a heavy cream. As soon as this has happened, you can relax, stop beating for a moment if you wish; then continue adding the oil in tablespoon dollops, beating thoroughly after each addition. When sauce thickens too much, thin out with drops of vinegar or lemon juice. When you have added as much oil as you wish, up to 2¼ cups, season to taste. If sauce is not used immediately, scrape into a small bowl and cover tightly so a skin will not form on its surface.

REMEDY FOR TURNED OR CURDLED SAUCE. Warm a bowl in hot water, dry it, and add 1 teaspoon of prepared mustard and 1 tablespoon of sauce. Beat for several seconds until the sauce and mustard have creamed and thickened. Add the rest of the sauce by teaspoons, beating each addition until it has thickened in the sauce.

SALADE MIMOSA
(Green Salad with Vinaigrette, Sieved Egg, and Herbs)
For 4 to 6 people

A peeled hard-boiled egg in a sieve
2 to 3 Tb fresh green herbs or parsley
Salt and pepper
A large head of Boston

lettuce or a mixture of greens, separated, washed, and dried
A salad bowl
⅓ to ½ cup vinaigrette

Push the egg through the sieve with your fingers; toss with the herbs, and salt and pepper to taste. Just before serving, toss salad greens in your salad bowl with the dressing, and sprinkle on the egg-and-herb mixture.

POMMES DE TERRE A L'HUILE
(French Potato Salad)
For about 6 cups

8 to 10 medium "boiling" potatoes (about 2 lbs.)
A 3-quart mixing bowl
2 Tb dry white wine or dry white vermouth

2 Tb chicken bouillon
½ cup vinaigrette
2 Tb minced shallots or scallions
3 Tb minced parsley

Boil or steam the potatoes in their jackets until just tender. Peel and slice while still warm. Toss gently in the mixing bowl with the wine and bouillon, and after several minutes, toss again. When liquid has been absorbed by the potatoes, toss with the vinaigrette, shallots or scallions, and parsley.

This salad is delicious served warm with hot sausages, or you can chill it and serve either as is, or with ½ cup mayonnaise folded in.

SALADE NIÇOISE
(*Mediterranean Main-course Salad*)
For 6 to 8 people

3 cups previously cooked
green beans in a bowl

3 quartered tomatoes in a
bowl

¾ to 1 cup vinaigrette

1 head Boston lettuce,
separated, washed, and
dried

A large salad bowl or
shallow dish

3 cups cold French potato
salad (preceding recipe)

½ cup pitted black olives,
preferably the dry Medi-
terranean type

3 hard-boiled eggs, cold,
peeled and quartered

12 canned anchovy fillets,
drained, either flat or
rolled with capers

About 1 cup (8 ounces)
canned tuna, drained

Just before serving, season beans and tomatoes with several spoonfuls of dressing. Toss the lettuce leaves in the salad bowl with ¼ cup of vinaigrette and place leaves about bowl. Arrange potatoes in bottom of bowl, decorate with the beans and tomatoes, interspersing them with a design of tuna, olives, eggs, and anchovies. Pour remaining dressing over salad, sprinkle with herbs, and serve.

The Eighteenth Show

CHICKEN LIVERS
A LA FRANÇAISE

Chicken livers by the pound used to be an unheard-of luxury; now that you can buy quantities of fresh ones in almost every supermarket, chicken livers have become relatively inexpensive as delicacies go. They are wonderfully nourishing besides, containing all kinds of body-building things that make the blood flow strong and red. Chicken livers are quick to cook, too; sauté them, fold them into a wine sauce with ham and mushrooms, and you have a delicious main course. Purée them, bake in a dish with eggs and seasonings, and they make an unusual lunch or supper dish.

FOIES DE VOLAILLE SAUTÉS, MADÈRE
(Sautéed Chicken Livers in Madeira Sauce)
For 4 to 6 people

1 lb. chicken livers (about 2
  cups)
Salt and pepper
½ cup flour in a plate
A large sieve
2 Tb butter
1 Tb cooking oil
A heavy 10-inch enameled
  or no-stick skillet

Optional: 1 cup diced
  boiled ham, previously
  sautéed in butter, and/or
1 cup quartered fresh
  mushrooms, previously
  sautéed in butter
½ cup beef stock or bouillon
⅓ cup dry Sercial Madeira
1 Tb soft butter
1 Tb fresh minced parsley

Pick over the chicken livers; cut out any filaments and black or greenish spots (these are caused by the bile sack which rested on the liver before cleaning). Dry on paper towels. Just before cooking, sprinkle lightly with salt and pepper, roll in flour, then shake in a sieve to remove excess flour.

Melt the butter and oil in the skillet over moderately high heat. When you see the butter foam begin to subside, add the chicken livers. Toss frequently for 3 to 4 minutes until livers are lightly browned; they are done when just springy to the touch of your finger. Do not overcook. Add optional sautéed ham and mushrooms, pour in the stock and the wine, and simmer for 1 minute. Taste and correct seasoning. (Set aside until later if you are not ready to serve.) Reheat just before serving, then remove from heat and toss with the soft butter and parsley.

SERVING SUGGESTIONS

Spoon the chicken livers into a ring of rice or around a mound of rice, and garnish with buttered peas or asparagus tips; or serve on a bed of creamed spinach and pass rice separately. A red Bordeaux would be your best choice in wines.

TIMBALE DE FOIES DE VOLAILLE
(*Chicken-liver Mold*)
For 4 cups serving 6 to 8 people

Served hot, this chicken-liver custard is delicious as a first course or as the mainstay for luncheon. It is attractive cold, as a light chicken-liver *pâté* for cocktails or the cold buffet table.

THE CUSTARD MIXTURE

1 lb. chicken livers (about 2 cups)
2 eggs (U. S. graded "large")
2 egg yolks
¼ tsp salt
⅛ tsp pepper

1 cup thick white sauce (1½ Tb butter, 2 Tb flour, and 1 cup milk)
Optional: ⅓ cup heavy cream
2 Tb port, Madeira, or cognac

Pick over chicken livers, cutting out any filaments and black or greenish spots. Place them in the jar of an electric blender with the eggs, egg yolks, salt, and pepper, and blend for 1 minute. Add the white sauce and the wine or cognac, blend for 15 seconds more, and strain through a sieve into a bowl. (Or purée chicken livers through a food mill or meat grinder into a bowl, beat in rest of ingredients, and push through a sieve.)

BAKING AND SERVING

A 4-cup baking dish 2½ to 3 inches deep, or 8 half-cup ramekins or custard cups
1 Tb softened butter
A pan of boiling water to hold baking dish or ramekins
2 cups *hollandaise* or *béarnaise*; or cream sauce flavored with 1 tsp tomato paste and tarragon or parsley (see p. 278)

(Preheat oven to 350 degrees.)

Smear a light film of butter inside baking dish or ramekins and fill to within ⅛ inch of the top with the liver mixture. When ready to bake, set in pan of boiling water, then place in middle level of preheated oven. Regulate water in pan so it is almost but not quite simmering. The timbale is done when it shows a very faint line of shrinkage from dish, and when a knife plunged into the center comes out clean. Allow about 30 minutes in the oven for a timbale made in a baking dish; about 20, if you use ramekins. (If not served immediately, leave in pan of water in turned-off oven, with door ajar—or reheat if necessary.)

To unmold timbale made in baking dish, allow to settle for 5 minutes if you have just finished baking, then run a knife around edge of timbale. Turn a lightly buttered hot serving dish upside down over mold, then reverse the two, giving a sharp downward jerk, and timbale will fall into place. To unmold ramekins, run a knife around edge of each one, and unmold onto hot plates or a platter, giving a sharp downward jerk for each just at the end.

Pour sauce over and around the timbale or ramekins, and serve immediately, passing the rest of the sauce in a warmed bowl.

Timbales are best as a separate course, with hot French bread and a chilled white Burgundy, Graves, or Traminer.

The Nineteenth Show

ROAST DUCK A L'ORANGE
≈§ • ?≈

One of the most well known of all duck dishes is *canard à l'orange*, roast duck decorated with fresh orange segments and accompanied by an orange-flavored brown sauce. Its most important element is its sauce—a rich, strong, meaty duck essence darkened with caramel, flavored with wine and orange peel, and given a light liaison of arrowroot. You can and should prepare the sauce well ahead of time so that when the duck is roasted, the dish is within 2 to 3 minutes of being done.

DUCK TALK. Only a genuine duckling—a bird under 6 months old—is good for roasting, and fortunately that is the only kind of bird you are likely to find in any American market. It generally weighs 4½ to 5½ pounds ready to cook, has been beautifully plucked and cleaned, and is usually frozen. To thaw it, leave it in its plastic bag in the refrigerator for 2 days, or unwrap and set it in a sinkful of cold water for several hours, removing the giblet package from cavity as soon as you can dislodge it.

To prepare the duck for roasting, pull out all loose fat from cavity and from around inside of neck. To make carving the breast meat easier, cut out the wishbone from inside the neck cavity. The lower part of the wing is mostly bone; chop it off at the elbow. Be sure the fat glands on the back end at the base of the tail have been removed; dig out any yellow residue that may remain, and rub the area with salt and lemon juice. To help the layer of subcutaneous duck fat escape during cooking, prick the skin at ½-inch intervals along the thighs, the back, and the lower part of the breast. Wrap and refrigerate the duck if you are not ready, but remove it and let come to room temperature before roasting (for accurate timing).

CANARD A L'ORANGE
(Roast Duck with Orange Sauce)
For 4 to 5 people

STOCK FOR THE SAUCE

(Prepare several hours or the day before your dinner.)

Duck wing ends, neck,
   giblets
2 Tb cooking oil
1 medium carrot, sliced
1 medium onion, sliced

1 cup beef bouillon
2 cups water
4 parsley sprigs, 1 bay leaf,
   and ¼ tsp sage

Chop the duck wing ends, neck, and giblets into 1-inch pieces. Brown in a frying pan in hot cooking oil with the sliced carrot and onion. Transfer to a heavy saucepan, add bouillon and enough water to cover by 1 inch. Bring to the simmer, skim off scum, then add the herbs and simmer 2 to 2½ hours. Strain, skim off all fat, and boil down until you have 2 cups of liquid. When cold, cover and refrigerate until needed.

THE ORANGE PEEL

(This may be done several hours ahead.)

4 brightly colored oranges,
   navel or Valencia, if
   possible

1 quart water

Using a vegetable peeler, remove just the orange part of the skin in strips. Cut into fine julienne (small strips no more than 1/16 inch wide and 1½ inches long). Simmer for 15 minutes in 1 quart of water, to remove bitterness; then drain, rinse in cold water, and dry in paper towels. Part of the peel goes into the sauce; part, inside the duck. Wrap it in waxed paper and refrigerate if you are not ready to use it. Wrap and refrigerate the partially peeled oranges until later.

ROASTING THE DUCK

Roasting time: 1 hour and 30 to 40 minutes.

A 5-lb. ready-to-cook
  duckling
½ tsp salt
⅛ tsp pepper

⅓ of the prepared orange
  peel
A shallow roasting pan with
  rack, just large enough to
  hold the duck easily

Prepare the duck as described at beginning of recipe; dry thoroughly, season cavity with salt and pepper, and add the orange peel. Truss wings and legs to body and close cavity. For accurate timing, duck must be at room temperature.

If you are roasting the duck on a rotary spit, use moderately high heat. For oven roasting, preheat to 450 degrees and set duck breast up on rack in roasting pan; after 15 minutes, turn oven down to 350 degrees, then turn duck from one side to the other every 15 minutes, and onto its back for the last 15 minutes. Basting is not necessary. Note that the meat of duck roasted in the French manner is juicy and cooked to just under the well-done stage. To tell when duck is done, prick thickest part of the drumstick deeply with a fork: the juices should run faintly rosy to clear; when duck is drained, the last drops of juice from vent should run faintly rosy to clear yellow.

CONTINUING WITH THE SAUCE; THE ORANGE SEGMENTS

3 Tb granulated sugar
¼ cup red wine vinegar
The 2 cups of duck stock

2 Tb arrowroot blended
  with 2 Tb port
The rest of the orange peel,
  and the oranges

Blend the sugar and vinegar in a small saucepan, swirl over heat to melt sugar completely, then boil rapidly until mixture is a caramel-brown. Remove from heat and beat in half the duck stock; simmer, stirring, to dissolve the caramel. Remove from heat, pour in rest of duck stock, and blend in the arrowroot mixture. Add orange peel and simmer for 3 to 4 minutes; carefully correct seasoning. The sauce will be lightly thickened, and clear.

Shortly before serving, cut white part of peel off oranges, and then cut the oranges into neat, skinless segments—if done too far ahead, segments will not taste fresh. Refrigerate in a covered bowl until serving time.

FINAL ASSEMBLY AND SERVING

½ cup dry port	Drops of orange bitters or
The prepared sauce base	lemon juice
2 to 3 Tb orange liqueur	2 to 3 Tb softened butter

When duck is done, place on serving platter and discard trussing strings; keep it warm in turned-off oven until ready to serve. Spoon fat out of roasting pan, pour in the port wine, and scrape up all coagulated roasting juices with a wooden spoon. Pour mixture into sauce and bring to the simmer, adding orange liqueur. Taste carefully; add drops of bitters or lemon juice if sauce seems too sweet. Just before serving, remove from heat and swirl in butter, a tablespoonful at a time. Decorate breast of duck with orange segments and pile rest of segments at either end of platter; spoon a bit of sauce and peel over duck, pour rest into a warm sauceboat, and serve.

VEGETABLE AND WINE SUGGESTIONS

Nothing but sautéed or shoestring potatoes or homemade potato chips should interfere with these flavors. Serve a red Bordeaux-Médoc or an excellent white Burgundy wine.

The Twentieth Show

CHOCOLATE MOUSSE

Here is a queen among chocolate *mousses*, lighter than some because beaten egg whites are folded in instead of whipped cream. But it is every bit as richly flavored as the most devout chocolate cultist could wish, and the subtle aroma of good liqueur brings out that chocolate essence to perfection. You will note that egg yolks and sugar are beaten over hot water before the rest of the ingredients go in; this step has the triple function of cooking the yolks, dissolving the sugar, and giving a lightness and cohesion to the mixture. Butter, which goes in later, gives it body and suppleness as well. Plan to make the *mousse* several hours or the day before serving, as it must be well chilled; you can even freeze it. Serve the *mousse* in a bowl, in dessert cups, or in little covered china pots; or for drama, you can mold it.

MOUSSELINE AU CHOCOLAT
(*Chocolate Mousse*)
For about 5 cups serving 6 to 8 people

MELTING THE CHOCOLATE

1 cup semisweet chocolate bits, or 6 squares semisweet baking chocolate
4 Tb strong coffee
A small saucepan and

wooden spoon for stirring the chocolate
A larger pan with almost-simmering water

Place the chocolate and coffee in the small saucepan. Remove the larger pan with water from heat and place chocolate pan in it. Stir for a minute or so until chocolate begins to melt, then let it melt slowly over the hot water while you go on with the recipe.

THE EGG YOLKS AND SUGAR

4 egg yolks
A 3-quart mixing bowl or the large bowl of an electric mixer
A large wire whip
¾ cup granulated sugar (instant superfine if possible)

¼ cup orange liqueur, rum, or Benedictine, or strained orange juice, or strong coffee
A pan of almost-simmering water

Place egg yolks in mixing bowl and start beating with whip while gradually pouring in the sugar in a thin stream. Continue beating for 2 to 3 minutes until mixture is thick, pale, and forms a slowly dissolving ribbon when a bit is lifted and falls back onto the surface. Beat in the liqueur or other liquid, and set the bowl in a pan of almost-simmering water. Beat at moderate speed for 4 to 5 minutes, or until foamy and warm when tested with your finger. Remove the bowl from the hot water and either beat the mixture in mixer for several minutes until cool, or set it in a bowl of cold water and beat with your wire whip. It should again form the ribbon, and have the consistency of thick, creamy mayonnaise.

ADDING BUTTER AND CHOCOLATE

1½ sticks (6 ounces)
   softened unsalted butter

Stir the chocolate again and continue until perfectly smooth. Gradually beat the softened butter into the chocolate. Beat the chocolate and butter into the yolks and sugar.

THE EGG WHITES

4 egg whites, room temperature	Pinch of salt
A very clean, dry bowl and beater	2 Tb instant superfine granulated sugar
	A rubber spatula

Beat egg whites slowly until they begin to foam, then beat in the salt. Increase speed gradually to fast until soft peaks are formed. Sprinkle on the sugar and continue beating until stiff peaks are formed. Stir one fourth of the egg whites into the chocolate mixture to lighten it; scoop the rest of the egg whites on top and delicately fold them in.

CHILLING AND SERVING

Immediately turn the *mousse* into a lightly oiled 6-cup metal mold, a serving bowl, or individual cups. Cover and chill for several hours or overnight.

If you are unmolding the *mousse*, dip mold for several seconds into hot water, run a knife rapidly between edge of *mousse* and mold, and turn a chilled serving dish upside down over mold; reverse the two, giving a sharp downward jerk, and the *mousse* should drop into place in a few seconds.

You may wish to pass with the *mousse* a bowl of lightly whipped cream flavored with powdered sugar and liqueur. If you are serving a ring-molded *mousse,* you could put the cream in the center and sprinkle with grated chocolate. Here is a recipe for French whipped cream.

Crème Chantilly
(Lightly Whipped Cream)
For about 2 cups

½ pint (1 cup) chilled
   heavy or whipping cream
A chilled 3-quart bowl
A large wire whip, chilled
2 Tb sifted confectioners'
   sugar

1 to 2 Tb liqueur or 1 tsp
   vanilla extract
2 thicknesses of damp,
   washed cheesecloth set in
   a sieve over a bowl

Pour the cream into the chilled bowl and beat slowly with the whip until the cream begins to foam. Gradually increase beating speed to moderate, and continue until beater leaves light traces on surface of cream and a bit lifted and dropped will softly retain its shape. (In hot weather, it is best to beat over cracked ice.) Gently fold in the sifted sugar and the flavorings. If you are doing the cream in advance, turn it into cheesecloth-lined sieve and refrigerate; the cream will stay beaten, and the delicious liquid that has seeped into bottom of bowl may be used for something else.

The Twenty-first Show

PÂTÉS

A French *pâté* is a luxurious cold meat loaf, which turns out to be very easy to make. It consists of an all-purpose mixture of ground lean pork, ground veal, and pork fat, to which you can add anything else you think appropriate, such as strips of ham or veal, liver, marinated game, pistachios, truffles, and always a bit of cognac, port, or Madeira, along with seasonings and spices. If the mixture is cooked and served in its baking dish, it is called either a *terrine* or a *pâté;* baked in a pastry crust it is a *pâté en croûte.* Boned chicken, turkey, or duck filled with the same type of mixture is a *galantine. Pâtés* will keep for about 10 days under refrigeration, and are wonderful to have on hand for cold impromptu meals; all you need to serve with them are a salad, French bread, and a light red, dry white, or *rosé* wine.

A NOTE ON PORK FAT. Fresh pork fat is an essential ingredient for the type of meat mixture that goes into a *pâté;* blended with the meats, it prevents them from cooking dry, and gives them a lightness of texture. Cut into thin sheets, pork fat is also used to line the inside of the baking dish. The best type is fat back, which comes from the back of the pig next to the skin; it is firm and does not disintegrate as easily as fat from other parts of the animal. Alternatives are fat trimmed from fresh ham (pork leg) or from around a fresh pork loin. Or take fat salt pork or thick strips of bacon simmered for 15 minutes in a large saucepan of water to remove salt and/or smoky taste before using.

BAKING DISHES. You may cook a *pâté* in almost any kind of a baking dish or pan, from a special rectangular or oval mold called a *terrine* to a soufflé dish, casserole, or bread pan.

TERRINE DE PORC, VEAU, ET JAMBON
(Pork and Veal Pâté with Ham)
For a 2-quart mold

A pork and veal *pâté* with strips of veal and ham makes slices with an attractive design. This is the most classic of mixtures, and all other *pâtés* follow this general pattern.

THE BASIC PÂTÉ MIXTURE   (For 4 cups)

½ cup finely minced onions	A 3-quart mixing bowl
2 Tb butter	½ cup dry port or Madeira,
A small skillet	or cognac

Cook the onions slowly in the butter until soft and translucent; then scrape them into the mixing bowl. Pour the wine into the skillet and boil until reduced by half; add to the onions in the mixing bowl.

¾ lb. (1½ cups) finely ground lean pork	2 lightly beaten eggs
¾ lb. (1½ cups) finely ground lean veal	½ tsp salt
	⅛ tsp pepper
½ lb. (1 cup) ground fresh pork fat (see notes at beginning of recipe)	½ tsp thyme
	Big pinch allspice
	A small clove mashed garlic

Vigorously beat the ground meats, fat, eggs, and seasonings into the onions until all is thoroughly blended and texture has softened and lightened—2 to 3 minutes. Sauté a small spoonful until cooked through; taste and correct seasoning if necessary.

THE VEAL STRIPS

½ lb. lean veal from the round or tenderloin, cut into ¼-inch strips	3 Tb cognac
	Salt and pepper
A bowl	Pinch each of thyme and allspice

1 Tb finely minced shallots   Optional: 1 or more canned
   or scallions   truffles cut into ¼-inch
                                        dice, and juice from can

While preparing other ingredients to follow, marinate the
veal in a bowl with the cognac and other seasonings, including
the optional truffles and the juice from their can. Before using,
drain the veal and truffles; reserve the marinade.

FORMING THE PÂTÉ

A 2-quart baking dish or pan   ½ lb. lean boiled ham cut
   (see notes at beginning of   into strips ¼ inch thick
   recipe)   1 bay leaf
Sufficient sheets or strips of   Aluminum foil
   pork fat to enclose *pâté*   A heavy cover for baking
   (see notes at beginning of   dish or pan
   recipe)   A pan to hold baking dish
4 cups of the basic *pâté*   in oven
   mixture

(Preheat oven to 350 degrees for next step.)
Line bottom and sides of dish with strips of pork fat, pressing
it firmly in place. Beat veal marinade into basic *pâté* mixture,
and spread one third in bottom of dish. Cover with half the
strips of marinated veal, alternating with half the strips of ham.
If using truffles, place them in a row down the center. Cover with
half the remaining *pâté* mixture, the rest of the veal and ham
strips, more truffles, and finally the last of the *pâté* mixture. Lay
the bay leaf on top; cover with a sheet or strips of pork fat. Enclose the top of the dish with aluminum foil and set on the
cover (put a weight on top if cover is loose or flimsy).

BAKING THE PÂTÉ

Set dish in a slightly larger pan and pour in enough water to
come two thirds the way up. Set in lower third of preheated 350-
degree oven and bake for about 1½ hours, or until *pâté* has
shrunk slightly from baking dish and all liquid and surrounding
juices are a clear yellow with no traces of rosy color.

COOLING, CHILLING, AND SERVING

When done, take the dish from the water and set on a plate. Remove lid, and on top of the foil covering put a piece of wood, a pan, or a dish which will just fit into the baking dish. On or in it, place a 3- to 4-pound weight or parts of a meat grinder; this will pack down the *pâté* so there will be no air spaces later. Cool at room temperature for several hours, then refrigerate, still weighted down, for 6 to 8 hours or overnight.

Cut serving slices right from the baking dish at the table, or unmold the *pâté*, peel off the pork fat, and serve the *pâté* decorated in aspic. (*Note:* If you are keeping it for more than 2 or 3 days in the refrigerator, unmold the chilled *pâté* and scrape all meat jelly off surface, as it is the jelly that spoils first. Wipe *pâté* dry and return to baking dish or wrap in waxed paper or plastic wrap.)

The Twenty-second Show

ASPICS
☙ • ❧
(*Duck with Cherries; Eggs in Aspic*)

There is nothing like aspic to dress up a cold duck or a poached egg; it will turn either one into an object of incomparable and glittering chic. Even if you have no particular flair for decoration, you will be surprised at what wonders you can perform with enough aspic, a bit of time, cracked ice, and a few simple tricks of the trade.

Gelée de Viande
(Wine-flavored Meat Jelly for Aspics)
For 2 cups

A meat jelly is the culinary term for any stock or consommé which stiffens when cold because it contains natural gelatin or because gelatin has been added to it. When you are using the jelly for decorations, it should be clear and sparkling for maximum eye appeal.

1 Tb (1 envelope) unflavored powdered gelatin	2 cups clear beef consommé in a saucepan 2 to 3 Tb cognac, or dry port or Madeira

Sprinkle the gelatin over the consommé and let soften for several minutes, then stir over gentle heat until all gelatin granules have dissolved completely. Remove from heat and stir in cognac or wine to taste. (*Note:* In very hot weather, it is safest to use 1 envelope of gelatin for each 1½ rather than 2 cups of consommé.)

You may refrigerate the jelly in a covered container for several days, or you may freeze it.

HOW TO WORK WITH JELLIES FOR ASPICS ❧

Allow yourself plenty of time, because the jelly must be given full opportunity to set, and have sufficient cracked ice available to speed things up. A complicated decoration need not be done all at once; you can complete various parts whenever you have a free moment and the process may go on in spurts for a day or two.

Always test the jelly before you work with it, just to be sure and safe: Pour ½ inch into a small saucer and refrigerate until set; break up with a fork and let stand at room temperature for 10 minutes. The pieces should hold their shape but not be rubbery. Add more gelatin if too soft; more consommé if too stiff.

COATING FOODS IN ASPIC. Jellies set very quickly once they are cold. To avoid continual warmings of the whole amount, heat just what you will need at one time in a small pan, stir over cracked ice until liquid turns syrupy and is about to set, then remove from ice and rapidly spoon a layer over the chilled food.

CHOPPED JELLY. Foods decorated with successive layers of jelly usually need a cover-up for dribbles on the platter, or an attractive something to fill up empty spaces. Chopped jelly is an easy and attractive solution. To make it, pour a ½-inch layer of warm jelly into a plate or pan and chill until set. Turn out onto a board and chop into ⅛-inch pieces with a big knife. Outline the food or fill up empty spaces in your decoration either by forcing the chopped jelly through a pastry bag or heaping it in place with a spoon.

JELLY CUTOUTS. Chill a ¼-inch layer of jelly in a plate or pan, then cut into squares, triangles, or diamonds, and place on top of food or around the edge of your platter. Cutouts are usually put in place at the very end, as a final touch to your decoration.

CANARD A LA MONTMORENCY
(*Duck in Aspic with Cherries*)
For 4 to 5 people

This is a handsome dish for a cold lunch, or to have on the cold buffet table. You can use the same general system for a cold *duck à l'orange*; the orange segments would be steeped in wine but not heated, and the orange peel would be used for added decoration.

36 to 48 pitted black cherries, fresh or canned	4 cups wine-flavored meat jelly in a saucepan
1 Tb lemon juice	A 12-inch serving platter
3 Tb port or cognac	A 4½-lb. roasted duck,
Sugar to taste (2 to 3 Tb)	chilled and carved into serving pieces

Toss the cherries in a bowl with lemon juice, port or cognac, and sugar. Let them macerate (steep) for 20 to 30 minutes. Then add the cherries and their maceration juices to the meat jelly. If using fresh cherries, heat at below the simmer for 3 to 4 minutes to poach gently without bursting; heat 1 minute only for canned cherries. Drain and chill.

Pour a ⅛-inch layer of warm jelly into a platter and chill for 15 to 20 minutes until set. Peel skin from carved duck, and arrange duck pieces in an attractive design over chilled jelly layer on platter. Spoon a layer of cold syrupy jelly over the duck (first layer will not adhere very well), chill 10 minutes, and repeat with successive layers until you have a 1/16-inch coating.

Dip chilled cherries into a bit of syrupy jelly, arrange over duck, and chill again until set. Spoon a final layer or two of jelly over duck and cherries. Pour remaining jelly into a plate, chill, chop, and spoon around duck. If you have extra jelly, you may also wish to make more decorations with jelly cutouts. Refrigerate the duck until serving time—you may complete the dish a day in advance.

OEUFS EN GELÉE
(*Poached Eggs in Aspic*)
For 4 servings

These individual servings of eggs molded in aspic are attractive as a first course or luncheon dish, or arranged around a platter of cold meat, fish, or vegetables. Look around for special egg-in-aspic molds, which are made of metal and are oval in shape; if you cannot find them, use muffin tins or custard cups. The object here is to line the bottom of each mold with a layer of set jelly, and arrange a decoration over it before the egg and the rest of the jelly go in; then you will have an interesting design over the egg when you unmold it for serving.

2 cups wine-flavored meat jelly	dropped into boiling water for 30 seconds
4 oval or round molds, ½-cup size	Rounds or ovals of boiled ham
4 chilled poached eggs	Slice of truffle or *foie gras*,
Decorative suggestions:	or 4 Tb liver *mousse*
Fresh tarragon leaves	

Pour a ⅛-inch layer of jelly into each mold and chill until set. Dip tarragon leaves, truffles, or ham into almost-set jelly and arrange over chilled jelly in each mold; if using *foie gras* or liver *mousse*, place a slice or spoonful on top. Cover with a chilled poached egg, its most attractive side down. Fill molds with cold syrupy jelly (if jelly is warm, you will dislodge the decoration); chill for an hour or more, until set. Unmold one by one, by dipping in hot water, rapidly running a knife around edge of aspic, and reversing the mold onto a plate, giving a sharp downward jerk as you do so.

The Twenty-third Show

BOUILLABAISSE

How to make the authentic bouillabaisse is always a subject of lively discussion among French experts; each always insists that his own is the only correct version. If you do not happen to live on the Mediterranean, you cannot obtain the particular rockfish, gurnards, mullets, weavers, sea eels, wrasses, and breams which they consider the absolutely essential fish for bouillabaisse, but you can make an extremely good facsimile even if you have only frozen fish and canned clam juice to work with, because all the other essential flavors of tomatoes, onions or leeks, garlic, herbs, and olive oil are always available.

Bouillabaisse is really a fish chowder; whole small fish or large fish cut into serving pieces are boiled in a deliciously aromatic fish broth. The fish are served on a platter, and the broth in a tureen, and you eat both together in large soup plates.

For the best and most interesting flavor, pick six or more varieties of fish, which is why a bouillabaisse is ideally made for at least six people. Some of the fish should be firm fleshed and gelatinous, like halibut, eel, and cusk; some should be tender and flaky, like hake, whiting, and sole. The firm fish hold their shape, and the tender fish partially disperse in the soup. Shellfish are optional, but always add glamour and color if you wish to include them.

Except for live lobsters and crabs, all the fish may be cleaned, sliced, and refrigerated several hours before the final cooking. The soup base may be boiled, strained, and refrigerated. The actual cooking of the fish in the soup will take only about 20 minutes, and then the dish should be served immediately.

THE FISH. Fish for bouillabaisse should be lean, and of the best and freshest-smelling quality. Here are suggestions: bass, cod, conger or sea eel, cusk, flounder, grouper, grunt, haddock, hake or whiting, halibut, perch, pollock, rockfish or sculpin, snapper, spot, sea trout or weakfish, wolffish. Shellfish—crab, lobster, mussels, clams, scallops.

Have the fish cleaned and scaled; discard gills. Save heads, bones, and trimmings for the soup base. Cut large fish into crosswise slices 2 inches wide. Scrub clams; scrub and soak mussels; wash scallops. If using live crab or lobster, split just before cooking; remove sand sack and intestinal tube from lobsters, and tail flap from under crabs.

BOUILLABAISSE A LA MARSEILLAISE
(Mediterranean Fish Chowder)
For 6 to 8 people

THE SOUP BASE

1 cup sliced yellow onions
¾ to 1 cup sliced leeks, white part only; or ½ cup more onions
½ cup olive oil
A heavy 8-quart kettle or casserole

2 to 3 cups chopped fresh tomatoes, or 1¼ cups drained canned tomatoes, or ¼ cup tomato paste
4 cloves mashed garlic

Cook the onions and leeks slowly in the olive oil for 5 minutes without browning. Stir in the tomatoes and garlic, and cook 5 minutes more.

2½ quarts water
6 parsley sprigs
1 bay leaf
½ tsp thyme or basil
⅛ tsp fennel
2 big pinches of saffron
A 2-inch piece or ½ tsp
   dried orange peel
⅛ tsp pepper

1 Tb salt (none if using
   clam juice)
3 to 4 lbs. fish heads, bones,
   and trimmings including
   shellfish remains; or, 1
   quart clam juice and 1½
   quarts of water, and no
   salt

Add the water, herbs, seasoning, and fish or clam juice to the kettle. Bring to the boil, skim, and cook, uncovered, at the slow boil for 30 to 40 minutes. Strain, correct seasoning. Set aside, uncovered, until cool if you are not finishing the bouillabaisse immediately, then refrigerate.

COOKING THE BOUILLABAISSE

The soup base
6 to 8 lbs. assorted lean fish,
   and shellfish if you wish,

selected and prepared
according to directions at
beginning of recipe

Bring the soup base to a rapid boil in the kettle about 20 minutes before serving. Add lobsters, crabs, and firm-fleshed fish. Bring quickly back to the boil and boil rapidly, uncovered, for 5 minutes. Then add the tender-fleshed fish, and the clams, mussels, and scallops. Bring back to the boil again for 5 minutes. Do not overcook.

SERVING

A hot platter
A soup tureen or soup
   casserole

Rounds of toasted French
   bread
⅓ cup roughly chopped
   fresh parsley

Immediately lift out the fish and arrange on the platter. Carefully taste soup for seasoning, place 6 to 8 slices of bread in the tureen, and pour in the soup. Spoon a ladleful of soup over the fish, and sprinkle parsley over both fish and soup. Serve immediately.

At the table, each guest is served or helps himself to both fish

and soup, placing them in a large soup plate. Eat the bouillabaisse with a large soup spoon and fork, helped along with additional pieces of French bread. If you wish to serve wine, you
have a choice of *rosé*, a strong dry white wine such as Côtes du
Rhône or Riesling, or a light, young red such as Beaujolais or
domestic Mountain Red.

The Twenty-fourth Show

LOBSTER A L'AMÉRICAINE

Homard à l'Américaine is live lobster chopped into serving
pieces, sautéed in oil until the shells turn red, then flamed in
cognac, and simmered with wine, aromatic vegetables, and
tomatoes. In France, unless you are at a formal dinner, you are
served the lobster right in its shell and you eat noisily and happily with your fingers as well as with knife and fork. Even if
finger bowls and large napkins are provided, wading into richly
sauced lobsters with such informality does not appeal at all to
a number of our countrymen. If this is the case, you will just
have to remove the lobster meat from the shells before serving,
which is too bad as it makes much more work for the cook.

A NOTE ON DEALING WITH LIVE LOBSTERS.   If your fishman splits
the lobsters for you, have it done within an hour or two of cooking. A lobster is killed instantly when you plunge the point of
a knife into the head between the eyes or sever the spinal cord
by making a small incision in the back of the shell at the junc-
ture of the chest and tail. Or you can place the lobsters in a
large kettle and run very hot water over them for 5 minutes.
Run your knife down the length of the belly on the under side,
then split the lobster in two lengthwise, remove stomach sack in
the head, and the intestinal tube which runs just under the out-

side curve of the tail meat. Reserve coral and green matter in a bowl. Remove claws and joints, and crack them with a heavy knife. Separate tails from chests.

HOMARD A L'AMÉRICAINE
(*Lobster Simmered in Wine, Tomatoes, and Herbs*)
For 6 people

SAUTÉING THE LOBSTER

Three 1½-lb. live lobsters	**A heavy 12-inch enameled**
3 Tb olive oil	**skillet or casserole**

Prepare the lobsters as described in preceding paragraph. Heat the oil in the skillet until very hot but not smoking. Add the lobster pieces, meat-side down, and sauté for several minutes, turning them, until the shells are bright red. Remove lobster to a side dish.

SIMMERING IN WINE AND FLAVORINGS

1 medium carrot, finely diced	**chopped; or ⅓ cup plain tomato sauce**
1 medium onion, finely diced	**2 Tb tomato paste, or more**
Salt and pepper	**tomato sauce if needed**
3 Tb minced shallots or scallions	**1 cup fish stock or ⅓ cup clam juice**
1 clove mashed garlic	**1 cup dry white vermouth**
⅓ cup cognac	**½ cup beef stock or bouillon**
1 lb. tomatoes, peeled, seeded, juiced, and	**2 Tb minced parsley**
	1 tsp dried tarragon, or 1 Tb fresh tarragon

(Preheat oven to 350 degrees.)

Stir the diced carrot and onion into the skillet, and cook slowly for 5 minutes or until almost tender. Season the lobster with salt and pepper, return to the skillet, and add the shallots or scallions and the garlic. With skillet over moderate heat, pour in the cognac. Avert your face, ignite cognac with a lighted match, and shake skillet slowly until flames have subsided. Stir in the rest of the ingredients, bring to the simmer, cover, and cook slowly either on top of the stove or in middle level of pre-heated oven. Regulate heat so lobster simmers quietly for 20 minutes.

FINISHING THE LOBSTER

The lobster coral and green matter	A sieve set over a 2-quart bowl
6 Tb softened butter	A wooden spoon

While the lobster is simmering, force the lobster coral and green matter with the butter through the sieve and into the bowl. Set aside.

When the lobster is done, remove it to a side dish. (Take the meat out of the shells if you must.) Set skillet with its cooking liquid over high heat and boil rapidly until sauce has reduced and thickened slightly; it will thicken more when the butter-and-coral mixture is added later. Taste very carefully for seasoning. Return the lobster to the sauce.

The recipe may be completed to this point, and finished later.

Bring the lobster to the simmer until well heated through. Remove from heat. Beat a half cupful of the hot sauce by driblets into the coral-and-butter mixture, then pour the mixture back over the lobster. Shake and swirl pan over low heat for 2 to 3 minutes to poach the coral and thicken the sauce, but do not bring to the simmer.

SERVING

A ring of steamed rice or *risotto* on a hot, lightly buttered platter	2 to 3 Tb minced parsley, or parsley and fresh tarragon

Arrange the lobster and sauce in the rice ring, decorate with herbs, and serve immediately. A strong, dry white wine such as a Burgundy or Côtes du Rhône would be your best choice.

The Twenty-fifth Show

ENTRÉE CRÊPES
❧ · ❧

(Rolled Crêpes with Shellfish Stuffing;
Mound of Crêpes with Spinach and Mushrooms)

Every French household makes use of those thin little pancakes
called *crêpes*, not only for flaming desserts, but also as an
attractive way to turn leftovers or simple ingredients into a
main-course dish. You may roll *crêpes* around a filling of
creamed fish, meat, or vegetables, or pile *crêpes* one upon the
other making a great mound of them with filling in between
each. Covered by a delicious sauce, sprinkled with cheese, and
browned in the oven, filled *crêpes* make a most appetizing, even
elegant dish.

Pâte à Crêpes
Batter for about 12 crêpes, 6½ inches in diameter

1 cup cold water	2 cups all-purpose flour (sift
1 cup cold milk	directly into dry-measure
4 eggs (U. S. graded	cups; sweep off excess)
"large")	4 Tb previously melted
½ tsp salt	butter

Either whirl all ingredients in an electric blender at high
speed for about 1 minute; or gradually blend eggs into flour
with an electric mixer or wooden spoon, beat in liquids gradually, and strain through a fine sieve. Refrigerate for at least
2 hours; this allows the flour particles to swell and soften so
that your *crêpes* will be light in texture. (*Note:* Since doing this
show, I have found that the granular "instant-blending" flour is

a much easier alternative. Place 1½ cups in a mixing bowl, grad ually blend in the liquids and then the rest of the ingredients with a wire whip, and you can make the *crêpes* immediately.)

METHOD FOR MAKING CRÊPES.   Provide yourself with a no-stick or cast-iron skillet 6 to 7 inches in diameter at the bottom. Rub pan with a piece of fresh pork rind or fat bacon, or brush lightly with cooking oil. Have a ladle, large spoon, or measure which will hold ¼ cup.

Set pan over moderately high heat until just beginning to smoke. Immediately remove from heat and, holding pan handle in your right hand, pour with your left hand a scant ¼ cup of batter into the middle of pan. Quickly tilt pan in all directions to run batter all over bottom of pan in a thin film. (Pour back any batter that does not adhere to the pan, and note the correct amount for your next *crêpe*.)

Immediately set pan over heat and cook for about 1 minute. The *crêpe* is ready for turning when you can shake and jerk it loose from bottom of pan; lift an edge to see that it is a nice brown underneath. Turn the *crêpe* and cook for about ½ min- ute on the other side; this is rarely more than a spotty brown and is kept as the nonpublic side. Slide the *crêpe* onto a plate and continue with the rest of the batter, greasing pan lightly each time if it seems necessary. When you get used to it, you can keep 2 pans going at once.

If you make the *crêpes* in advance, it is best to stack them between layers of waxed paper or foil to prevent them from sticking together. *Crêpes* may be frozen; to thaw, heat them in a covered dish in a 300-degree oven.

CRÊPES ROULÉES ET FARCIES
(*Crêpes Rolled Around a Creamed Shellfish Stuffing, Gratinéed in Wine and Cheese Sauce*)
For 12 pieces

THE CREAMED SHELLFISH MEAT

2 Tb butter
An 8-inch enameled or no-
   stick skillet

3 Tb minced shallots or
   scallions

1½ cups diced or shredded cooked or canned shellfish meat

Salt and pepper
¼ cup dry white vermouth
A bowl

Heat the butter to bubbling in the skillet, stir in the shallots or scallions, then the shellfish. Toss and stir over moderately high heat for 1 minute. Season with salt and pepper, then add the vermouth and boil rapidly until liquid has almost entirely evaporated. Scrape into a bowl.

THE WINE AND CHEESE SAUCE

⅓ cup dry white vermouth
2 Tb cornstarch blended in a small bowl with 2 Tb milk

1½ cups heavy cream
¼ tsp salt
White pepper
½ cup grated Swiss cheese

Add the vermouth to the skillet and boil rapidly until reduced to a tablespoon. Remove from heat; stir in the cornstarch mixture, cream, seasonings. Simmer 2 minutes, stirring, then blend in the cheese and simmer a minute more. Correct seasoning.

ASSEMBLING AND BAKING

12 cooked *crêpes*, 6 to 7 inches in diameter
¼ cup grated Swiss cheese

2 Tb butter
A lightly buttered baking dish

Blend half the sauce into the shellfish, then place a big spoonful of the shellfish mixture on lower third of each *crêpe*, and roll *crêpes* into cylindrical shapes. Arrange the *crêpes* closely together in a lightly buttered baking dish, spoon over rest of sauce, sprinkle with the cheese, and dot with bits of the butter. Refrigerate until you are ready to bake. Fifteen to 20 minutes before serving, set in upper third of a preheated 425-degree oven until bubbling hot and cheese topping has browned lightly, or heat and brown under a low broiler.

GÂTEAU DE CRÊPES A LA FLORENTINE
(*Mound of Crêpes Filled with Spinach and Mushrooms, Baked with Cheese Sauce*)
For 4 to 6 people

CREAM SAUCE WITH CHEESE, SPINACH, AND MUSHROOMS

4 Tb butter
5 Tb flour
2¾ cups hot milk
½ tsp salt
Pepper and nutmeg
¼ cup heavy cream
1 cup coarsely grated Swiss
cheese

1½ cups cooked chopped
spinach
1 cup cream cheese or
cottage cheese
1 egg
1 cup diced fresh mush-
rooms, previously sautéed
in butter with 2 Tb
minced shallots or scal-
lions

For the sauce, melt the butter, stir in the flour, and cook slowly for 2 minutes without coloring; remove from heat, beat in the milk, salt, and pepper and nutmeg to taste. Boil, stirring, for 1 minute, then beat in the cream and all but 2 tablespoons of the Swiss cheese; simmer a moment, then correct seasoning.

Blend several tablespoons of sauce into the spinach and carefully correct seasoning. Beat the cream cheese or cottage cheese with the egg, mushrooms, and several tablespoons of sauce to make a thick paste; correct seasoning.

ASSEMBLING AND BAKING

24 cooked *crêpes*, 6 to 7
inches in diameter

A lightly buttered baking
dish
1 Tb butter

(Preheat oven to 375 degrees.)

Center a *crêpe* in the bottom of a lightly buttered baking dish, spread with spinach, cover with a *crêpe*, spread with a layer of the cheese-and-mushroom mixture, and continue this way with the rest of the *crêpes* and the 2 fillings, ending the mound with a *crêpe*. Pour the remaining cheese sauce over the mound, sprinkle with the remaining 2 tablespoons of grated Swiss cheese, and dot with a tablespoon of butter. Refrigerate until 30 to 40 minutes before serving, then set in upper third of preheated oven until bubbling hot and cheese topping has browned lightly.

The Twenty-sixth Show

DESSERT CRÊPES
◦⋧ • ⋦◦
(*Crêpes with Orange-Butter and Almonds; Crêpes with Apples and Macaroons; Crêpes Suzette*)

Few of us can say *"crêpes"* without adding *"Suzette,"* so famous and popular has this flaming dessert of paper-thin, orange-flavored pancakes become. Chef Henri Charpentier, who died some years ago in California at a ripe old age, is said to have created them at the Café de Paris in Monte Carlo, while still a very young apprentice, when he was asked by the then-Prince of Wales to dream up an especially fine dessert for the royal party. Young Henri remembered a dish of fruit-filled *crêpes* his grandmother used to make; he substituted orange butter for the fruit, flamed his *crêpes* in brandy, and thereby created the legend which is now part of the repertoire of every chef from the shores of Montezuma to the wilds of Hohokus, New Jersey. While *crêpes Suzette* require you to perform like an accomplished *maître d'hôtel* in front of your guests, there are other *crêpe* recipes which you can assemble in the kitchen and simply ignite at the table. For all dessert *crêpes*, you need an especially light, somewhat different pancake batter from that for entrée *crêpes*, and here it is:

Crêpes Fines Sucrées

Batter for about 18 dessert crêpes,
5 to 6 inches in diameter

¾ cup milk
¾ cup cold water
3 egg yolks
1 Tb granulated sugar
3 Tb orange liqueur, rum,
  or cognac

1½ cups all-purpose flour
  (measure by sifting
  directly into dry-measure
  cups and leveling off)
5 Tb melted butter

Either whirl all ingredients at top speed in an electric blender for about 1 minute; or gradually work the liquids into the flour with an electric mixer or wooden spoon, beat in the dry ingredients, and strain through a fine sieve. Refrigerate for at least 2 hours, allowing flour particles to swell and soften. (Note: Since doing this show, I have found that the granular "instant-blending" flour is a much easier alternative. Place 1 cup plus 2 tablespoons in a mixing bowl, gradually blend in the liquids and then the rest of the ingredients with a wire whip, and you can make the *crêpes* immediately.) Cook the *crêpes* in a 5- to 6-inch no-stick or cast-iron skillet. If batter seems too thick after you've tried your first *crêpe*, beat in a tablespoon or so of water. If made in advance, stack *crêpes* between layers of waxed paper or foil so they will not stick together.

Beurre d'Orange

(*Orange Butter for Filling and Flavoring Crêpes*)
For 3 cups

4 large lumps of sugar
2 large, firm, bright-skinned
  oranges
¼ cup granulated sugar
Small electric-mixer bowl

An electric beater and/or
  a wooden spoon or pestle
½ lb. unsalted butter
⅔ cup strained orange juice
3 Tb orange liqueur

Rub sugar lumps hard over the oranges to extract as much oil from the orange skins as the sugar will absorb. Remove orange part of peel of both oranges with a vegetable peeler.

Place the peel on a board and chop up very fine with the granulated sugar. Then crush the sugar lumps and the peel-and-sugar mixture in the small bowl of an electric mixer with a pestle or wooden spoon. Add the butter and beat until light and fluffy; gradually beat in the orange juice and liqueur. Cover and refrigerate until needed. (Orange butter may be frozen.)

CRÊPES FOURRÉES ET FLAMBÉES
(Crêpes Stuffed with Orange Butter and Almonds)
For 18 crêpes serving 6 to 8 people

½ cup pulverized blanched almonds (you can use an electric blender for this)
¼ tsp almond extract
1 cup orange butter (preceding recipe)
18 cooked *crêpes*, 5 to 6 inches in diameter

A lightly buttered baking-serving dish
3 Tb granulated sugar
⅓ cup each of orange liqueur and cognac warmed in a small saucepan

Beat the almonds and almond extract into the orange butter. Spread a spoonful of this mixture on the lower third of each *crêpe*, roll into cylinders, and arrange in a lightly buttered baking-and-serving dish. Cover and refrigerate until ready to use. About 15 minutes before serving, sprinkle with the sugar and bake in upper third of a preheated 350- to 375-degree oven until sugar topping has begun to caramelize lightly. Just before serving, pour on the warm liqueur and bring to the table. Ignite with a match, and spoon the liqueur over the *crêpes* until flames die down.

GÂTEAU DE CRÊPES A LA NORMANDE
(Flaming Mound of Crêpes with Baked Apple Slices and Macaroons)
For 12 crêpes serving 6 to 8 people

4 to 5 cups sliced apples (about 2 lbs.)
A large heavy-bottomed baking pan

⅓ cup granulated sugar
4 Tb melted butter
12 cooked *crêpes*, 5 to 6 inches in diameter

A lightly buttered baking-
  serving dish
6 to 8 stale macaroons,
  crumbled

More melted butter and
  sugar and cognac

Spread apples in the baking pan, sprinkle with sugar and melted butter, and set in middle level of a preheated 350-degree oven for about 15 minutes or until apple slices are tender. Center a *crêpe* in the buttered baking-and-serving dish, spread with a layer of apple slices, sprinkle with macaroons, and with a few drops of butter and cognac if you wish. Lay a *crêpe* on top, cover with apples, and continue thus, ending with a *crêpe*. Sprinkle with melted butter and sugar. About 30 minutes before serving, bake in middle level of a preheated 375-degree oven until bubbling hot. Serve as is, or flame as in the preceding recipe.

CRÊPES SUZETTE

For 18 crêpes serving 6 people

3 cups orange butter
A chafing dish
18 cooked *crêpes*, 5 to 6
  inches in diameter

2 Tb granulated sugar
⅓ cup each of orange
  liqueur and cognac

Heat the orange butter in a chafing dish until bubbling and the mixture is slightly caramelized—this will take several minutes. Dip both sides of a *crêpe* in hot butter, fold *crêpe* in half its best side out, and in half again to form a wedge shape. Place at side of dish and repeat rapidly with the rest of the *crêpes*. Sprinkle 2 tablespoons of sugar over the *crêpes*, and pour on the liqueurs. Shake pan gently while liqueurs heat, and if they do not flame up automatically, ignite with a match. Spoon the liqueur over the *crêpes* until the flames die down. Serve on very hot plates.

The Twenty-seventh Show

STEAKS AND HAMBURGERS
❧ · ❧

Hamburger is every bit as good as steak, and steaks even better than ever when you cook them the French way, sautéed and served with a delicious sauce which uses every bit of the flavorful meat juices left in the sauté pan.

HAMBURGERS A LA FRANÇAISE
For 6 medium-sized hamburgers

¾ cup finely minced onions, previously cooked in 2 Tb butter
1½ lbs. lean, ground beef from the neck and plate
2 Tb ground beef suet, beef marrow, or softened butter
1½ tsp salt

⅛ tsp pepper
⅛ tsp thyme
1 egg
A big mixing bowl
Flour on a plate (about ½ cup)
A heavy skillet
1 Tb butter and 1 Tb oil
A hot serving platter

Place all ingredients except flour, butter, and oil in the mixing bowl and beat to blend thoroughly. Form hamburgers into cakes. Just before cooking, dredge in flour and shake off excess. Sauté in very hot butter and oil and remove to a hot platter. Keep warm while making the following sauce—2 to 3 minutes.

Sauce Bordelaise
(*Red Wine and Marrow Sauce for Hamburgers or Steak*)
For 6 servings

A 4-inch piece of beef marrow
2 Tb minced shallots or scallions

1 tsp cornstarch blended with 1 tsp water

| ½ cup beef bouillon | Salt and pepper |
| ⅔ cup red wine | 2 Tb minced parsley |

Stand bone on one end and split with a cleaver to expose marrow. Dig out marrow in one piece using a small knife. Then dipping knife in hot water for each cut, slice or dice marrow. Bring bouillon and wine to the boil in a small saucepan, remove from heat, add marrow, and set aside. When meat is done, remove to hot platter and pour fat out of frying pan. Stir in shallots or scallions, drain marrow and reserve; add liquid to pan. Boil rapidly, scraping up coagulated sauté juices with a wooden spoon. When reduced to about ½ cup, remove from heat and stir in cornstarch. Simmer 1 minute; add salt and pepper to taste. Remove from heat, fold in marrow and parsley, and pour over meat.

STEAK CUTS ࢞

(Allow 1 pound trimmed and boneless steak for 2 to 3 people; ¾ pound of bone-in steak per person)

> *Most expensive:* trimmed *filet* or tenderloin
> *Very expensive:* trimmed loin strip
> *Expensive:* boneless hip or sirloin; trimmed porterhouse, T-bone, rib, Delmonico
> *Moderate:* trimmed boneless shoulder arm and blade
> *Least expensive:* trimmed boneless chuck and flank

SAUTÉED STEAK, HENRI IV
(Filet Steaks with Artichokes or Mushrooms, Béarnaise Sauce)
For 4 people

1½ Tb butter	previously sautéed in
½ Tb cooking oil	clear melted butter
A heavy frying pan	Salt and pepper
4 *filet* steaks, or other cuts	2 Tb minced shallots or
from the preceding list,	scallions
1 inch thick	⅓ cup Madeira wine
4 rectangles white bread,	

4 cooked artichoke bottoms, or large broiled mushroom caps	½ cup *béarnaise* (*hollandaise* with wine vinegar and tarragon flavoring) (see p. 278)

Heat butter and oil in the frying pan until butter foam has almost subsided; dry steaks on paper towels and sauté for 3 to 4 minutes on each side. Meat is medium rare as soon as a little pearling of juice appears on top, and meat feels slightly springy when pressed. Place steaks on toast rectangles and arrange on a hot platter; season with salt and pepper. Pour fat out of pan, add shallots or scallions and wine, boil down rapidly, scraping up meat juices, then pour over steaks. Place a hot artichoke bottom or mushroom cap on each steak and fill with *sauce béarnaise*. Garnish platter with buttered asparagus tips or peas, and sautéed potatoes. Serve with hot French bread and red Bordeaux wine.

The Twenty-eighth Show

THE POTATO SHOW

Be the edible ever so humble, it can be made wonderfully gastronomical when subjected to the imagination of the French. As they can dress the egg in a thousand ways, so can they do wonders with the potato, in many instances making it almost a meal in itself. Here are two for the oven, and two for the pan.

GRATIN DAUPHINOIS
(Scalloped Potatoes au Gratin)
For 6 people

2 lbs. "boiling" potatoes, peeled	1 small clove mashed garlic
1 cup milk	1 tsp salt
A 6-cup flameproof baking dish, 2 inches deep	⅛ tsp pepper
	3 to 4 Tb butter

(Preheat oven to 425 degrees.)

Slice potatoes ⅛ inch thick and drop into a bowl of cold water. Bring milk to the boil in baking dish with garlic, salt, and pepper. Drain potatoes, add to boiling milk, and distribute butter over them. Bake in middle level of preheated oven for about 25 minutes, until milk is absorbed, potatoes are tender, and top has browned. (If not served immediately, keep warm, uncovered, adding a bit more milk if potatoes seem dry.)

SERVING

Serve with roasts, steaks, or chops.

GRATIN DE POMMES DE TERRE ET SAUCISSON
(Sausage and Potato Casserole)
For 4 people

3 cups sliced, previously boiled potatoes (about 1 lb.)	in diameter and 2 inches deep
1 cup minced onions, previously cooked in butter	3 eggs
½ lb. sliced Polish sausage	1½ cups light cream
A lightly buttered baking dish or pie plate, 8 inches	¼ tsp salt
	⅛ tsp pepper
	¼ cup grated Swiss cheese
	1 Tb butter

(Preheat oven to 375 degrees.)

Arrange layers of potatoes, onions, and sausage in baking dish. Blend eggs, cream, salt, and pepper in a bowl, pour into baking dish, sprinkle with cheese, and dot with the butter. Bake in upper third of preheated oven for 30 to 40 minutes, until top has nicely browned.

SERVING

Serve as main-course lunch or supper dish.

POMMES DE TERRE BYRON
(Baked-potato Pancake)

Split potatoes as soon as baked. Scoop out flesh and break up in a bowl with a mixing fork. Fluff in salt, pepper, and softened butter to taste, and moisten slightly with heavy cream. Sauté in a frying pan in hot butter until bottom is crusty, then *either* flip over and brown other side; *or* slip onto a lightly buttered baking dish, sprinkle with grated Swiss cheese, cream, and melted butter, then brown under a moderately hot broiler.

SERVING

Serve with roasts or steaks.

CRÊPES DE POMMES DE TERRE
(Grated-potato Pancakes)
For about 15 pancakes 3 inches in diameter, or 2 pancakes
8 inches in diameter

8 ounces cream cheese	2½ lbs. "baking" potatoes
3 Tb flour	(4 cups when grated)
2 eggs	3 to 4 Tb heavy cream
½ tsp salt	A 10-inch frying pan
⅛ tsp pepper	About 1½ Tb butter, more
6 ounces (1¼ cups) Swiss	if needed
cheese, cut into ⅛-inch	About 1½ Tb oil, more if
dice	needed

Blend the cream cheese, flour, eggs, salt, and pepper in a

large mixing bowl with a mixing fork. Stir in the diced cheese. Peel potatoes, grate through large holes of grater. A handful at a time, twist potatoes into a ball in the corner of a towel and extract as much juice as possible. Blend into the cheese and eggs, then stir in enough cream to make mixture the consistency of creamy cole slaw.

Heat butter and oil in a frying pan, ladle in small or large mounds of potato batter about ⅜ inch thick. Cook over moderately high heat for 3 to 4 minutes, until bubbles appear through batter. Lower heat slightly, turn, and cook 4 to 5 minutes more on the other side. If not served immediately, arrange in one layer on a baking sheet, and leave uncovered. Crisp for several minutes in a preheated 400-degree oven.

SERVING

Serve with roasts, steaks, poached or fried eggs.

The Twenty-ninth Show

FISH SOUFFLÉ ON A PLATTER
(Sauce Mousseline Sabayon)

A soufflé is nothing but a thick sauce into which stiffly beaten egg whites are incorporated: the egg whites automatically force the mixture to puff up in a hot oven. As the puff is automatic, baking a soufflé on a platter is far more dramatic than baking it in a dish. This lovely recipe is the specialty of a small restaurant on the edge of Móntmartre, where three generations of family cooks have made both the soufflé and the restaurant famous.

FILETS DE POISSON EN SOUFFLÉ
(Fish Soufflé Baked on a Platter)
For 6 people

POACHING THE FISH

½ lb. skinless flounder or sole fillets
An enameled or stainless-steel saucepan
½ cup dry white vermouth

plus water, or 1½ cups white-wine fish stock
1 Tb minced shallots, green onions, or scallions
Salt and pepper

Place the fish in the saucepan with the vermouth or fish stock and enough cold water to cover. Add shallots and seasonings. Simmer uncovered for about 6 minutes, or until fish is just cooked through; remove fish to a side dish. Rapidly boil down cooking liquid until you have about ½ cup; reserve half for the soufflé mixture and the rest for the sauce.

THE SOUFFLÉ MIXTURE

2½ Tb butter
3 Tb flour
A 2½-quart saucepan
¾ cup hot milk
Salt, pepper, and nutmeg

1 egg yolk
5 stiffly beaten egg whites
½ cup coarsely grated Swiss cheese

Cook the butter and flour together in the saucepan for 2 minutes without coloring. Remove from heat. Beat in the hot milk with a wire whip, then ¼ cup of the fish-cooking liquid. Bring to the boil, stirring, for 1 minute. Remove from heat. Beat in the egg yolk. Stir in one fourth of the beaten egg whites, then delicately fold in the rest of the egg whites and all but 2 tablespoons of the cheese.

BAKING THE SOUFFLÉ

(Preheat oven to 425 degrees.)
Lightly butter an oval fireproof platter about 16 inches long.

Spread a ¼-inch layer of soufflé mixture in the bottom of the platter. Flake the poached fish fillets and divide into 6 portions on the platter. Heap the rest of the soufflé mixture over the fish, making 6 mounds. Sprinkle with the remaining cheese and set on rack in upper third of preheated oven. Bake for 15 to 18 minutes, or until soufflé has puffed and browned on top. Serve immediately with the following sauce:

Sauce Mousseline Sabayon
(Hollandaise with Cream for Fish)
For 1½ cups

¼ cup reduced fish-cooking
   liquid
3 Tb heavy cream
4 egg yolks
A 6-cup enameled saucepan
   and a wire whip

1½ to 2 sticks (6 to 8
   ounces) softened butter
Salt, white pepper, and
   drops of lemon juice

Blend the fish stock, cream, and egg yolks in the saucepan with a wire whip. Then stir over low heat until mixture slowly thickens into a light cream that coats the wires of the whip—be careful not to overheat or the egg yolks will scramble, but you must heat them enough to thicken. Remove from heat and at once begin to beat in the butter, a tablespoon at a time. Sauce will gradually thicken into a heavy cream. Season to taste with salt, pepper, and drops of lemon juice. Keep over tepid—not hot—water until ready to use.

The Thirtieth Show

MOUSSAKA AND RATATOUILLE
❧ · ❧
(Eggplant)

With its sleek purple skin, bright-green topknot, and graceful shape, the eggplant is one of our handsomest vegetables, and here are two splendid recipes that do it justice. The *ratatouille* is a vegetable casserole with eggplant, zucchini, and the flavors of Provence; the *moussaka* is an exotic meat loaf enclosed in eggplant skin. You will notice that in both cases the eggplant is salted and allowed to steep for about half an hour: salt draws out all the bitterness and also all that excess liquid which otherwise would turn your creation into a mushy stew.

RATATOUILLE
(*Provençal Eggplant and Zucchini Casserole with Onions, Tomatoes, Peppers, and Herbs*)
For 4 to 6 people

When a *ratatouille* is made as it should be, it is a casserole of cooked vegetables in which each of them retains its shape and its own special character. Therefore, the eggplant and the zucchini are sautéed separately; the onions, peppers, and tomatoes are also cooked apart, and then everything is combined for a brief communal simmer. General proportions are an equal weight each of eggplant, zucchini, and onions, twice the weight of tomatoes, and a modicum of other ingredients for additional flavor. *Ratatouille* may be served either hot or cold.

PRELIMINARY SALTING

½ lb. eggplant
½ lb. zucchini

A 3-quart mixing bowl
1 tsp salt

Peel eggplant and cut into lengthwise slices ⅜ inch thick. Scrub zucchini under cold water, cut off and discard two ends, and slice zucchini into lengthwise pieces ⅜ inch thick. Toss the vegetables together in a bowl with the salt and let stand 30 minutes. Drain; dry in a towel.

SAUTÉING

4 or more Tb olive oil
A 10- to 12-inch enameled
  or no-stick frying pan
½ lb. (1½ cups) sliced
  onions
1 cup sliced green peppers
  (about 2 peppers)
2 cloves mashed garlic

Salt and pepper
1 lb. tomatoes, peeled,
  seeded, and juiced (1½
  cups pulp), or 1 cup
  drained canned pear-
  shaped tomatoes
3 Tb minced parsley

Heat olive oil in the frying pan, then sauté eggplant and zucchini slices to brown lightly on both sides. Remove to side dish. Add more oil if necessary, and cook onions and peppers slowly until soft. Stir in garlic and season with salt and pepper. Slice tomato pulp into strips and place over onions and peppers. Cover pan and cook for 5 minutes, then uncover, raise heat, and boil for several minutes until tomato juice has almost completely evaporated. Season with salt and pepper; fold in parsley.

ASSEMBLING AND BAKING

A 2½-quart flameproof casserole 2 inches deep

Spoon a third of the tomato mixture in the bottom of the casserole. Arrange half of the eggplant and zucchini on top, then half the remaining tomatoes. Cover with the remaining eggplant and zucchini, and the last of the tomato mixture. Cover casserole and simmer over low heat for 10 minutes. Uncover, tip casserole and baste with the juices rendered, and correct seasoning if necessary. Raise heat slightly and boil slowly until juices have almost entirely evaporated.

SERVING

Serve hot with roasts, steaks, hamburgers, broiled fish.
Serve cold with cold meats and fish, or as a cold hors d'oeuvre.

MOUSSAKA
(Lamb and Eggplant Mold)
For 8 people

The origin of *moussaka* appears to be Rumanian, but it is a dish often served in the Near East, where the eggplant and lamb are cooked in layers in a baking dish. In this attractive French version, a cylindrical dish is lined with the skins of cooked eggplant, then filled with sautéed eggplant, mushrooms, ground cooked lamb, and various flavorings. After baking, the *moussaka* is unmolded. Surrounded with tomato sauce if served hot, with fresh greenery if served cold, it is as delicious to eat as it is wonderful to look at.

PRELIMINARY SALTING AND BAKING OF THE EGGPLANT

5 lbs. of eggplant (4 to 5 eggplants, each 7 to 8 inches long)	2 Tb olive oil A shallow roasting pan
1 Tb salt	1 Tb olive oil A 3-quart mixing bowl

(Preheat oven to 400 degrees.)
Remove green caps and slice eggplants in half lengthwise; cut deep gashes in the flesh of each half. Sprinkle with salt and let stand 30 minutes. Squeeze out water, dry flesh side, and brush with olive oil. Pour ½ inch water in a roasting pan, add eggplants, flesh side up, and bake 30 to 40 minutes in preheated oven, or until tender. Scoop out flesh, leaving eggplant skins intact (use a spoon or grapefruit knife). Chop flesh and sauté for a minute or two in hot olive oil. Turn into mixing bowl.

ASSEMBLING AND BAKING

A lightly oiled cylindrical 2-quart baking dish 3½	to 4 inches deep and 7 inches in diameter

2½ cups ground cooked lamb

⅔ cup minced onions, previously cooked in butter

1 cup minced mushrooms, previously cooked in butter

1 tsp salt

⅛ tsp pepper

½ tsp thyme

½ tsp ground rosemary

1 small clove mashed garlic

⅔ cup beef stock or bouillon simmered 2 minutes with

½ Tb cornstarch

3 Tb tomato paste

3 eggs (U. S. graded "large")

A pan of boiling water

A serving dish

Line mold with eggplant skins, pointed ends meeting at center-bottom of mold, purple sides against mold. Beat all the above ingredients into the chopped eggplant, turn into lined mold, and fold dangling eggplant skins up over the surface. Cover with aluminum foil and a lid. Bake in a pan of boiling water in a 375-degree oven for 1½ hours. Let cool 10 minutes, then unmold on a serving dish.

SERVING

Serve hot with tomato sauce, steamed rice, French bread, and *rosé* wine.

Serve cold with tomato salad, French bread, and *rosé* wine.

The Thirty-first Show

DINNER IN A POT
⋑⋐ • ⋑⋐

Beef, pork or veal, chicken, sausage, and vegetables all cook together with aromatic liquid in a big kettle, providing you with a sumptuous dinner, and a delicious bouillon for other meals.

Various items are added to the kettle at different times, according to how long each takes to cook; if one part is done before the rest, it is removed, then added again to the kettle to warm up before serving. Count on about 5 hours from start to finish, but the kettle does not need more than occasional attention as you go about your business elsewhere in the house. Be sure to choose a kettle large enough to hold all the ingredients listed. Estimated cooking times are as follows:

> *Beef:* 3 to 4 hours, depending on quality
> *Pork* or *veal:* 2½ to 3 hours
> *Whole chicken:* 2½ to 3 hours
> *Cut-up chicken:* 2 to 2½ hours
> *Vegetable garnish:* 1½ hours
> *Sausage:* ½ hour

POTÉE NORMANDE: POT-AU-FEU
(*French Boiled Dinner*)
For 12 to 14 people

THE BEEF AND PORK OR VEAL

A kettle large enough to hold all ingredients listed in recipe
A 4-lb. boneless beef-chuck pot roast
A 4-lb. boneless pork or veal shoulder
2 each of celery ribs, carrots, onions

1 lb. beef and veal bones, cracked
A large herb bouquet: 8 parsley sprigs, 6 peppercorns, 4 cloves, 3 cloves garlic, 2 tsp thyme, 2 bay leaves, all tied in washed cheesecloth
2 Tb salt

Have the beef and pork or veal tied securely; to each piece of meat, attach a string long enough to fasten to handle of kettle. Place beef in kettle; tie string to handle. Add vegetables, bones, herb bouquet, and salt, and cover by 6 inches with cold water. Bring to simmer, skim off scum, and simmer for 1 hour. Then add veal or pork.

CHICKEN AND STUFFING

(If you wish to use cut-up rather than stewing chicken, tie in washed cheesecloth before adding to kettle.)

4 cups stale white bread crumbs	½ tsp thyme
A large mixing bowl	1 egg
¼ to ½ cup bouillon or milk	The chopped chicken liver, heart, and peeled gizzard, previously sautéed in butter with ⅔ cup minced onions
¼ cup melted butter	
¼ cup diced boiled ham	
3 ounces (½ package) cream cheese	Salt and pepper to taste
	A 4-lb. stewing chicken

Place bread crumbs in bowl, moisten with a little bouillon or milk, then beat in the butter, ham, cheese, thyme, egg, and giblets, and season to taste with salt and pepper. Stuff and truss the chicken, tie a long string to it, place in kettle and tie end of string to handle. Bring kettle rapidly back to simmer, skimming as necessary.

VEGETABLE GARNISH AND SAUSAGE

Carrots, peeled and quartered	Leeks, cut to 6 to 8 inches long, green part split lengthwise, thoroughly washed
Turnips, peeled and quartered	
Onions, peeled, root ends pierced	Whole Polish sausage or individual Italian sausages

Prepare vegetables and tie each group in washed cheesecloth; add to kettle 1½ hours before end of estimated simmering time. Add sausage, or sausages (tied in cheesecloth), ½ hour before end.

Meats and chicken are done when a fork pierces the flesh easily. If *potée* is done before you are ready, it will stay warm for a good 45 minutes, or may be reheated.

SERVING

To serve, drain meats, cut and discard strings, and arrange

meat and chicken on a large, hot platter. Distribute vegetables around, sprinkle with parsley, and baste with a bit of the cooking stock. Strain and degrease a bowlful of cooking stock to serve with the platter.

Suggested accompaniments: boiled rice or potatoes; tomato, caper, or horseradish sauce; Kosher salt; pickles; French bread; red or *rosé* wine.

The Thirty-second Show

QUICK-CHANGE PASTRY
⮜⋑ · ⋐⮞
(Pâte à Choux)

Pâte à choux is a very thick *panade*—meaning flour, water, and butter cooked together—into which whole eggs are beaten. However you cook it, the eggs make the *panade* swell up. A tremendously versatile mixture, it can become cream puffs, cheese puffs, shrimp puffs, dumplings, or *gnocchi*, and is the base for many a mousse. Even leftover *pâte à choux* is useful: beat in some cream, a bit of cheese, and diced ham, clams, or whatever you have of that nature, and it is a spread for hot puffed hors d'oeuvre.

PÂTE A CHOUX
(*Choux Paste or Cream-Puff Pastry*)
For about 2 cups

1 cup water	⅛ tsp pepper
6 Tb butter, cut into	Pinch nutmeg
pieces	A heavy-bottomed 2-quart
1 tsp salt	saucepan

1 cup all-purpose flour   cup; sweep off excess
(measure by sifting   flour)
directly into dry-measure   4 eggs (U. S. graded
                                    "large")

Place water, butter, salt, pepper, and nutmeg in the saucepan and bring to the boil. When butter has melted and water is bubbling, remove from heat; immediately pour in all the flour and beat with a wooden spoon to blend thoroughly. Set over moderate heat and beat with a wooden spoon for a minute or two, until mixture leaves sides of pan clean, leaves spoon clean, and films on bottom of pan; this is to evaporate excess moisture. Remove from heat.

Make a depression in the center, break an egg into it, and beat thoroughly until egg is absorbed. Continue with the rest of the eggs, beating them in one by one until thoroughly absorbed.

This is now a *pâte à choux*, and you should use it while still warm or it will stiffen too much for handling. You can refrigerate or freeze leftover *pâte à choux*. To use again, bring to room temperature, then beat over hot water until pastry is just tepid; if overheated, eggs will loose their puffing ability.

FOR SWEET DESSERT PUFFS: Omit salt, pepper, and nutmeg; add 1 teaspoon sugar to the preceding proportions.

Forming and Baking Small Puffs
For about 36 puffs 1½ inches in diameter

2 lightly buttered baking   2 cups *choux* paste
sheets (14 by 18 inches if   1 egg and ½ tsp water
possible)   beaten in a small bowl
A pastry bag with ½-inch   A pastry brush
tube, or a soup spoon

(Preheat oven to 425 degrees.)
Either with a pastry bag or with a soup spoon, form circular blobs of *choux* paste 1 inch in diameter and 1 inch high spaced 1½ to 2 inches apart on the baking sheets. Glaze tops of puffs

with egg, pushing them into shape, if necessary, with the flat of your pastry brush. Do not let glaze dribble down sides of puffs onto baking sheet; this will prevent proper rising.

Bake in upper- and lower-middle levels of preheated oven for about 20 minutes, or until puffs are a nice golden brown and crisp to the touch. They should double in size. Pierce each puff with a knife to let out steam; return to turned-off hot oven for 10 minutes to dry out. (Cooled baked puffs may be frozen.)

The easiest way to fill small puffs is with a pastry bag and ¼-inch tube; plunge it into side or bottom of puff and squeeze in the filling.

Small Cheese Puffs

Beat 1 cup finely grated Swiss cheese into the warm *choux* paste; form the puffs as in the preceding recipe but top each egg-glazed blob with a pinch of grated cheese before baking.

Forming and Baking Large Puffs
For 10 to 12 puffs 3 inches in diameter

Same equipment as for small puffs
2 cups *choux* paste

1 egg and ½ tsp water, beaten together

(Preheat oven to 425 degrees.)

Use a ¾-inch tube opening for your pastry bag. Squeeze paste into 2¼-inch mounds 1 inch high and spaced 2 inches apart on lightly buttered baking sheets. Paint with beaten egg. Bake 20 minutes in preheated oven until doubled in size and lightly browned. Reduce oven heat to 375 degrees and bake 10 to 15 minutes more. When firm and crusty, make a 1-inch slit in the side of each and return to turned-off hot oven for 15 minutes. Open puffs, scoop out damp interiors, and let puff shells cool on a rack before re-assembling.

Gnocchi
(*Cheese-flavored Potato Dumplings*)
For about 1 dozen 3-inch gnocchi

Serve these delicious sausage-shaped objects as a hot first course, as a main-course luncheon or supper dish, or to accompany a roast, chops, or steaks.

THE GNOCCHI PASTE

2 cups plain mashed potatoes A heavy-bottomed saucepan	1 cup warm *choux* pastry ⅓ cup grated Swiss cheese Salt and pepper

Stir the mashed potatoes in the saucepan over moderately high heat until potatoes begin to film bottom of pan; this is to remove excess moisture. Remove from heat and beat in the *choux* pastry, cheese, and salt and pepper to taste. Roll spoonfuls of the mixture on a lightly floured board to form cylinders about 2½ inches long and 1 inch in diameter.

POACHING OR PRELIMINARY COOKING

Arrange in a lightly buttered skillet or chicken fryer, cover by 1½ inches with boiling water, and add salt to taste. Cook, uncovered, at below the simmer for about 15 minutes—if water actually simmers, *gnocchi* may disintegrate. *Gnocchi* are done when they rise to the surface and roll over easily. Remove with a slotted spoon and drain on paper towels. (Cooked *gnocchi* may be refrigerated for several days or frozen.)

FINAL COOKING

(Preheat oven to 375 degrees.)
Arrange the poached *gnocchi* in a heavily buttered shallow baking dish, sprinkle with grated cheese and melted butter, and bake in upper third of preheated oven for about 25 minutes, or until bubbling hot and nicely browned on top.

The Thirty-third Show

CARAMEL DESSERTS

∽§ · §∾

(Caramel Custard and Apple Custard)

Folding the tongue around a spoonful of caramel custard is certainly one of life's precious moments. The gentle texture of the custard, the lingering savor of vanilla and caramel, and that lovely brown syrup of which there never seems to be quite enough—it all tastes so good one rather hates to eat it. Caramel is simply sugar and water boiled rapidly together until the syrup turns a light brown. In the two following recipes, one for the classic custard and one for caramelized apple slices, the hot syrup is rolled around in a baking dish before the custard mixture is poured in; when the dessert is baked and unmolded, it is enrobed in a brown cloak of caramel.

HOW TO CARAMELIZE A MOLD OR BAKING DISH. For a 6- to 8-cup mold, bring ½ cup granulated sugar and 2½ tablespoons water to the boil in a small, heavy saucepan, slowly swirling the pan by its handle until sugar has dissolved completely and liquid is perfectly clear. Then boil, swirling pan frequently, until sugar has turned a caramel-brown—2 to 3 minutes. Immediately pour the hot caramel into your mold or dish and turn in all directions to film bottom and sides. When caramel ceases to run, reverse mold onto a plate.

CRÈME RENVERSÉE AU CARAMEL
(Molded Caramel Custard)
For 6 to 8 people

5 eggs (U. S. graded
   "large")
4 egg yolks
A 2½-quart mixing bowl
   and wire whip
¾ cup granulated sugar
3¾ cups simmering milk

A vanilla bean steeped for
   10 minutes in the hot
   milk, or 1½ tsp vanilla
   extract
A 6-cup caramelized cylindrical mold or baking dish
   about 3½ inches deep
A pan of boiling water

(Preheat oven to 350 degrees.)

Beat eggs and yolks in the mixing bowl with a wire whip; gradually beat in sugar. When mixture is light and foamy, beat in hot milk in a very thin stream. (Beat in vanilla extract if used.) Strain through a fine sieve into caramelized mold. Set in a pan of boiling water and bake in lower third of preheated oven. To ensure a smooth custard, regulate heat so water in pan never quite simmers. Custard is done in about 40 minutes, or when a knife plunged down through center comes out clean.

SERVING

To serve warm, let settle for 10 minutes in a pan of cold water. Turn a warm serving dish upside down over custard, then reverse the two to unmold the custard.

To serve cold, let cool to room temperature; chill several hours, then unmold.

POMMES EN BELLE VUE
(Molded Apple Custard)
For 6 to 8 people

10 cups peeled and sliced
   apples (about 4 lbs.)
½ cup granulated sugar
2 Tb lemon juice

¼ tsp cinnamon
⅓ cup butter, previously
   melted
A large, shallow roasting pan

(Preheat oven to 350 degrees.)

Fold the apple slices with the sugar, lemon juice, cinnamon, and butter in the roasting pan. Bake for 20 to 30 minutes in preheated oven until barely tender and slightly caramelized.

4 eggs (U. S. graded "large")	A 2-quart caramelized cylindrical mold or baking dish
1 egg white	3½ to 4 inches deep
¼ cup rum or orange juice	A pan of boiling water
A large mixing bowl	

Beat eggs, egg white, and rum or orange juice in the mixing bowl until blended. Fold in the apple slices and turn into the caramelized mold. Set mold in a pan of boiling water and bake in lower third of preheated oven for about 1½ hours, until dessert shows a faint line of shrinkage from mold. Unmold as described in preceding recipe. Serve hot or cold with custard sauce or lightly whipped cream.

PRALIN

(Nut Brittle for Almonds, Walnuts, Hazelnuts, Pecans, Peanuts)
For about 2 cups

1 cup shelled nuts, with or without their skins	⅓ cup water
A shallow roasting pan	An oiled marble slab or roasting pan
1 cup granulated sugar	

Spread nuts in a shallow roasting pan and dry them out for 20 to 30 minutes in a 300-degree oven. If they are moist, they will soften in the brittle.

Make a caramel with the sugar and water. Stir the nuts into the hot syrup, bring just to the boil, and turn out onto a lightly oiled marble or roasting pan. When cool, in about 20 minutes, break up into pieces. Pulverize in an electric blender or meat grinder, or pound in a mortar or heavy bowl.

Store in an airtight jar, and freeze if weather is humid. Use as a topping for desserts or ice cream, or fold into dessert creams or sauces.

The Thirty-fourth Show

COOKING YOUR GOOSE
~§·§~

There are many who prefer braised goose to roast goose because the meat is tenderer and juicier, and the closed, moist cooking of a braise renders out more fat than open-pan roasting. You can use any stuffing you wish for braised goose, from the conventional sage and bread crumb, or sausage and chestnut, to this unusual combination of prunes and liver *pâté*. When you buy your goose, be sure the label states that it is a "young roasting goose," and it should not weigh more than around 11 pounds, ready-to-cook. Most American geese now come frozen; to defrost, either leave the goose in its plastic wrapping and thaw for 2 to 3 days in the refrigerator, or unwrap and set in a sinkful of cold water for several hours, removing giblet package as soon as you can pry it loose.

OIE BRAISÉE AUX PRUNEAUX
(*Braised Goose with Prune and Liver Stuffing*)

For 8 people

PRUNE AND LIVER STUFFING

40 to 50 large prunes
The goose liver, minced
2 Tb finely minced shallots
   or scallions
1 Tb butter
⅓ cup port wine

½ cup (4 ounces) *foie gras*
   or canned liver paste
Pinch each of allspice and
   thyme
Salt and pepper
3 to 4 Tb dry white bread
   crumbs

Drop prunes into boiling water and soak for 5 minutes, or until tender. Remove pits as neatly as possible. Sauté goose liver and shallots or scallions in hot butter for 2 minutes; scrape into a mixing bowl. Rapidly boil down port wine in sauté pan until reduced to 1 tablespoon; scrape into mixing bowl. Beat in *foie gras* or liver paste, allspice and thyme, and season to taste. If necessary, beat in bread crumbs by spoonfuls until mixture is firm enough for stuffing. Fold ½ teaspoon into each prune.

PREPARING AND BROWNING THE GOOSE

A 9-lb. ready-to-cook goose   A broiling pan
1 Tb salt

Cut out wishbone (for easier carving), chop wings off at elbows, and pull loose fat from inside goose. Rub cavity with salt, stuff loosely with prunes, and truss. Prick skin at ½-inch intervals around sides of breasts, thighs, and back. Set goose in a broiling pan and brown under a moderately hot broiler, turning frequently, for about 15 minutes, removing accumulated fat from pan as necessary.

BRAISING THE GOOSE

Estimated Cooking Time: 2 hours and 20 to 30 minutes.

The goose neck, wing ends,
    gizzard, and heart
½ cup each of sliced carrots
    and onions
2 Tb goose fat
A covered roaster just large
    enough to hold the goose
½ cup flour

2 cups red wine (such as
    Beaujolais, Médoc, or
    California Mountain Red)
Salt
1 Tb sage
2 cloves garlic
4 to 6 cups beef stock or
    bouillon

(Preheat oven to 350 degrees.)
Chop the giblets into 1-inch pieces, dry, and brown with the vegetables in hot goose fat in the roaster over moderately high heat. Lower heat, stir in flour, and cook, stirring, for 3 minutes to brown lightly. Remove from heat; stir in the wine. Salt the goose and place on its side in the roaster. Add sage, garlic, and enough beef stock or bouillon to come halfway up the goose.

Bring to the simmer, cover, and set in lower third of preheated oven. Regulate heat so liquid simmers slowly throughout cooking; turn goose on other side in 1 hour, on back after 2 hours. Goose is done when drumsticks move slightly in sockets and, when fleshiest part of one is pierced, the juices run pale yellow. Do not overcook.

SAUCE AND SERVING

Drain goose and place on a hot platter; cut and discard trussing strings. Skim as much fat as you can off braising sauce; you will have several cupfuls, which you can save for sautéing potatoes, chicken, or for basting roasts. Ladle about 4 cups sauce through a strainer into a saucepan and skim off fat again. Bring to the simmer, skimming, and carefully correct seasoning. Spoon a bit of sauce over goose and pour rest into a hot gravy bowl.

Serve with braised onions and chestnuts, or Brussels sprouts and mashed potatoes; red Burgundy wine.

The Thirty-fifth Show

CHESTNUT COOKERY
❧ • ☙

Chestnut trees used to be the glory of eastern America from Maine to Florida, some trees reaching a height of one hundred feet with trunks eight and even twelve feet in diameter. In 1900 they were attacked by a virulent fungus, and the 1930's saw the very last of our American chestnuts. Fortunately, the European variety, *Castanea sativa*, still survives, and Europe is where all our fresh chestnuts come from during the late fall and winter months. Chestnuts have been a source of food for centuries, not only as nuts, but dried and ground into flour. They are delicious as a vegetable, braised, glazed, or puréed and served with turkey, goose, or pork. When fresh chestnuts are out of season, you can buy them canned. Here are recipes for both, including a quick and handsome dessert using canned chestnuts.

PREPARATION OF FRESH CHESTNUTS FOR COOKING. Peel a thin strip of shell off the side of each chestnut. Drop prepared chestnuts in a saucepan of cold water to cover by 1 inch. Bring to the boil, simmer 1 minute, and remove from heat. Immediately start lifting out chestnuts, three at a time, with a slotted spoon. With a small knife, peel off shell and brown inner skin, being sure to dig out all pieces of skin between cracks of nut. Set aside any nuts with recalcitrant skins; drop them into boiling water, boil 1 minute, then peel one by one. (Chestnuts must be hot for easy peeling.)

COOKING OF FRESH CHESTNUTS
(As a Vegetable)

Set peeled chestnuts in a saucepan and cover with beef stock or half-and-half mixture of canned beef bouillon and water, covering with the liquid by 1 inch. Tie 2 celery stalks, 1 bay leaf, ½ teaspoon thyme, and 6 parsley sprigs (per 2 quarts peeled chestnuts) in washed cheesecloth, add to saucepan, and bring to the simmer. Simmer very slowly, uncovered, for about 40 minutes, adding more liquid if necessary, to keep chestnuts covered. Chestnuts are done when just tender (eat one as a test); do not overcook or chestnuts will become mushy. Set aside in liquid until needed.

CANNED WHOLE CHESTNUTS
(As a Vegetable)

Use the same beef stock, herb, and vegetable mixture as in the preceding recipe; bring to the boil and simmer 20 to 30 minutes. Empty 1 or more cans of "whole unflavored" chestnuts into another saucepan, bring to the simmer, drain, and add the chestnuts to the flavored stock. Bring to the boil, simmer uncovered for 5 minutes, then remove from heat and let the chestnuts steep in the hot liquid for 30 minutes so they will absorb its flavor. Drain when ready to use in any of the following recipes.

GLAZED CHESTNUTS
(As a Vegetable Garnish)
For 4 cups cooked chestnuts

¾ cup liquid (chestnut-
cooking stock, or stock
and dry port or Madeira)

1½ Tb arrowroot or corn-
starch in a small bowl
2 Tb butter

Gradually blend the liquid into the cornstarch to form a smooth mixture. Pour into a wide saucepan or chicken fryer, bring to the simmer for 2 minutes, stirring. Add the drained cooked chestnuts; toss and swirl for several minutes until well heated through, adding a bit more liquid if necessary. Remove from heat, fold in the butter, and toss to cover chestnuts with a glaze of buttery sauce. Serve immediately.

PURÉED CHESTNUTS
(As a Vegetable)

Prepare fresh or canned chestnuts as described in preceding recipes. Drain and purée through a food mill or sieve. Beat in spoonfuls of cooking stock to make a mixture the consistency of mashed potatoes. Beat in spoonfuls of butter and/or cream to taste (2 to 3 tablespoons per cup), and salt and pepper. Set aside uncovered; reheat over simmering water, stirring frequently, until heated through—this will take a good half hour if purée has been refrigerated.

PALISSADE AUX MARRONS
(*Molded Chestnut and Chocolate Dessert*)
For 8 to 12 people

Two 1-pound-5-ounce cans whole unflavored chestnuts

½ lb. softened unsalted butter

1⅓ cups (8 ounces) semi-sweet chocolate morsels, previously melted with ¼ cup kirsch or rum and 1 Tb vanilla extract

½ to ¾ cup granulated sugar, previously melted with 3 Tb each of port wine and strong coffee and ⅛ tsp salt

A 6-cup cylindrical dish 3 to 4 inches deep

About 12 finger-shaped sugar cookies

2 to 3 cups heavy cream or sweetened whipped cream

Pour contents of the 2 cans of chestnuts into a saucepan, bring to the simmer, drain, and purée through a food mill into a large mixing bowl. Beat in the butter, melted chocolate, and sugar syrup.

Line bottom of cylindrical dish with waxed paper. Turn a 1-inch layer of chestnut mixture into the dish, being careful not to touch the sides. Then line the sides of the dish with upright sugar cookies, to make a columnar effect (the chestnut mixture will hold the cookies in place). Fill the dish with the remaining chestnut mixture, cover with waxed paper, and chill for 6 hours or overnight (or for 2 or 3 days). At serving time, run a knife between the cookie column and the sides of the dish, then reverse onto a serving platter. Accompany with the cream. You might also serve a bottle of champagne *demi-sec* or a Sauternes.

The Thirty-eighth Show

COQ AU VIN
◈ · ◈
(*Chicken in Red Wine*)

Coq au vin is probably the most famous of all French chicken dishes, and certainly one of the most delicious, with its rich red-wine sauce, its tender onion and mushroom garniture, and its browned pieces of chicken with their wonderful flavor. Ideal for a party because you may prepare it completely a day or more before serving, *coq au vin* seems to be even better when done ahead so all its elements have time to steep together.

COQ AU VIN
(*Casserole of Chicken in Red Wine, Garnished with Onions, Mushrooms, and Bacon*)
For 4 to 6 people

THE BACON

A 3- to 4-ounce chunk of lean bacon	A 10-inch flameproof casserole or an electric skillet
	2 Tb cooking oil

Remove rind and cut bacon into sticks 1 inch long and ¼ inch across. Simmer for 10 minutes in 2 quarts of water, drain, rinse in cold water, and dry. Sauté slowly in the casserole (260 degrees for the electric skillet) with the oil. When bacon is very lightly browned, remove to a side dish, leaving fat in pan.

BROWNING THE CHICKEN

2½ to 3 lbs. cut-up frying chicken	⅛ tsp pepper
½ tsp salt	¼ cup cognac

Dry chicken thoroughly in a towel. Brown on all sides in the hot fat (360 degrees). Season chicken with salt and pepper, return bacon to pan, cover pan, and cook slowly (300 degrees) for 10 minutes, turning chicken once. Then uncover, pour in cognac, ignite with a lighted match. Shake pan back and forth for several seconds until flames subside.

SIMMERING IN RED WINE

3 cups Burgundy, Mâcon, Chianti, or California Mountain Red wine
1 to 2 cups beef stock or bouillon

1 Tb tomato paste
2 cloves mashed garlic
¼ tsp thyme
1 bay leaf

Pour wine into pan, and add just enough bouillon to cover the chicken. Stir in tomato paste, garlic, and herbs. Bring to the simmer, then cover and simmer slowly for about 30 minutes, or until chicken meat is tender when pierced with a fork.

THE ONIONS

12 to 24 small white onions
Salt to taste

1 to 2 Tb cooking oil

While chicken is cooking, drop onions into boiling water, bring water back to the boil, and let boil for 1 minute. Drain, shave off two ends of onions, peel carefully, and pierce a deep cross in the root end with a small knife (to keep onions whole during cooking). Heat oil in a frying pan, add onions, and toss for several minutes until lightly browned (this will be a patchy brown). Add water to halfway up onions and ¼ to ½ teaspoon salt, cover pan, and simmer slowly for 25 to 30 minutes, or until onions are tender when pierced with a knife.

THE MUSHROOMS

½ lb. fresh mushrooms
1 Tb butter

½ Tb cooking oil

Trim base of mushroom stems, remove base from stems,

wash stems and caps rapidly in cold water and dry in a towel. Cut caps into quarters, stems into bias chunks (to resemble, roughly, the cut caps). Heat butter and oil in frying pan; when bubbling hot, toss in mushrooms and sauté over high heat for 4 or 5 minutes until lightly browned.

SAUCE AND SERVING

3 Tb flour   **2 Tb softened butter**

When chicken is done, drain out cooking liquid into a sauce-pan. Skim off fat and boil down liquid, if necessary, to concentrate flavor. You should have about 2¼ cups. Remove from heat. Blend butter and flour together in a saucer; beat into the cooking liquid with a wire whip. Bring to the simmer, stirring, and simmer for a minute or two until sauce has thickened. Scrape onions and mushrooms into sauce and simmer a minute to blend flavors. Carefully taste sauce, adding more salt and pepper if you feel it necessary. Then pour sauce over chicken. (Chicken is now ready for final reheating, but can be set aside until cool, then covered and refrigerated for a day or two.)

Shortly before serving, bring to the simmer, basting chicken with sauce. Cover and simmer slowly for 4 to 5 minutes, until chicken is hot through. (Do not overcook at this point!)

Serve from casserole, or arrange on a hot platter and decorate with sprigs of parsley.

Accompany with parsley potatoes, rice, or noodles; buttered green peas or a green salad; hot French bread; and the same red wine you used for cooking the chicken.

The Thirty-ninth Show

CASSOULET
◆ · ◆
(French Baked Beans)

Cassoulet is a rich combination of beans baked with meats, as much a part of southwestern France as Boston baked beans are of New England. The following recipe makes no attempt to cut corners, for the concoction of a good *cassoulet* is a fairly long process. You can prepare it in one day, but two or even three days of leisurely on-and-off cooking make it easier. The recipe calls for a roast loin of pork, shoulder of lamb braised in wine, homemade sausage cakes, and for beans cooked with pork rind, fresh bacon or salt pork, and aromatic vegetables. The meats are cut into serving pieces and arranged in a casserole with the beans and various cooking juices, then the dish is baked in the oven for an hour to blend flavors.

Any or all of the steps leading up to the final assembly of the *cassoulet* may be carried on at various times; the assembled *cassoulet* may be refrigerated and baked a day or two later.

CASSOULET
(Beans Baked with Pork, Lamb, and Sausages)
For 10 to 12 people

THE BEANS

An 8-quart kettle containing 5 quarts of rapidly boiling water
5 cups (2 lbs.) dry white beans (Great Northern or small white California)
½ lb. fresh or salt pork rind
1 lb. lean salt pork simmered for 10 minutes in 2 quarts water
A heavy saucepan
1 cup sliced onions

A large herb bouquet: 8
parsley sprigs, 4 unpeeled
cloves garlic, 2 cloves, ½
tsp thyme, and 2 bay

leaves all tied in washed
cheesecloth
Salt

Drop beans into the boiling water. Bring rapidly back to the boil and boil for 2 minutes. Remove from heat and let beans soak for 1 hour. Meanwhile, place pork rind in a saucepan with 1 quart water, bring to boil, and boil 1 minute. Drain, rinse in cold water, and repeat the process. Then, with shears, cut rind into strips ¼ inch wide; cut strips into small triangles. Place again into saucepan, add 1 quart water, and simmer very slowly for 30 minutes; set saucepan aside.

As soon as beans have soaked for 1 hour, add the salt pork, onions, herb packet, and pork rind with its cooking liquid to the kettle. Bring to simmer, skim off scum, and simmer slowly, uncovered, for about 1½ hours or until beans are just tender. Add boiling water, if necessary during cooking, to keep beans covered. Season to taste with salt near end of cooking. Leave beans in cooking liquid until ready to use.

THE PORK

2½ lbs. boned pork roast
(loin or shoulder), excess
fat removed

Roast the pork to an internal temperature of 175 degrees. Set aside, reserving cooking juices.

THE LAMB

2½ lbs. boned shoulder of
lamb
3 to 4 Tb cooking oil
A heavy flameproof casserole
or large skillet
1 lb. cracked lamb bones
2 cups minced onions
4 cloves mashed garlic

6 Tb tomato paste
½ tsp thyme
2 bay leaves
2 cups dry white vermouth
3 cups beef bouillon
1 cup water
Salt and pepper

Cut lamb into 2-inch chunks, dry thoroughly, and brown a

few pieces at a time in very hot cooking oil in the flameproof casserole or large skillet. Remove meat to a side dish, brown the bones, remove them, and brown the onions lightly. Drain out browning fat, return meat and bones, and stir in the garlic, tomato paste, thyme, bay leaves, wine, and bouillon. Bring to the simmer, season lightly, cover, and simmer slowly for 1½ hours. Discard bones and bay leaves, skim off fat, and season cooking juices to taste with salt and pepper.

HOMEMADE SAUSAGE CAKES

1 lb. (2 cups) lean ground
  pork
⅓ lb. (⅔ cup) fresh,
  ground pork fat
2 tsp salt
⅛ tsp pepper
Big pinch allspice

⅛ tsp crumbled bay leaf
A small clove mashed garlic
Optional: ¼ cup cognac or
  armagnac and/or 1 small
  chopped truffle and juice
  from can

Beat all ingredients together; form into cakes 2 inches in diameter and ½ inch thick. Brown lightly in a skillet, and drain on paper towels.

FINAL ASSEMBLY

2 cups dry white bread
  crumbs
½ cup minced parsley
An 8-quart flameproof

casserole or baking dish
5 to 6 inches high
3 Tb pork-roasting fat or
  melted butter

Drain the beans, discard herb packet, and cut the salt pork into ¼-inch serving slices. Cut the roast pork into 1½- to 2-inch serving chunks. Arrange a layer of beans in the bottom of the casserole or baking dish. Cover with a layer of lamb, pork, salt pork, and sausage cakes. Repeat with layers of beans and meat, ending with a layer of sausage cakes. Pour in the lamb-cooking juices, pork-roasting juices, and sufficient bean-cooking liquid barely to cover the top layer of beans. Mix bread crumbs and parsley together, spread over the beans and sausage cakes, and dribble on the fat or butter. Set aside or refrigerate until ready for final cooking.

BAKING

(Preheat oven to 400 degrees.)

Bring casserole to the simmer on top of the stove, then set in upper third of preheated oven. When top has crusted lightly, in about 20 minutes, turn oven down to 350 degrees. Break the crust into the beans with the back of a spoon, and baste with the liquid in the casserole. Repeat several times as the crust forms again, but leave a final crust intact for serving. If liquid becomes too thick, add a few spoonsful of bean-cooking juice. *Cassoulet* should bake for about an hour.

OTHER MEAT CHOICES

Roast or braised goose, duck, turkey, or partridge; ham hock or veal shank; Polish or Italian sausage. Any of these may be added to or substituted for the meats in the recipe, but if the *cassoulet* is to be a masterpiece, you must have some excellent flavoring juices to give it the right taste.

SERVING

This is a heavy dish, best served as a noonday dinner on a cold day. First course of clear soup or oysters; a green salad with the *cassoulet*, and a strong, dry white or *rosé* wine. Fruit for dessert, followed by a brisk walk.

The Fortieth Show

VEGETABLE ADVENTURES
≈§ · §≈
(*Braised Lettuce and Sauerkraut*)

Common garden lettuce becomes a fascinating new cooked vegetable when you braise it, as the French do, with wonderful flavorings. And if you have never been wild about sauerkraut, you may well become an addict when you try it this way. Braising literally means a long slow cooking, so that there is an exchange and a blending of flavors between the vegetable and the braising ingredients; this process does not begin, however, until the vegetable is tender enough to absorb its savory surroundings. You may braise lettuce or sauerkraut several hours or even a day before serving; like a good stew, it will taste even better when reheated.

LAITUES BRAISÉES

(*Braised Lettuce*)
(*A green vegetable to go with steaks, chops, roast beef, veal, or chicken*)
Amounts per person: 2 medium heads Boston lettuce;
1 head escarole or chicory

WASHING

Trim stems of lettuce and remove wilted leaves. Holding lettuce by end of stem, pump up and down gently in a basin of cold water to remove all dirt.

BLANCHING (Preliminary Cooking)

A large kettle containing 7 to 8 quarts of boiling water	1½ tsp salt per quart of water Salt and pepper

Plunge 2 or 3 heads washed lettuce into the boiling water and boil slowly, uncovered, 3 to 5 minutes until lettuce is limp. Remove limp lettuce, plunge it into cold water, and continue with the rest. One at a time, squeeze heads gently but firmly in both hands to eliminate as much water as possible. Slice large heads in half lengthwise; leave small heads whole. Sprinkle with salt and pepper; fold heads in half crosswise to make triangular shapes.

BRAISING For 6 heads chicory or escarole; 12 heads Boston lettuce

A 12-inch flameproof cas-
serole with cover
6 thick slices bacon, previously simmered for 10
minutes in 2 quarts water,
then drained
2 Tb butter
½ cup sliced onions

½ cup sliced carrots
Optional: ½ cup dry white
vermouth
About 2 cups beef bouillon
A medium herb bouquet:
4 parsley sprigs, ¼ tsp
thyme, and a bay leaf tied
in washed cheesecloth

(Preheat oven to 325 degrees.)

In the casserole sauté the bacon in butter for a minute or two to brown very lightly. Remove bacon, stir in onions and carrots, and cook slowly for 8 to 10 minutes until tender but not browned. Remove half the vegetables, arrange the lettuce over the rest, then cover with the cooked vegetables and the bacon. Pour in optional vermouth and enough bouillon barely to cover the lettuce. Bring to the simmer, place a piece of waxed paper over the lettuce, cover the casserole, and bake in middle level of preheated oven. Lettuce should simmer very slowly for about 2 hours. (May be cooked ahead to this point; reheat before next step.)

SAUCE AND SERVING

A hot serving dish
1 tsp cornstarch mixed with

1 Tb vermouth or cold
bouillon
1 Tb butter

Remove lettuce to serving dish. Rapidly boil down cooking liquid, if necessary, to about ½ cup. Remove from heat. Beat cornstarch mixture into cooking liquid, and simmer, stirring, for 2 minutes. Remove from heat, swirl in butter, pour over lettuce, and serve.

CHOUCROUTE BRAISÉE A L'ALSACIENNE
(Braised Sauerkraut)
(To serve with duck, goose, pheasant, pork, ham, or sausages)
For 2 lbs. or 5 cups sauerkraut serving 6 people

WASHING

Drain sauerkraut and soak in a large basin of cold water for 15 to 20 minutes, changing water three times. Drain, squeeze by small handfuls to eliminate as much water as possible, and pick apart to separate strands.

PRELIMINARY COOKING

½ lb. thick-sliced bacon
A 2½- to 3-quart flameproof
  casserole with cover

3 Tb rendered goose or pork
  fat, or cooking oil
½ cup sliced carrots
1 cup sliced onions

Cut bacon into 2-inch pieces, simmer 10 minutes in 2 quarts water, drain, and dry. In the casserole, sauté the bacon slowly in fat or oil with the vegetables for 10 minutes without browning. Stir in the sauerkraut, toss to cover with the fat and vegetables, cover casserole and cook slowly for 10 minutes.

BRAISING

4 parsley sprigs, 1 bay leaf,
  6 peppercorns and, if
  available, 10 juniper
  berries all tied in washed
  cheesecloth

Optional: 1 cup dry white
  wine or ¾ cup dry white
  vermouth
3 to 4 cups chicken bouillon
Salt

(Preheat oven to 325 degrees for next step.)

Bury the herb and spice packet in the sauerkraut. Pour in the optional wine, and enough chicken bouillon just to cover the sauerkraut. Bring to the simmer, season lightly with salt, lay a piece of waxed paper over the sauerkraut, cover the casserole, and set in middle level of preheated oven. Sauerkraut should simmer very slowly for about 4 hours, and should absorb all the cooking liquid by the time it is done. (May be cooked ahead, left uncovered until cold, then covered and refrigerated.)

Choucroute Garnie
(*Sauerkraut Braised with Meats*)
For 6 people

A classic combination is pork chops and sausages (Italian or Polish), browned in hot fat in a skillet, and added to finish cooking with the sauerkraut about ½ hour before the end of the braising. Thinly sliced cooked ham may be laid over the sauerkraut the last 5 minutes in the oven. Serve with boiled potatoes and dry white wine or beer.

The Forty-first Show

PUFF PASTRY
◆⊰ • ⊱◆
(*Using Granular "Instant-Blending" Flour; Roquefort Case*)

French puff pastry dough is paper-thin layers of dough separated by paper-thin layers of butter; when it goes into the oven, the dough layers puff and the pastry rises. Properly made, it is flaky, light as a feather, and tender. It is used for making patty shells, turnovers, puffed cases for various foods, Napoleons and other dessert pastries, and cookies.

(*Note:* Granular "instant-blending" all-purpose flour needs no sifting. To measure it for this recipe, dip a dry-measure cup into the bag of flour, shake cup to level flour even with lip of cup, and pour measured flour into mixing bowl.)

FRENCH PUFF PASTRY
(*Pâte Feuilletée*)
(*Made with Granular Flour*)
For 2 sixteen-inch cases

THE DÉTREMPE

⅓ cup salad oil
3 cups granular "instant-blending" flour
A mixing bowl

2 tsp salt dissolved in ¾ cup cold water
2 or more Tb additional cold water if needed

With a rubber spatula, blend the oil into the flour in the mixing bowl. When mixed, blend in the salted water, pressing firmly with your spatula, then with your fingers. Add more water by droplets until you have a firm but pliable dough. Knead as briefly as possible into a cake 6 inches in diameter. Wrap in waxed paper and refrigerate for 1 hour.

THE DOUGH AND BUTTER PACKAGE

**2 sticks (½ lb.) chilled
unsalted butter**

Just before proceeding to next step, pound the butter with a rolling pin, then knead with the heel of the hand to smooth out butter and get out all lumps. Butter must be cold but malleable. Form it into a 5-inch square.

Roll the dough into a 10-inch circle, place the butter in the center of the dough-circle, then bring the edges of the circle up over the butter to enclose it completely. Do not stretch dough at sides of butter; press dough well together on top and seal by pressing with fingers.

FIRST TURN ("Premier Tour")

Sprinkle board and top of dough lightly with granular flour, and roll dough rapidly and evenly into as perfect a rectangle as possible, about 6 by 16 inches. Keep lifting dough and sprinkling underside and top lightly with flour as necessary, to prevent sticking.

Then, as though you were folding a long sheet of letter paper, lift up the bottom (one of the small ends) of the dough and fold it over a third of the dough; lift the top and fold it down to meet the bottom edge of the first fold, making three even layers of dough.

SECOND TURN

Turn dough so that top edge of top layer is to your right; roll into a rectangle as before, and fold again in thirds. Wrap in a large sheet of waxed paper, then in a plastic bag or damp towel, and chill for 1 hour.

THIRD AND FOURTH TURNS

Make two more turns in the same manner, wrap and chill again for 1 hour.

FIFTH AND SIXTH TURNS

Repeat with the two final turns, then let the dough rest for at least 2 hours or overnight before rolling and shaping. Dough will keep for several days in the refrigerator, or may be frozen.

(*Notes:* Work as rapidly as possible so butter does not soften; if dough softens and is hard to handle, stop where you are, and chill. Whenever dough seems rubbery and is hard to roll, or retracts after rolling, stop where you are; wrap and chill dough until it has relaxed. If dough is too cold, leave at room temperature until butter has again become malleable.)

Feuilletée au Roquefort

(*Roquefort Cheese Case*)
(*As a first course, or main-course luncheon dish*)
For a 16-inch case serving 6 to 8 people

Puff pastry (½ the amount made in preceding recipe)	About ⅔ cup thick cream sauce
½ lb. Roquefort cheese	Egg glaze (1 egg beaten with 1 tsp water)

Roll puff pastry into a rectangle 16 inches long and about 8 inches wide. Cut in half lengthwise and refrigerate one half until you are ready to use it. Roll out other half to widen it by 2 or 3 inches. (It should be about ¹⁄₁₆ inch thick.) Run cold water over a cookie sheet and shake off excess. Fold the widened dough strip in several places so you can lift it easily. Unfold it on the cookie sheet. Prick a 4-inch strip down the center at ¼-inch intervals with a fork, to keep bottom from rising when baked.

Cut the Roquefort cheese into slivers and place them down the center of the dough strip, leaving a 1-inch margin all around. Cover with the cream sauce, then fold the margin of the dough up over the cheese filling on all four sides.

Paint the dough margin with cold water, cover rectangle completely with the second strip, and seal the 2 dough layers firmly by pressing with your fingers. Refrigerate for 1 hour. Just before baking, preheat oven to 425 degrees, paint top of case with egg glaze. Then draw the tines of a fork over the glaze. Bake for 20 minutes at 425 degrees; lower thermostat to 350 degrees and bake 30 minutes more.

Serve hot with a white Burgundy wine or a *rosé*. If it is to be used as a main course for lunch or supper, serve a green or mixed vegetable salad.

The Forty-second Show

MORE ABOUT PUFF PASTRY
⌁⑊ • ⑊⌁
(*Using Pastry Flour; Vol-au-Vents and Bouchées*)

French puff pastry, which rises up so magically to form *vol-au-vents*, turnovers, and other delicacies, is difficult to make with ordinary all-purpose flour. Because the dough must be rolled six times in a special way before you can form and bake it, just the fact that regular all-purpose flour is high in gluten means that the dough becomes stiff, rubbery, and recalcitrant when rolled repeatedly. Flour with a low gluten content, which is the kind the French use, is very easy to handle. Low-gluten flour is called pastry flour in this country and is made from soft wheat; it comes in a sack, not a box, and is not to be confused with cake flour. When you make a mixture of ⅔ pastry flour and ⅓ all-purpose flour, you will have a blend that almost resembles French flour and that is perfect for making puff pastry. However, as there is little demand for pastry flour, you will have to look around for it, or order by mail.

FLOUR NOTE: Since this book was first published, we have found that a combination of 1 part plain bleached cake flour to every 3 parts all-purpose flour makes an excellent formula for puff pastry.

PÂTE FEUILLETÉE

(French Puff Pastry Made with Pastry Flour)
For 1 seven- to eight-inch vol-au-vent and
3 to 4 patty shells, or 8 three-inch patty shells and
8 two-inch appetizer shells

THE DÉTREMPE

1 cup regular all-purpose flour and 3¾ cups pastry flour (measure by sifting directly into dry-measure cups and sweeping off excess)

A mixing bowl
6 Tb chilled unsalted butter
2 tsp salt dissolved in ¾ cup very cold water (more water by droplets if necessary)

Place flour in the mixing bowl, add butter, and rub together rapidly with tips of fingers, or work with a pastry blender, until mixture resembles coarse meal. Rapidly blend in the water with the slightly cupped fingers of one hand, pressing mixture firmly together and adding more water by droplets to make a firm but pliable dough. Knead briefly into a cake 6 inches in diameter, working dough as little as possible. Wrap in waxed paper and chill for 30 to 40 minutes. Then roll out into a 10-inch circle.

THE PACKAGE

2 sticks (½ lb.) chilled unsalted butter

Beat and knead butter until it is perfectly smooth, free from lumps, malleable, yet still cold. Shape into a 5-inch square and place in middle of dough circle. Bring edges of dough up over butter to enclose it completely. Seal edges with fingers.

TURNS 1 THROUGH 6   (Rolling and Folding)

Flour lightly and roll out rapidly into an even rectangle about 16 by 6 inches. As though folding a letter, bring bottom edge up to middle and top edge down to cover it, making three even layers. Turn pastry so top edge is to your right, roll dough again into a rectangle. Fold in three's, wrap in waxed paper and a plastic bag; and chill 45 minutes to 1 hour. Repeat with two more rolls and folds; chill again, then complete the final two rolls and folds, making six in all. (These are called turns.) After a final chilling of 45 to 60 minutes, the puff pastry dough is ready for shaping. Securely wrapped, the dough may be refrigerated for several days or may be frozen.

(*Notes*: It is best to complete the first four turns within 45 minutes to 1 hour; if dough is too cold, the butter will congeal into lumps. But if you cannot complete them in the allotted time, leave the dough out of the refrigerator for half an hour or more, until the butter has softened for easy rolling. However, in hot weather, you must work rapidly so dough does not soften so much it is hard to handle. Keep every piece of dough you are not working on, and all scraps in the refrigerator until they are needed.)

Vol-au-Vent

(*Large Patty Shell*)

Puff pastry dough (preceding recipe)	Egg glaze (1 egg beaten with 1 tsp water)

Roll the chilled puff pastry dough into a rectangle about ⅜ inch thick, 18 inches long, and 10 inches wide. Cut 2 seven- to eight-inch circles in the dough, centering them well on the pastry so they do not touch the edges.

Run cold water over a baking sheet. Place one dough circle in the center, paint around its top circumference with cold water. Cut a 5- to 6-inch circle from the center of the second circle, thus making a ring and a smaller circle. Lay the ring in place on the first circle, sealing the two pieces of dough together with your fingers. You now have a flat cylinder of two layers. Prick the center of the bottom layer all over with a fork, to keep center from rising during baking.

Roll the smaller circle out and cut it into a 7- to 8-inch circle to form a cover for the pastry cylinder. Wet the top of the cylinder with cold water, and press the final circle in place.

Seal the three layers of dough together with the back edge of a knife, holding it vertically, and pressing indentations into the edges of the dough every ⅛ inch all the way around. Chill for 30 minutes before baking. Just before baking, paint top with egg glaze, and draw the tines of a fork over the glazed surface to make decorative crosshatch marks.

Bake for 20 minutes in the middle level of a preheated 400-degree oven. When about tripled in height and beginning to brown nicely, lower heat to 350 degrees and bake 30 to 40 minutes longer, until sides are brown and crisp.

Cut under top cover, remove it, and dig uncooked pastry out of shell with a fork. Bake uncovered 5 minutes more to dry out interior, then cool on a rack. Reheat for several minutes at 400 degrees before serving with whatever hot filling you have chosen.

Bouchées
(Individual Patty Shells)
(Same ingredients as for vol-au-vent)

Make and bake small patty shells in exactly the same way as for *vol-au-vent*, but you need only 2 layers: the bottom circle and the ring. Use a 3- to 3½-inch cutter for the bottom circles plus a 2-inch one for the rings. The centers of the rings may be baked as is for appetizers: simply outline a ⅜-inch circle in the top of each to make a removable cover after baking.

FREEZING PATTY SHELLS

Uncooked shells may be frozen; to bake them, remove from freezer, paint with egg glaze, and pop into a preheated oven. Baked shells may be frozen if securely wrapped; to reheat, place for 5 minutes or so in a 400-degree oven.

The Forty-third Show

FISH MOUSSELINES
✎§ • §✎
(Beurre Blanc—White Butter Sauce)

A *mousseline* is a delicate French fish cake made of any lean white fish that is ground up raw, beaten with egg white and cream, then formed into patties, and cooked very slowly in butter. Laid on a bed of creamed mushrooms and garnished with asparagus tips, it is a delectable dish to serve when you want to be especially chic. This recipe includes an attractive way to cook frozen asparagus, and the famous French white butter sauce, *beurre blanc*. This is a speciality of the Loire Valley, and is usually associated with pike; it is a strong concentrate of white wine, vinegar, and shallots into which butter is whipped to make a warm, pale-yellow cream the consistency of *hollandaise*.

MOUSSELINES DE POISSON A LA MARÉCHALE
(Fish Mousselines with Beurre Blanc)
For 6 to 8 people

THE MOUSSELINE MIXTURE

1½ cup finely ground raw
flounder, sole, or baby
halibut
¾ tsp salt
Big pinch white pepper

Pinch nutmeg
1 egg white (2 Tb)
A bowl of cracked ice
6 to 8 Tb chilled heavy
cream

Beat the ground fish, seasonings, and egg white vigorously for several minutes over cracked ice until mixture has enough body to hold solidly when lifted in a spoon. Then add 2 tablespoons of chilled cream and beat for 1 minute, adding more cream by tablespoonfuls and beating vigorously for a minute after each addition. Mixture must retain enough body so it will hold its shape when formed into cakes—add a bit more cream if you think the paste will absorb it.

FORMING AND COOKING THE MOUSSELINES

6 Tb butter (3 for each skillet)	or no-stick skillets about 9 inches in diameter
2 heavy-bottomed enameled	Covers for the skillets

Melt the butter in the skillets, and set aside. With your hands or with a flexible spatula dipped into cold water, form the *mousseline* mixture into 6 to 8 cakes on a floured board. Place the cakes, as they are formed, into the skillets. Set skillets over low heat, cover, and cook very slowly for 6 minutes. Turn and cook for 6 minutes more. The *mousselines* should not brown at all, and are done when just firm and lightly springy to the touch. (They may be cooked ahead of time and reheated slowly in covered skillets just before serving, on top of stove, or in a 325-degree oven.)

BEURRE BLANC—WHITE BUTTER SAUCE   (For 1 to 1½ cups)

¼ cup wine vinegar, preferably white	½ tsp salt ⅛ tsp white pepper
2 Tb each of lemon juice and dry white vermouth	A 6-cup enameled saucepan 2 to 3 sticks (½ to ¾ lb.)
1 Tb finely minced shallots or scallions	chilled butter cut into ¼-inch pieces

Boil the vinegar, lemon juice, vermouth, shallots or scallions, salt, and pepper in the saucepan until liquid has reduced to 1½ tablespoons. Remove saucepan from heat and immediately beat in 2 pieces of chilled butter with a wire whip. As butter softens and creams in the liquid, beat in another piece. Then set pan over very low heat and, beating constantly, continue adding successive pieces of butter as each previous piece has almost creamed into the sauce. Sauce should become a thick ivory-colored cream, the consistency of a light *hollandaise*. Immediately remove from heat and season to taste. (If not served immediately, set over barely tepid water to keep butter from congealing; do not reheat or sauce may thin out and turn oily.)

CREAMED MUSHROOMS

¾ lb. finely minced fresh mushrooms	2 Tb minced shallots or scallions
2 Tb butter and 1 Tb cooking oil	2 Tb flour
	About ½ cup medium cream
	Salt and pepper

Sauté the mushrooms in hot butter and oil for several minutes, until the pieces begin to separate from each other. Stir in the shallots or scallions and cook a moment more. Lower heat, stir in the flour and cook, stirring, for 2 minutes. Remove from heat and stir in half the cream. Simmer, stirring, for a moment, and adding more cream by spoonfuls. Mushrooms should just hold their shape when lifted in a spoon. Season carefully with salt and pepper. Reheat just before serving.

ASPARAGUS

1 box frozen cut asparagus	2 Tb butter in a skillet
2 Tb salt	Salt and pepper

Allow the asparagus to thaw until the pieces separate from each other. Then drop into 4 quarts of rapidly boiling water. Add 2 tablespoons salt, bring rapidly back to the boil, and boil uncovered for 3 or 4 minutes, until asparagus is barely tender. Drain. If not to be served immediately, run cold water over asparagus to stop the cooking and set the fresh color and texture. Several minutes before serving, toss gently in 2 tablespoons hot butter to finish cooking. Season to taste with salt and pepper.

SERVING

Place mushrooms in a mound on a hot, lightly buttered serving dish. Arrange the *mousselines* over the mushrooms. Decorate spaces with buttered asparagus and spoon the sauce over the fish.

Serve with hot French bread and a chilled white Burgundy, Traminer, or Graves wine.

The Forty-fourth Show

CAKE FOR COMPANY
 ⋅❧
(*Yellow Spongecake; Orange-Butter Filling*)

Biscuit au beurre, or butter spongecake, is one of the two classic French recipes for yellow cakes that are to be filled and iced. You will note that there is no baking powder; the lightness of the cake depends entirely on beautifully beaten egg whites which are folded into the batter with such speed and delicacy that they retain their volume and the maximum of their puffing abilities. Like most French cakes, this is barely 2 inches high when filled and iced; if you want a taller cake, double the recipe, use two pans, and make a four-layer cake.

BISCUIT AU BEURRE
(*Butter Spongecake*)
For an 8-inch cake

PRELIMINARIES

A round cake pan, 8 inches in diameter and 1½ inches deep	½ tsp butter for the pan 2 Tb flour for the pan 3 Tb butter

(Preheat oven to 350 degrees.)
Butter the cake pan lightly, roll flour around inside it to coat it completely, knock out excess flour. Melt the butter and set it aside. Measure out the rest of the ingredients listed.

SUGAR AND EGG YOLKS

A 3-quart mixing bowl An electric mixer or large wire whip	½ cup granulated sugar 3 egg yolks 1½ tsp vanilla extract

Using a wire whisk or an electric mixer, gradually beat the sugar into the egg yolks and continue beating for several minutes until mixture is thick, pale yellow, and forms a slowly dissolving ribbon when a bit is lifted and dropped back onto the surface. Beat in the vanilla extract.

BEATING THE EGG WHITES

3 egg whites	A scant ¼ tsp cream of
A mixing bowl	tartar
Pinch of salt	1½ Tb granulated sugar

Beat the egg whites in a separate bowl until foamy, then beat in the salt and the cream of tartar. Continue beating until soft peaks are formed, sprinkle on the sugar, and beat until stiff peaks are formed.

FOLDING

1 cup plain bleached cake	off excess and return flour
flour (sift directly into	to sifter)
dry-measure cup; sweep	

Fold one fourth of the egg whites into the egg yolk mixture; sprinkle on one fourth of the flour, add one fourth the remaining egg whites, and rapidly fold in. Continue with one third of the remaining flour, one third of the remaining egg whites, then half of each, and finally the last of each, folding rapidly and delicately. When almost blended, fold in the melted butter by spoonfuls, omitting the milky residue at the bottom of the pan. Do not overmix and deflate the egg whites.

BAKING AND UNMOLDING

A cake rack

(Preheat oven to 350 degrees.)

Immediately turn batter into prepared cake pan, tilting pan to run batter to the rim all around. Set in middle level of preheated oven and bake for about 25 minutes. Cake is done when it has puffed, is lightly brown, and has just begun to show a faint line of shrinkage from the edges of the pan.

Remove from oven and let cool in pan for about 8 minutes, then unmold onto a rack.

FOURRAGE À LA CRÈME D'ORANGE—ORANGE-BUTTER FILLING (For about 2 cups, enough to fill 2 or 3 eight-inch cakes)

A 6-cup enameled saucepan	2 egg yolks
6 Tb unsalted butter	The grated rind of 1 orange
1⅔ cups granulated sugar	¼ cup strained orange juice
2 eggs	1 Tb orange liqueur

Place all the ingredients together in the saucepan and beat over low heat or not-quite-simmering water until mixture thickens like honey and is too hot for your finger. Do not overheat or eggs will scramble, but they must thicken. Mixture will thicken a little more as it cools. May be refrigerated for several days, or frozen.

FILLING, ICING, AND DECORATING THE CAKE

The butter spongecake	boiled with 2 Tb sugar
⅔ to 1 cup orange-butter filling	until last drops from spoon are sticky)
½ cup apricot glaze (⅔ cup apricot jam forced through a sieve, then	1 cup pulverized almonds
	Whole almonds or glacéed fruits

When cake is cold, cut a small vertical wedge up the edge, and slice cake in half horizontally. Spread with filling, and re-form the cake, lining up two halves with vertical wedge. Paint top and sides of cake with apricot glaze. Brush pulverized almonds around sides of cake; decorate top with almonds or glacéed fruits.

The Forty-fifth Show

ARTICHOKES FROM
TOP TO BOTTOM

❧ · ☙

Cynara scolymus, the French or globe artichoke, is said to be good for the liver; the flowers of artichokes-gone-to-seed can be used for souring milk; and a powder made from the dried leaves is a remedy for noxious fevers. In addition to the foregoing esoterica, the delicately nutty flavor of plain boiled artichoke is so delicious you can eat it all by itself: artichokes are therefore good for dieters. For those so fortunate as to be wasp-waisted, artichokes are the best of excuses for indulging in oceans of melted butter, *hollandaise*, and mayonnaise.

Fresh artichokes are in season from October through June; April and May are the abundant months when prices are most reasonable. Artichoke quality depends not on size but on freshness: pick them heavy, compact, with fleshy, close-clinging, crisp leaves and fresh green stems. In some of the winter months artichokes can have tinges of brown; frost has touched them, and this is considered desirable because frost is supposed to tenderize the leaves.

Serve whole boiled artichokes hot, tepid, or cold, as a first course, in place of a salad, or as a luncheon dish with cold ham, cheese, and French bread. Serve artichoke bottoms whole as a container for other vegetables, poached eggs, or sauces, or slice them and toss with other vegetables to accompany the main course.

ARTICHAUTS AU NATUREL
(Whole Boiled Artichokes)

PREPARATION FOR COOKING

One artichoke at a time, remove the stem by bending it at the base of the artichoke until the stem snaps off, then break off small leaves at the base. Trim base with a knife so artichoke will stand solidly upright. Finally lay the artichoke on its side and slice three fourths of an inch off the top; trim off points of remaining leaves with scissors. Wash under cold running water, and drop into a basin of cold water containing 1 tablespoon vinegar per quart. The vinegar prevents artichokes from discoloring before you cook them. (*Note:* If the artichokes are very fresh and tender, you can peel the stems down to the moist flesh and boil them along with the artichokes.)

COOKING

Plunge the prepared artichokes into a large kettle of rapidly boiling salted water, and drape a double layer of washed cheese-cloth over them to keep the exposed portions moist during cooking. Cook, uncovered, at the slow boil for 35 to 45 minutes, depending on size. The artichokes are done when lower leaves pull out—eat one as a test: the lower half inch or so should be tender—and when a knife will pierce the bottom easily. Remove immediately and drain upside down in a colander.

SERVING AND EATING

Stand artichokes upright and serve in salad-size plates about 8 inches in diameter, or special artichoke plates. To eat an artichoke, pull off a leaf and hold its tip in your fingers. Dip bottom of leaf in melted butter or one of the sauces suggested, then scrape off its tender flesh between your teeth. When you have gone through the leaves, you will come to the bottom, which you eat with a knife and fork after you have scraped off and discarded the choke or hairy center growth which covers it.

SAUCES

Melted butter, lemon butter, or *hollandaise* for hot or warm artichokes; vinaigrette (French dressing), mustard sauce, or mayonnaise for cold artichokes.

FONDS D'ARTICHAUTS
(*Artichoke Bottoms*)

The tender, meaty bottom of the artichoke, after all the leaves and the choke have been removed, is even more of a delicacy in this country than it is in France, owing to the price of artichokes. The stems are prepared from raw artichokes: the lower leaves are broken off in such a way as to lose as little of the meat as possible, then the heart is trimmed and given a preliminary cooking in a *blanc* to prevent discoloring. If you wish to serve them whole and use them as containers, choose the largest artichokes you can find, 4 to 5 inches in diameter if possible.

PREPARATION FOR COOKING

Bend the stem at the base of a whole raw artichoke until it snaps off. Holding the artichoke bottom up, bend a lower leaf back on itself until it snaps, then pull it off. Continue all around the artichoke until you have gone beyond the curve of the heart and the leaf structure folds inward; slice off the rest of the leaves at this point. You are thus left with the artichoke bottom trimmed of all but the meaty base of the leaf structure; the choke which is buried in the center will be removed after cooking. Rub cut parts of artichoke with half a lemon to keep from darkening. Then, holding the trimmed artichoke bottom up in your left hand, rotate it slowly against the blade of a knife held firmly in your right hand, and cut off all bits of green to expose the whitish flesh. Rub cut portions frequently with lemon. Drop each bottom as it is finished into cold water containing 1 tablespoon of lemon juice per quart.

PRELIMINARY COOKING

Prepare a *blanc* as follows: place ¼ cup of flour in a saucepan and beat in enough cold water by spoonfuls to make a smooth paste, then beat in 1 quart of water, 2 tablespoons of lemon juice, and 1½ teaspoons salt. Bring to the boil, beating with a wire whip, then add the prepared artichoke bottoms. Add boiling water if necessary, to be sure artichokes are covered with liquid; simmer 30 to 40 minutes, uncovered, until tender when pierced with a knife. Leave artichokes in liquid until ready to use (they will keep under refrigeration for several days); drain, wash under cold water, and delicately remove the choke with a spoon, trimming off remaining leaf ends if you wish.

SERVING WHOLE ARTICHOKE BOTTOMS

To serve cold, season cavity with salt, pepper, lemon juice, and oil, and fill with seafood or chicken salad, or vegetables in mayonnaise. To serve hot, season with salt and pepper, paint all over with melted butter, then place bottom up in a hot baking dish; lay buttered waxed paper over the artichokes, cover the dish, and bake in the middle level of a preheated 325-degree oven for about 20 minutes, or until well heated through. The artichokes are then ready to receive any filling your recipe directs.

The Forty-sixth Show

ELEGANCE WITH EGGS
ᘐᘐ · ᘐᘐ
(Baked, Molded, Shirred; Omelettes)

The French, who do not eat eggs for breakfast, have put much of their ingenuity into eggs for any other meal. A French textbook on the subject is entitled One Thousand Ways to Prepare

Eggs. Here are three out of that number, and these can be varied in scores of ways. Use them for main-course lunch or supper dishes, or for an especially important breakfast or brunch.

OEUFS EN COCOTTE A LA CRÈME
(Eggs Baked in Ramekins)
For each serving

½ tsp butter	1 or 2 eggs
2 Tb heavy cream	Salt and pepper

(Preheat oven to 375 degrees.)

Choose a porcelain or fireproof glass dish 2½ to 3 inches in diameter and about 1½ inches deep. Arrange in a pan containing ¾ inch of water and set over a burner; bring water to the simmer. Place all but a dot of butter in the ramekin; add a tablespoon of cream, and break in the egg or eggs. When egg white has begun to coagulate in bottom of ramekin, add the remaining spoonful of cream, seasonings, and the dot of butter. Place in lower third of preheated oven and bake for 7 to 8 minutes. The eggs are done when just set, but still tremble slightly. If you wish to wait a bit before serving, remove from oven when slightly underdone; they will finish cooking, and stay warm in the water for 10 to 15 minutes. Season with salt and pepper before serving.

VARIATIONS ❧

(1) Add chopped green herbs to the cream—such as parsley, chives, or tarragon.

(2) Instead of cream, use cheese sauce, tomato sauce, onion, sauce, or curry sauce.

(3) Place in bottom of ramekin a spoonful of minced, cooked vegetables, fish, or chicken livers, then proceed with recipe.

OEUFS MOLLETS
(Molded Eggs)
(A substitute for poached eggs)

Smear ramekins or muffin tins heavily with butter. Set in a pan of simmering water, break an egg in each; bake as in the preceding recipe. Unmold the eggs and use hot or cold in any way you would use poached eggs.

OEUFS SUR LE PLAT
(Shirred Eggs)
For each serving

½ **Tb butter**   **Salt and pepper**
1 or 2 eggs

Choose a shallow fireproof baking-and-serving dish about 4 inches in diameter. Place the dish over moderate heat or in a pan of simmering water. Add butter; as soon as it has melted, break in 1 or 2 eggs. When bottom of egg has coagulated in dish, remove from heat, tilt dish, and baste top of egg with the butter in the dish. Place on a baking sheet, and a minute before serving, set so surface of egg is about 1 inch from red-hot broiler element. Slide dish out every few seconds, tilt, and baste top of egg with the butter in the dish. In less than a minute, the white will be set, and the yolk filmed and glistening. Remove from oven, season with salt and pepper, and serve immediately.

VARIATIONS ⁊

(1) Use half the amount of butter. After bottom of egg has set, pour on 2 tablespoons of heavy cream and sprinkle with a tablespoon of Swiss cheese. Proceed as above, but basting under broiler is not necessary.

(2) Use one of the ideas suggested in the variations for *oeufs en cocotte,* or garnish the cooked eggs with sautéed mushrooms, kidneys, chicken livers, or vegetables.

OMELETTE GRATINÉE AUX CHAMPIGNONS
(Mushroom Omelette Gratinéed with Cheese Sauce)
For a 3-egg omelette serving 2 people

1 cup cream sauce
½ cup coarsely grated Swiss cheese
½ lb. sliced mushrooms, previously sautéed in butter
A saucepan
3 eggs

Salt and pepper
1½ Tb butter
An omelette pan or non-sticking skillet 7 inches in diameter at the bottom
A mixing bowl and a table fork
A warm fireproof serving plate

Into the cream sauce stir all but 2 tablespoons of the grated cheese. Place half the mushrooms in a saucepan, stir in one third of the sauce, and heat just before making your omelette.

When ready to make the omelette, beat the eggs, a big pinch of salt, and a pinch of pepper in a mixing bowl with a fork until yolks and whites are blended—20 to 30 seconds. Place a tablespoon of butter in the omelette pan or skillet, set over high heat, and as the butter melts tilt pan in all directions to coat bottom and sides. When butter foam has almost subsided, pour in the eggs.

Let eggs settle 3 or 4 seconds, then grasp pan handle with left hand and, moving pan rapidly back and forth over heat, stir eggs with the flat of your table fork. When eggs have coagulated into a very soft custard, in about 8 seconds, spoon the hot sauced mushrooms across the center of the omelette at right angles to the pan handle. Lift handle to tilt pan away from you, flip near end of omelette over onto the filling with the fork, and shake pan to slide omelette to far lip of pan.

Turn pan around and grasp handle with your right hand, thumb on top. Hold a warm fireproof serving plate in your left hand. Tilt plate and pan together at an angle, resting lip of pan on plate. Quickly turn omelette pan upside down over plate, and omelette will fall into place.

Spread the rest of the mushrooms on top of the omelette,

cover with remaining sauce, sprinkle with the reserved 2 table-spoons of cheese, and dot with the remaining butter. Run ome-lette close under a red-hot broiler for about a minute, to brown cheese delicately.

Serve at once, accompanied by a green salad, French bread, and a dry white wine or a *rosé*.

The Forty-seventh Show

BAVARIAN CREAM—
COLD SOUFFLÉ

When the ancients wrote of ambrosia, they might well have had French Bavarian cream in mind. It is velvet to the tongue, it melts in the mouth, and caresses the palate in a most sensuous fashion. Lightly held in shape by just the right amount of gel-atin, it may stand alone in molded splendor, or may rise up from the dish like a majestic soufflé.

BAVAROIS A L'ORANGE
(Orange Bavarian Cream)
For about 2 quarts, serving 8 to 10 people

THE ORANGE CUSTARD

2 large bright-skinned oranges	⅔ cup strained orange juice
2 large sugar lumps	1½ Tb (1½ envelopes)
A saucepan	unflavored gelatin

One at a time, rub the sugar lumps over the oranges until all sides of each lump are impregnated with orange oil. Crush the lumps and place in a saucepan; grate the rind and add to saucepan. Squeeze the juice of the oranges, strain ⅔ cup into a measure, and sprinkle the gelatin on top so that it will soften when ready to be used.

1 cup granulated sugar	saucepan with the orange-
7 egg yolks	sugar and rind
2 tsp cornstarch	An enameled or stainless-
1½ cups milk heated in the	steel saucepan and a
	wooden spoon

Gradually beat granulated sugar into the yolks in a mixing bowl, using a wire whip or electric beater. Continue beating for a minute or more, until mixture is pale and lemon-colored. Beat in the cornstarch. Then, in a thin stream of droplets, beat in the hot milk. Pour mixture into the saucepan and stir with a wooden spoon over moderate heat until mixture thickens enough to coat the spoon lightly, around 170 degrees on a candy thermometer. Do not let custard come to boil or yolks may curdle, but you must let it heat enough to thicken properly. Remove from heat and immediately beat in the orange juice and gelatin.

THE EGG WHITES AND PRELIMINARY CHILLING

5 egg whites	¼ tsp cream of tartar
Pinch of salt	2 Tb granulated sugar

Beat the egg whites in a clean, dry bowl for a moment until foamy, then beat in the salt and cream of tartar. Continue beating until soft peaks are formed; add sugar and beat until stiff peaks are formed. Fold the egg whites into the hot custard sauce and chill over cracked ice or in the refrigerator, folding occasionally to keep mixture from separating. When cold but not set, proceed with next step.

WHIPPED CREAM AND FINAL FLAVORING

½ cup chilled whipping	A chilled beater
cream	2 Tb orange liqueur
A chilled mixing bowl	

Beat the chilled cream until it has doubled in volume and

beater leaves light traces on its surface. Fold the cream, then the liqueur, into the cold orange mixture.

TO SERVE AS A MOLDED DESSERT

An 8-cup cylindrical mold or ring mold, preferably

of metal as unmolding is easier

A chilled serving dish

Rinse mold in cold water. Pour in the Bavarian cream mixture, cover with waxed paper, and chill for at least 4 hours or overnight. To unmold, dip in hot water for several seconds, quickly run a knife around inside edge of mold, then invert the serving dish over the mold. Quickly reverse the two, and in a few seconds the dessert should fall into place; if not, repeat the process. Decorate top and/or sides of the Bavarian cream with fresh, skinless orange segments flavored with sugar and a spoonful or two of orange liqueur. (*Note:* Bavarian cream may be frozen, and served as a frozen dessert.)

TO SERVE AS A COLD SOUFFLÉ

A 5- to 6-cup soufflé dish

Surround soufflé dish with a waxed paper collar which stands 3 inches above the dish. Pour in the Bavarian cream mixture and chill until set. Peel off paper just before serving.

The Forty-eighth Show

THE CASE FOR SALMON
❧ · ❧
(*Coulibiac*)

Here is a magnificent dish for those who love to play around with pastry. It is a rectangular case or shell of pie dough baked until set in the oven, then filled with a delicious mixture of rice, mushrooms, and salmon, topped with mock puff pastry, decorated with pastry cutouts, and returned to the oven to brown and finish cooking. A handsome party dish, the various parts of it can be cooked and assembled well in advance.

COULIBIAC DE SAUMON EN CROÛTE
(*Salmon, Rice, and Mushrooms Baked in a Rectangular Pastry Case*)
For 6 people

THE PASTRY DOUGH

4 cups all-purpose flour
  (sifted directly into each
  cup, and leveled off with
  flat of knife)
A large mixing bowl
1¾ sticks (7 ounces)
  chilled butter

4 Tb chilled vegetable
  shortening
2 tsp salt dissolved in ¾ cup
  cold water
1 or more Tb cold water, as
  needed
2 Tb softened butter (for
  cover)

Place flour in mixing bowl and work the chilled butter and shortening into it with a pastry blender or the tips of your fingers until mixture resembles coarse cornmeal. With cupped fingers of one hand, rapidly blend in the water, pressing dough together, adding more water by droplets if needed, to make a pliable but not damp and sticky dough. Gather it into a ball, place on a board, and rapidly push two spoonful bits of it out and away from you with the heel of your hand in a 6-inch smear. This constitutes the final blending of fat and flour. Press into a ball, wrap in waxed paper, and chill for 2 hours or until firm.

THE BOTTOM CASE

(Preheat oven to 425 degrees.)

Roll two thirds of the dough into a rectangle ⅛ inch thick and large enough to fit on the outside bottom of a loaf pan 13 to 14 inches long and 3 inches wide. Butter outside of pan, turn it upside down, and fit the dough over it, letting dough come down to a depth of 2 inches. Trim dough evenly all around and prick all over with the tines of a fork. Bake for 6 to 8 minutes in a preheated oven, until dough has just set and begins to color. Remove and unmold on a rack.

THE TOP COVER   (Mock Puff Pastry, or Flaky Pastry)

2 Tb softened butter

Roll the remaining dough into a rectangle, spread bottom half with 1 tablespoon softened butter, and fold over top half to cover with bottom. Repeat with another tablespoon of butter. Wrap in waxed paper and chill.

THE RICE

2 Tb minced onions	3 cups fish or chicken
2 Tb butter	bouillon
A heavy 2-quart saucepan	Salt and pepper
1½ cups dry, raw, plain rice	

Sauté the onions in butter in the saucepan for 5 minutes without letting them brown. Stir in the rice, cook slowly for several minutes until grains are milky, then stir in the bouillon. Bring to the boil, stir once, then cover pan and cook at a moderately fast simmer without stirring for about 18 minutes, until rice has absorbed liquid. Fluff lightly with a fork and season with salt and pepper. (May be done in advance.)

THE SALMON AND MUSHROOMS

2 cups finely diced mush-
rooms, previously sautéed
in butter
½ cup finely minced shallots
or scallions
2 Tb butter
½ cup dry white vermouth

¼ cup cognac
2½ cups skinless and boneless salmon, canned or
previously cooked
½ cup minced fresh parsley
1 tsp oregano or tarragon
Salt and pepper

Cook the shallots or scallions slowly in the butter for 2 minutes; stir in the mushrooms, vermouth, and cognac, and boil for several minutes to evaporate alcohol. Then stir in the salmon, parsley, and tarragon, and heat for several minutes to blend flavors. Season to taste with salt and pepper. (May be done in advance.)

FILLING AND DECORATING THE CASE

2 cups well-flavored cream
sauce, incorporating
salmon juices, if any

Egg glaze (1 egg beaten
with 1 tsp water)

(Preheat oven to 425 degrees.)

Place pastry case on a lightly buttered baking sheet. Arrange a layer of rice in the bottom of the case, cover with a layer of mushrooms and salmon, then with a layer of sauce. Repeat with layers of rice, salmon, and sauce, mounding your filling in a dome if it overflows the case.

Roll the dough reserved for your top cover into a rectangle 1½ inches longer and wider on each side than your pastry case. Paint the sides of the case with beaten egg, lay on the dough cover and press closely against the case, to seal firmly. Roll out leftover dough; cut into fancy shapes. Paint cover with egg glaze, affix decorations, and paint with egg. Draw the tines of a fork over the egg glaze to make crosshatch markings. Poke 2 one-eighth-inch holes in dough cover and insert paper or foil funnels; these will allow steam to escape. (If you wish to fill and decorate the case ahead of time, omit egg glaze, using it only to affix decorations. Refrigerate until baking time, then glaze with egg.)

Bake in middle level of preheated oven for 45 to 60 minutes (longer if case has been chilled) until pastry is nicely browned and you can hear bubbling noises coming up through funnels.

SERVING

You will probably want a sauce with this; it needs a bit of moistening as you eat it—melted butter, lemon butter, light cream sauce with lemon flavoring, mock *hollandaise*. Buttered peas go nicely with it, or a green or mixed vegetable salad. Serve a white Burgundy or Traminer wine.

The Forty-ninth Show

LEST WE FORGET
BROCCOLI AND CAULIFLOWER
(Mock Hollandaise Sauce)

Both broccoli and cauliflower will cook in less than half the usual time, and will retain their maximum freshness and texture, if the stems are peeled before cooking. Trimmed, peeled, washed, and refrigerated several hours ahead of time, either vegetable requires only 5 to 6 minutes cooking time, and this can be done just before serving.

BROCCOLI
1 bunch serves 4 people

PREPARATION FOR COOKING

Cut the top portion of each head 2½ to 3 inches long, usually down to where the branches separate from the central stem. Halve or quarter the branches, if necessary, to make all pieces about ½ inch thick at the base. Using a small knife, and starting at the bottom of each piece, peel off the outside skin in strips, coming almost up to the flower buds. Make a ½-inch slit through the bottom of each branch, for quicker cooking. Cut off and discard the tough ¼- to ½-inch butt of the central stems, and peel off the skins; cut down through the tough woody portions, if necessary, to expose the tender flesh.

Wash the broccoli thoroughly and rapidly in cold water; with modern growing methods, prolonged soaking is rarely necessary.

Refrigerate in a covered bowl until ready to cook. Prepare your sauce and heat your serving dish before cooking the broccoli.

COOKING BROCCOLI

Bring 6 quarts of water and 3 tablespoons of salt to the rapid boil in a large saucepan or kettle. Place the broccoli in a salad basket or vegetable rack, lower into the water, and boil uncovered for about 5 minutes. Test by eating a piece; the stem should be just tender, but still slightly crunchy. Drain, and serve immediately. (If broccoli must be done ahead, drain and cool quickly; plunge into rapidly boiling water for a moment just before serving.)

Broccoli à la Polonaise

1 stick (¼ lb.) butter
A frying pan
½ cup fresh bread crumbs
Salt and pepper

1 hard-boiled egg, peeled
A sieve set over a bowl
A hot serving dish

Melt butter, skim off the foam, and spoon the clear liquid into a frying pan. Stir in bread crumbs. Sauté, stirring with a wooden spoon, for several minutes until bread crumbs are lightly browned. Season with salt and pepper, set aside, and reheat just before serving. Push the hard-boiled egg through a sieve into a bowl; fluff in salt and pepper.

When broccoli is done, arrange on a hot serving dish, and sprinkle with the bread crumbs and sieved egg. Serve immediately.

OTHER SERVING SUGGESTIONS

Salt, pepper, and lemon juice; melted butter; lemon butter; *sauce hollandaise*; cream sauce, cheese sauce; mock *hollandaise* (recipe follows that for cauliflower).

CAULIFLOWER
A 7- to 8-inch head serves 4 people

PREPARATION FOR COOKING

Remove leaves, cut out central stem, and break the cauliflower into buds or flowerets. Peel the stems of each, and slit them (for quicker cooking). Peel the central stem, cutting down to the tender flesh, then cut the stem into bias pieces about ½ inch in diameter. Wash the cauliflower rapidly in cold water, drain, and refrigerate in a covered bowl until ready to cook. Prepare your sauce and heat your serving dish before cooking the cauliflower.

COOKING CAULIFLOWER

Cook cauliflower in exactly the same way as broccoli, timing it about 6 minutes.

MOLDING CAULIFLOWER

To re-form the cauliflower into a head shape after cooking, choose a bowl approximately the same size as the original, uncut head. Heat the bowl over simmering water, and when the cauliflower is done, pack in the flowerets, head down, pouring a spoonful of sauce or butter over it as you go. When bowl is filled, press the cauliflower down with a saucer, to pack it. Turn a heated serving dish upside down over the bowl, and reverse the two. Remove the bowl, sauce or decorate the cauliflower, and serve immediately.

SAUCES FOR CAULIFLOWER

Serve with mock *hollandaise* (recipe follows) or with one of the other sauces suggested for broccoli.

Mock Hollandaise Sauce (Bâtarde)

(For Cauliflower, Broccoli, Asparagus, Boiled Lamb, Chicken, or Fish)
For about 1½ cups

3 Tb softened or melted butter	1 egg yolk blended in a bowl with ¼ cup heavy cream
3 Tb flour	Salt and pepper
1¼ cups hot vegetable-cooking water or milk	1 to 2 Tb lemon juice
	2 or more Tb softened butter

Blend the butter and flour in a small saucepan with a rubber spatula. Using a wire whip, beat in the hot liquid, then bring to the boil, beating slowly. By driblets, beat this hot sauce into the egg yolk and cream, pour back into saucepan, and bring to the boil, stirring. Remove from heat and season to taste with salt, pepper, and lemon juice. If not to be served immediately, clean off sides of pan with rubber spatula and dot top of sauce with softened butter to prevent a skin from forming. Reheat just before serving, remove from heat, and beat in softened butter by tablespoons.

The Fiftieth Show

VEAL FOR A KING

VEAU SYLVIE
(Veal Roasted with Ham and Cheese)
For 8 people

This is a roast of veal split lengthwise, stuffed with slices of ham and cheese, then reformed and tied. Browned top and bottom, the veal is roasted in a covered casserole and served with a sauce made from its roasting juices.

The ideal cut for this would be the top of the round from a large leg of veal, as it is a long, cylindrical piece with no muscle separations. Alternate cuts would be a whole small boned leg, or boned loin or rib.

SLITTING AND MARINATING THE VEAL

A 3½-pound boneless roast of veal
Optional marinade ingredients:
⅓ cup cognac
⅓ cup dry Sercial Madeira
½ cup each of sliced carrots and onions
A large herb bouquet: 4 parsley sprigs, 1 bay leaf, ½ tsp thyme, and 4 peppercorns tied in washed cheesecloth

Make a series of deep, parallel cuts in the roast, about 1 inch apart, starting at the top of the roast, and going with the grain the length of the meat from one end to the other, and to within ½ inch of the bottom of the roast. You will thus have 3 or 4 thick slices of meat which are free at the top and sides, but which are all attached together at the bottom. If your meat contains many muscle separations it will look very messy, but will be tied in shape again later. If you wish to marinate the meat, mix the marinade ingredients in a large bowl, add the meat, and baste with the liquid. Turn and baste every hour or so for 6 hours at least, or overnight, in the refrigerator. Drain the meat, and dry thoroughly before proceeding to next step.

STUFFING THE VEAL

6 or more slices of boiled ham 1/16 inch thick	If you can find it or order it: A piece of caul fat (pig's
12 or more slices of Swiss cheese 1/16 inch thick	caul)
	Heavy white string

Place roast so its bottom rests on your cutting board. Completely cover each leaf of meat with a layer of ham between two layers of cheese, then close the leaves of meat together to re-form the roast. (If you have caul fat, wrap the roast in it; it will hold the stuffing in place, and melt during cooking.) Tie loops of string around the meat to hold it in shape. Dry the roast again in paper towels so it will brown nicely.

BROWNING THE ROAST

3 Tb butter	roaster large enough to
1 Tb cooking oil	hold the meat
A covered casserole or	

(Preheat oven to 450 degrees.)

Strain the marinade, to separate vegetables from liquid (or use fresh vegetables). Heat butter and oil in the roaster and cook the marinade vegetables slowly for 5 minutes. Push them to the sides of the pan, raise heat to moderately high, put in the veal, uncut side down, and let bottom brown for 5 minutes. Baste with the fat in the pan, then place casserole uncovered in upper third of preheated oven to brown top and sides of meat for about 15 minutes. Baste every 4 or 5 minutes with butter in casserole. (If you have used caul fat, you may simply brown the roast in a frying pan, if you wish, then proceed to next step, omitting the blanched bacon.)

ROASTING THE VEAL

½ tsp salt
⅛ tsp pepper
2 strips fat bacon simmered
   for 10 minutes in 1 quart
of water, rinsed, and
dried (or a strip of suet)
A piece of aluminum foil

Turn oven down to 325 degrees. Pour in the marinade liquid, if you have used it, and season the meat with salt and pepper. Place the bacon or suet over the meat, and the foil. Cover the casserole, and set in lower third of oven. Regulate heat so meat cooks slowly and steadily for about 1½ hours. The meat is done when, if pricked deeply with a fork, the juices run clear yellow.

SAUCE AND SERVING

A hot serving platter
1 cup beef stock or bouillon
1 Tb cornstarch blended in a
small bowl with 2 Tb
   Madeira or stock
2 Tb softened butter

Remove meat to serving platter, discard trussing strings and bacon or suet. Skim fat off juices in casserole, pour in stock or bouillon, and simmer, skimming off fat, for a minute or two. Raise heat and boil rapidly, tasting, until flavor has concentrated. Remove from heat, beat in cornstarch mixture, then boil, stirring, for 2 minutes. Carefully correct seasoning. Remove from heat and swirl in enrichment butter until it has absorbed. Strain into a hot gravy bowl and spoon a bit over the meat.

VEGETABLE AND WINE SUGGESTIONS

Braised lettuce, celery, or spinach; broiled tomatoes; and either potatoes sautéed in butter or buttered noodles. Serve a red Bordeaux wine from the Médoc district.

The Fifty-first Show

THE SOUP SHOW
◦৯ • ৫◦
(*Leek and Potato, Vichyssoise, Watercress*)

In this busy can-opener world, a homemade soup often seems like a new taste sensation. The old French standby, leek and potato soup, tastes so good you cannot believe it is nothing but vegetables, water, and salt simmered together. It is also versatile: add watercress and you have a *potage au cresson,* or chill it, lace it with cream, and you have *vichyssoise.* Another delicious soup is cream of watercress with its final enrichment of egg yolks. Hot or cold, most French soups are very easy, and can be made ready hours before serving time.

POTAGE PARMENTIER
(*Leek or Onion and Potato Soup*)
For about 2 quarts, serving 6 to 8

PRELIMINARY COOKING

A 3- to 4-quart saucepan or pressure cooker	3 cups thinly sliced leeks or yellow onions
3 to 4 cups peeled potatoes sliced or diced	2 quarts water
	1 Tb salt

Either simmer the vegetables, water, and salt together, partially covered, for 40 to 50 minutes until vegetables are tender; or cook under 15 pounds pressure for 5 minutes, release pressure, and simmer uncovered for 15 minutes to develop the flavor.

Mash the vegetables in the soup with a fork, or pass the soup through a food mill. Correct seasoning. Set aside uncovered until just before serving, then reheat to the simmer.

FINAL ENRICHMENT

⅓ cup heavy cream or 2 to   2 to 3 Tb minced parsley
3 Tb softened butter   or chives

Remove from heat just before serving, and stir in the cream or butter by spoonfuls. Pour into a tureen or soup cups and decorate with herbs.

VARIATIONS ତ

Potage au Cresson
(Watercress Soup)

Follow preceding recipe but before puréeing the soup stir in 1 bunch of watercress (about 1 cup) and simmer for 5 minutes. Then purée the soup, and finish the recipe.

Vichyssoise

Follow the main recipe but use only the white part of leeks. Purée the soup in an electric blender or food mill, then through a fine sieve. Stir in ½ to 1 cup heavy cream, oversalt slightly, and chill. Serve in chilled soup cups and decorate with minced chives. (Note: You may use part chicken stock and part water to cook the vegetables.)

POTAGE CRÈME DE CRESSON
(Cream of Watercress Soup)
For 6 servings

COOKING THE WATERCRESS

½ cup minced onions   watercress leaves and
3 Tb butter   tender stems, washed, and
A 3-quart covered saucepan   dried in a towel
3 to 4 packed cups fresh   ½ tsp salt

Cook the onions slowly in the butter in the saucepan for about 10 minutes. When tender and translucent, stir in the watercress and salt, cover, and cook slowly for 5 minutes or until thoroughly wilted.

SIMMERING

3 Tb flour	5½ cups boiling chicken stock

Sprinkle the flour into the watercress mixture and stir over moderate heat for 3 minutes. Remove from heat, blend in the hot stock, and simmer for 5 minutes. Purée through a food mill, return to the saucepan, and correct seasoning. Set aside until shortly before serving, and reheat again to the simmer.

FINAL ENRICHMENT

2 egg yolks blended in a mixing bowl with ½ cup heavy cream	1 to 2 Tb softened butter

Beat a cupful of hot soup by driblets into the yolks and cream, gradually beat in the rest of the soup in a thin stream. Return soup to saucepan and stir over moderate heat for a moment or two to poach the egg yolks, but do not bring to the simmer. Remove from heat and stir in the enrichment butter a tablespoon at a time.

SERVING

To serve cold, omit final butter enrichment and chill. If too thick, stir in more cream before serving.

The Fifty-second Show

FLAMING SOUFFLÉ
ঙ্গ • ঙ্গ
(*Crème Anglaise*)

Here is a soufflé which rises nicely, is slow to sink, and which is baked in a low serving dish. Flame it with hot liqueur, if you wish a dramatic presentation.

SOUFFLÉ A L'ORANGE, FLAMBÉ
(*Rum, Orange, and Macaroon Soufflé, Flambé*)
For 4 to 6 people

The grated rind of 2 oranges
⅔ cup granulated sugar
A mixing bowl
6 egg yolks
A stainless-steel bowl or
    saucepan

¼ cup dark rum or orange
    juice
A wire whip
An electric mixer

(Preheat oven to 375 degrees.)

Mash the orange rind and sugar together in a bowl with a wooden spoon, to extract as much of the orange oil as possible. Place the egg yolks in the bowl or saucepan. Gradually beat in the orange sugar and continue beating until egg yolks are pale yellow and thickened. Beat in the rum or orange juice, then set over barely simmering water and beat with a wire whip (2 strokes per second) until mixture turns into a warm, thick cream. This will take 3 or 4 minutes, and mixture will be thick enough to form a slowly dissolving ribbon when a bit is dropped from the beater and falls back onto the surface. Remove from heat and beat in an electric mixer 4 to 5 minutes until cool and thick.

¼ cup sifted cornstarch
6 egg whites
A clean bowl for beating egg
   whites

¼ tsp cream of tartar
2 Tb granulated sugar

Beat the sifted cornstarch into the egg yolk mixture. Beat the egg whites until foamy, then beat in the cream of tartar and continue beating until soft peaks are formed. Sprinkle in the sugar and beat until stiff peaks are formed. Stir one fourth of the egg whites into the yolk mixture; delicately fold in the rest.

A lightly buttered baking
   dish, 9 inches in diameter
   and 2 inches deep
¾ cup crumbled macaroons

Powdered sugar in a fine-
   meshed sieve
Optional: ⅓ cup warmed
   rum or brandy

Turn one third of the soufflé mixture into the buttered baking dish, sprinkle on half of the macaroons, cover with half the remaining soufflé mixture, continue with the last of the macaroons, the last of the soufflé mixture, and sprinkle top with ¹⁄₁₆-inch layer of powdered sugar. Bake in middle level of preheated 375-degree oven for about 25 minutes, or until soufflé has puffed and the top has browned. If you wish to flame the soufflé, pour the warm rum or brandy over it just as you enter the dining room, then ignite with a lighted match. Serve with the following sauce, or with lightly whipped cream.

Crème Anglaise

(French Custard Sauce)
For about 1½ cups

3 egg yolks
A 1½-quart stainless-steel or
   enameled saucepan
⅓ cup granulated sugar

1¼ cups hot milk
2 tsp vanilla extract
Optional: 1 Tb rum
1 Tb softened butter

Beat the egg yolks in the saucepan until thick and sticky (1 minute), gradually beat in the sugar, then beat in the hot milk by droplets. Stir over moderately low heat with a wooden spoon until sauce thickens enough to coat the spoon—do not let sauce come near the simmer or the egg yolks will curdle. Remove from heat and stir in vanilla, then the optional rum, and the butter. Serve warm or cool.

The Fifty-third Show

SMALL ROAST BIRDS

◆§ · §◆

PIGEONNEAUX SUR CANAPÉS
(*Roast Squabs on Liver Canapés*)
For 6 people, ½ bird apiece

This is one of the classic French methods for serving small roast birds, such as squab, game hen, partridge, quail, dove, woodcock. The roasting time given in the recipe is for squab pigeon; game hens, with their firmer flesh, will take 10 to 15 minutes longer to cook.

PREPARATION FOR ROASTING

3 young squabs or other tender small birds of about ¾ lbs. each
Salt and pepper
1½ Tb finely minced shallots or scallions
¾ tsp tarragon
3 Tb softened butter

3 or more strips (4 x 2 x ⅛ inches) fresh pork fat or suet; or thick-sliced bacon simmered for 10 minutes in 1 quart of water
A shallow roasting pan
⅓ cup each of sliced carrots and onions

Chop the birds' wings off at the elbows; reserve all trimmings and giblets. Sprinkle salt, pepper, ½ tablespoon shallots or scallions, and ¼ teaspoon tarragon into the cavity of each, and add ½ tablespoon of butter. Dry each bird thoroughly, rub skin with butter, place the pork fat, suet, or bacon over the breasts and thighs, and truss for roasting. Lay birds on their sides in the roasting pan, and strew the vegetables about them. (May be prepared ahead to this point; refrigerate until ½ hour before roasting.)

ROASTING

2 Tb butter melted with
1 Tb good cooking oil

(Preheat to 400 degrees.)
Place birds in middle level of preheated oven. Every 5 to 6 minutes, turn birds on another side and baste with a spoonful of butter and oil. When almost tender, in about 25 minutes, remove the fat strips, turn the birds breast up, and salt lightly. Continue roasting, basting every 2 or 3 minutes, until birds are browned and tender—5 to 10 minutes more. They are done when the last drops of juice drained from their vents run clear yellow with no trace of rose. Do not overcook!

SAUCE AND GARNITURE

(Prepare ahead of time, or while birds are roasting.)

SAUCE BASE

A heavy saucepan
Necks, gizzards, hearts, and
  wing tips from birds
2 Tb each of sliced carrots
  and onions

2 Tb good cooking oil
1½ cups beef bouillon or
  brown chicken stock

In the saucepan, lightly brown the necks, gizzards, hearts, and wing tips and the carrots and onions in the oil. Cover with bouillon or stock and simmer for 30 minutes or longer. Strain and reserve.

LIVER CANAPÉS

Homemade-type of white
  bread

⅓ cup butter
A frying pan

| The livers from the birds | Salt and pepper |
| 1½ Tb fresh pork fat or suet | ½ Tb Madeira or port |

Remove crusts from 3 slices of bread; cut into rectangles 2 by 3½ inches. Melt the butter, and pour the clear liquid (not the milky residue) into the frying pan. Sauté the bread on each side until lightly browned.

Chop the bird livers into a fine purée with the pork fat or suet. Then blend in a bowl with salt, pepper, and the Madeira or port. Spread mixture over one side of the sautéed bread. Just before serving the birds, run canapés close under a hot broiler for a minute, until liver is bubbling.

MUSHROOMS

1 lb. fresh mushrooms, quartered	1 Tb minced shallots or scallions
2 Tb butter	Optional: ½ clove mashed garlic
1 Tb oil	3 Tb minced fresh parsley

Sauté the mushrooms in oil and butter until lightly browned, adding the minced shallots or scallions at the end, and, if you wish, ½ small clove of mashed garlic. Just before serving, reheat, season, and sprinkle with parsley.

FINAL ASSEMBLY AND SERVING

A hot serving platter	1 Tb softened butter
¼ cup Madeira or port	A handful of parsley sprigs or watercress leaves
Salt and pepper	

When the birds are done, split them in half lengthwise. Place each half, cut side down, over a hot liver canapé on the serving platter. Set in turned-off oven, door ajar, while finishing the sauce.

Skim all but a tablespoon of fat from the roasting pan, pour in the sauce base and the Madeira or port. Boil down rapidly, scraping up coagulated roasting juices, until liquid has reduced to about ½ cup. Correct seasoning, remove from heat, and swirl in the butter.

Arrange the sautéed mushrooms around the roast birds, decorating with parsley sprigs or watercress, spoon the sauce (omitting the sliced vegetables) over the birds, and serve immediately.
Wine suggestion: Red Bordeaux-Médoc.

The Fifty-fourth Show

BOEUF A LA MODE

Braised beef is a wonderful party dish because it can be cooked ahead, doesn't mind waiting, and can be served either whole or sliced. Leftovers are delicious, hot or cold. This recipe calls for a solid piece of braising beef which will slice into neat serving pieces. Because the meat shrinks considerably during cooking, choose a boneless piece of at least 4 pounds, and, however long it is, it should be at least 4 inches in diameter. Recommended cuts are: Top Round, Bottom Round, Knuckle or Sirloin Tip, Undercut of Chuck.

LARDING NOTE. When a piece of beef is larded, ¼-inch strips of fresh pork fat-back, fat salt pork, or suet are inserted through the length of the raw meat going with the grain, at ¾- to 1-inch intervals. These strips serve to baste the interior of the meat as it cooks, and show a decorative pattern when the meat is sliced. Some fancy butcher shops will do this for you. If you wish to lard the meat yourself, you will have to find a "lardoir" or larding needle, a metal trough about ⅜ inch in diameter and 12 to 14 inches long, with a handle at one end and a point at the other. These can often be found at butcher supply houses or French import shops. Larding is not necessary for this recipe, though it adds a traditional French touch.

BOEUF A LA MODE
(*Pot Roast of Beef Braised in Red Wine*)
For 10 to 12 people

THE MARINADE

(A marinade tenderizes and flavors the meat, but if you do not have time to do it simply add all the listed ingredients to the braising casserole where indicated in the recipe.)

1 cup each of thinly sliced carrots, onions, celery stalks
2 halved cloves unpeeled garlic
An herb bouquet: 1 Tb thyme, 2 bay leaves, 6 parsley sprigs, 4 allspice berries, 6 peppercorns tied in washed cheesecloth
1 Tb salt
5 cups full-bodied young

red wine—Burgundy, Côtes-du-Rhône, Mountain Red, or Chianti
⅓ cup brandy
½ cup olive oil or salad oil
A stainless-steel or enameled bowl or casserole large enough to hold all the ingredients listed
A 5-lb. piece of braising beef trimmed and tied securely with white string

Mix all the marinade ingredients in the bowl or casserole, add beef. Baste with the marinade, cover, and let soak for at least 6 hours, though 12 to 24 are advisable. (Refrigerate meat in warm weather.) Turn and baste the meat every hour or so. Half an hour before cooking, drain meat on a rack. Just before browning, dry thoroughly with paper towels.

BROWNING AND BRAISING THE BEEF

4 or more Tb cooking oil
A heavy covered roaster just large enough to hold the beef
4 to 6 cups beef stock or bouillon

Optional for additional flavor and consistency: cracked veal knuckles, split calf's feet, pork rind simmered 10 minutes in water

(Preheat oven to 350 degrees.)

Heat the oil in the roaster until almost smoking; add the meat and brown on all sides. Discard browning oil. Add marinade ingredients and boil down liquid by half. Then pour in enough stock or bouillon to come two thirds the way up the beef. Add optional ingredients and bring to simmer on top of the stove.

Cover tightly and place in lower third of preheated oven. Regulate oven heat so liquid remains at a gentle simmer for 2¾ to 4 hours, depending on the grade and quality of the beef. It is done when a sharp-pronged fork will pierce it easily.

SAUCE AND SERVING

A hot serving platter
1 Tb cornstarch mixed with
  2 Tb Madeira or port,
  stock, or water, if needed

Parsley sprigs or watercress
  leaves or vegetables

When meat is tender, remove it to a hot serving platter. Discard trussing strings. Trim off any loose fat, and keep meat warm while finishing the sauce (5 to 10 minutes).

Skim the fat off the braising juices in the roaster, strain juices through a sieve into a saucepan. Simmer for a minute, skimming off fat, then boil rapidly until liquid has reduced to about 3½ cups and is full of flavor. Taste carefully for seasoning. Sauce should be lightly thickened; if too liquid, beat in cornstarch mixture and simmer for 2 minutes.

Pour a bit of sauce over meat, decorate platter with parsley, watercress, or vegetables, and send rest of sauce to table in a warmed bowl.

VEGETABLE AND WINE SUGGESTIONS

Braised carrots and onions, or braised lettuce, celery, or leaks, and broiled tomatoes; buttered noodles, parsley potatoes, or steamed rice. A full red wine served at room temperature, such as Burgundy, Côtes-du-Rhône, Châteauneuf-du-Pape, or Mountain Red.

AHEAD-OF-TIME NOTES

For a wait of up to 1 hour, return meat, vegetables, and sauce to casserole, cover loosely, and set over barely simmering water.

For a longer wait, you can slice the meat and arrange it on a fireproof platter. Place your vegetable garnish around the meat and baste with the sauce. Half an hour before serving, cover and reheat in a 350-degree oven until bubbling—but do not overcook.

The Fifty-fifth Show

TIMBALES
◦ ◦
(Spinach Custard; Ham Custard)

Timbales are quickly assembled mixtures of cooked fish, meat, or vegetables, plus eggs, milk, and seasonings. There are two kinds, one with whole eggs, and one with separated eggs. They are both baked in soufflé dishes, individual ramekins, or ring molds, and are unmolded for serving. Attractive as a first course or a main-course luncheon or supper dish, vegetable timbales may also accompany roasts, steaks, or chops, making a nice change from the conventional vegetable garniture.

PREPARATION OF BAKING DISHES, MOLDS, OR RAMEKINS. So that the timbale will unmold easily after baking, smear the inside of the dish fairly heavily with softened butter, and line the bottom with buttered waxed paper.

TIMBALE AUX ÉPINARDS

(Molded Spinach Custard)

For 5 to 6 cups serving 4 to 6

½ cup minced onions

2 Tb butter

A stainless-steel or enameled covered saucepan (spinach will pick up metallic taste if cooked in plain metal pans)

2½ to 3 lbs. fresh spinach trimmed and blanched for 3 minutes in boiling

water; or 2 packages (10 ounces each) frozen leaf spinach thawed in cold water

A stainless-steel knife for chopping spinach

¼ tsp salt

Pinch each of pepper and nutmeg

Cook the onions slowly in the butter. Meanwhile, squeeze the spinach, a small handful at a time, to remove as much water as possible. Chop into a fine purée. When onions are tender, stir in the spinach and the salt, pepper, and nutmeg. Cover pan and cook very slowly, stirring occasionally to prevent sticking, until spinach is tender (about 5 minutes).

1 cup milk

5 eggs

2 Tb butter

A mixing bowl

⅔ cup stale white bread crumbs (use homemade-

type bread or French bread)

½ cup grated Swiss cheese

Salt and pepper

A 6-cup ring mold or soufflé dish, or 4 ramekins of 1½-cup capacity

When spinach is done, stir in the additional butter and the milk. Beat the eggs in a mixing bowl, then gradually beat into them the warm spinach mixture. Stir in the bread crumbs and cheese, and correct seasoning. Pour into prepared mold. (May be assembled ahead to this point and refrigerated. Baking time will be about 10 minutes longer if done this way.)

BAKING AND SERVING

A pan containing about 1½
   inches of boiling water
Optional: cream sauce, light

cheese sauce, or *hol-
landaise* (see p. 278)

(Preheat oven to 325 degrees.)

Set mold in a pan of boiling water (water should come ½ to ⅔ the way up the mold), and place in bottom third of oven. Bake for 30 to 40 minutes, depending on shape of mold, until a knife, plunged into center of custard, comes out clean. Let settle for 5 minutes before unmolding, or keep warm in pan of water in a 150-degree oven.

To unmold, run a knife around edge of custard; turn a hot serving dish upside down over the mold, reverse the two and custard will drop onto dish. Peel waxed paper off top. No sauce is needed if the timbale is to take the place of a vegetable; if it is to be a first or main course, spoon a cream sauce, light cheese sauce, or *hollandaise* over it.

VARIATIONS ⅋

Using the same ingredients and proportions, substitute 2 to 2½ cups of any of the following for the spinach: cooked and chopped asparagus, broccoli, green peas, cauliflower, Brussels sprouts, mushrooms, chicken livers, or cooked or canned tuna, salmon, or shellfish.

TIMBALE AU JAMBON
(Molded Ham Custard)
For about 6 cups serving 4 to 6

This main-course timbale may be made with ham or with cooked fish, shellfish, chicken, chicken livers, meat leftovers, or vegetables. You may cook it in a ring mold, soufflé dish, loaf pan, or individual ramekins.

(Preheat oven to 325 degrees.)

1½ cups boiled noodles
¾ cup mushrooms, previ-
   ously sautéed in butter

⅔ cup boiled ham
½ cup onions, previously
   sautéed in butter

Salt and pepper
1 cup thick cream sauce
½ cup grated Swiss cheese
3 egg yolks
1 Tb tomato paste
¼ cup minced parsley

3 stiffly beaten egg whites
A 6-cup ring mold, soufflé
   dish, or loaf pan, or 4
   ramekins of 1½-cup
   capacity

Put the noodles, mushrooms, ham, and onions through the medium blade of a food mill or food chopper. Beat the mixture in a bowl with the seasonings, cream sauce, cheese, egg yolks, tomato paste, and parsley. Fold in the beaten egg whites and turn into prepared mold or ramekins. Set in a pan of boiling water and bake for about 30 minutes, depending on shape of mold (a ring mold will bake more quickly than a soufflé dish). Timbale is done when mixture has risen about ½ inch and browned nicely on top. It will sink slightly as it cools, but may be kept warm for a good half hour before serving. Unmold on a hot serving dish.

SAUCE AND GARNITURE

If you have used a ring mold, you can fill the timbale with cooked green vegetables; otherwise you might surround it with the vegetables. Tomato sauce, cream sauce mixed with herbs or a spoonful of tomato paste, or a light cheese sauce would go well, spooned over the timbale.

The Fifty-sixth Show

FISH FILLETS SYLVESTRE
❦ · ❦
(Steamed Rice)

With a bit of sole and a bottle of wine you can take off on a vast exploration of fish dishes. Cooking the sole is always the same, and making the sauce hardly changes from one recipe to another; the variety and excitement you achieve comes from what else you add. Here the fish is poached with a very finely diced vegetable garnish and white wine, making a deliciously aromatic liquid for the sauce. When you serve the fish surrounded with perfectly steamed rice and buttered fresh peas, you will find yourself compelled to celebrate it with your best bottle of white Burgundy wine.

FILETS DE SOLE SYLVESTRE
(Fish Fillets Poached in White Wine with
a Brunoise of Aromatic Vegetables)
For 4 people

THE BRUNOISE OF AROMATIC VEGETABLES

The following cut into ¹⁄₁₆-inch dice, making 1¾ cups in all: 2 medium onions, 2 medium carrots, 1 medium celery stalk, 8 parsley stems
A small, heavy covered saucepan

2 Tb butter
½ bay leaf
¼ tsp tarragon
⅛ tsp salt
Pinch of pepper
¼ lb. fresh mushrooms cut into ¹⁄₁₆-inch dice

After cutting the first group of vegetables into the finest

possible dice, cook them over low heat with the butter, herbs, and seasonings for about 20 minutes. They should be perfectly tender and the palest golden color. Then add the mushrooms and cook slowly for 10 minutes more.

COOKING THE FISH

8 fillets of sole, flounder, or whiting measuring 9 by 2 inches (2 per person)	Salt and pepper
	A 10- to 12-inch baking-serving dish, 1½ to 2 inches deep, buttered
1 cup dry white French vermouth	¼ to ½ cup cold water

(Preheat oven to 350 degrees.)

Score the fish lightly on the side which was next to the skin; this is the rather milky side, and drawing a knife over it cuts the surface membrane, thus preventing the fillet from curling as it cooks. Lightly salt and pepper the fillets, place a spoonful of cooked vegetables over half the scored side and fold in two, wedge-shaped. Arrange the fish in one layer in the baking dish. Pour on the vermouth, and add enough cold water almost to cover the fish. (If you happen to have the fish frame [bone structure] lay it over the fish.) Cover with waxed paper. If your baking dish is flameproof, bring barely to the simmer on top of the stove, then set in lower third of preheated oven for about 8 minutes. Otherwise, set dish directly in oven for about 12 minutes. Fish is done when a fork pierces the flesh easily, and flesh barely flakes. Do not overcook. Keep warm in turned-off oven, with door ajar, while making sauce.

SAUCE AND SERVING

2 stainless-steel or enameled saucepans	1 Tb flour
	1 Tb tomato purée or paste
1 Tb butter	4 or more Tb softened butter

Drain all the cooking liquid into one of the saucepans and boil down rapidly until liquid has reduced to about ⅔ cup. In the other saucepan, melt butter, blend in flour, and cook slowly without coloring for 2 minutes. Remove from heat and vigorously beat in the reduced cooking liquid, then the tomato flavoring. Just before serving, remove from heat and beat in the softened butter, ½ tablespoon at a time. (Sauce cannot be reheated once butter has gone in.) Drain fish again, adding liquid to sauce. Spoon sauce over fish and serve immediately.

MISCELLANEOUS NOTES

If you wish to cook the fish and make the sauce (minus final butter enrichment) in advance, set fish aside and reheat either in oven or over simmering water. Be careful not to overcook! Film sauce with a tablespoon of butter to keep a skin from forming.

Riz Étuvé au Beurre
(Steamed and Buttered Rice)
For 4½ cups, about 6 servings

1½ cups clean, unwashed, raw rice
A large kettle containing 7 to 8 quarts rapidly boiling water
1½ tsp salt per quart of water

2 to 3 Tb butter
Salt and pepper
A heavy 3-quart saucepan or casserole
A round of buttered waxed paper

Gradually sprinkle the rice into the boiling salted water, adding slowly enough so water does not drop below the boil. Stir up once, to be sure none of the grains are sticking to the bottom of the kettle.

Boil uncovered and moderately fast for 10 to 12 minutes. Start testing after 10 minutes by biting successive grains of rice. When a grain is just tender enough to have no hardness at the center, but is not yet fully cooked, drain the rice in a colander. Fluff it up under hot running water for a minute or two to wash off any traces of rice flour. (It is this, plus overcooking, which makes rice sticky.)

In the saucepan or casserole, melt the butter and stir in the salt and pepper. As soon as rice has been washed, turn it into the pan, fluff with a fork to mix with the butter and seasonings.

Cover with buttered waxed paper, then put on the lid. Steam over simmering water or, still in water, in a 325-degree oven for 20 to 30 minutes, until grains have swelled and rice is tender. If not to be served immediately, remove from heat and set aside covered only by the waxed paper. To reheat, cover and set over simmering water for 10 minutes or so. Fluff in more salt and pepper to taste just before serving.

The Fifty-seventh Show

BABAS AU RHUM

These little cakes made of a simple yeast dough are soaked, after baking, in a rum-and-sugar syrup. After they have absorbed the syrup, they are drained, painted with apricot jam, decorated with glacéed fruit, and served either individually in paper cups or together on a platter. Baked *babas* freeze perfectly and need only to be warmed in the oven before soaking and decorating.

A NOTE ON YEAST DOUGHS. As indicated in the recipe, you can, if necessary, stop a yeast dough from rising by pushing it down, covering with a plate and a weight, and placing it in the refrigerator; the dough will remain stable for several hours and no harm is done. You can also freeze it.

When dough has risen to double its bulk, it should not be allowed to rise further or the yeast will overferment, lose its strength, and impart an unpleasant "yeasty" flavor to the baked dough.

PÂTE A BABA
(Dough for Babas)
For 12 babas

MIXING THE DOUGH

4 Tb butter
1 package compressed fresh
yeast; or 1 envelope dry
active yeast dissolved in
3 Tb warm water
A large mixing bowl
2 Tb granulated sugar
⅛ tsp salt

2 eggs (U. S. graded
"large")
1½ cups all-purpose white
flour (measured by scoop-
ing cup into bag, and
leveling off excess even
with lip of cup, using a
knife)

Melt the butter and let cool to tepid while preparing other ingredients. Mash yeast cake with a fork in mixing bowl, beat in sugar and salt, and let yeast melt into a damp paste while measuring flour. (Or add dissolved dry yeast to bowl, with sugar and salt.) When yeast is ready, break in the eggs and beat to blend well, then beat in the flour and the tepid melted butter. With the fingers of one hand held together and slightly cupped, knead the dough by lifting it, slapping it, and pulling it vigorously against the sides of the bowl. (If you have used dry yeast, add 2 or 3 more tablespoons of flour if, after kneading for a moment, the dough seems excessively damp and sticky. On the other hand, if the dough seems too firm—it should be quite sticky at first—add a tablespoon of beaten egg; this might be necessary when you are using fresh yeast.) Dough will stick to your hand for about a minute of kneading; as soon as it begins to be less sticky, remove it from the bowl and slap and knead it roughly on the table. It has been kneaded to sufficient elasticity when you can roll it out a foot in length and give it a full twist without breaking it. At this point it will not stick to your hands.

FIRST RISING

1 tsp flour

Form the dough into a ball and place in the mixing bowl. With scissors, cut a 2-inch cross 1 inch deep in the top of the dough and sprinkle dough with the flour. Cover with several thicknesses of damp towel and let rise in a warm place, 80 to 90 degrees, for 1½ to 2 hours, or until the dough has doubled in bulk; if you poke your finger into the dough, the impression will remain without springing back.

SECOND RISING

Again with the cupped fingers of one hand, gently deflate the dough by gathering it from the sides of the bowl to the center.

12 *baba*, popover, or muffin cups or tins, about 2	inches in diameter and 2 inches deep
	1 Tb butter

Butter insides of the cups. Lightly break off about a table-spoon of dough, enough to fill ⅓ of a cup, and press lightly into the bottom of each cup. Do not bother to even top of dough; it will smooth as it rises. Place uncovered in a warm place; let rise until dough is ¼ inch over the rim of the cups. (May be refrigerated when partially risen, if necessary; continue rising in an hour or two.)

BAKING

As soon as dough has risen, bake in upper third of a preheated 375-degree oven for about 15 minutes. The *babas* are done when slightly shrunk from sides of cups and nicely browned. Unmold and let cool on a cake rack.

Babas au Rhum

THE SUGAR SYRUP

Both the *babas* and the syrup should be lukewarm before the soaking begins. If *babas* are cold or have come from the freezer, warm them in the oven.

2 cups water	1 cup granulated sugar
A 1-quart saucepan	½ cup dark rum

Bring 1 cup of the water to the boil in a saucepan with the sugar, stirring until sugar has dissolved completely and liquid is clear and limpid. Remove from heat, stir in the second cup of water, and the rum.

SOAKING THE BABAS

12 lukewarm *babas* (preced-ceding recipe)	just large enough to hold the *babas* easily
A dish 2 inches deep and	Optional: a bulb baster
	A cake rack set over a tray

Prick the tops and sides of the tepid *babas* at ¾-inch intervals with a sharp-pronged fork. Arrange in the dish and pour over them the lukewarm syrup; let stand for ½ hour, basting frequently with the syrup in the dish (a bulb baster is useful for this). The *babas* should imbibe enough syrup so they are moist and spongy but still hold their shape. Drain on the rack for ½ hour before decorating.

Babas au Rhum, Classique

½ cup apricot jam	Slivered almonds
1 Tb sugar	Frilled paper cups (cup-cake type)
2 Tb dark rum	
12 glacéed cherries	

Force the apricot jam through a sieve to eliminate bits of skin, then boil with the sugar in a small saucepan until last drops from spoon are sticky (228 degrees). Sprinkle a few drops of rum over the *babas*, paint each with warm apricot glaze, and set in paper cups. Decorate top with cherries and almonds. (Decorated *babas* will keep for a day or two in the refrigerator, but are best if eaten promptly.)

VARIATION ❧

Arrange the soaked and glazed *babas* in a serving dish. Surround them with blueberries or strawberries which have been flavored with leftover *baba* syrup. Serve with lightly whipped cream, passed in a bowl.

The Fifty-eighth Show

CHICKEN DINNER FOR FOUR
IN HALF AN HOUR
∾⟨ · ⟩∾

MENU:

Cold Hors d'Oeuvre
Herbal Chicken, Sautéed Potatoes and Zucchini
Fresh Pears, Brie or Camembert Cheese, Crackers
Red Bordeaux or Rosé Wine

With a minimum of advance planning, a moderately fast operator can have this whole dinner prepared and ready to serve in
half an hour. The cold hors d'oeuvre, consisting of watercress,
thin salami slices, tomatoes, and halved hard-boiled eggs with
mayonnaise, is merely a matter of rapid assembly if you boil
and shell the eggs at breakfast time—though you can do the
eggs along with the zucchini. The dessert of fruit and cheese
takes no preparation at all. Thus your chief emphasis is on the
main course. Here is a suggested step-by-step schedule of events.

1) FIRST STEP

Fill a kettle with 6 quarts of hot water, add 3 tablespoons of
salt, cover, and set over highest heat. This is for boiling the
zucchini, peeling the tomatoes—and boiling the eggs if need be.

2) COOKING THE CHICKEN   (Poulet à la Sicilienne)

3 Tb butter
2½ to 3 lbs. cut-up broiler/
   fryer chicken
Salt and pepper
½ Tb tarragon or mixed

dried herbs, such as
   "Italian Seasoning"
A heavy frying pan, cas-
   serole, or an electric
   skillet

Melt the butter in the pan; when bubbling, add the chicken and turn to coat with butter on all sides. Season with salt, pepper, and half the herbs. Cover and cook slowly, allowing the butter to bubble quietly but not to brown (260 degrees).

3) BOILING THE ZUCCHINI

4 to 6 medium zucchini

Scrub the zucchini with a vegetable brush under cold water. Cut off green cap at one end and button at the other end of each. Drop into the rapidly boiling water, and boil uncovered for about 8 minutes. (If zucchini water is not yet boiling, start on next step, adding zucchini when water does boil.)

4) TOMATOES AND EGGS

3 to 4 ripe tomatoes,   **4 eggs**
   medium size

Place tomatoes in a skimmer and hold in the boiling zucchini water for exactly 10 seconds to loosen skin for peeling; set aside. If you haven't boiled your eggs, add them now to the zucchini water, timing them 11 minutes (for graded "large eggs").

5) THE POTATOES

3 to 4 medium all-purpose   **A 10-inch frying pan (no-**
   potatoes   **stick type is recom-**
1 Tb butter   **mended)**
½ Tb cooking oil   **Salt and pepper**

Peel the potatoes and cut into ⅜-inch dice. Dry thoroughly in a towel. Heat butter and oil in frying pan until butter foam is beginning to subside, then add the potatoes. Let cook for a minute at high heat, toss, let cook another minute, and continue thus for several minutes until the potatoes just start to brown. Sprinkle with salt and pepper, toss, cover, and let cook over moderate heat for about 15 minutes, tossing occasionally. (Do not overfill the pan, maximum depth is 1 inch; if you try to cook too many, they will steam and stick rather than brown.)

6) INTERIM DETAILS

4 scallions   6 to 8 parsley sprigs

In between potato tossings, turn the chicken and season again lightly with salt, pepper, and the rest of the herbs. Mince the white part of the scallions and stir into the chicken. Chop the parsley and set aside in a jar for later. Cut out the stem-button, peel the tomatoes, and set aside. Remove eggs when done, tap shells with a spoon to crack them, and place in cold water.

7) FINISHING THE ZUCCHINI

2 Tb olive oil   Optional: ½ clove garlic,
Salt and pepper   finely chopped or mashed

The zucchini is done as soon as it is barely soft when pressed; do not overcook it. Remove immediately from water. With a two-pronged fork and sharp knife, cut into quarters lengthwise, then cut into ¾-inch pieces. Heat oil in a large saucepan or frying pan; when hot, toss in the zucchini and sauté, tossing, over high heat to evaporate moisture and brown very lightly. Toss with salt and pepper to taste, and optional garlic. Set over low heat, tossing occasionally as you continue with the menu.

Remove zucchini kettle from heat; place serving platter on top of kettle, to warm.

8) ASSEMBLING THE HORS D'OEUVRE

Watercress   The peeled tomatoes
12 slices salami   Salt and pepper
4 peeled hard-boiled eggs
Mayonnaise (homemade if
    possible)

Arrange the watercress around the edge of a serving dish and insert the salami around the outside edge. Halve the eggs and lay against the watercress; cover each with a spoonful of mayonnaise. Cut the tomatoes in wedges, and place in the center. Sprinkle with salt, pepper, and the chopped parsley. (Cover and refrigerate if not served immediately.)

9) FINAL ASSEMBLY

The chicken is done when it is tender if pressed, and the juices, when pricked deeply with a fork, run clear yellow. It takes about 25 minutes, in all, to cook. When done, arrange on the hot serving platter, turn the sautéed potatoes out on one side, and the zucchini on the other. Cover and keep warm over zucchini kettle until ready to serve; sprinkle with parsley just before bringing it into the dining room.

The Fifty-ninth Show

ROGNONS SAUTÉS ET FLAMBÉS
✑ • ✑
(*Veal and Lamb Kidneys, Sautéed and Flambéed*)

Veal and lamb kidneys should be absolutely fresh, with a pleasant fresh odor, and no suggestion of an ammonia smell. When they come from the animal, they are encased in a layer of fat which, when peeled off, reveals a thin membrane surrounding the kidney; this should also be peeled off. Cut out most of the fat on the underside of the kidneys. Veal kidneys should weigh from 6 to 8 ounces; allow ¾ to 1½ per person, depending on your menu. Lamb kidneys weigh about 2 ounces; allow 2 or 3 per person. Raw kidneys may be frozen.

ROGNONS DE VEAU EN CASSEROLE

(Kidneys Cooked in Butter, with Mustard Sauce)
For 4 people

4 Tb butter

A heavy sauté pan just large enough to hold the kidneys comfortably in one layer

3 to 4 veal kidneys or 8 to 12 lamb kidneys

Heat the butter and when foam begins to subside, roll the kidneys in the butter, then cook, uncovered, turning every minute or two. Regulate heat so butter is hot but not browning. A little juice will exude from kidneys. Kidneys should stiffen but not become hard; they should brown a little bit, and should be pink at the center when sliced. Timing: about 10 minutes for veal kidneys; 5, for lamb kidneys. Remove kidneys to a plate.

1 Tb minced shallots or scallions

½ cup dry white vermouth

1 Tb lemon juice

1½ Tb prepared mustard of the Dijon type mashed with 3 Tb softened butter

Salt and pepper

Stir the shallots or onions into the butter in the pan and cook for 1 minute. Add vermouth and lemon juice. Boil rapidly until liquids have reduced to about 4 tablespoons. Remove from heat and swirl in the mustard-butter, and a sprinkling of salt and pepper. Cut the kidneys into crosswise slices ⅛ inch thick. Sprinkle with salt and pepper and turn them and their juices into the pan.

Just before serving, shake and toss over moderate heat for a minute or two to warm through without boiling.

Serve on very hot plates. If used as a main course rather than a hot hors d'oeuvre, accompany with potatoes sautéed in butter, braised onions, and a red Burgundy wine.

Rognons de Veau Flambés

(Sautéed Kidneys Flambéed, with Mushroom Sauce)
For 4 to 6 people

Kidneys cooked this way are best as a separate course, served with hot French bread and a red Burgundy wine. If you wish to finish them off in a chafing dish, sauté the kidneys in the kitchen and assemble all the rest of the ingredients in the dining room with your chafing dish.

A heavy sauté pan large enough to hold kidneys	3 to 4 veal kidneys or 8 to 12 lamb kidneys 4 Tb butter

Sauté the whole kidneys in butter, as in the preceding recipe. If you are finishing them at the table, bring the sautéed kidneys in the chafing dish.

⅓ cup cognac ½ cup beef bouillon mixed with 1 tsp cornstarch ⅓ cup Sercial Madeira or port wine ½ lb. sliced mushrooms, previously sautéed in butter with 1 Tb minced scallions or shallots	1 cup heavy cream Salt and pepper ½ Tb prepared mustard of the Dijon type blended with 2 Tb softened butter and ½ tsp Worcestershire sauce

Pour the cognac over the kidneys. Heat to bubbling, avert your face, and ignite liquid with a lighted match. Shake pan and baste kidneys with flaming liquid until the fire subsides. Remove kidneys to a plate or carving board.

Pour the beef bouillon and wine into the pan; boil for a few minutes until reduced and thickened. Add the mushrooms and cream and boil a few minutes more; sauce should be thick enough to coat a spoon lightly. Season carefully with salt and pepper. Remove from heat and swirl in the mustard mixture.

Cut the kidneys into crosswise slices ⅛ inch thick and season lightly with salt and pepper. Return kidneys and juices to pan. Shake and toss over heat to warm the kidneys through without boiling. Serve on very hot plates.

The Sixtieth Show

LOBSTER BUFFET

⊰ • ⊱

HOMARD GRATINÉ AU FROMAGE
(*Lobster Steamed in Wine and Gratinéed with Cheese*)
For 4 people, 1 lobster each

Here is a delicious way to serve stuffed broiled lobsters. It is particularly recommended for the cook who wants a splendid main course that can be assembled at leisure. This is a much simpler recipe than lobster Thermidor, and every bit as good. The lobsters are steamed in wine and herbs, then this liquid is used to make the light cheese sauce, which bubbles around the lobster meat as it heats in the oven.

STEAMING THE LOBSTERS

A large fish kettle or steamer
2 cups dry white vermouth
2 cups water
1 large onion, thinly sliced
1 medium carrot, thinly
  sliced
1 medium celery stalk,
  thinly sliced

6 parsley sprigs
1 bay leaf
1 Tb tarragon
2 tsp salt
4 peppercorns
4 live lobsters, 1¼ lbs. each

Simmer the above ingredients for 15 minutes. Meanwhile, wash the live lobsters rapidly under cold running water and tie them to a rack (if possible) so they will stay flat during cooking. Bring liquid to a rapid boil, add lobsters, cover tightly, and steam for 18 to 20 minutes or until head feelers can be pulled easily from sockets.

THE SAUCE

3 Tb butter   ½ cup heavy cream
A 3-cup enameled saucepan   ½ cup grated Swiss cheese
4 Tb flour   Salt and pepper

When lobsters are done, remove them. (If you did not tie the lobsters before cooking, tie or weight the tails so they will flatten while cooling.) Rapidly boil down cooking liquid until it has reduced to 2 cups. Melt butter in saucepan, blend in flour, and cook slowly for 2 minutes without browning. Remove from heat, and let cool for a moment. Strain in a cupful of the hot lobster-cooking liquid, vigorously blend with a wire whip, then strain in the rest of the liquid. Bring to the boil, stirring, for 1 minute. Thin out with spoonfuls of cream until sauce coats a spoon nicely. Stir in all but 2 tablespoons of the cheese, and correct seasoning.

BROWNING UNDER THE BROILER

1 Tb butter   A shallow broiling pan

Cut off claws and legs. Turn lobsters on their backs and, being careful to keep chest and tail sections attached, cut out underpart of shells to expose tail meat and the chest meat and green matter. Remove sand sack at head. Remove tail meat and slit it up the back so that you can take out and discard the intestinal vein. Cut tail meat into ¼-inch slices. Spread a bit of sauce in the tail and chest cavities. Replace the tail meat; remove joint and claw meat and place in chest cavity. Cover with sauce, sprinkle with remaining grated cheese, and dot with the butter. Arrange lobsters in the pan and set under a moderate broiler to heat through thoroughly and brown top. (Or refrigerate until about 20 minutes before serving time. Then set in upper third of a preheated 425-degree oven until lobsters are bubbling hot and cheese topping has browned.)

Serve with watercress, shoestring potatoes, and a chilled, dry white wine such as a Burgundy.

The Sixty-first Show

THE MUSHROOM SHOW

~§ • §~

HOW TO BUY FRESH, CULTIVATED MUSHROOMS §~

The freshest of fresh mushrooms are closed on the underside of the cap so that you cannot see the gills. Caps and stems should be smooth, unblemished, fresh-looking, and fresh-smelling. As a mushroom ages, the cap expands to expose the gills. It is best to buy mushrooms in bulk rather than in a package, so that you can hand-pick each one.

PREPARATION FOR COOKING §~

Trim the base of the stems. If gills are even partially exposed, break the stem off inside the cap so you can wash out any sand that may have lodged in the gills.

Just before using, drop the mushrooms in a large basin of cold water. Rapidly rub them between your hands for several seconds to dislodge dirt particles; immediately lift mushrooms into a colander. If there are more than a few grains of sand in the bottom of the basin, wash and drain again. Dry the mushrooms in a towel.

WAYS OF CUTTING MUSHROOMS §~

MINCED OR DICED. Place washed mushrooms in a heap on your board and chop with a long straight-edged knife, holding an end of the blade in the fingers of each hand. Use rapid up-and-down movements, and repeatedly sweep mushrooms back into a heap with the knife. Chop until pieces are smaller than ⅛ inch.

SLICED. Place mushroom cap hollow-side down on board; make ⅛-inch vertical slices straight across cap. Slice stems into ⅛-inch crosswise pieces.

QUARTERED. Place cap hollow-side down; cut straight down the center, making 2 halves; cut each half into 2 or 3 pieces, depending on the size you wish. Cut stems into bias pieces, approximately the same size as the caps.

FLUTED OR TURNED CAPS. Cultivated mushroom caps need not be peeled, but fluting (or turning) removes the peel and gives a decorative design to the cap. Hold the cap domed-side up in the fingers of your left hand. Hold a very sharp small knife rigidly in your right hand, its blade pointing away from you. Rest the thumb of your right hand on the mushroom cap, then rotate the cap toward you against the blade of the knife starting at the crown, thus removing a very shallow strip or flute down one half of the cap. Continue in the same manner all around the cap. Note that the knife remains almost stationary; the mushroom cuts itself as you rotate it against the blade of the knife. (Fluted mushrooms are either stewed or broiled.)

CHAMPIGNONS A BLANC
(Stewed Mushrooms)

For use in sauces, fricassées, or in recipes where cooked mushrooms must remain white.

¼ lb. fresh mushrooms
⅓ cup water
⅛ tsp salt
½ Tb lemon juice

1 Tb butter
An enameled or stainless-
  steel saucepan

Trim and wash the mushrooms and cut them in any way your recipe specifies. Bring the water, salt, lemon juice, and butter to the boil in the saucepan. Add the mushrooms and toss to cover them with the liquid. Cover and boil moderately fast, tossing occasionally for 5 minutes. Set aside until ready to use. (Add cooking juices to sauces or soup.)

CHAMPIGNONS SAUTÉS AU BEURRE
(Sautéed Mushrooms)

Sautéed mushrooms are used alone as a vegetable garnish for steak, broiled chicken, or roasts, or in a combination with other vegetables such as carrots or onions, or as an integral part of such dishes as beef stews, chicken in red wine, or baked chicken. (*Note:* Mushrooms will steam rather than brown if you have more than one layer in the pan: sauté in several batches if you have a large quantity to do.)

A 10-inch no-stick skillet
2 Tb butter
1 Tb light olive oil or cooking oil
½ lb. fresh mushrooms, washed and dried (small whole mushrooms, or sliced or quartered mushrooms)
1 to 2 Tb minced shallots or scallions
Optional: 1 clove crushed garlic, 2 to 3 Tb minced parsley
Salt and pepper

Place skillet over high heat and add the butter and oil. As soon as you see the butter foam begin to subside, add the mushrooms. Toss and shake the pan frequently so mushrooms will cook evenly. At first, mushrooms will absorb the fat in the pan; in a few minutes the fat will reappear on the surface and the mushrooms will begin to brown. When lightly browned, add the shallots or scallions and optional garlic. Toss for a moment more and remove from heat. Reheat and season to taste with salt, pepper, and optional parsley just before serving.

CHAMPIGNONS SOUS CLOCHE
(Mushrooms Baked Under Glass)
For each serving

This buttery essence of mushrooms makes an exquisite first-course or luncheon dish.

A crustless round of home-made-type white bread,
¼ inch thick and 3 inches in diameter

A 3-inch mushroom cap, or
2 to 3 smaller caps
An individual fireproof serving dish or a large baking
dish
The Flavored Butter:
½ Tb butter
Pinch salt and pepper

½ tsp minced parsley
½ tsp minced shallots or
scallions
⅛ tsp lemon juice
A mixing bowl
½ to 1 tsp heavy cream
A fireproof glass bell, bowl,
or baking dish

(Preheat oven to 400 degrees.)

Either toast the bread and butter it on one side, or sauté in butter until lightly browned on each side. Shave the bottom of the mushroom cap (or caps) so it (or they) will lie flat, and place curved side down on the toast. Set on an individual serving dish, or if you have a group, on a baking dish. Beat the butter, salt and pepper, parsley, shallots or scallions, and lemon juice in the bowl until soft and well mixed, then fill the cap (or caps) with this mixture and drop a half teaspoon or so of heavy cream on each cap. Cover with a bell, bowl, or baking dish. Twenty to 25 minutes before serving, set in middle level of preheated oven until mushrooms have softened but have not become limp. Serve immediately. Individual glass bells or *cloches* are removed at the table; otherwise remove cover in the kitchen. Serve with a dry white Graves, a Traminer, or a light red Bordeaux.

The Sixty-second Show

VEAL OR PORK DINNER
FOR FOUR IN HALF AN HOUR
⋰⋱ · ⋰⋱

MENU:

Vichyssoise à la Russe
Sauté de Veau (ou de Porc) aux Champignons
Braised Rice
Green Salad
Poires au Gratin
Red Bordeaux or Rosé Wine
French Bread

To prepare this three-course dinner in half an hour, start with the dessert, which takes longest to cook. The rice and veal are carried on simultaneously, and while they finish cooking, the soup is assembled. The green salad needs no recipe.

POIRES AU GRATIN
(Pears Baked with Wine and Macaroons)

A baking dish 2 inches high
and 8 inches in diameter
1 Tb softened butter
3 to 4 firm, ripe pears

⅓ cup apricot jam
¼ cup dry white vermouth
2 to 3 stale macaroons
2 Tb butter cut into dots

Smear the baking dish with the butter. Peel, quarter, and core the pears; cut into lengthwise slices about ⅜ inch thick, and arrange in the dish. Force the apricot jam through a sieve into a bowl; blend with the vermouth, and pour over the pears. Crumble the macaroons over all, and top with the butter dots.

Set in a middle level of preheated oven and bake for 20 to 25 minutes, until top has browned lightly. Serve hot, warm, or cold and accompany, if you wish, with a pitcher of heavy cream.

RISOTTO A LA PIÉMONTAISE

(Rice Braised in Chicken Stock)

2 Tb butter
A heavy-bottomed 2-quart
  saucepan
1¼ cup unwashed raw
  white rice

¼ cup dry white vermouth
2½ cups chicken stock or
  bouillon
Salt and pepper

Melt the butter over moderate heat. Add the rice and stir slowly with a wooden fork until grains turn translucent, then gradually a milky white—about 2 minutes. Add the vermouth and let absorb, then stir in a third of the chicken stock or bouillon. Lower heat and let rice cook at the barest simmer for 3 to 4 minutes, stirring occasionally. (Start on the veal at this point, and carry on the two operations simultaneously.) When liquid is absorbed, stir in half the remaining stock and continue cooking slowly, stirring occasionally with your wooden fork, and when liquid is again absorbed add the last of the stock. When this is finally absorbed, taste the rice. If not as tender as you wish, add a bit more stock or water and cover the pan for a few minutes. Rice should take 15 to 18 minutes total cooking time. Season to taste with salt and pepper. (If done ahead, cover and reheat over hot water.)

SAUTÉ DE VEAU (OU DE PORC) AUX CHAMPIGNONS

(Tenderloin of Veal or Pork Sautéed with Mushrooms)

1½ to 2 lbs. veal or pork
  tenderloin cut into ¾-inch
  slices
A heavy 10-inch skillet
2 Tb butter
1 Tb cooking oil

An 8- to 10-ounce can of
  mushroom stems and
  pieces
½ tsp tarragon, thyme, or
  mixed herbs
¼ tsp salt; pinch of pepper

Optional: small clove of
 mashed garlic
2 or 3 Tb finely minced
 scallions

¼ cup Sercial Madeira or
 dry white French
 vermouth

Dry the veal or pork on paper towels. Heat the oil and butter in the skillet. When butter foam has almost subsided, add the meat and sauté over high heat, tossing frequently, until it has browned lightly on all sides. Lower heat and continue cooking, tossing occasionally, until meat has stiffened when pressed with your finger. (Total cooking time is 7 to 10 minutes; during this period you will have time to mind the rice, chop scallions and parsley, and assemble the soup.)

Drain the mushrooms and add to the meat. Sprinkle on the herbs, salt and pepper; add the optional garlic, and scallions; toss for a moment, then pour in the mushroom juices and the wine. Boil down to reduce by half. Set aside if you are not ready to serve and reheat when needed.

SAUCE AND SERVING   (Sauce Hollandaise aux Herbes)

2 egg yolks
A small enameled saucepan
1 Tb cold stock or vermouth

4 to 6 Tb softened butter
2 Tb minced parsley

Beat the egg yolks vigorously in saucepan with a wire whip until yolks are thick and sticky. Beat in the cold liquid and ½ tablespoon of butter, then gradually beat in the meat-cooking juices. Stir over low heat until mixture has thickened into a cream; remove from heat and beat in the butter by teaspoonfuls. Sauce will be the consistency of a *hollandaise*. (Keep over tepid water if not used immediately.) Arrange the rice on either side of an oval platter; place the meat in the middle; spoon the sauce over, and sprinkle with parsley.

VICHYSSOISE A LA RUSSE
(Cold Leek and Potato Soup with Beets and Sour Cream)

2 twenty-ounce cans of
 vichyssoise or leek and
 potato soup, chilled

Salt, pepper, lemon juice
Optional: chicken stock or
 milk, chilled

About 1 cup sour cream
1 cup canned julienne of
    beets (matchstick size),

drained and seasoned
    with salt and pepper
2 to 3 Tb finely minced
    chives or scallion tops

Turn the chilled soup into a bowl; season to taste with salt, pepper, and lemon juice. If too thick, dilute with chicken stock or milk; if too thin, beat in a few tablespoons of sour cream. Just before serving, pour chilled soup into bowls; place a big spoonful of cream in the center; top with another big spoonful of beets, and sprinkle with minced chives or scallion tops.

The Sixty-third Show

BROILED CHICKEN
PLAIN AND SAUCY

⊷ક • ੴ⊶

Broiled chicken is a heavenly dish when the skin is crisply brown, and the meat juicy. The only two secrets to succulent broiling are moderate heat, which prevents the outer layer of meat from drying out before the chicken is cooked through, and constant basting. Basting helps sear and brown the outside, seals in the juices, and gives the skin a delicious, buttery flavor. Here are directions for splitting a whole chicken the French way, and recipes for plain broiled chicken and chicken with mustard and herb coating. As fresh peas go beautifully with chicken, an excellent French recipe for them is also included.

THE FRENCH SPLIT—HOW TO PREPARE A WHOLE BROILER FOR COOKING

For this, the chicken is split down the back, spread out, and broiled whole. To split the chicken, take a sharp knife or poultry shears and remove whole length of backbone, cutting close against it on each side starting either at the neck or the tail end. Then, to make the chicken lie flat, spread it breast up on a flat surface and bang the breast with your fist to snap some of the rib bones. To keep the legs and wings in place during cooking, locate ball joints connecting wings to shoulder and cut through the tendons; reaching up under the lower breast skin, cut through the tendons at the joints connecting the drumsticks and second joints. So that the drumsticks will stay in place, make a ½-inch slit at the lower sides of the breast skin, and push the drumstick ends through the slits. Fold the wings akimbo, a wing tip tucked under each shoulder. The chicken is now ready for broiling.

POULET GRILLÉ AU NATUREL
(Plain Broiled Chicken)
For 4 people

A 2½-lb. broiling chicken	Salt
2 Tb butter	2 Tb minced shallots or
1 Tb cooking oil	scallions
A shallow broiling pan or	½ cup beef or chicken
baking dish	bouillon

Dry the chicken thoroughly with paper towels. Melt the butter with the cooking oil, brush chicken all over, and arrange skin side down in the broiling pan or baking dish. Place chicken so surface of meat is 5 to 6 inches from hot broiler element; chicken should cook slowly and not start to brown for 5 minutes. After 5 minutes, brush chicken with butter and oil; it should just be starting to brown. Regulate heat accordingly. Baste again with butter and oil in 5 minutes, and at the end of 15 minutes, give a final basting, sprinkle with salt, and turn chicken skin side up. Continue broiling, basting every five minutes (using fat and juices in pan) for another 15 minutes or until drumsticks are tender when pressed and juices run clear yellow when fleshiest part of dark meat is pricked deeply.

Remove chicken to a hot platter, skim all but 2 tablespoons

of basting fat out of pan, and stir in shallots or scallions. Cook on stove, stirring, for a moment, then add bouillon. Boil rapidly, scraping coagulated cooking juices into bouillon until liquid has reduced to a syrupy consistency. Pour over chicken and serve. (To serve, cut in half lengthwise through breastbone, then lift each leg portion and pull free from breast.)

VEGETABLE AND WINE SUGGESTIONS

Green peas and broiled tomatoes, or *ratatouille* (eggplant and tomato casserole), and sautéed potatoes. Serve with a light red wine such as Beaujolais, Bordeaux, Sauvignon, or Zinfandel, or a *rosé*.

POULET GRILLÉ A LA DIABLE
(Broiled Chicken with Mustard, Herb, and Bread-Crumb Coating)
For 4 people

A 2½-lb. broiling chicken	¼ tsp thyme, basil, or
2 Tb butter	tarragon
1 Tb cooking oil	3 drops Tabasco sauce
3 Tb Dijon-type (strong)	1 cup fresh white bread
prepared mustard	crumbs (from homemade-
1½ Tb minced shallots or	type bread)
scallions	

Broil the chicken as described in the preceding recipe, but cook it for 10 minutes only on each side. Beat the mustard, shallots or scallions, herbs, and Tabasco in a small bowl; then, drop by drop, beat in half the basting fat and juices from the broiling pan, to make a mayonnaise-like sauce. Reserve the rest of the fat and juices for later.

Spread the underside (not the skin side) of the chicken with half the mustard mixture, and cover with a layer of bread crumbs. Place chicken skin side down on a rack in a broiling pan and baste with half the reserved broiling juices. Return chicken to hot broiler for 5 to 6 minutes, until crumbs have browned nicely. Turn chicken skin side up, spread with remaining mustard, cover with crumbs, and baste with the last of the broiling juices. Return to broiler for 5 to 6 minutes more, or until chicken is done.

AHEAD-OF-TIME SUGGESTION

After second side of chicken has its coating of mustard, crumbs, and juices, set aside. Cover and refrigerate when cool. To finish off cooking, bake in upper third of preheated 375-degree oven for about 20 minutes or until top coating has browned.

VEGETABLE AND WINE SUGGESTIONS

Same as for preceding recipe.

POIS FRAIS EN BRAISAGE

(Fresh Peas Braised with Lettuce and Scallions)
4 to 6 servings

This is an excellent French cooking method for the rather large, tough, store-bought peas usually available to us in the markets. The peas remain green after cooking, become tender, and have a delicious flavor, though they will look a bit wrinkled.

2 lbs. fresh peas (about 3 cups, shelled)	1 to 2 Tb sugar (depending on sweetness of peas)
1 medium head Boston lettuce, washed and shredded	4 Tb minced scallions
	4 Tb softened butter
½ tsp salt	A heavy-bottomed saucepan

Place peas and rest of ingredients in saucepan and squeeze them all together roughly with your hands, to bruise the peas slightly. Add cold water so peas are barely covered. Set over moderately high heat, cover pan closely, and boil for 20 to 30 minutes; after about 20 minutes, test peas for tenderness by eating one. Continue boiling until peas are tender and liquid has evaporated; add 2 to 3 more tablespoons water if necessary. Correct seasoning and serve. (If not served immediately, set aside uncovered. Reheat with 2 tablespoons water, cover, and boil for a moment or two, tossing frequently, until peas are hot through.)

The Sixty-fourth Show

LAMB STEW IS FRENCH TOO

෴ᵇ • ᶜ෴

NAVARIN PRINTANIER

(*Lamb Stew with Carrots, Onions, Potatoes,*
Turnips, and Fresh Green Peas and Beans)
For 6 people

CUTS AND PREPARATION OF LAMB FOR STEWING

The most interesting lamb stew is made from a mixture of cuts, to give texture, flavor, and body to the sauce. The following are recommended (1 pound of boneless meat will serve 2 to 3 people):

Breast, for fat and texture
Shoulder, for lean, solid pieces
Short Ribs, for texture and flavor
Neck, for texture and sauce consistency

Have all excess fat removed, and the fell or covering membrane. Cut the meat into 2-inch cubes weighing 2 to 2½ ounces. Any bones left in the meat will give added flavor to the sauce; most of them may be removed before serving.

BROWNING THE LAMB

3 lbs. lamb stew meat
3 to 4 Tb cooking oil
A 10- to 12-inch skillet
A 5- to 6-quart flameproof
    casserole or Dutch oven

1 Tb granulated sugar
1 tsp salt
¼ tsp pepper
3 Tb flour

Dry the lamb pieces thoroughly in paper towels. Heat oil in skillet until almost smoking, and brown the lamb on all sides, a few pieces at a time. Transfer the lamb, as it is browned, to the casserole or Dutch oven. Sprinkle on the sugar and toss the lamb over moderately high heat for 3 to 4 minutes, until sugar has browned and caramelized—this will give a fine amber color to the sauce. Then toss the meat with the seasonings and flour and cook over moderate heat for 2 to 3 minutes, tossing, to brown the flour.

BRAISING

2 to 3 cups brown lamb or beef stock or canned beef bouillon
3 medium tomatoes, peeled, seeded, juiced, and

chopped; or 3 Tb tomato paste
2 cloves mashed garlic
¼ tsp thyme or rosemary
1 bay leaf

(Preheat oven to 350 degrees.)

Pour fat out of browning skillet, pour in 2 cups of stock or bouillon, and boil, scraping up coagulated browning juices. Pour into casserole over lamb and bring to simmer, shaking casserole to blend. Then add the tomatoes or tomato paste, garlic, herbs, and enough additional stock or bouillon almost to cover the lamb. Bring to simmer, cover the casserole, and simmer slowly on top of the stove or in preheated oven for 1 hour. Then pour the contents of the casserole into a colander set over a pan. Rinse out casserole. Remove any loose bones and return lamb to casserole. Skim fat off sauce in pan, correct seasoning, and pour sauce back over meat. Then add the root vegetables, which have been prepared as follows:

ADDING THE ROOT VEGETABLES

6 to 12 "boiling" potatoes
6 turnips
6 carrots

12 to 18 small white onions about 1 inch in diameter

Peel the potatoes and trim into ovals about 1½ inches long; place in cold water. Peel and quarter carrots and turnips; cut into 1½-inch lengths. Peel the onions and pierce a cross in root ends so they will cook evenly. When lamb is ready, press vegetables into casserole around and between the pieces of meat, and baste with the sauce. Bring to simmer, cover, and cook for about an hour longer or until meat and vegetables are tender when pierced with a fork. Skim off fat, correct seasoning, and add green vegetables, which have been prepared as follows:

ADDING THE GREEN VEGETABLES

1 cup shelled green peas
  (about ⅔ lb. unshelled)
1 cup green beans (about ¼
  lb.) cut into ½-inch
  pieces

3 to 4 quarts boiling water
1½ to 2 Tb salt

Drop the peas and beans into the boiling salted water and boil rapidly, uncovered, for about 5 minutes, or until vegetables are almost tender. Immediately drain in a colander, then run cold water over for 3 minutes to stop cooking and set color. Set aside until ready to use. (Stew may be prepared ahead to this point. Set meat aside, cover askew. Bring to simmer on top of stove before proceeding with recipe.)

SERVING

Shortly before serving, place the peas and beans in the casserole on top of the other ingredients and baste with the bubbling sauce. Cover and simmer about 5 minutes, until green vegetables are tender. Serve the stew from its casserole, or arrange on a hot platter. Accompany with hot French bread and a red Beaujolais, Bordeaux, or Mountain Red wine, or a chilled *rosé*.

The Sixty-fifth Show

INTRODUCING
CHARLOTTE MALAKOFF

❧ • ☙

CHARLOTTE MALAKOFF AU CHOCOLAT
(Chocolate-Almond Cream Molded in Ladyfingers)

This delectable dessert is fast to assemble if you have lady-fingers on hand; but the ladyfingers must be of excellent home-made quality. As these are hard to buy and easy to make, here is the recipe.

BISCUITS À LA CUILLER   (For 24 to 30 ladyfingers)

2 large baking sheets (18 by 24 inches)
1 Tb softened butter
Flour
A pastry bag with round tube opening ⅜ inch in diameter, or a large kitchen spoon
1½ cups powdered sugar in a sieve
A 3-quart mixing bowl

½ cup granulated sugar
3 egg yolks
1 tsp vanilla extract
3 egg whites
Pinch of salt
⅛ tsp cream of tartar
1 Tb granulated sugar
⅔ cup plain bleached cake flour (sift directly into cups, level off with knife, return flour to sifter)

(Preheat oven to 300 degrees.)

Prepare the baking sheets by rubbing lightly with butter, dusting with flour, and knocking off excess flour. Assemble pastry bag, if you are using one; prepare the powdered sugar, and measure out the rest of the ingredients listed.

In the mixing bowl, gradually beat the sugar into the egg yolks, add the vanilla, and continue beating for several minutes until mixture is thick, pale yellow, and forms the ribbon. In a separate bowl, beat the egg whites until foaming, beat in the salt and cream of tartar, and continue beating until soft peaks are formed. Sprinkle in a tablespoon of granulated sugar and beat until stiff peaks are formed.

Scoop one fourth of the egg whites over the top of the egg yolks and sugar, sift on one fourth of the flour, and delicately fold until partially blended. Then add one third of the remaining egg whites; sift on one third of the remaining flour, fold until partially blended again. Repeat with half, and then with the last of each. Do not attempt to blend too thoroughly; the batter must remain light and puffy.

Either with the pastry bag, or with a large kitchen spoon, make even lines of batter 4 inches long, 1½ inches wide, spaced 1 inch apart on the pastry sheets. Sprinkle with a $\frac{1}{16}$-inch layer of powdered sugar. Bake immediately in middle and upper-third levels of oven for about 20 minutes. Ladyfingers are done when a very pale brown underneath the sugar coating. They should be slightly crusty outside, tender but dry inside. Remove from baking sheets with a spatula; cool on cake racks.

LINING THE DESSERT MOLD WITH LADYFINGERS

A 2-quart cylindrical mold, 4 inches high, if possible, and 7 inches in diameter	⅔ cup water
	24 ladyfingers, 4 inches long and about 2 inches wide
Waxed paper	
⅓ cup orange liqueur	

Line the bottom of the dry mold with a round of waxed paper. Pour the liqueur and water into a soup plate. One by one, dip the ladyfingers into the liquid for a second, then drain on a cake rack. Arrange a row of upright ladyfingers inside the mold, pressed closely together, their curved sides against the mold. Reserve the remaining dipped ladyfingers.

THE ALMOND CREAM

A 4-quart mixing bowl
½ lb. softened unsalted
  butter
1 cup instant superfine
  granulated sugar
¼ cup orange liqueur
⅔ cup semisweet chocolate
  bits melted with ¼ cup
  strong coffee
¼ tsp almond extract

1⅓ cups powdered almonds
  (blanched almonds
  ground in a blender or
  put through a meat
  grinder with a bit of the
  instant sugar)
2 cups heavy cream, chilled
A chilled bowl and beater

Cream the butter and sugar together for several minutes,
until pale and fluffy. Beat in the orange liqueur, melted chocolate, and almond extract; continue beating for several minutes
until sugar is no longer grainy in texture. Beat in the almonds.
Whip the chilled cream in a chilled bowl with a chilled beater
just until beater leaves light traces on cream—do not whip any
more than this or cream may not chill smoothly. Fold the cream
into the chocolate-almond mixture. Turn a third of the mixture
into the lined mold, arrange over it a layer of ladyfingers, and
continue with layers of chocolate-almond cream and ladyfingers,
ending with ladyfingers if there are any left. Trim off any ladyfingers protruding above edge of mold and press bits into top of
cream. Cover mold with waxed paper, set a saucer over the
paper, and place a weight over it (2-cup glass measure of water,
for instance). Refrigerate for 6 hours or overnight; butter must
be chilled firm, so dessert will not collapse when unmolded.
(Dessert will keep for several days under refrigeration, or may
be frozen.)

UNMOLDING AND SERVING

To serve, remove waxed paper from top, run a knife around
inside edge of mold, pushing gently to dislodge dessert. Turn a
chilled serving dish upside down over mold, and reverse the two,
giving a sharp downward jerk so dessert will drop onto dish.
Decorate the top of the charlotte with grated chocolate. Refrigerate if not served immediately.

The Sixty-sixth Show

HOT TURKEY BALLOTTINE

～ა · ჰ⌀

HOT TURKEY BALLOTTINE

If you have never boned a turkey in your life, or never seen it done, you may think it an impossibly difficult, long, and probably fruitless task. However, boning is not complicated once you start in with a few directions, and it does not take very long to do—your second attempt will go much faster than your first. It is a wonderful bird for a party: an 8-pound turkey, boned and stuffed, can serve 20 people. Finally, a boned turkey is so easy to carve: you just slice it from end to end like a sausage.

HOW TO BONE A TURKEY—OR ANY OTHER BIRD

The object, in boning, is to remove the flesh from the carcass bones without piercing the skin of the bird except at the back, where the opening slit is made. The skin is to serve as a container, folded around whatever stuffing you have chosen.

The opening move is to cut a deep slit down the back of the turkey, from neck to tail, exposing the backbone. Then, with a small, sharp knife, its edge always cutting against the bone, scrape and cut the flesh from the carcass down one side of the bird, pulling the flesh away from the bones with your fingers. When you come to the ball joints connecting the wings and the second joints to the carcass, sever them, and continue down the carcass until you reach the ridge of the breast, where skin and bone meet. Stop at this point; you must be careful here as the skin is thin and easily slit. Repeat the same operation on the other side of the bird, cutting against the bone and not slitting any skin. When you finally arrive at the ridge of the breastbone on this opposite side, stop again. Then lift the carcass frame and cut very closely against the ridge of the breastbone to free it, being very careful indeed that you do not cut the covering skin. Chop off the wings at the elbows, leaving just the upper wing bones attached.

Now arrange this mass of skin and flesh on a board, flesh side up. You will see, protruding from the flesh, the pair of ball joints which are the wings, and the second pair at the opposite end which are the second joints. Remove the second-joint bones by detaching the meat from around the exposed joint, then scraping meat from bone while holding onto the free end of the joint; when you come to the end of the bone, cut it free from the ball joint of the drumstick. If you want to roast the turkey, and have it still look like a turkey, leave on the drumsticks and upper wings. If you want all bones removed, chop off the outside ball joints of the drumsticks and wings, then scrape meat off bone from inside the bird, pulling the skin inside out. You will have four creases in the outside skin, where these appendages were. With pliers, pull out the tendons imbedded in the flesh of the drumsticks.

You may now wish to slice off some of the thick layers of breast and thigh meat. The larger pieces may be cut into strips or cubes, and make decorative patterns in the stuffing; the small pieces may be ground up and mixed into the stuffing.

The chopped-up carcass will make the best turkey soup imaginable, simply simmered in water with carrots, onions, celery, herbs, and seasonings.

THE STUFFING

You may use any of the conventional turkey stuffings you wish, such as bread crumbs, rice, or sausage. The following is a French *pâté* mixture. For an 8- to 9-pound turkey, 5 to 6 cups of stuffing are required. Any leftover stuffing may be frozen, or cooked like hamburger or meat loaf. (If you do not wish to use pork and pork fat, use chicken or turkey meat, or beef tongue, and beef suet.)

1 cup finely minced onions
2 Tb butter
⅓ cup cognac
⅓ cup Madeira or port
A large mixing bowl
1 lb. lean ground pork
1 lb. lean ground veal
½ lb. ground pork fat (fat
    back if possible)

Optional: ground turkey
    meat and turkey liver
1½ Tb salt
1 tsp thyme
½ tsp allspice
⅛ tsp pepper
3 eggs

Cook the onions in the butter until soft and translucent; add the cognac and Madeira or port and boil down by half. Scrape into mixing bowl, add the rest of the ingredients, and beat vigorously until thoroughly mixed.

STUFFING AND TYING THE TURKEY

½ Tb salt
⅛ tsp pepper
⅛ tsp allspice
3 Tb cognac
Optional: strips ⅛ inch

thick, or cubes, of turkey
meat, boiled ham, boiled
tongue; diced truffles;
pistachio nuts

Spread the boned turkey skin side down and season with salt, pepper, allspice, and cognac. Heap the stuffing in the center, shaping it into a loaf. (If you wish, make layers of stuffing alternating with layers of turkey meat, ham, tongue, etc.) Bring the turkey skin up over the loaf to enclose it completely. Sew skin in place with a needle and white string, or secure with skewers and string. Make 3 or 4 ties around the circumference of the turkey to give it a cylindrical shape.

ROASTING THE TURKEY

A shallow roasting pan

(Preheat oven to 350 degrees.)
Place turkey on its side in the roasting pan. Roast for ½ hour, then turn the turkey on its other side. In ½ hour, turn the turkey breast up, insert a meat thermometer in the side, and lower oven temperature to 325 degrees. Continue roasting to a thermometer reading of 185 degrees, basting with fat in pan every 20 to 30

minutes. An 8- to 9-pound turkey will take about 3½ hours. When done, remove thermometer and strings and set on a hot platter.

SERVING

Serve the turkey hot, with the usual turkey accompaniments. Or allow it to cool, then chill it, and serve it with a salad, French bread, and a chilled *rosé* wine.

The Sixty-seventh Show

COLD TURKEY GALANTINE

A *galantine* is a boned turkey, duck, or chicken stuffed with a meat *pâté* mixture; rolled into a sausage shape, it is cooked in wine-flavored bouillon, then chilled, and usually decorated with aspic. It makes a handsome *pièce de résistance* on any buffet table, and although it looks very difficult to make, it is not. But it is a dish for those who enjoy cooking. As a *galantine* is not built in a day, you will need one for the cooking and chilling, and part of another for the decorating.

STUFFING AND ROLLING THE TURKEY

An 8- to 9-lb. turkey, all
  bones removed (see "The
  Sixty-sixth Show")
5 to 6 cups stuffing (French
  pâté mixture; see "The
  Sixty-sixth Show")
Optional: strips ⅜ inch

thick of boiled ham or
  tongue; chopped or quar-
  tered truffles
Salt, pepper, cognac
A large clean towel
Strong white string

Lay the boned turkey skin side down on a board, being sure the leg and wing skin-sleeves have been pulled inside out, leaving neat folds of skin on the outside of the bird. Slice off breast and dark meat, leaving only a ¼-inch layer attached to the skin. Cut the white meat into strips about ⅜ inch thick, and set aside, sprinkled with salt, pepper, and a tablespoon or so of cognac. Grind dark meat and add to *pâté* mixture.

Dipping your hands in cold water, arrange one third of the stuffing in a strip 3½ inches wide, down the length of the turkey; arrange over this a lengthwise layer of white meat strips interspersed, if you wish, with strips of ham or tongue, and truffles. Cover with half the remaining stuffing, another layer of strips, and top with the last of the stuffing. Then roll the turkey around the stuffing to make a cylinder about 5 inches in diameter and 12 to 14 inches long. (The turkey skin does not have to enclose the stuffing at the two ends of the cylinder.)

Rinse the towel in cold water, wring it out, and, stretching it tight as you go, wrap the rolled turkey in the towel. Tie the two ends of the towel securely with string, twisting the towel against the ends of the turkey cylinder to make a tight bundle. Tie string around the circumference of the turkey in several places to preserve its cylindrical shape during cooking. Insert a meat thermometer through the towel, being sure point reaches center of meat.

COOKING THE TURKEY

The bottom of a covered roaster, just large enough to hold turkey and all ingredients listed
The turkey carcass bones, chopped
Optional for added flavor: 2 cups chopped veal knuckle bones
3 medium onions, sliced
2 medium carrots, chopped
3 medium celery stalks, sliced
A large herb bouquet: 8 parsley sprigs, 1½ tsp thyme, and 1 bay leaf tied in washed cheesecloth
6 cups canned chicken broth
1½ cups dry white vermouth
Salt as needed

Lay the turkey in the roaster and add the bones, vegetables, herb bouquet, chicken broth, vermouth, and enough cold water to cover ingredients by about 1½ inches. Bring to the simmer, correct seasoning, and cook at a very slow simmer, liquid barely bubbling, for about 3 hours or to a meat-thermometer reading of 180 to 185 degrees.

Allow turkey to cool in cooking liquid for 1 hour, so it will pick up flavor and juiciness. Then remove it to a tray, cover with a board or tray, and place weights on top which will pack meat down as it cools and prevent air spaces. When turkey is cold, unwrap it, wipe it off with paper towels, and chill overnight.

The *galantine* may now be sliced and served as is with a green salad, French bread, and a *rosé* wine, or you may decorate it with aspic as follows:

CLARIFICATION OF COOKING STOCK, AND ASPIC   (For about 6 cups)

3 packages (3 Tb) unflavored powdered gelatin	A clean 3-quart saucepan 3 layers of washed cheese-cloth, 14 inches square
3 egg whites in a clean 2-quart mixing bowl	¼ cup port wine

Strain cooking stock into a large pan and thoroughly degrease it either by skimming off fat with a spoon or by chilling it and removing congealed fat; then bring to the simmer, remove from heat, and skim off remaining fat globules by drawing strips of paper towel across the surface. Stock is now ready to be turned into an aspic: gelatin is to be added so the liquid will set when chilled, and egg whites are to simmer with it, rendering it clear and sparkling.

Measure 5 cups of the degreased stock into a clean saucepan, sprinkle the gelatin over it and allow to soften for several minutes. Heat, stirring, until gelatin has dissolved completely.

Beat another cup of degreased stock gradually into the egg whites, using a large wire whip. Gradually beat in the hot gelatined stock. Pour back into saucepan and bring slowly to the simmer, constantly agitating liquid with your wire whip. When simmer is reached, stop stirring. Set saucepan over low heat, maintaining liquid just below simmer for 10 to 15 minutes. Egg whites will rise to the surface.

Line a sieve with the washed cheesecloth; place in a large colander set over a clean bowl. Gently ladle the stock mixture into the cheesecloth, disturbing the egg-white layer as little as possible. Allow to drain for 5 minutes undisturbed, then remove colander and sieve. Liquid in bowl should be clear and limpid; stir in the port wine.

DECORATING THE GALANTINE

The *galantine* is now to be laid on a bed of aspic; it is to be glazed with aspic and decorated with whatever vegetable and aspic designs you choose. For the bed of aspic, pour a ⅛-inch layer of unset aspic into a serving platter and chill until set— about 20 minutes. For the aspic designs, line a 12-by-14-inch pan with waxed paper lightly oiled on both sides, pour in a ¼-inch layer of unset aspic, and chill.

Cut ⅓ to ½ the chilled *galantine* into serving slices; arrange the uncut portion and the slices on the bed of aspic in the platter. Pour a cup of unset aspic into a small saucepan and stir over crushed ice until syrupy and almost set. Spoon over the meat and chill—this first layer will not adhere very well. Repeat with several additional layers, building up a ¹⁄₁₆-inch glaze. If you wish to use vegetable decorations, arrange them now over the meat and glaze with two coats of aspic.

For aspic designs, cut squares, triangles, or diamonds in your pan of chilled aspic; arrange over the meat and around the edge of the platter. Chop the remaining chilled aspic with a large knife and spoon into any unfilled spaces and over dribbles. The *galantine* is now ready; keep refrigerated until serving time.

The Sixty-eighth Show

LE MARQUIS AU CHOCOLAT
•◦§ • ◦§•
(Chocolate Spongecake)

LE MARQUIS AU CHOCOLAT
(*Chocolate Butter Spongecake; Butter-Cream Frosting
and Chocolate Glaze*)
For an 8-inch cake serving 6 to 8 people

˒ Here is a splendid cake for chocolate lovers with sylphid figures. Filled and frosted with rum-flavored butter cream, covered with a light cloak of melted cholocate, it can be served as a dessert or at high tea.

HOW TO MELT CHOCOLATE. Perfectly melted chocolate is a smooth and shining cream; badly melted chocolate, which has usually been overheated, is dark and granular. For best results, use chocolate bits or morsels, or break block chocolate into ¼-inch pieces, and place in a small saucepan with whatever liquid your recipe specifies; fill a larger saucepan one third full of water, bring to a boil, remove from heat, and set chocolate pan in the hot water. Stir for a moment until chocolate begins to melt, then set aside for several minutes. When you are ready to use it, stir vigorously until chocolate is perfectly smooth and velvety. Keep, if necessary, over warm but not hot water.

PRELIMINARIES ◦§•

Biscuit au Chocolat
(*The Chocolate Spongecake*)

1 Tb softened butter	**A round one-piece cake pan**
Flour	**8 inches in diameter and**
	1½ inches deep

⅔ to 1 cup (4 to 6 ounces)
semisweet chocolate bits
(lesser amount gives a
lighter cake)

1 heaping Tb instant coffee
dissolved in 2 Tb boiling
water

(Preheat oven to 350 degrees.)

Lightly butter inside of cake pan, roll flour inside to cover surface completely, and knock out excess flour. Melt the chocolate with the coffee, then let cool to tepid.

THE CAKE BATTER ✑

3 eggs (U. S. graded
"large")
A large mixing bowl
½ cup granulated sugar
⅔ cup cake flour (sift directly into cups, level off
with knife, and return
flour to sifter)
3½ Tb softened unsalted
butter

For the egg whites: pinch of
salt, ⅛ tsp cream of
tartar, and 1 Tb granulated sugar
An electric mixer with large
and small bowls and, if
possible, extra blades (or
2 bowls and 2 large
whips); rubber spatulas

Separate the eggs, placing the yolks in the large bowl and the whites in another bowl (or small bowl of mixer). Measure out the cake flour, and mash the butter to soften it.

Either with your mixer or with a large whip, gradually beat the sugar into the egg yolks and continue beating for several minutes until mixture is thick and lemon-colored. If you are using a mixer, beat in the tepid melted chocolate, then the butter; otherwise, beat butter gradually into chocolate until smooth, then beat into yolks and sugar.

With clean dry beaters or a large wire whip, beat the egg whites until foamy, then beat in the salt and cream of tartar. Continue beating until soft peaks are formed; sprinkle in the sugar and beat until stiff peaks are formed.

Using a rubber spatula, stir ¼ of the egg whites into the chocolate and egg-yolk mixture; when partially blended, sift on ¼ the cake flour. Fold in rapidly and delicately with rubber spatula; when partially blended, start folding in ⅓ the remaining egg whites. When this is partially blended, sift on ⅓ the remaining flour and continue thus, alternating with flour and egg whites, folding rapidly until all is incorporated.

BAKING

Turn into prepared cake pan; tilt pan to run batter up to top all around. Set immediately in middle level of preheated oven and bake for about 30 minutes. Cake will rise slightly above edge of pan and top will crack. It is done when a needle or fork, plunged down through center of cake, comes out clean; a very faint line of shrinkage will also show between edge of cake and pan. Remove from oven and let cool 5 minutes, then unmold on a cake rack.

If cake is not iced when cold, wrap airtight and refrigerate or freeze. (Note that a paper-thin layer will usually flake off from top and bottom of cake; this is normal.)

Crème au Beurre à l'Anglaise
(Custard Butter Cream)
For about 2½ cups

A 2½-quart mixing bowl	rum, kirsch, orange
4 egg yolks	liqueur, or strong coffee;
⅔ cup granulated sugar	or 1 Tb vanilla extract;
½ cup hot milk	or ⅓ cup (2 ounces)
½ lb. softened unsalted	semisweet chocolate bits,
butter	melted
Flavoring choices: 3 Tb	

Place egg yolks in the mixing bowl; gradually beat in the sugar and continue beating until mixture is thick and lemon-colored. Then gradually beat in the milk. Turn into a clean saucepan and stir with a wooden spoon over moderately low heat until mixture slowly thickens enough to coat the spoon with a light cream. (Be careful not to overheat or egg yolks will curdle, but mixture must thicken.) Set pan in cold water and stir until tepid; rinse out mixing bowl and strain custard back into it. Then, using a wire whip or an electric mixer, gradually beat in the softened butter by tablespoonfuls. Beat in the flavoring. If cream looks grainy, beat in more butter by spoonfuls. Chill or stir over crushed ice, if necessary; cream should be smooth, thick, and homogeneous. (Leftover butter cream may be frozen.)

FILLING AND ICING THE CAKE ଛ—

When cake is thoroughly cold brush crumbs off surface. Leave cake upside down, as you want sides to slant inward slightly. Cut a tiny vertical wedge up the edge of the cake; this will guide you in re-forming it. Then slice cake in half horizontally. Spread a ¼-inch layer of butter cream on the bottom half (formerly the top); replace second half, lining up the two halves with the wedge. Spread icing on top and sides of cake, smoothing with a spatula dipped in hot water, and keeping sides slanting slightly inward. Chill until frosting is firm.

Chocolate Glaze

1 cup (6 ounces) semisweet   ¼ cup coffee
    chocolate bits

Melt chocolate bits with the coffee and let cool to tepid. Place chilled cake on a rack over a tray and pour all the chocolate over the top, letting it fall down over the sides, which, if nicely smoothed and slightly slanting, should take the chocolate coating perfectly. When glaze is set, transfer cake to serving plate. (Cake should be kept under refrigeration.)

The Sixty-ninth Show

VEGETABLES FOR THE BIRDS
ܐ܇ • ܇ܐ
(*Garlic Potatoes; Cucumbers; Turnips*)

In French cooking, interesting vegetables are just as important a part of the meal as the carefully cooked roast. Here is a trio of out-of-the-ordinary recipes for three old friends: potatoes, cucumbers, and turnips. They go especially well with roast birds.

PURÉE DE POMMES DE TERRE A L'AIL
(*Garlic Mashed Potatoes*)
For 6 to 8 people

Serve these with roast turkey, goose, or duck, or with sausages, pork, beef, or lamb. The amount of garlic may seem astonishing, but it is not too much. A preliminary blanching and a slow cooking in butter remove the strong taste, leaving just a tantalizing flavor when mixed with the potatoes.

THE GARLIC SAUCE

2 heads garlic, about 30 cloves	2 Tb flour
4 Tb butter	1 cup hot milk
A 3- to 4-cup covered saucepan	¼ tsp salt and a pinch of pepper

Separate garlic cloves and drop into boiling water; boil 2 minutes, drain, and peel. Then cook the garlic slowly in the butter for about 20 minutes in the covered saucepan, until very tender but not at all browned. Blend in the flour, cook slowly for 2 minutes. Remove from heat, beat in hot milk and seasonings, and boil, stirring, for 1 minute. If not to be used immediately, set aside and reheat later.

BLENDING WITH THE POTATOES (For about 5 cups mashed potatoes)

2½ lbs. baking potatoes	3 to 4 Tb heavy cream
4 Tb butter	¼ cup minced fresh parsley
Salt and pepper	

Peel and quarter the potatoes. Either boil in salted water, or steam until just tender; put through a ricer into a heavy saucepan. Stir briefly over moderately high heat until potatoes film bottom of pan, then stir in the butter, and salt and pepper to taste. Keep uncovered over simmering water until ready to serve —but the sooner they are served the better. Just before entering the dining room, rub the garlic through a sieve into the potatoes; beat in the cream and parsley, and turn into a hot, buttered serving dish.

CONCOMBRES PERSILLÉS, OU A LA CRÈME
(Parslied or Creamed Cucumbers)
For 6 to 8 people

Cooked cucumbers are particularly nice with chicken, turkey, and veal. As cucumbers contain a large amount of moisture, you must treat them first to remove most of this water or you will end up with cucumber mush: a salt maceration is far better than a preliminary blanching, as the salt draws out the water but leaves all the flavor. Also, if your cucumbers are bitter, the salt removes the bite.

MACERATING THE CUCUMBERS

6 cucumbers about 8 inches long	1½ tsp salt
	⅛ tsp sugar
2 Tb wine vinegar	

Peel the cucumbers, cut in half lengthwise, and scoop out the seeds with a teaspoon. Cut into lengthwise strips about ⅜ inch wide, then cut the strips into 2-inch pieces. Toss in a bowl with the vinegar, salt, and sugar and let stand at least 20 minutes. Drain, and dry in paper towels just before using.

COOKING

2 to 3 Tb butter
A large heavy-bottomed
  enameled skillet or saucepan
Salt and pepper
2 Tb minced shallots or
  scallions

Optional: 1 cup heavy
  cream simmered down by
  half in a small saucepan
3 Tb fresh minced parsley

Heat the butter to bubbling in the skillet or saucepan. Add the cucumbers and shallots or scallions; cook slowly, tossing frequently, for about 5 minutes, until cucumbers are tenderly crisp but not browned. Just before serving, toss with the optional cream and the parsley. Turn into a hot dish.

NAVETS A LA CHAMPENOISE
(*Turnip and Onion Casserole*)
For 6 to 8 people

If you are one who hates, abominates, abhors, and loathes the turnip, this savory casserole should so fill you with rapture that you will cherish this lowly vegetable forevermore. Serve it with roast goose, duck, or turkey, or with pork, beef, sausages, or ham.

2½ lbs. yellow turnips or
  rutabagas (about 8 cups
  diced)
⅔ cup finely diced fat-and-
  lean fresh pork butt or
  side pork; or 3 Tb butter
  or cooking oil

⅔ cup finely diced onions
1 Tb flour
¾ cup beef bouillon
¼ tsp sage
Salt and pepper
2 to 3 Tb fresh minced
  parsley

Peel the turnips, cut into quarters, then into ½-inch slices; cut slices into ½-inch strips, and the strips into ½-inch cubes. Drop into boiling salted water and boil uncovered for 3 to 5 minutes, or until slightly tender. Drain.

If you are using the pork, sauté slowly in a 3-quart saucepan until very lightly browned; otherwise, add the butter or oil to the pan. Stir in the onions, cover, and cook slowly for 5 minutes without browning. Blend in the flour and cook slowly for 2 minutes. Remove from heat, beat in the bouillon, return to heat and bring to the simmer. Add the sage, then fold in the turnips. Season to taste with salt and pepper.

Cover the pan and simmer slowly for 20 to 30 minutes, or until turnips are tender. If sauce is too liquid, uncover and boil slowly for several minutes until liquid has reduced and thickened. Correct seasoning. (May be cooked ahead. Cool uncovered; cover and simmer a few moments before serving.)

To serve, fold in the parsley and turn into a hot serving dish.

The Seventieth Show

FRENCH TARTS, APPLE STYLE

⊷§ • §⊶

(Pastry Dough and Tart Shells)

Every serious cook should be able to produce a tender, crunchy, buttery pastry crust that is a delight to eat in tarts, *quiches*, turnovers, or quick hors d'oeuvre. The mastery of pastry dough is simply a matter of practice, as there is a definite feel in the hands you must acquire for mixing and rolling. Do a batch of pastry every day, if you are determined to learn, and keep notes as you go along. Here are detailed directions for making an all-purpose dough and for forming and baking pastry shells, as well as a short recipe for French apple tart.

Pâte Brisée Fine

(French pastry dough for pies, tarts, quiches, and turnovers)
For an 8- to 10-inch tart shell

1½ cups all-purpose flour
(see measuring note below)
1 stick (¼ lb.) chilled butter cut into ½-inch pieces
3 Tb chilled white vegetable shortening

For sweet tart dough: a pinch of salt and 2 Tb granulated sugar
For regular dough: ½ tsp salt and a pinch of sugar
⅓ cup cold water (iced water in hot weather)

Measure flour by scooping cup into bag, then leveling off with the straight edge of a knife. Place flour, butter, and shortening in a large mixing bowl. *Either* rapidly rub fat and flour together between tips of fingers until mixture resembles small oatmeal flakes, *or* (and this is highly recommended) use a pastry blender, chopping fat and flour rapidly together until mixture resembles very coarse meal. In any case, do not overmix: butter should soften no more than necessary; further blending takes place later.

Then dissolve the salt and sugar in the cold water, pour into the flour and fat, and blend rapidly with a rubber spatula, pressing mixture against sides of bowl to form a rough mass.

Turn dough out onto a board or marble. With the heel of one hand (not the palm, which is too warm), rapidly press pastry by two-spoonful bits down on the board and away from you in a firm, rough, quick 6-inch smear. This constitutes the final blending of fat and flour. Scrape dough again into a mass, briefly press it into a smooth ball, and sprinkle lightly with flour. Consistency of dough should be fairly soft and pliable. Wrap in waxed paper and chill for 2 hours or overnight; this is to harden the butter, and to relax the rubbery gluten in the flour. (Raw pastry dough may be frozen.)

Croûte à Tarte Cuite à Blanc
(How to Mold and Bake Pastry Shells for Tarts and Quiches)

THE PAN OR MOLD

(Preheat oven to 425 degrees.)

A French tart or *quiche* is served in an open-faced, free-standing pastry shell. The shell is formed in a bottomless metal flan ring set on a baking sheet; when baked, the ring is removed and the tart is slid onto a serving plate. If you do not have a flan ring, use a false-bottomed cake pan 1 to 1½ inches deep. Butter inside of ring and baking sheet, or inside of cake pan, before rolling dough.

ROLLING THE DOUGH

Beat your ball of chilled dough with a rolling pin and knead dough briefly around edges to soften slightly. Lightly flour top and bottom of dough, then place rolling pin across center; roll back and forth to start dough moving. Finally, with a firm, even stroke, and pushing your pin down and away from you, start just below center of dough and roll to within an inch of the far edge. Lift dough, turn it at a slight angle, and give another roll. Continue lifting, turning, and rolling; as necessary, sprinkle board and top of dough lightly with flour to prevent sticking. Roll into a circle 3/16 inch thick and at least 2 inches larger than your ring or pan. Work as rapidly as possible so dough will not soften; if it does soften, refrigerate on waxed paper and continue rolling in 10 to 15 minutes.

INTO THE MOLD

Fold dough in half, in half again, and center the point of the dough-wedge in your buttered mold. Unfold the dough. Lift edges and, with your thumbs, work about ⅜ inches of dough gently down inside of mold all around circumference. Roll pin over top of mold to remove excess dough. With your thumbs, push dough ⅛-inch above edge of mold to make an even, rounded rim at top of mold. Press a decorative edge around rim of dough with the dull edge of a knife or the tines of a fork. Prick bottom of pastry with a fork at ¼-inch intervals; this is to prevent puffing during baking.

BRACING THE PASTRY

Whether or not your pastry shell is to be cooked with a filling, preliminary baking will prevent a soggy bottom crust. To brace the sides and weight down the bottom, either butter the outside of a slightly smaller tin or saucepan, set into the pastry-filled mold, and weight down with dried beans; or line the pastry with buttered lightweight foil and fill with beans, spreading them up to the rim all around. (Unbaked shells may be frozen.)

BAKING

Bake in middle level of preheated 425-degree oven for 5 to 6 minutes, until pastry is set but still slightly soft. Remove liner and prick bottom of pastry again; if sides of shell have sunk down, push them up gently with a rubber spatula. Return to oven for another 3 or 4 minutes, until shell has begun to shrink slightly from mold and pastry has barely started to color. For a fully cooked shell, bake 7 to 10 minutes more, until shell has browned lightly. (Baked shells may be frozen.)

PATCHING NOTES

If sides or bottom of a baked shell crack, patch with a thin piece of raw dough and set in oven for several minutes to set the dough. An inside patch will never show.

TARTE AUX POMMES
(French Apple Tart)
For 6 people

An 8-inch partially baked pastry shell set on a buttered baking sheet
3 to 4 cups thick, unflavored applesauce

½ to ⅔ cup granulated sugar
3 Tb apple brandy, cognac, or rum, or 1 Tb vanilla extract

The grated rind of 1 lemon
2 Tb butter
2 to 3 apples, peeled and cut
into ⅛-inch lengthwise
slices

½ cup apricot jam, strained,
and boiled to 228 degrees
with 2 Tb sugar

(Preheat oven to 375 degrees.)

Stir ½ to ⅔ cup sugar into the applesauce, add the liqueur or vanilla and lemon rind. Boil down, stirring frequently, until sauce is thick enough to hold in a mass in the spoon. Stir in the butter, and turn applesauce into pastry shell, filling it almost to the brim. Arrange closely overlapping raw apple slices over the top in concentric circles. Bake for 30 minutes in preheated oven. Unmold the tart onto a serving plate; paint top and sides with warm apricot jam. Serve hot, warm, or cold accompanied, if you wish, with lightly whipped cream.

The Seventy-first Show

FEASTING ON THE REMAINS

✎ • ☙

(Turkey Soup; Creamed Turkey; Giant Crêpe)

The remains of a feast can spell feasting again on the remains, and that can be even more fun for all concerned than the original banquet. All you need is the glint of adventure in your eye when you tackle that turkey carcass and those nice little bowls of leftover vegetables.

BOUILLON DE VOLAILLE
(Poultry Stock—Chicken, Turkey, Goose, Duck, or Game Bird)

An excellent stock, bouillon, or soup can be made of any poultry carcass, especially if you add some raw bones and poultry scraps to it, which your butcher will either give you or sell at a most reasonable price. Or you can keep a supply on hand, simply by packaging and freezing necks, gizzards, and scraps anytime you serve poultry. Mix all kinds of poultry together for this all-purpose bouillon. The following recipe is for the carcass of a 15-pound turkey; vary the proportions according to your larder, as exact measures are not important here.

A large kettle
A poultry carcass
1 to 2 lbs. sawed, raw beef
  and/or veal bones
2 to 3 lbs. raw poultry
  necks, hearts, and
  gizzards, fresh or frozen
2 Tb salt
2 large carrots, 2 celery

stalks, 2 leeks (if available), roughly chopped
2 peeled onions stuck with
  2 cloves
A large herb bouquet: 8
  parsley sprigs, 1 bay leaf,
  and 1 tsp thyme or sage
  tied in washed cheese-
  cloth

Chop up the carcass and put into kettle with the bones and poultry scraps. Cover by 2 inches with water, add the salt, and bring to the simmer. Skim off surface scum for about 5 minutes, or until it almost ceases to rise. Then add the vegetables and herbs, bring again to the simmer, and simmer uncovered for 3 to 4 hours, skimming off accumulated fat and scum occasionally. Add water, if needed, so ingredients are always covered. To keep the stock clear and unclouded, do not let liquid boil, and do not cover pot. You may stop the cooking at any time and continue cooking later, but do not cover a warm kettle or your stock may sour.

When you feel you have simmered all the flavor out of your ingredients, strain the liquid into a large bowl or pan. Let cool uncovered, then chill. When chilled, scrape off and discard all surface fat. If stock is weak, boil down slowly to concentrate flavor. Season to taste, and the stock is ready to use for soups, stews, and sauces. Keep under refrigeration, boiling up every 3 days, or freeze.

VELOUTÉ DE VOLAILLE A LA SÉNÉGALAISE
(Curried Turkey Soup, Hot or Cold)
For 6 people

You can make a delicious main-course soup with poultry stock, a bit of curry, and whatever you think would enhance your brew. Here is a suggested recipe.

4 Tb butter
A heavy-bottomed 3- to 4-quart saucepan
1 Tb curry powder
4 to 8 Tb flour (depending on your amount of potatoes)
5 to 6 cups poultry stock
Optional cooked ingredients: mashed potatoes, creamed

onions, broccoli, cucumbers, carrots, peas, asparagus tips
½ cup (more or less) heavy cream
About 1 cup diced or thinly sliced cooked turkey meat
4 Tb fresh minced parsley or chives, or 2 Tb minced chervil or tarragon

Melt the butter in the saucepan. Stir in the curry powder and cook slowly for 1 minute. (If you have no cooked onions, add ½ cup raw minced onions and cook for about 10 minutes without browning.) Stir in the flour and cook slowly for 2 minutes. Remove from heat, let cool a moment, then vigorously beat in the hot poultry stock with a wire whip. Simmer, stirring with a whip, for 1 minute. If you are using cooked onions, chop them and add to the soup; if you are using mashed potatoes, beat them in a tablespoon at a time until the soup is as thick as you wish it to be. Stir in cream by spoonfuls, simmering slowly, then season carefully to taste. Stir in the turkey meat, optional vegetables, and herbs, and bring to the simmer again just before serving. (If not served immediately, or if to be served cold, film top of soup with stock or cream to prevent a skin from forming. Chill if to be served cold; you may wish to stir in more cream and top each bowl with more fresh herbs.)

Smelling a vanilla bean to make sure it is fragrant. Smell herbs, smell fish, smell everything before using.

Taste the sauce very carefully for seasoning.

TIPS FROM JULIA CHILD: SMELLING AND TASTING

Tasting the broccoli. Don't overcook fresh vegetables; they should remain slightly crunchy.

How does it taste? That's the final test.

Look for heavy frying pans that hold and spread the heat: the oval cast-iron pan (1) is useful for browning meat and poultry as well as sautéing fish, and the long-handled round pan (4) is perfect for omelettes; these are French imports. The straight-sided skillet or chicken fryer of heavy aluminum with no-stick interior (3) is for general browning and top-of-stove cooking; the slant-sided skillet of the same material (8) is right for sautéing. A heavy 7- to 8-quart oval casserole of enameled iron (2) can be used for stews, soups, and covered roasting. The oval baking or *au gratin* dish of enameled iron (5) can go on top of the stove, in the oven, and on the table. Two examples of the ever-useful baking, serving, molding, and soufflé dish are the French charlotte mold of tinned metal (7) and its American counterpart in flameproof ceramic (6). [*Above*]

These gadgets are designed to make cooking easier. A French pastry scraper (1) or its American equivalent, the painter's spatula (3), keep your work surface clean when you are kneading pastry, dough, or fondant. The flat-sided French wooden spatula (2) is better than a spoon for beating sauces. A mixing fork with spatula-like tines (4) will mash as well as blend soft foods. The giant balloon wire whip (5) is for beating egg whites, the medium size (6) is for general work, and the mini-whip (7) fits in where others cannot beat. The bulb baster (8) and the rubber spatula (9) are two of America's great culinary contributions. Be sure to get a pepper grinder that really works, like the French "Peugeot" (10). Buy yourself a big, heavy rolling pin like the American ball-bearing chef's pin (11) or the French hardwood pastry model (12); a 10-inch lightweight dime-store rolling pin is almost useless (13). [*Top right*]

Razor-sharp tools make for professional work and happy cutting. Carbon steel rather than stainless is recommended, as carbon takes the best edge easily. If you cannot find proper knives, ask your butcher where he gets his. General-purpose chef's knives for paring, slicing, and chopping range in size from the 10-inch blade down to the two tiny ones (1, 3, 6, and 7). The Japanese hatchet (2) is a fine chopper, and the butcher's scimitar (5) is great for meat as well as slab bacon. A professional-size sharpening steel (4) keeps them all in shape. Get lobster shears (8) if you go in at all for shellfish, and heavy-duty shears (9) for anything from fish fins to waxed paper. [*Bottom right*]

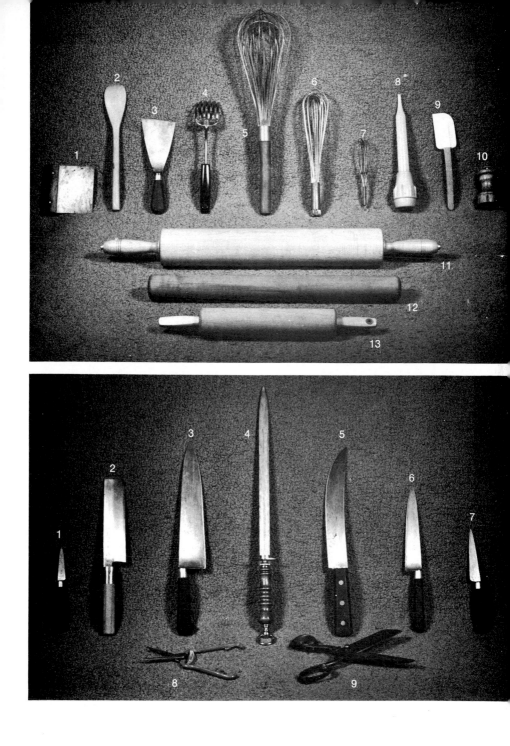

For puréeing soups, fruits, and vegetables, the imported French food mill with removable disks (1) is hard to improve upon. A lid that will cover a variety of saucepan sizes is a space-saver; good examples are the long-handled French copper pot lids (2 and 3), or the graduated aluminum cover (13). A trustworthy meat thermometer (4) will take the guesswork out of roasting. Sturdy saucepans, such as ones of aluminum lined with stainless steel (5), enameled ironware (10 and 12), and heavy-duty tin-lined copper (8), will last for years. A tin-lined metal fish poacher with removable rack and cover (6) is a useful luxury. Free-standing pastry shells are easy to form in French metal flan rings (7) set on pastry sheets. Graduated glass pitchers (9 and 11) measure liquids accurately, and dry-measure cups are essential for flour and sugar, like this set in stainless steel with long handles (14).

To flute a mushroom: turn it against the knife and it cuts itself.

This is a fluted mushroom cap.

DECORATIVE TOUCHES

A pastry bag has many uses; here it makes a professional-looking border of mashed potatoes.

1   Yeast: be sure it is thoroughly dissolved and has begun to foam before mixing.

MAKING

2   Mix the flour and eggs in a bowl with a rubber spatula; then add the yeast.

3   Turn the dough out on a board; it will be very sticky at first.

4   Knead with heel of hand.

5   When dough has body, lift it and slap it onto board.

6 Soften chilled butter by beating it with a rolling pin.

7 Then smear it out with heel of hand.

BRIOCHES

8 Start kneading cold but malleable butter into the dough.

9 Place in bowl; clip the dough with scissors; let it rise to double its volume.

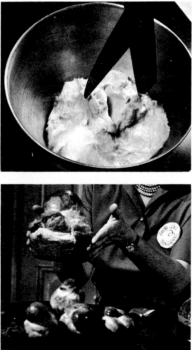

10 Baby *brioche* and middle-sized *brioche*, before and after cooking.

11 *Les voilà*—the baby and the middle-sized *brioches* ready for eating.

Asparagus is done when the stalks
droop just slightly. They are easy
to remove when tied with string.

A French wire salad basket
can be used as a container to hold
vegetables while boiling them.

In making a soufflé the egg whites are the key. Beat them
until they are smooth and glossy and hold their shape,
in order to produce a soufflé that rises to its supreme height.

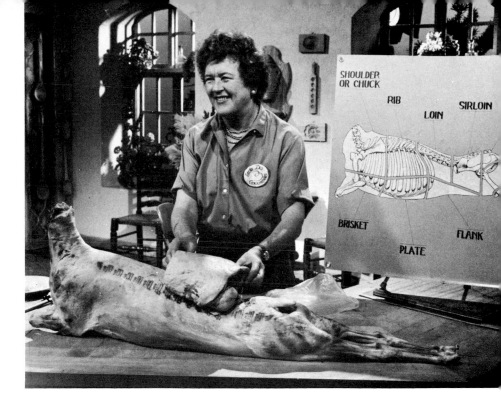

LEARN WHERE THE MEAT COMES FROM

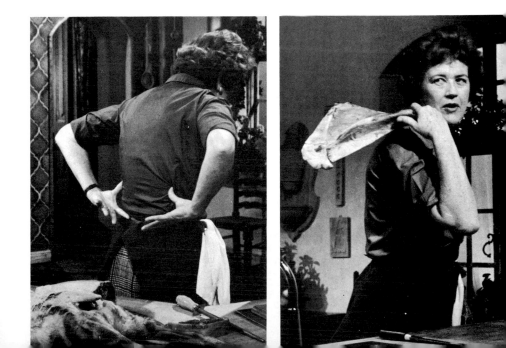

You don't need a fancy fish poacher to boil a salmon; use a washtub.

To keep the lobster's tail straight, tie it onto a board or rack before cooking.

If you're a fisherman, save
all sculpin and other rockfish
for bouillabaisse.

The French consider the roe the
most delicate part of the scallop
(it looks like an orange tongue).

When decorating a cold fish,
slip waxed paper under the edges;
remove when aspic has set.

A turban of sole is a decorative
dish cooked in a ring;
here it is ready for serving.

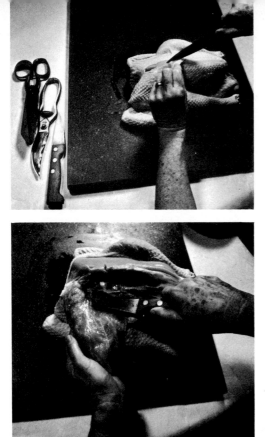

1   Slit breast skin from neck to tail.

BONING OUT THE

2   Peel back skin and remove breast meat on each side.

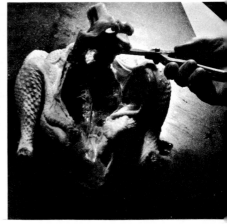

3   When breast meat is off, you are ready to cut off the breastbone.

4   After cutting through rib cage on either side, the breastbone is still attached at the shoulder as shown here; the next step is to cut it off.

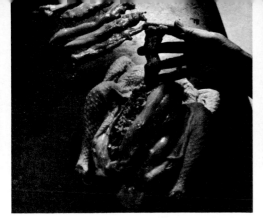

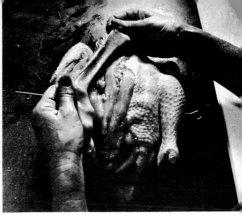

5   Fill the cavity with stuffing and cover with strips of breast meat.

6   Fold breast skin back into place.

BREAST OF A CHICKEN

8   Truss the chicken—and it is ready for roasting or poaching.

7   Sew up breast skin.

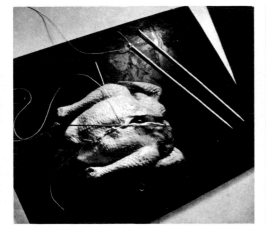

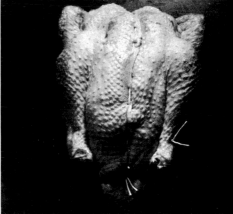

After pressing it on the mold, trim the dough with a ravioli wheel.

Prick the dough with a fork.

UPSIDE-DOWN PASTRY SHELLS

You can form upside-down shells on any shape; here are some examples, ranging from muffin tins to a horseshoe.

You can put two rolls together
as shown here to make
the large party-size *bûche*.

JELLY ROLLS AND BÛCHES

Spread on butter cream,
scumbling it to give a bark effect.

Scoop out meringue mushroom cap
to make a hollow for the stem.

Sprinkle powdered sugar over
decorated *bûche*.

Le Vacherin—meringue cake.

TWO TRIUMPHANT DESSERTS

Génoise cake.

SALPICON DE VOLAILLE
(*Diced Turkey or Chicken in White Wine Sauce*)
For 6 people

A little wine and other judicious additions can turn leftover poultry meat into an elegant feast. Again this is the type of recipe one plays by tongue and taste, enhancing flavors according to one's imagination and kitchen resources as suggested here.

3 Tb butter
A large skillet or saucepan
3 to 4 Tb minced shallots
    or scallions
3 to 4 cups chicken or turkey
    meat cut into ⅜-inch dice
About 2 cups diced cooked
    ham or tongue
Salt and pepper
½ tsp tarragon or oregano

½ cup dry white vermouth
Optional additions: a cup or
    so of cooked mushrooms,
    cucumbers, green peppers,
    peas, asparagus, or broc-
    coli; 1 or 2 diced hard-
    boiled eggs
2 to 3 cups thick *velouté*
    sauce (see note below)

(*Note:* Make the *velouté* sauce following the recipe for the turkey soup base, using curry if you wish, and cooked onions and mashed potatoes, but less liquid, as sauce should be thicker than soup.)

Melt the butter in the saucepan or skillet, stir in the shallots or scallions, and cook slowly for 1 minute. Stir in the chicken or turkey, ham or tongue, season with salt, pepper, and herbs. Raise heat and toss together for 2 minutes, to warm the meat with the seasonings. Pour in the wine; boil down rapidly until liquid has almost evaporated. Fold in optional additions, and enough *velouté* sauce to enrobe all ingredients. Taste carefully for seasoning. If not to be used immediately, film top with cream or melted butter, and reheat when needed.

SERVING SUGGESTIONS

Serve the hot *salpicon* in patty shells, or over steamed rice or buttered noodles, or browned with cheese in the oven. Or turn it into a buttered, fireproof serving dish and cover with a giant *crêpe* (pancake); spread with grated Swiss cheese, sprinkle with butter, and brown lightly under a hot broiler. Here is the *crêpe* recipe: Beat ¼ cup cold water and ¼ cup cold milk into ⅓ cup "instant-blending" flour; beat in 1 egg, ¼ teaspoon salt, a pinch of pepper, and 1 tablespoon melted butter; cook in a 10- to 12- inch skillet. Leftover batter may be refrigerated, or mixed into soups, sauces, or creamed dishes.

The Seventy-second Show

THE FRENCH JELLY ROLL
◄§ • §►
(*Orange-Almond Cake; Strawberry Filling*)

Jelly-roll cakes are quick to make and dramatic to serve. You can fill and dress them in any manner that suits your fancy, from jelly, fresh fruits, whipped-cream mixtures or custards, to creamy cake fillings and frostings. For the cake itself, use a regular spongecake batter, or try the following orange and almond mixture, which surrounds your filling with a tender crunch and delicious flavor.

BISCUIT ROULÉ A L'ORANGE ET
AUX AMANDES
(*Orange and Almond Sponge Sheet*)
For 8 to 10 servings

PRELIMINARIES

3 Tb butter
A jelly-roll or cake pan, 11
    inches in diameter, 17

inches long, and 1 inch
deep
Flour

Preheat oven to 375 degrees and place rack in middle level. Melt the butter and let cool to tepid: part is for the pan, part for the cake. Paint inside of cake pan with melted butter, and line with 12-by-21-inch piece of waxed paper, letting ends extend beyond edges of pan. Butter the paper, roll flour over it, covering entire inside surface, and knock out excess flour. Assemble the following ingredients:

⅔ cup granulated sugar
3 eggs (U. S. graded "large") (place yolks in a large mixing bowl, whites in small bowl of an electric mixer or an egg-white beating bowl: be sure egg-white bowl is absolutely dry and clean, and that no specks of yolk are mixed with the whites)
The rind of 1 orange (grate it into the mixing bowl containing the yolks)
⅓ cup strained orange juice
¾ cup pulverized blanched almonds (grind them in an electric blender, or put through a meat grinder with part of the ⅔ cup granulated sugar)
¼ tsp almond extract
¾ cup sifted plain bleached cake flour (place dry-measure cups on waxed paper, sift flour directly into cups, and sweep off overflow with a straight-edged knife)
A scant ¼ tsp cream of tartar
Pinch of salt
1 Tb granulated sugar
1½ Tb tepid melted butter
Powdered sugar in a sieve

MIXING THE CAKE BATTER

Using a large wire whip, gradually beat the sugar into the egg yolks and orange rind; beat vigorously for a minute or two until mixture is thick and pale yellow. Beat in the orange juice, then the almonds, almond extract, and flour.

Beat the egg whites for a moment at moderate speed; when they begin to foam, add the cream of tartar and salt. Beat at top speed until egg whites form soft peaks, sprinkle in the sugar and beat a few seconds more until egg whites form stiff peaks when lifted with a spoon or spatula.

Scoop the egg whites over the yolk mixture. Rapidly and delicately fold together, using a rubber spatula; when almost blended, rapidly fold in the tepid butter ½ Tb at a time.

Immediately turn the batter into your prepared pan, smoothing over the entire surface. Bang pan briefly on table, to even the mixture, and set in middle level of preheated oven.

BAKING

Bake for about 10 minutes. Cake is done when barely starting to color, when top is lightly springy or spongy if pressed with fingers, and when the faintest line of separation shows between cake and sides of pan. Do not overcook, or cake will break when rolled; it must be soft and spongy.

COOLING AND UNMOLDING

Remove from oven and sprinkle top of cake with a ⅟₁₆-inch layer of powdered sugar. Cover with a sheet of waxed paper. Rinse a towel in cold water, wring it out, and lay over the waxed paper. Turn cake upside down and let cool for 20 minutes.

To unmold, loosen paper lining at one end of pan. Holding paper flat on table, gradually lift off pan, starting at the loose-paper end. Carefully dislodge paper from long sides of cake, then peel it off the top. Trim brown edges all around cake; they will crack when rolled. The cake is now ready for filling, which should be done immediately.

AHEAD-OF-TIME NOTE

It is usually safest to fill and roll the cake promptly. But if you have not overbaked it, you can risk storing it as follows: sprinkle with powdered sugar, cover with waxed paper, roll up in the damp towel, and refrigerate in a plastic bag. The risk is that the cake may dry out, lose its sponginess, and then be unrollable.

FARCE AUX FRAISES CIO-CIO-SAN
(Fresh Strawberry Filling with Almonds and Kumquats)

4 cups sliced fresh strawberries and about ½ cup sugar; or 3 ten-ounce packages frozen sliced strawberries, defrosted and drained
2 Tb dry white vermouth
2 Tb cognac, orange liqueur, or kirsch
2 packages (2 Tb) unflavored powdered gelatin
⅔ cup sliced almonds
½ cup kumquats preserved in syrup, seeded and diced
Decorative suggestions: powdered sugar, sliced almonds, and kumquats, or powdered sugar and whole strawberries

If you are using fresh strawberries, toss them in a bowl with the sugar and let stand for 20 minutes. Put the wine and liqueur in a small saucepan, add ¼ cup of strawberry juice, and sprinkle on the gelatin. Let soften for several minutes, then stir over heat to dissolve gelatin completely. Fold into the strawberries, along with the almonds and diced kumquats. Chill or stir over ice until thickened, then spread over the cake.

Roll up the cake either from the short or the long end, depending on whether you prefer a long or a fat roll; use bottom layer of waxed paper to help you as you flip cake over onto itself.

Transfer cake to a serving board or platter; cover with waxed paper and refrigerate if not served fairly soon. Just before serving, sprinkle with powdered sugar (waxed paper slipped under sides and ends will keep serving board neat), and decorate with almonds and kumquats, or strawberries. Accompany, if you wish, with more strawberries and sweetened whipped cream.

The Seventy-third Show

BÛCHE DE NOËL
◆ ꙮ ◆
(Yule Log; Meringue Mushrooms; Spun Sugar)

BÛCHE DE NOËL
For 10 to 12 people

What could be more handsome on the Christmas table than an edible yule log with chocolate bark, meringue mushrooms, and spun sugar moss! Though it looks like a tricky work of art you will find it quite easy to do, for a *bûche de Noël* is merely a spongecake batter baked in a jelly-roll pan, rolled with a filling, and decorated log-fashion with chocolate frosting and various woodsy trimmings.

THE SPONGECAKE SHEET (APPROXIMATELY 11 BY 17 INCHES). Follow the recipe as given on The Seventy-second Show for orange-almond cake, or use the plain spongecake (The Forty-fourth Show), or the chocolate cake (The Sixty-eighth Show).

FILLING AND FROSTING. About 2½ cups of each will be needed. Select any filling you wish, and any chocolate frosting that is easy to spread and that will not soften too much while waiting for service. The following meringue mixture may be used for both filling and frosting, and for forming decorative mushrooms.

Meringue Italienne
(Sugar-syrup Meringue Mixture)
For about 3 cups

3 egg whites	1⅓ cups granulated sugar
An electric beater	⅓ cup water
Pinch of salt	A small heavy saucepan
A scant ¼ tsp cream of tartar	

(For this, the egg whites should be beaten and the sugar syrup cooked at approximately the same time; work them together if you can. You will need an electric beater for the egg whites; if you have a two-bowl mixer, beat the whites in the small bowl, and transfer them to the large bowl when you add the sugar syrup.)

Beat the egg whites at moderate speed for a moment until they begin to foam; add the salt and cream of tartar and beat at fast speed until egg whites form stiff peaks when lifted in a spoon or spatula.

Place sugar and water in saucepan and set over high heat. Swirl pan—do not stir—gently until sugar has dissolved completely and liquid is perfectly clear. Cover pan and boil rapidly, without stirring, for a moment or two: condensing steam falls from cover, washing down sides of pan and preventing the formation of crystals. Uncover pan when bubbles begin to thicken, and boil rapidly to the soft-ball stage, 238 degrees.

Beating egg whites at moderately slow speed, pour in the sugar syrup in a thin stream. Continue beating at high speed for at least 5 minutes, until mixture is cool. It will be satin-smooth, and form stiff peaks when lifted with a spoon or spatula.

Reserve ¼ cup for the meringue mushrooms.

Crème au Beurre à la Meringue
(Meringue Butter Cream)
For about 2 cups

2 cups (12 ounces) semi-sweet chocolate bits melted with 3 Tb strong coffee or rum	1 Tb vanilla extract ½ lb. (2 sticks) softened unsalted butter

Beat the melted chocolate and vanilla into the cool meringue mixture. Gradually beat in the butter. Chill the butter cream until of easy spreading consistency. (Leftover butter cream may be frozen.)

FILLING AND FROSTING THE LOG

Spread half the filling on the spongecake sheet, and roll up starting at one of the short ends. (Wrap and chill if you are not yet ready to frost it.)

When ready to frost, cut off the two ends on the bias, to give the appearance of a sawed log. For branches, cut holes about ½ inch deep in the surface of the cake; insert 2-inch lengths from trimmed-off ends. (Don't make branches too long, or they will not support the frosting.) Transfer cake to a serving board or rectangular dish. Insert waxed-paper strips under sides and ends of cake to keep frosting off your serving board; remove after frosting. Then, using either a small spatula or a pastry bag with ribbon tube, cover the top and sides of the cake, leaving the two ends unfrosted. Scumble the frosting with a fork or spatula to give a barklike effect. Refrigerate to set frosting.

MERINGUE MUSHROOMS

(Preheat oven to 200 degrees.)

Lightly butter a small baking sheet, roll flour over the surface, and knock off excess. Force the reserved meringue mixture through a pastry tube with ¾₆-inch tube-opening or drop off the end of a teaspoon onto the baking sheet, making ½-inch domes for mushroom caps, and pointed cones for stems. You should have 10 or 12 of each. Bake for 40 to 60 minutes, until you hear the meringues crackle softly. They are done when dry, and when they come off the baking sheet easily. To assemble, pierce a hole in the bottom of each cap, fill with butter cream, and insert the stem. (*Note:* Mushrooms should be baked soon after the meringue mixture is made, otherwise mixture softens too much for mushrooms to be formed.)

SPUN-SUGAR MOSS

Arrange an oiled broom handle between two chairs, and spread plenty of newspapers on the floor. Boil ½ cup sugar and 3 tablespoons water, following directions for *meringue italienne*, until sugar turns a light caramel color. Let syrup cool a few seconds until slightly thickened, then dip a fork into the syrup and wave fork over broom handle; syrup will form threads over handle.

FINAL DECORATIONS

Press clusters of mushrooms into the log wherever you think mushrooms should grow, and sprinkle with a light dusting of cocoa shaken through a sieve. Sprinkle a little powdered sugar over the log, to give a snowy effect. Decorate with holly or leaves, if you wish, and drape spun-sugar moss in strategic places. (Final decorations are done just before serving, as log should be under refrigeration until the last moment.)

The Seventy-fourth Show

BEEF GETS STEWED TWO WAYS

Here are two easy-to-assemble, hearty, fragrant beef stews from the south of France: *carbonnade de boeuf* and *daube de boeuf*. The name *carbonnade* comes from *carbonata*, or coals; originally it described slices of grilled meat, but in Provence it has come to mean slices of meat stewed with onions. *Daube* derives from the French covered stew pot, *daubière*, and usually indicates chunks of beef stewed with vegetables. Both dishes may be prepared well ahead of time, and take nicely to reheating.

MEAT CUTS AND MARINATION. Both recipes are based on the Swiss-steak type of beef cuts, which cook tender in 1½ to 2 hours: an excellent choice is trimmed and boneless chuck steak. In both recipes, the marinade is optional: it serves to tenderize and flavor the meat. If you have not the time to marinate, simply add the listed ingredients to the casserole as you are assembling it. Recipes are for 6 people.

CARBONNADE DE BOEUF A LA PROVENÇALE

(Casserole of Beef, Onions, and Potatoes)

For 6 people

3 lbs. chuck steak cut into
slices approximately 3½
by 2 by ⅜ inches

THE MARINADE

¼ cup wine vinegar	⅛ tsp pepper
1 Tb olive oil	2 tsp salt
2 large cloves garlic, peeled and minced	¾ tsp savory
	¾ tsp thyme

Mix the marinade in a glazed, glass, or stainless-steel bowl. Turn and baste the meat with the liquid, cover, and refrigerate for 6 hours or overnight, basting and turning the meat several times.

THE ONIONS

Optional but traditional: 4 ounces (about ⅔ cup) fresh side pork, or fat-and-lean slices from a fresh pork butt	A heavy skillet
	1 to 3 Tb olive oil
	5 to 6 cups sliced onions

Cut the optional pork into 1-inch pieces about ¼ inch thick. Sauté slowly in a tablespoon of oil to render the fat and brown very lightly. (If pork is omitted, pour 3 tablespoons oil into your pan.) Stir in the onions, cover closely, and cook slowly for about 20 minutes, stirring occasionally until onions are tender and just starting to brown.

BAKING

A 6-quart flameproof casserole	Salt and pepper
7 to 8 cups sliced all-purpose potatoes	Beef bouillon
	¼ cup Parmesan cheese (for final step)

(Preheat oven to 350 degrees.)

Drain meat and season with salt and pepper. Alternate layers of onions and meat in casserole. Pour in marinade ingredients, then arrange layers of potato slices on top, seasoning each with salt and pepper. Pour in enough bouillon to cover the meat; bring to simmer on top of stove.

Cover casserole and set in middle level of preheated oven for about 1 hour, or until meat is almost tender when pierced with a fork. Timing will depend on quality of meat; it cooks about half an hour more in final step.

Raise oven heat to 425 degrees. Tip casserole and spoon out accumulated fat. Sprinkle the Parmesan cheese over the potatoes and baste with a spoonful or two of the cooking liquid. (If done ahead to this point, set aside uncovered. Reheat to simmer before proceeding.)

Place uncovered casserole in upper third of 425-degree oven and bake for about 30 minutes, to brown top of potatoes and reduce and thicken cooking liquid. Serve from casserole.

SUGGESTED ACCOMPANIMENTS

Fresh green beans or peas, French bread, and either a red wine such as Beaujolais or Mountain Red or a *rosé*.

DAUBE DE BOEUF A LA PROVENÇALE
(*Casserole of Beef with Wine and Vegetables*)
For 6 people

3 lbs. chuck steak cut into
2½-inch squares 1 inch
thick

THE MARINADE

2 Tb olive oil
1½ cups dry white ver-
mouth
¼ cup brandy or gin
2 tsp salt
¼ tsp pepper

½ tsp thyme or sage
1 bay leaf
2 cloves peeled and minced
garlic
2 cups thinly sliced carrots
2 cups thinly sliced onions

Marinate the beef as directed in the preceding recipe.

ASSEMBLING

A 6-quart flameproof cas-
serole
Salt, pepper, flour
1½ cups firm, ripe tomatoes,
peeled, seeded, juiced,
and chopped
1½ cups sliced fresh mushrooms

Optional: about 8 slices,
¼ inch thick, fresh side
pork; or fat-and-lean slices
from a fresh pork butt
Beef bouillon if necessary

Scrape off marinade and season meat lightly with salt and pepper, then roll in flour and set aside on waxed paper. Drain marinade liquid into a bowl; toss tomatoes and mushrooms with marinade vegetables. Place several strips of optional pork in bottom of casserole and cover with one third of the mixed vegetables. Then alternate with layers of meat and vegetables, covering top layer of vegetables with slices of optional pork. Pour in the marinade liquid.

COOKING AND SERVING

Cover casserole, set over moderate heat, and simmer for about 15 minutes. If vegetables have not rendered enough liquid almost to cover meat, add a bit of bouillon. Cover and cook at the simmer for 1½ to 2 hours, or until meat is tender when pierced with a fork. Tip casserole, skim out fat, and taste for seasoning. If liquid has not reduced and thickened, drain out into a saucepan and thicken with a tablespoon of cornstarch mixed with bouillon. Boil 2 minutes, then pour into casserole. (If not served immediately, cool uncovered, then cover and refrigerate. Simmer covered for 5 minutes before serving.)

FINAL PROVENÇAL FILLIP

For added flavor, chop or purée 2 cloves of garlic and place in a bowl with 3 to 4 tablespoons drained capers. Pound or mash into a paste, then beat in 3 tablespoons of strong Dijon-type mustard. Gradually beat in 3 tablespoons olive oil to make a thick sauce; stir in ¼ cup minced fresh basil or parsley. Stir into the finished *daube* just before serving.

SUGGESTED ACCOMPANIMENTS

Steamed rice, buttered noodles, or boiled potatoes; French bread; Beaujolais, Mountain Red, or *rosé* wine.

The Seventy-fifth Show

HAM DINNER FOR FOUR IN HALF AN HOUR

(Egg-Stuffed Tomatoes; Puréed Peas and Watercress; Braised Leeks; Cherries Jubilée)

There comes a time when you have no time, yet it's company time. That's when you want a roster of fast, chic little meals. This three-course dinner featuring ham can be assembled in about half an hour if you follow the events in the order suggested.

MENU

Tomates Farcies à la Portugaise—
Tomatoes Filled with Scrambled Eggs
Tranches de Jambon à la Crème—Ham Slices in Madeira Sauce
Purée of Peas and Watercress *Braised Leeks*
Hot French Bread *Rosé Wine*
Cherries Jubilée *Vanilla Ice Cream*

1) **MACERATING THE CHERRIES**

A 1-lb. can of pitted sour red cherries
The grated rind of 1 lemon
¼ cup granulated sugar
⅛ tsp powdered cinnamon
3 to 4 Tb kirsch or cognac

Drain the cherries (save the juice), and toss in a bowl with the lemon rind, sugar, cinnamon, and kirsch or cognac; let steep until needed.

2) BRAISING THE LEEKS

4 to 8 leeks, depending on size	Salt 2 Tb butter

Discard roots and cut lower part of leeks about 5 inches long (tops may be saved for soup). Slice leeks in half lengthwise and wash thoroughly under running water. Arrange in one layer in a wide saucepan or shallow flameproof baking dish. Add about ½ inch water, sprinkle with salt, and distribute the butter on top. Bring to the boil, cover, and boil slowly until leeks are tender. (*Note:* Leeks will take 15 to 20 minutes to cook; when tender, liquid should have almost entirely evaporated. If cooked ahead of time, set aside uncovered and either reheat with a tablespoon or so of water, or spread with grated Swiss cheese, dots of butter, and brown lightly under the broiler.)

3) COOKING THE PEAS

2 ten-ounce packages frozen green peas (partially defrosted, if possible, for faster and more even cooking)	½ cup chicken stock or bouillon ¼ tsp salt 1 Tb butter

Break up frozen block of peas and place in a heavy, large saucepan with the chicken stock, salt, and butter. Cover and let boil moderately fast while working on the next step. (*Note:* After peas have cooked about 5 minutes and are almost tender, the watercress goes in for 5 minutes more of cooking before both are puréed.)

4) THE STUFFED TOMATOES

2 firm, ripe, red tomatoes Salt, pepper, and butter	1 Tb minced shallots or scallions

3 eggs
Decorative suggestions:
   watercress or lettuce
   leaves, anchovies, capers,

canned green or red pep-
pers, minced parsley or
other fresh herbs

Cut tomatoes in half, squeeze out juice and seeds; remove central pulp with a grapefruit knife. Sprinkle interior with salt; drain tomatoes upside down on a rack. Beat the eggs in a bowl with a pinch of salt and pepper; heat a tablespoon of butter in a heavy pan, stir in the shallots or scallions and cook slowly for a moment. Then add the eggs and scramble over low heat until they form soft curds. Season to taste, fill the tomatoes, and place on a bed of watercress or lettuce. Decorate top of egg fillings with whatever you have chosen; cover and refrigerate until serving time.

5) THE VEGETABLES AGAIN

When peas are almost tender, place a handful of watercress, stems and all, on top; cover and continue cooking for 4 to 5 minutes until cress has wilted. Check on leek cooking, and add a bit of water if necessary.

6) THE HAM

1½ to 2 lbs. cooked ham
   slices, ¼ inch thick
Cooking oil and butter
2 Tb strong Dijon-type
   mustard
½ Tb tomato paste
½ cup heavy cream

2 Tb minced shallots or
   scallions
¼ cup dry port or Madeira
   wine
⅓ cup ham or beef stock, or
   canned beef bouillon

Trim off fat, cut ham into serving pieces, and dry on paper towels. Heat 1 tablespoon of oil and 2 of butter in a heavy frying pan; when bubbling hot, add ham and brown lightly for a minute or two on each side, then remove ham.

While browning ham, beat the mustard and tomato paste in a small bowl with half the cream; set aside.

Stir shallots, wine, and stock or bouillon into ham-cooking pan and boil down for several minutes until liquid has reduced by half and is slightly syrupy.

(At this point, you might purée the peas and watercress through the coarse blade of a food mill, or in an electric blender; correct seasoning and return to pan. Reheat when needed, and stir in a tablespoon of butter if you wish.)

When liquid in ham pan has boiled down, stir in the mustard mixture and boil for a moment. Return ham to pan, baste with the sauce, and simmer a moment to blend flavors. (If ham is not fork-tender, cover and simmer 5 minutes or so.) Add more cream if you wish, and boil until thickened. Set aside until ready to serve, then cover and reheat for a moment.

7) ASSEMBLING THE MAIN COURSE

Place the puréed peas and watercress in a mound on a hot serving dish. Cover with the ham, and pour the sauce over. Arrange the braised leeks around the edge of the dish.

8) THE CHERRIES JUBILÉE

Blend a tablespoon of arrowroot or cornstarch in a bowl with the cherry macerating juices, then beat in a few tablespoons of canned cherry juice. Pour into chafing-dish pan and stir over heat until thickened, adding more cherry juice if needed. Before entering dining room, stir in cherries and heat thoroughly. To flame, set over chafing-dish flame, sprinkle with 3 tablespoons granulated sugar, and add ½ cup cognac. Heat, then set afire with a lighted match. Spoon up the flaming mixture until blaze dies down; serve over vanilla ice cream.

The Seventy-sixth Show

CROISSANTS

❦ · ❧

CROISSANTS

A NOTE ON FLOUR. Although you can produce excellent *croissants* from all-purpose flour, bread flour, or frozen packaged white dough, the high gluten content makes for hard and rubbery rolling out. A mixture of 2 parts unbleached pastry flour and 1 part unbleached all-purpose flour gives a dough that is much easier to handle. *Croissants* made from unbleached flour are more tender in texture than those made from bleached flour; oil added to the basic dough helps to tenderize bleached flours. Measure flour by scooping cup into bag; sweep off excess with the straight edge of a knife. (Sources for pastry flour are given in The Forty-second Show, "More About Puff Pastry.")

The Basic Yeast Dough
For 1 dozen 5½-inch croissants

1 package (¼ ounce) dry active yeast
¼ cup warm water (not over 110 degrees)

¼ tsp salt
½ Tb sugar

Sprinkle the yeast over the warm water, add the salt and sugar, and let yeast stand until it has dissolved and risen in a soft mass on top of the liquid. This will take 5 minutes or so; prepare rest of ingredients while waiting for yeast to prove itself.

2 cups white flour (about 9 ounces; see notes above)

¾ tsp salt
1 Tb sugar

A mixing bowl
For bleached flour: 4 Tb
    tasteless cooking oil

For unbleached flour: 2 Tb
    tasteless cooking oil
⅓ to ½ cup tepid milk

Place flour, salt, sugar, and oil in mixing bowl; add the dissolved yeast and ⅓ cup of tepid milk. Blend with a rubber spatula, pressing dough into a mass, then turn out onto a board. Begin lifting dough and throwing it roughly down on the board with one hand—it should be fairly soft and somewhat sticky at first; if it seems stiff, work in more milk by droplets. Continue lifting and throwing and, as dough becomes more elastic, folding and kneading it with the heel of your hand. Be rough, rapid, and energetic; in about 3 minutes dough should have enough body so it is smooth, elastic, and does not stick to your hand. (If still sticky at this point, knead in a bit more flour.)

RISING

Place dough in a clean bowl, set in a plastic bag, and let the dough rise until doubled in bulk; it should be light, and recede slightly to the pressure of your finger. At room temperature, rising time will be 1 to 1½ hours. If room is cold, place dough in a warming oven, on a pillow over a radiator, or on an electric pad or blanket: rising temperature should be no more than 85 degrees, or yeast will overferment, and either lose its strength or impart an unpleasant taste to the dough. You can retard rising time by placing bowl in refrigerator: cover with a plate and a weight, and leave overnight. In any case, dough must rise to double, but it must not overrise, or again the yeast will overferment.

PUNCHING DOWN AND CHILLING

When dough has risen, remove from bowl and punch down into a flat circle. Wrap in waxed paper and chill for about 20 minutes; this will make the next step easier. (Dough may be frozen at this point.)

Basic Yeast Dough Becomes Croissant Dough

(You may use frozen packaged white dough: following the thaw-and-rise directions on the package, you will have arrived at this point. Half of a 1¼-pound frozen package equals the amount of homemade dough in this recipe.)

**1 stick (¼ lb.) chilled
butter**

Work the butter into a smooth consistency by beating it with a rolling pin, then pushing it out rapidly by bits with the heel of your hand; it must be entirely free of lumps, cold, and malleable, so it will roll easily with the dough. Form butter into a 5-inch square.

With palms of hands, press cold dough into a flat 9-inch circle; set the butter square on top. Fold edges of dough up over butter, pinching edges together to seal in butter completely. Flour package lightly on both sides, and place on board, enclosure side up.

TURNS 1 AND 2

With a lightly floured rolling pin, and pushing down and away from you, rapidly roll the package into a rectangle about 15 inches long and 5 inches wide. Keep sides of rectangle as straight as possible, and remember that your object is to spread the layer of butter evenly between the two layers of dough the length and width of the rectangle. Sprinkle board and top of dough lightly with flour as necessary, to prevent sticking.

Fold the dough in three, as though folding a business letter, by lifting bottom of rectangle up over half the dough, and bringing top of rectangle down, making 3 even layers. Turn dough so top flap is to your right; roll again into a 15 x 5-inch rectangle, and fold again into 3 layers. Flour lightly, wrap in waxed paper, and refrigerate for 1 to 2 hours; this chills the butter and relaxes the gluten or rubbery quality in the dough so that it may be rolled and folded again.

TURNS 3 AND 4

Repeat the process, with 2 more rollings and foldings into three. You now have 82 layers of dough and 81 layers of butter! Wrap and chill for 2 hours before forming the *croissants*. (Dough may be frozen at this point.)

Forming the Croissants

Lightly butter a 12 x 14-inch baking sheet. Roll the chilled dough into a rectangle about 20 inches by 5 inches; cut in half crosswise and chill one half.

Roll reserved dough into a 12 x 5-inch rectangle and cut into thirds. Refrigerate two of the thirds. Roll one of the thirds into a 5½-inch square and cut in half on the bias. You now have two triangles; roll one triangle to extend its point, making triangle about 7 inches long. With your fingers, fold top over onto itself, and continue rolling up dough toward point of triangle with the palm of your hand. Bend the two ends to make the crescent shape, and place on baking sheet, point of triangle underneath. Continue with rest of dough, making 12 *croissants* in all. (Keep unformed dough chilled, for easy handling.)

RISING

Let *croissants* rise for an hour or more at room temperature, until almost doubled, and light in texture. (Risen *croissants* may be frozen, then baked while still frozen.)

GLAZING AND BAKING

1 egg beaten with ½ tsp
water

(Preheat oven to 475 degrees.)

Set rack in middle level. Paint *croissants* with the egg to glaze them. Bake for 10 to 12 minutes, until nicely browned. Cool on a rack for 10 to 15 minutes before serving. (Cooled baked *croissants* may be frozen; to serve, reheat for a few minutes at 400 degrees.)

The Seventy-seventh Show

CHOCOLATE SOUFFLÉ
❧ · ☙

Chocolate soufflé, that marvelously light, delicious, dramatic dessert, is nothing but a thick chocolate-flavored sauce into which beaten egg whites are incorporated; the eggs automatically puff the soufflé when it goes into a hot oven. The only requisites are to have a sauce that is thick but not heavy—cornstarch takes care of that—egg whites that are correctly beaten and folded in, and a reliable oven. You must also be able to time your meal so that the soufflé can be served immediately it is done, for this type of soufflé will not wait for anyone.

THE BAKING DISH OR MOLD. Choose a baking dish of any flame-proof material, such as tinned metal, glass, or porcelain. For this recipe, the dish should hold 7 to 8 cups, be about 6 to 7 inches in diameter at the top, and have sides 3½ to 4 inches high, which may slant outward very slightly. If you are serving more than 6 people, double the recipe and use 2 dishes: a soufflé will not rise to its dramatic height if its baking dish is too wide.

SOUFFLÉ AU CHOCOLAT
(Chocolate Soufflé)
For 6 to 8 people

MELTING THE CHOCOLATE

3 Tb instant coffee
3 Tb boiling water
1 cup semisweet chocolate morsels or bits (or 6

ounces or squares of semi-sweet baking chocolate, broken into small pieces)

Bring a small saucepan one third full of water to the boil and remove from heat. Place instant coffee in a slightly smaller saucepan, add 3 tablespoons boiling water, and dissolve coffee; stir chocolate into coffee and set in the pan of hot water. Stir briefly until chocolate starts to melt, then set aside; finish later.

PREPARING THE BAKING DISH; THE OVEN

A 6-cup soufflé dish 3½ to 4 inches deep	½ Tb softened butter 2 to 3 Tb cake flour

Smear inside of baking dish with softened butter to cover bottom and sides with a light film. Roll cake flour or cornstarch around in dish; knock out excess. Preheat oven to 375 degrees.

THE COLLAR   Soufflé will rise to a height of 6 to 7 inches, or about 3 inches over rim of dish; sides of soufflé must be supported during baking. Make a collar as follows: Cut a piece of aluminum foil 12 inches wide and 1½ inches longer than the circumference of the dish. Fold in half lengthwise, butter one side, and surround dish with foil, buttered side of foil against sides of dish. Secure with a straight pin, head down for quick removal.

THE SOUFFLÉ SAUCE BASE

⅓ cup cornstarch (sift starch into ⅓-cup measure; sweep off excess with straight edge of a knife)	A 1½-quart saucepan 1½ cups milk ½ cup granulated sugar 3 Tb softened butter

Place starch in saucepan, add a few tablespoons of milk, and beat vigorously with a wire whip to blend completely. Beat in the rest of the milk and the sugar. Stir over moderately high heat, reaching all over sides, corners, and bottom of pan until sauce comes to the boil and thickens. Boil, stirring, ½ minute. Clean sauce off sides of pan with a rubber spatula; spread the butter over the top of the sauce. (If not used immediately, keep warm over simmering water; sauce lumps when cold and is difficult to smooth out.)

FINISHING THE SAUCE BASE

5 eggs

Just before baking the soufflé, scrape the sauce base into a large mixing bowl (for easy blending); beat in the melted chocolate, which should be perfectly smooth and tepid. Separate the eggs, beating the yolks into the sauce base and dropping the whites into your egg-white bowl (being sure bowl is absolutely clean and dry, and that you have no specks of yolk mixed in with the whites).

THE EGG WHITES

2 extra egg whites, making   Pinch of salt
    7 in all   2 Tb granulated sugar
¼ tsp cream of tartar

Using a large, clean, dry wire whip (balloon size) or an electric mixer, beat the egg whites at moderate speed for a moment until they begin to foam. Beat in the cream of tartar and salt, and continue beating at fast speed until egg whites form soft peaks. Sprinkle on the sugar and continue beating until egg whites form stiff peaks, like a clown's pointed cap, tip bending slightly down.

FOLDING IN THE EGG WHITES

With a rubber spatula, stir one fourth of the beaten egg whites into the chocolate sauce base, to lighten it. Scrape the rest of the egg whites on top and fold them delicately and quickly into the sauce base by cutting down from top to bottom of bowl, bringing spatula toward you to side of bowl, turning blade flat with side of bowl, and lifting out. You are thus bringing a bit of the chocolate mixture up over the egg whites. Continue rapidly, turning bowl as you go. The object is to blend the chocolate and egg whites quickly, and to deflate the egg whites as little as possible; the whole operation should take less than a minute.

BAKING

(Oven has been preheated to 375 degrees.)

Set soufflé over high heat for 30 seconds, to warm it. Then place in middle or lower-middle level of oven. Do not open oven door for 35 to 45 minutes; soufflé will be done in about 55 minutes. It is ready when it has risen up to or slightly over the aluminum collar, and will usually show the faintest line of shrinkage from the collar. A trussing needle or straw inserted through the side of the puff should come out almost clean. (If soufflé is not baked long enough, the sides will collapse.) Remove from oven, set on a serving dish, take out the collar pin, and gently dislodge collar all around. Serve immediately, accompanied by sweetened, lightly beaten cream.

HOW TO SERVE A SOUFFLÉ

Hold a serving spoon and fork back to back above soufflé and plunge sharply into the top crust, spreading crust apart quickly. Serve, and repeat for each serving.

The Seventy-eighth Show

FOUR-IN-HAND CHICKEN

Chicken simmered in white wine and aromatic vegetables gives you four recipes in one. Serve it just as it is, hot or cold, and you have a delicious simple main course when your mood is noncaloric. When you're looking for a party dish, turn it into an aspic, serve it *au gratin,* or try the Belgian *waterzooi* with its smooth cream-and-egg-yolk sauce.

POULET POCHÉ AUX AROMATES

(*Chicken Simmered in White Wine and Vegetables*)
For 4 to 6 people

THE VEGETABLE FLAVORING

2 medium carrots, peeled
2 medium onions, peeled
3 medium celery stalks,
 trimmed and washed
For the two final recipes

only: 2 Tb butter, ½ bay
leaf, and ½ cup chicken
broth
A 4-quart covered flame-
proof casserole or an
electric skillet

For the first two recipes, simply cut the vegetables in thin slices. For the last two recipes, cut the vegetables into julienne matchsticks 1½ inches long and cook them slowly in the butter, bay leaf, and chicken broth for about 10 minutes, or until tender.

SIMMERING THE CHICKEN

A 3½-lb. frying chicken, cut
 up, giblets included
Salt and pepper
¼ tsp tarragon or "Italian
Seasoning"

1 cup dry white vermouth
About 2 cups clear chicken
broth

Remove any loose fat, and place the giblets in the bottom of the casserole or electric skillet, then arrange layers of chicken and vegetables on top, sprinkling each with salt, pepper, and herbs. Pour in the wine; add enough chicken broth almost to cover chicken. Bring to the simmer, cover, and simmer slowly either over low heat or in a 325-degree oven for about 30 minutes. Chicken is done when drumsticks, pricked with a fork, are tender. Remove giblets; skim off fat; carefully correct seasoning of cooking liquid. Serve in any of the following ways.

1) Served "au Naturel"

Serve the chicken just as it is, decorated with parsley. Accompany it with boiled rice or potatoes, or green peas or beans and French bread. A red Bordeaux wine or a *rosé* would go nicely. If chilled, chicken stock will set slightly, like jellied consommé; serve it then with a green salad.

2) Served *"en Aspic"*

For each 2 cups of cooking liquid, soften 1 package (1 tablespoon) unflavored gelatin for 5 minutes in ¼ cup cold chicken broth. Stir into the hot cooking liquid until gelatin has dissolved completely. Rearrange chicken (and vegetables too, if you wish) attractively in the casserole, in a serving dish, or in a mold. Pour the liquid around, and chill until set. (Remove any congealed fat.) Chicken may be served either as is, or unmolded. Accompany with a green salad, French bread, and chilled white wine, such as a Traminer.

3) Served *"à la Bretonne"*

When you want a party dish that can be prepared in advance, this is a casserole of chicken in white wine sauce. Besides the cooked chicken, you will need the following:

2 stainless-steel or enameled	**½ cup heavy cream**
saucepans	**3 Tb grated Swiss cheese**
5 Tb flour	**1 Tb butter**
4 Tb butter	

(Preheat oven to 375 degrees.)

Drain chicken-cooking liquid into one saucepan and boil down rapidly until liquid has reduced to 2 cups. In another saucepan, cook the flour and butter slowly together for 2 minutes without coloring. Remove from heat; let cool a moment, then pour in all the hot chicken stock at once, beating vigorously with a wire whip to blend thoroughly. Boil, stirring, for 1 minute. Thin out sauce with about ½ cup heavy cream, added by spoonfuls; sauce should coat a spoon nicely. Carefully correct seasoning.

Lightly butter a baking-and-serving dish. Pour a few spoonfuls of sauce into dish; arrange chicken on top. Fold the vegetables (which cooked with the chicken) into the sauce, and pour over the chicken. Sprinkle top with cheese; cut the tablespoon of butter into small pieces and distribute over cheese. (Set aside uncovered; cover and refrigerate when cold.)

About half an hour before serving, place in upper third of preheated oven; bake until bubbling hot and top has browned nicely.

Accompany with rice or noodles; buttered peas, asparagus, or green salad; French bread; and a red Bordeaux, white Graves, or *rosé* wine.

4) Served "à la Waterzooi"

This is a Flemish recipe which originated in Ghent; the Belgians use the same general idea for fish. Besides the cooked chicken, you will need the following:

6 egg yolks	**2 to 3 Tb chopped fresh**
½ cup heavy cream	**parsley**

Just before serving, blend the egg yolks and cream in a mixing bowl with a wire whip. By driblets, beat in a ladleful of the hot chicken-cooking liquid, then another ladleful (slow warming of the egg yolks prevents them from curdling). Pour egg-yolk mixture back into casserole with chicken and vegetables. Slowly swirl casserole over moderate heat for several minutes until sauce thickens slightly; be very careful sauce does not come near the simmer and curdle the egg yolks—this is the only trick to this recipe, and is why the thickening is done at the last moment. Sprinkle on the chopped parsley.

Serve immediately in large soup plates, accompanied with boiled potatoes, French bread, and a white Graves or Burgundy wine. The *waterzooi* is eaten with soup spoon, fork, and knife.

The Seventy-ninth Show

BRIOCHES

ᴥᠷ • ᠻᴥ

The very special, unbelievably light and airy texture of *brioches* is due to the large amount of butter and eggs worked into their yeast dough. Delicious with breakfast or tea, eaten plain or with jam, *brioches* may be baked in loaf or muffin tins, formed in the traditional cylinder shape with round headpiece, or baked in a ring. Stale *brioches* may be sliced and toasted, or hollowed out and used as edible containers for sauced foods.

PÂTE A BRIOCHE
(Brioche Dough)
For a 6- to 7-cup baking mold, or 8 muffin cups

MIXING AND KNEADING THE DOUGH

1 package (¼ ounce) dry active yeast	¼ tsp salt
	½ Tb granulated sugar
3 Tb hot water (not over 110 degrees) in a cup	

Sprinkle the yeast over the hot water, add the salt and sugar, and let yeast dissolve and rise in a soft mass on top of the liquid. This will take 5 minutes or so; prepare rest of ingredients while yeast is proving itself.

2 cups (9 ounces) all-purpose flour (measure by dipping dry-measure cup into flour; level off excess with straight-edged knife)	½ Tb granulated sugar
	¾ tsp salt
	3 eggs (U. S. graded "large")
	1½ sticks (6 ounces) chilled butter

Blend flour, sugar, salt, eggs, and dissolved yeast in a mixing bowl with a rubber spatula, then turn out onto a pastry board or marble. Begin lifting dough and throwing it roughly down on the board with one hand; it will be very soft and sticky. Continue lifting, throwing, and scraping dough back into a mass; when dough has enough body, begin kneading with the heel of your hand. After a few minutes of vigorous work, dough should have enough elasticity and body so that it barely sticks to your hand; it is now ready to receive the butter. Soften the butter by beating it with a rolling pin, then smearing it out on your board with the heel of your hand until it is perfectly smooth and about the same consistency as the dough. Take a 2-tablespoon bit in your fingers and work it into the dough by beating, stirring vigorously, and smearing the dough around on the board. Dough will seem ropy and stringy, but smooths out as it absorbs the butter. Continue working in butter by bits until all has been incorporated and dough again barely sticks to your hand.

Then place dough in a clean bowl, sprinkle top with a teaspoon of flour, and cut a cross in the top with scissors (to help in rising). Put bowl in a plastic bag, or cover with a damp towel.

RISING

Brioches are lighter in texture if the dough has two risings before its final rising in the baking molds. For the first rising, set at room temperature for 1½ to 2 hours or longer, until dough has risen by at least ⅔ and retreats slightly to the pressure of your finger. (Because of high butter content, rising temperature should not be over around 70 degrees; let rise several hours in refrigerator in hot weather.)

Remove from bowl, punch down, and knead for a moment. Replace in bowl, sprinkle lightly with flour, and set in refrigerator for 4 to 5 hours until doubled in bulk. (If left overnight, cover with a plate and weight to prevent overrising.) Do not allow dough to rise more than double or yeast will overferment; before forming dough, punch down again. (Dough may then be frozen.)

FORMING BRIOCHES À TÊTE (CYLINDRICAL
BRIOCHES WITH BALL-SHAPED HEADS)

For a large *brioche*, lightly butter a 6- to 7-cup round mold or baking dish 4 to 5 inches deep (or any straight-sided, oven-proof container); roll flour in it and knock out excess. Form ¾ of the chilled dough into a ball and place in mold. With your finger, work a hole 2 inches deep into the top of the ball, widening the hole slightly at the opening. Form the remaining dough into the shape of a teardrop, and insert the pointed end into the hole. Let rise an hour or more at room temperature, or until dough has almost doubled.

Form small *brioches* the same way, in buttered and floured muffin tins, fireproof glass cups, or fluted molds.

FORMING BRIOCHE EN COURONNE (RING-SHAPED BRIOCHE)

Ring-shaped *brioche* may be formed in a buttered and floured 4-quart ring mold, or may be shaped by hand. For hand shaping, knead the dough into a smooth ball. Make a hole in the center with your finger and twirl the dough around your finger, inserting more fingers and finally your hand as the inner circle widens. Continue widening inner circle, finally using both hands; object is to make a doughnut 8 to 10 inches in diameter. Rinse a baking sheet in cold water, shake off excess, and place *brioche* upon it. In about 10 minutes, when dough has relaxed, you may widen the circle more. Let rise to almost double (an hour or more).

GLAZING AND CLIPPING

(Preheat oven to 375 degrees.)

When *brioches* have risen, beat 1 egg in a bowl with 1 tea-spoon of water and paint the *brioches* with the glaze. (Do not glaze under top portion of *brioches* with heads, or heads will not rise properly in oven.)

Brioches are now to be clipped with scissors, to help them shape up nicely while baking. For *brioches* with heads, make 4 or 5 scissor clips in the large ball, close under the head and slanting inward about half the width of the head. For the ring *brioche*, clip top at 1 inch intervals, making cuts about 1 inch deep and pointing scissors toward outside of ring at a 45-degree angle.

BAKING

(Preheat oven to 475 degrees.)

Bake in middle level of oven. Small *brioches* are done in about 15 minutes, when nicely browned and easily unmolded. Large *brioches* bake for about 20 minutes until risen and beginning to brown, and should finish cooking at 350 degrees for about 30 minutes. They are done when a knife or straw, plunged down through center, comes out clean. Ring *brioches* take 20 to 30 minutes at 475 degrees, until a knife or straw comes out clean. The center frequently closes in as the *brioche* bakes.

If large or ring *brioches* brown too much during the latter part of the baking, cover loosely with aluminum foil.

When done, cool *brioches* on a rack for 15 to 20 minutes before serving. Baked, cooled *brioches* may be frozen. Defrost and reheat for a few moments in a 350-degree oven.

The Eightieth Show

VEAL PRINCE ORLOFF

Veal, unlike lamb or beef, has little pronounced flavor, and therefore is greatly enhanced when cooked with herbs, aromatic vegetables, and sauces. In the following recipe, the veal is roasted, carved, stuffed with onions and mushrooms, and covered with a cheese sauce; it makes a perfect party dish as all but the final browning in the oven may be readied in advance.

But as it is a dish that requires several separate preparations, it will seem far less complicated if you do the onion and mushroom stuffing the day before.

VEAL PRINCE ORLOFF

(Roast Veal Stuffed with Onions and Mushrooms)
For 6 to 8 people

COVER-ROASTING THE VEAL

A delicious roasting method, whether veal is stuffed or not.

A 3½-lb. boneless roast of veal, tied for roasting	½ tsp salt
	1 bay leaf
Cooking oil	½ tsp thyme
A large heavy frying pan	A strip of fresh pork fat or
½ cup sliced carrots	suet to cover top and sides
½ cup sliced onions	of roast
3 Tb butter	Aluminum foil
A large heavy casserole	A meat thermometer

(Preheat oven to 325 degrees.)

Dry the veal thoroughly on paper towels. Pour a ¹⁄₁₆-inch layer of cooking oil into the frying pan and set over moderately high heat. When oil is almost smoking, add the veal and brown on all sides and the two ends, turning frequently. Meanwhile, cook the vegetables slowly in the butter in a heavy casserole (just large enough to hold veal comfortably later). When veal is browned, sprinkle with salt and place in casserole with vegetables. Add bay leaf and thyme and cover meat with pork fat or suet (this acts as an automatic baster). Place aluminum foil over meat and cover the casserole.

Set hot casserole in lower third of oven and bake for about an hour. Remove cover and insert thermometer through foil into center of meat. Continue baking for 15 to 20 minutes; meat is done at a thermometer reading of 175 degrees, or when juices run clear yellow with no trace of rosy color.

When meat is done, remove to a carving board and let rest at room temperature for 20 to 30 minutes; juices should retreat back into meat tissues before carving. Veal will have rendered about a cup of flavorful liquid; strain liquid, degrease, and set aside for the sauce.

SOUBISE—BRAISED RICE AND ONIONS

The rice, onion, and mushroom stuffing may be prepared while veal is roasting, or a day ahead. *Soubise* is also a tasty vegetable combination by itself.

¼ cup dry, raw white rice	3½ to 4 cups thinly sliced
4 Tb butter	yellow onions
	½ tsp salt

(Preheat oven to 325 degrees.)

Drop the rice into 3 quarts of boiling salted water, bring rapidly back to the boil, and boil, uncovered, for exactly 5 minutes. Drain immediately. Melt the butter in a casserole or baking dish, stir in the onions and salt to coat with butter, then stir in the rice. Cover and cook for about an hour in preheated oven (along with the veal, if you wish). Onion juices contain enough liquid to moisten the rice. *Soubise* is done when both rice and onions are tender and lightly golden. Set aside until needed. (If served as a vegetable rather than a stuffing, you may wish to stir in a few tablespoons of grated Parmesan cheese, and some cream along with salt and pepper to taste.)

DUXELLES—FINELY DICED SAUTÉED MUSHROOMS FOR STUFFING
(For about 1 cup)

2 cups finely diced fresh	An 8-inch no-stick or en-
mushrooms (about ½ lb.)	ameled skillet
2 Tb butter	Salt and pepper

A handful at a time, twist the mushrooms in the corner of a towel, squeezing out as much juice as you can; this is so the mushrooms will be as dry as possible, and will not dilute stuffing. Then sauté them in hot butter, stirring frequently for several minutes, until pieces begin to separate from each other and to brown very lightly. Season to taste and set aside. (Any leftover mushrooms may be frozen; use in soups, sauces, or other stuffings.)

THICK SAUCE VELOUTÉ—FOR STUFFING AND FINAL COVERING
(For about 2 cups)

A heavy-bottomed stainless-steel or enameled saucepan	The hot veal-cooking liquid
	1½ to 2 cups hot milk
	About ½ cup heavy cream
4 Tb butter	Salt, pepper, and nutmeg
5 Tb flour	

In the saucepan stir the butter and flour over moderate heat for 2 minutes without browning. Remove from heat, and beat in the hot veal-cooking liquid with a wire whip; then beat in 1 cup of the milk. Boil, stirring, for 1 minute, adding a bit more milk by spoonfuls, to make a very thick sauce. Season to taste with salt and pepper.

Place 2 cups of the rice-and-onion *soubise* in a bowl, stir in about ⅔ cup of the sauce, 2 to 3 tablespoons of cream, and purée the mixture through a food mill, a sieve, or an electric blender. Stir in half a cup of the mushroom *duxelles*. Purée should be quite thick, so that when it is spread on the slices of meat it will stay in place; cook down, stirring constantly, if too thin. Carefully correct seasoning.

Film remaining sauce with 4 tablespoons of cream and set aside.

CARVING AND ASSEMBLING THE VEAL

Carve veal into neat serving slices about ³⁄₁₆ inch thick, piling slices to one side, in the order in which you cut them. Lightly butter a fireproof serving platter about 1½ inches deep and 12 to 14 inches long. Place the last slice of veal at one end of the platter, sprinkle lightly with salt and pepper, then spread with a spoonful of the stuffing. Overlap the next slice on the first, season, spread with stuffing, and continue to fill the platter. Spread any extra filling around and over the veal.

SAUCE VELOUTÉ BECOMES SAUCE MORNAY

Salt and pepper
½ cup grated Swiss cheese

2 Tb butter, previously
melted

Bring the *velouté* to the simmer and correct seasoning. It should be thick enough to coat a spoon fairly heavily; thin out with more cream as necessary. Remove from heat and beat in ⅓ cup of the cheese. The *velouté* is now *sauce Mornay*.

Spoon sauce over veal; sprinkle on the remaining cheese and the butter. Set aside or refrigerate until you are ready to finish the cooking.

BAKING AND SERVING

(Preheat oven to 375 degrees.)

About 30 minutes before serving, set in upper third of oven until sauce is bubbling hot and top has browned nicely. Serve, accompanied with braised lettuce or endive, or buttered peas or asparagus tips, and either a red Bordeaux-Médoc or a white Burgundy.

The Eighty-first Show

GREAT BEGINNINGS
(*Clams; Snails*)

A great beginning always adds excitement to a meal. Here are two suggestions that are available on short notice, as the main ingredients can be stored on your kitchen shelf.

CLAMS EN GELÉE

(Clams in Aspic on the Half Shell)

For 4 people

Clams in aspic are relatively quick to do, may be refrigerated for several hours before serving, and look very pretty with their shimmering topknot of aspic. If you do not have fresh clams, use minced canned clams, as indicated in the recipe.

OPENING FRESH CLAMS

8 hard-shell clams about 3 inches across	A heavy-bottomed saucepan and cover

Be sure clams are tightly closed and feel heavy. Scrub them thoroughly with a vegetable brush under cold running water. Place in the saucepan, add ½ inch of water, cover pan, and set over moderately high heat. As soon as shells swing open, in 5 to 6 minutes, remove from heat. Place clam meat in a chopping bowl, reserve shells and juice.

CLAM JUICE ASPIC   (For about 1 cup)

¼ cup combined diced carrots, onions, celery	1 cup clam juice (be sure there is no sand in fresh
¼ cup dry white vermouth	clam juice), plus water if
¼ tsp oregano	necessary
¼ bay leaf	1 package (1 Tb) un-
6 to 8 parsley stems (not the leaves)	flavored powdered gelatin softened in 3 Tb vermouth
An enameled or stainless-steel saucepan and cover	or clam juice

Place all ingredients except gelatin in the saucepan, cover, and simmer slowly for 20 to 30 minutes. Then add the softened gelatin, and stir over moderate heat for a minute or two, until it has dissolved completely.

THE CLAM-MEAT MIXTURE

1 peeled hard-boiled egg (save ½ for later)	1 Tb drained capers
	2 Tb parsley

¾ to 1 cup clam meat   Optional: 1 to 2 Tb heavy
  (either fresh or drained   cream
  canned minced clams)

Chop half the egg and the capers, parsley, and clams together into pieces of about ⅛ inch. Scrape into a bowl, strain in two thirds of the gelatined clam juice, stir in the optional cream (for color), and chill until gelatin has almost set. Strain the rest of the clam juice into a pie plate and chill until set.

ASSEMBLING THE CLAMS IN THEIR SHELLS AND SERVING

8 clam shells or small rame-   The remaining ½ hard-
  kins set on a rack over   boiled egg
  a tray   2 Tb finely minced parsley

Fork up the almost-set clam mixture, to break it up, and spoon into the shells or ramekins. Push the half hard-boiled egg through a sieve and toss to mix with the parsley; sprinkle over the clams. Turn the set aspic in the pie plate out onto a board, chop into small pieces with a knife, and spoon a mound of chopped aspic on top of each clam. Chill until serving time.

Accompany with French bread and a light white wine, such as Riesling or Traminer.

ESCARGOTS A LA BOURGUIGNONNE

(*Snails Baked in Their Shells with Garlic Butter*)
For 4 people, 6 snails each

You can buy canned snails and snail shells in the import sections of many grocery stores, and they are rapidly made ready for baking. However, they will have more flavor if you have time to prepare them for baking several hours ahead, so the snails will absorb the flavor of the butter. Bake and serve the snails in special snail dishes, or in ovenproof plates lined with crumpled aluminum foil, making depressions in the foil to hold each shell. The usual serving is 6 snails per person, each serving on its separate dish.

BEURRE POUR ESCARGOTS   (Butter for about 2 dozen snails)

1 stick (¼ lb.) butter
1 to 2 cloves mashed garlic
2 Tb minced fresh parsley
Salt, pepper, and lemon
   juice

Optional: 1 to 2 Tb very
   finely minced fresh pork
   fat

Cream butter until fluffy (using a wooden spoon and mixing bowl or an electric mixer). Beat in the garlic and parsley, salt, pepper, and lemon juice to taste, and optional pork fat (which fortifies butter in oven, and gives added flavor).

FILLING THE SNAIL SHELLS

2 dozen snail shells
2 dozen canned snails,
   drained

Put a ¼ teaspoon bit of butter into shell opening, then twist the snail into the shell following its natural spiral (tail or small end goes in first). Push snail down into shell as far as it will go, cover shell opening with another ¼ teaspoon of butter, and place snail in baking dish. Continue with rest of snails. If possible, refrigerate for several hours or overnight.

BAKING AND SERVING

(Preheat oven to 450 degrees.)

Bake in middle level of oven for about 10 minutes, until butter is bubbling out of snail shells. Serve immediately, accompanied by hot French bread and a young red wine, such as Beaujolais or Mountain Red.

To eat snails, pick up shell with special snail clamp, or hold shell steady with a fork in one hand; twist snail out of shell with a small fork or pick. Place meat on a bit of French bread, pour the butter over, and eat. When you've eaten all the snails, sop up the remaining garlic butter in the plate with bits of French bread.

The Eighty-third Show

STRAWBERRY TARTS
⋘ · ⋙
(French Pastry Cream)

Big or little, round or rectangular, fresh strawberry tarts are a feast for the eye as well as the tongue. All you need to have for these glittering eye-catchers is pastry dough, fresh strawberries, a jelly glaze, and if you wish a filling, French pastry cream.

TARTES AUX FRAISES
(Fresh Strawberry Tarts)

The Pastry Dough

Use your favorite mixture, or the following French sweet dough. Proportions are for an 8- to 10-inch shell, a 12-by-3-inch rectangle, or about 30 tartlet shells 2 inches in diameter.

1½ cups all-purpose flour (dip dry-measure cups into flour sack, sweep off excess with a straight-edged knife)	butter cut into ½-inch pieces
	A 3-quart mixing bowl
	¼ tsp salt
3 Tb chilled shortening	2 Tb granulated sugar
1 stick (¼ lb.) chilled	⅓ cup iced water

Rapidly blend flour and fat together in mixing bowl, either with tips of fingers or with a pastry blender, until mixture is like very coarse meal. Dissolve salt and sugar in the iced water, blend into flour and fat with a rubber spatula, pressing mixture into a rough mass. For final blending, turn out onto a pastry board; with heel of hand rapidly press dough by two-spoonful bits down on board and away from you in a firm, rough, quick 6-inch smear. Gather dough into a ball, flour lightly, wrap in waxed paper, and chill for 2 hours or overnight.

TART SHELLS

(Preheat oven to 425 degrees.)

For the classical round tart shapes, roll dough about ⅛ inch thick and line a buttered flan ring set on a buttered baking sheet, or buttered cake, pie, or tartlet tins. Prick bottom of dough at ¼-inch intervals with a fork, weight down pastry with foil and beans or another buttered tin. Bake 5 minutes, remove liner, and prick bottom of dough again to keep it from puffing. Bake 6 to 8 minutes more, or until dough has browned lightly; unmold shells and cool on a rack.

For a free-form shell, roll the dough into a rectangle about 15 by 6 inches and ³⁄₁₆ inch thick; cut off uneven edges. Fold dough lightly in half, in half again, and unfold on a lightly buttered baking sheet. Cut a 1½-inch square out of each corner, and moisten a 1½-inch border around rectangle with cold water. Roll up the 2 ends and the 2 sides, to make raised edges. Prick flat bottom of dough with a fork at ⅛-inch intervals. Press inside of raised edges to bottom of dough with tines of a fork to seal; holding fork vertically, press fork marks around outside edges. Bake for about 20 minutes in middle level of preheated oven, until lightly browned. Remove from baking sheet and cool on a rack.

Apricot or Red Currant Glaze
(For Waterproofing Pastry Shells and for Glazing Fruits)

1 cup apricot jam or red currant jelly	2 Tb granulated sugar

(If you are using apricot jam, push it through a sieve to eliminate bits of skin.) Boil the jam or jelly with the sugar for several minutes until last drops falling from a spoon are thick, sticky, and make a thread when taken between thumb and forefinger (228 degrees on a candy thermometer). Keep over hot water until ready to use.

Crème Pâtissière

(French Pastry Cream, for Tart and Cream-puff Fillings)
For about 2½ cups

6 egg yolks
A heavy-bottomed 2½-quart
stainless-steel or enameled
saucepan
½ cup granulated sugar
½ cup all-purpose flour (see
measuring directions for
pastry)

2 cups hot milk
2 Tb butter
1 Tb vanilla extract; or ½
Tb vanilla and 1 or 2 Tb
rum or kirsch

Place the egg yolks in the saucepan, and with a wire whip gradually beat in the sugar. Continue beating for a minute or two until mixture is thick, pale yellow, and forms the ribbon. Beat in the flour, then beat in the hot milk in a thin stream. Set over moderately high heat and stir slowly and continuously with a wire whip, reaching all over bottom and sides of pan, until mixture thickens. As it turns lumpy, beat vigorously to smooth it out. Lower heat and continue stirring for several minutes to cook the flour and thicken the cream. Be very careful about scorching cream in bottom of pan; be sure your pan is heavy, be sure to keep stirring, and do not use high heat, particularly after cream has started to thicken.

Remove from heat; beat in the butter and the flavoring. Clean off sides of pan with a rubber scraper. Film top of cream with a ½ tablespoon of milk, rum, or kirsch to prevent crusting. Chill. (Pastry cream will keep 3 or 4 days under refrigeration, or may be frozen.)

ASSEMBLING STRAWBERRY TARTS

Paint the inside of the cooked pastry shells with warm glaze; this waterproofs the shell, keeping it crisp under the filling. If you are using French pastry cream, spread a ⅜- to ½-inch layer in the shell (do not make layer too thick, or cream will spill out when tart is cut and served). Arrange fresh, hulled strawberries, stem ends down, and berries close together, in the shell or over the cream. Spoon warm glaze over the strawberries (if glaze has thickened too much for easy spooning, stir in a few drops of hot water). Tarts should be served within about an hour, so strawberries will retain their fresh texture.

The Eighty-fourth Show

THE SHRIMP SHOW
❧ · ☙

What do they do to make things taste so good, those French cooks? One thing they do, those French, is to use every possible bit of everything, as in this shrimp recipe where even the shells lend their special flavor to the dish.

BUYING SHRIMP.   Shrimp of the finest, freshest quality are essential for this recipe. Whether fresh or frozen, they should not have the faintest suggestion of "fishyness," iodine, or ammonia; they should smell sweet and appetizing. A limp shrimp is a stale shrimp: if you are buying fresh shrimp with heads and shells on, be sure the tails spring back into their curly shape. Buy frozen shrimp in their shells and keep them frozen at zero degrees until you are ready to cook them.

CROÛSTADES AUX CREVETTES
A LA NANTUA
(Shrimp in White Wine Sauce Served in Toast Cases)
For 4 people

COOKING THE SHRIMP

A 10-inch stainless-steel or
   no-stick frying pan
3 Tb butter

3 Tb each of diced carrots,
   onions, and celery

2 lbs. washed, fresh, whole
   medium shrimp; or 1½
   lbs. raw-frozen, headless
   medium shrimp in their
   shells
Salt and pepper

¼ cup cognac
½ cup dry white vermouth
1 medium tomato, chopped
½ bay leaf
⅛ tsp thyme
½ tsp tarragon or basil

Melt the butter, stir in the diced vegetables, and cook slowly for 8 to 10 minutes until vegetables are limp but not browned. Raise heat to moderately high, add the fresh or the still-frozen shrimp, and toss for a minute or two until shells turn bright pink. Sprinkle lightly with salt and pepper, pour in the cognac, and set aflame with a lighted match. Toss for a minute, then add the vermouth, chopped tomato, and herbs. Cover pan closely and cook at a slow simmer for 5 to 7 minutes, until shrimp are just firm when pressed. Let cool for 20 minutes in cooking liquid. Peel the shrimp and place in a bowl; reserve the shells and the cooking stock.

Beurre de Crevettes

(Shrimp Butter, for Sauce Enrichments, Sandwich Spreads, Egg Fillings, or the Decoration of Cold Dishes)
For about ⅔ cup

¼ lb. (½ cup) butter

1 cup cooked shrimp
   peelings

The object here is to pound and/or purée the shrimp shells with butter; the resulting sieved butter has a pale rosy color and lovely shrimpy taste. Use ¼ pound of butter for each cup of peel; if your shrimp were headless, add 3 or 4 whole cooked unpeeled shrimp for more flavor.

The old-fashioned method extracts the maximum flavor: Pound the shrimp and butter in a heavy bowl or mortar with a wooden masher, reducing the shells to a fine purée, then rub the mixture through a fine-meshed sieve, leaving all the shell bits behind.

The modern method is quick: Heat the butter to bubbling in a small saucepan, warm the jar of your electric blender in hot water; blend shells and hot butter at top speed for about a minute, then rub through a sieve. Beat the strained butter over cold water for a moment until it is cold and creamy.

Reserve the shell debris. The butter will keep for 3 or 4 days under refrigeration, or may be frozen.

Sauce Nantua

(*White Wine Shrimp Sauce with Shrimp Butter*)

For 1½ cups

The shrimp shell debris	stainless-steel saucepan
The shrimp-cooking stock	1 egg yolk
Fish stock, chicken broth, or milk	⅓ to ½ cup heavy cream
A small saucepan	The cooked, peeled shrimp (about 2 cups)
2 Tb butter	Salt, pepper, and lemon juice
2 Tb flour	
A 2-quart enameled or	3 or more Tb shrimp butter

Scrape the shrimp peelings into the cooking stock, simmer 5 minutes, then strain into a measure. Add fish stock, chicken broth, or milk to make 1 cup; pour into a small saucepan and heat to the simmer. Melt the butter in the large saucepan, blend in the flour, and stir over moderate heat for 2 minutes without browning. Remove from heat, let cool a moment, then beat in the hot cooking stock with a wire whip. Boil, stirring, for 1 minute; remove from heat. You now have a thick *sauce velouté*.

Blend the egg yolk and ⅓ cup of cream in a bowl with your wire whip; beat in the hot sauce by driblets. Stir over moderately high heat until sauce comes to the boil; simmer for a moment, adding more cream by spoonfuls to thin out sauce—it should coat a spoon nicely. Taste carefully for seasoning, adding salt, pepper, and drops of lemon juice as you feel it necessary. This is now a *sauce parisienne*.

Fold in the cooked shrimp. If you are not serving immediately, float a spoonful of cream over top to prevent crusting, and refrigerate.

Just before serving, bring to the simmer for a minute or two, to warm the shrimp and blend flavors. Immediately before serving, remove from heat and fold in as much shrimp butter as you wish, added by spoonfuls. With the addition of the butter you now have shrimp in *sauce Nantua*; do not bring near the simmer again or sauce will thin out. Serve in a ring of boiled rice, in a *vol-au-vent*, in patty shells, or in the following toast cases.

Croûstades
(*Toast Cases*)

(Preheat oven to 450 degrees.)

These are simply thick pieces of white bread hollowed out, buttered, and browned in the oven. To make them, cut the crust off a loaf of day-old white bread and slice bread 2½ to 3 inches thick. Hollow out one side with a small knife to make an open-topped box with sides and bottom about ¼ inch thick. Tamp sides and bottom with your fingers, then paint the inside and outside but not the underside of each case with melted butter. Place on a baking sheet in the upper third of oven for 5 to 7 minutes, until cases are lightly browned. If done ahead, reheat for a moment before filling. (Baked *croûstades* may be frozen.)

SERVING SUGGESTIONS

Croûstades aux crevettes may be the first course for a dinner, or the main course for luncheon or supper. If they are the main course, you could accompany them with fresh asparagus, peas, or broccoli. A fairly full-bodied white wine would go well, such as a Graves, a Meursault, or a Gewürztraminer.

The Eighty-fifth Show

SALAD FIXINGS

What a beautiful, appetizing, and satisfying creation the salad is—and what a simple one, too. Nature provides; you combine. Here are a few French ideas to toss around in your salad bowl, beginning, naturally enough, with salad greens.

SALAD GREENS. Keep your eye out for crispness, freshness, and for variety when you snoop about the markets for salad makings. Look for the tender-leafed Boston or oak-leaf lettuces, the frizzy chicory or curly endive, the tousled escarole with its pleasantly bitter taste, the lengthy romaine. Don't forget the peppery watercress, the pale short spears of Belgian endive, tender young spinach leaves, and parsley.

If you do not wash your greens immediately, keep them moist and fresh under refrigeration, either in your hydrator drawer or in a plastic bag. Salad greens must be dry when they are tossed with dressing, so you should prepare them several hours before serving. Tight crisp heads of iceberg lettuce need little if any washing, other varieties do. Separate the leaves from the central stems and swish in a sinkful of cold water, then remove leaves one by one, discarding wilted ones and tearing off blemishes. Toss and shake them in a large colander or salad basket to drain off as much water as you can, then spread on a large towel. Roll up loosely, refrigerate for several hours, and you are ready to toss up a salad, the towel having absorbed excess moisture.

VINAIGRETTE

(French Dressing for Green Salads, Combination Salads,
and Marinades)
For about ½ cup, enough for 2½
to 3 quarts of salad greens

The basic French dressing of France is very simple indeed—
oil, wine vinegar or lemon juice, salt, and pepper; mustard,
herbs, and garlic are optional. Although dressing will keep for
a day or two, it is usually best when freshly made.

1 to 2 Tb excellent wine
vinegar, or a combination
of vinegar and lemon
juice
⅛ tsp salt
Optional: ¼ to ½ tsp dry
or Dijon mustard

6 to 8 Tb best-quality olive
oil or salad oil
Fresh ground pepper
Optional: 1 Tb minced
shallots or scallions and/
or ¼ tsp dried herbs such
as tarragon or basil

Either make the dressing in your empty salad bowl: Beat
vinegar or vinegar and lemon juice, salt, and optional mustard
in the bowl to dissolve the salt. Then beat in the oil by droplets,
and finally the optional shallots or scallions, and such seasonings
as you feel necessary.

Or place all ingredients in a covered jar, shake vigorously to
blend, and correct seasoning.

SALADE VERTE

(Tossed Green Salad)
For 6 people

½ cup vinaigrette
2½ to 3 quarts salad greens
(all of one kind or a
mixture), washed and
dried
A large salad bowl with

nonporous interior (14 by
5 inches is a good size)
A long-handled spoon and
fork
Fresh minced herbs if avail-
able: parsley and chives,
tarragon, chervil, or basil

Just before serving, add the dressing and greens to the bowl;
lift and turn the greens with your spoon and fork to coat every

leaf with dressing. Sprinkle with fresh herbs if you have them, and serve as soon as possible.

GARLIC FLAVORING

Either rub the bowl hard with a cut clove of garlic before dressing the salad, or rub one or several small pieces of stale toasted bread with cut garlic, toss with the salad—these are called *chapons*.

SALAD COMBINATIONS

Salads for first courses, salads for salad courses, salads for cold meats, or salad for the main course—proportions are not given here, just a few ideas.

Salade d'Endives avec Betteraves
(Endive and Beet Salad)

Drain a can of sliced or julienne beets, toss with a few spoonfuls of vinaigrette, and let stand for 20 to 30 minutes. Prepare Belgian endives, slicing half crosswise and leaving the rest of the leaves whole. Just before serving, so beet juices will not run over the endives, toss the endive slices with a bit of vinaigrette in your salad bowl. Mound the beets on top, and decorate edges of bowl with whole leaves of endive placed like the spokes of a wheel. Spoon dressing over all, and decorate with parsley or chives.

Salade de Tomates à l'Huile
(Sliced Tomatoes Vinaigrette)

Cut out the stems from firm, ripe, red tomatoes. Place stem-end down; slice tomatoes vertically. Sprinkle a spoonful of chopped parsley and shallots or scallions in the bottom of your serving dish. Arrange the tomato slices on top and dust with salt, pepper, and a pinch of sugar. Spoon over enough vinaigrette to moisten; sprinkle with minced shallots, scallions or chives, parsley, and fresh basil or dill if you have any. Cover and let stand for 30 minutes or so before serving.

Salade Composée
(Main-Course Combination Salad)

A handsomely arranged combination salad can be the solution for what to serve at an informal spur-of-the-moment meal. The trick is to toss all of the elements separately in vinaigrette, letting some of them marinate for 10 to 20 minutes if they need to take on flavor. Then when you arrange your work of art, each part of it is perfectly seasoned. Here is a hearty meatless combination:

Marinate the following in vinaigrette for 20 to 30 minutes: canned kidney beans drained and rinsed under cold water; sliced raw zucchini; sliced raw mushrooms. At serving time, toss mixed salad greens in a bowl with vinaigrette and arrange around the edge of a large serving dish. Mound the beans in the center, and decorate base with groups of marinated mushrooms and zucchini interspersed with hard-boiled eggs, tomatoes, olives, anchovies, chunks of tuna or other fish. Pour a bit more vinaigrette over all, sprinkle with chopped parsley or other herbs, and serve with French bread and a chilled *rosé* wine.

The Eighty-sixth Show

THE NONCOLLAPSIBLE
CHEESE SOUFFLÉ
⋅⋅⋅ ⋅ ⋅⋅⋅

Most soufflés are prima donnas in the kitchen: they have to be baked just so, and served just when, and are always trembling on the verge of collapse. They are the boss of things, not you. Here's a recipe that turns the tables on the soufflé, and puts you in command: you can keep it warm in the oven, you can reheat it, and best of all, you can serve it unmolded so it makes a splendid effect, standing serenely on its platter.

SOUFFLÉ DÉMOULÉ, MOUSSELINE

(*The Noncollapsible Unmolded Cheese Soufflé*)
For 6 to 8 people

PRELIMINARIES

A baking dish to hold the soufflé dish
A 2-quart straight-sided baking dish 4 to 5 inches deep, for the soufflé
½ Tb softened butter
2 Tb finely grated Swiss cheese

(Preheat oven to 350 degrees.)
Put enough water in the baking dish so it will come at least halfway up the soufflé dish; place dish of water in lower third of oven. Spread butter inside soufflé dish, being sure bottom is especially well coated; roll cheese around in dish to cover bottom and sides.

THE SOUFFLÉ SAUCE BASE

2½ Tb butter
A heavy-bottomed 2½-quart saucepan
A wooden spoon
3 Tb flour
¾ cup hot milk
A wire whip
½ tsp salt
⅛ tsp pepper
A pinch of nutmeg

Melt the butter in the saucepan, stir in the flour with a wooden spoon and cook slowly, stirring, for 2 minutes without browning. Remove from heat, let cool a moment, then beat in all the hot milk, stirring vigorously with a wire whip. Boil, stirring, for ½ minute. Remove from heat and beat in the salt, pepper, and nutmeg.

ADDING EGGS TO SAUCE BASE

3 eggs (U. S. graded "large")
A clean, dry bowl
3 extra egg whites (6 to 7 Tb)

A balloon whip or electric
   mixer
A pinch of salt

¼ tsp cream of tartar
1 cup (4 ounces) coarsely
   grated Swiss cheese

Break the eggs one by one, dropping the whites into the clean bowl and beating the yolks into the hot sauce. Add the 3 extra egg whites to those in the bowl, and with a clean, dry whip or electric mixer, beat them for a moment at moderate speed until they begin to foam. Add the salt and cream of tartar, and beat at top speed until egg whites hold in a mass in the beater, and when beater is lifted the egg whites form stiff peaks with slightly drooping points.

Stir one fourth of the egg whites into the hot sauce, to lighten it. Stir in the cheese; scoop the rest of the egg whites on top. Fold the egg whites into the sauce, using a rubber spatula and plunging it down through the center of the mixture, drawing it to the side of the pan, turning it, and lifting it out. You will thus bring a bit of the sauce up over the egg whites, and prevent the whites from collapsing. Fold rapidly, turning the pan as you go; the whole operation should not take more than half a minute.

BAKING

Scoop the soufflé mixture into the prepared dish, which the mixture should fill by no more than about two thirds. Set in the dish of hot water in the preheated oven and bake for about 1¼ hours. The soufflé should cook slowly, which is why it is set in hot water; regulate oven heat so water in dish never quite simmers.

Soufflé is done when it has risen about ½ inch over the top of its dish: the top will be brown, and the sides will show the faintest line of shrinkage from the dish.

If you are not ready to serve, leave soufflé in hot turned-off oven. It will gradually sink about 2 inches as it cooks—which is why you want a deep dish.

UNMOLDING

When you are ready to serve, turn a warm, lightly buttered serving dish over the soufflé. Reverse the two, giving a sharp downward jerk, and the soufflé will drop onto the plate. If the baking dish was properly buttered, and the soufflé sufficiently cooked, it will unmold perfectly.

SERVING SUGGESTIONS

Either surround the soufflé with tomato, mushroom, or shellfish sauce, or with cooked peas, asparagus tips, mushrooms, chicken livers, or shellfish. A dry white wine, such as a Riesling, would go nicely, along with French bread and a tossed green salad.

VARIATIONS ৯~

Make any of the usual soufflés in the same way: instead of cheese only, use ¼ cup of cheese and about ¾ cup of such cooked chopped items as spinach, asparagus, mushrooms, fish, ham, or chicken livers.

The Eighty-seventh Show

QUICHES
৽ঌ · ৯~

A *quiche* hot out of the oven, a salad, and a cool bottle of white wine—there's the perfect light meal. Baked in an open-faced pastry shell, the *quiche* is really just a custard in fancy dress, a mixture of eggs and flavorings. Quick to assemble and practically foolproof, it requires an expert hand only for its crust. And if you've been having troubles with pastry dough, give this recipe a whirl in your electric mixer.

Pâte à Croûstade

*(Pastry Dough for Upside-down Tart Shells,
Pastry Cases, and Turnovers)*
For a 10-inch shell

2 cups granular "instant-
blending" flour
1 stick (4 ounces) chilled
butter
3 Tb chilled white vege-
table shortening

⅓ cup ice water
1 egg
1 tsp salt
⅛ tsp sugar

Place flour in the large bowl of your electric mixer. Cut the chilled butter and shortening into ¼-inch pieces, and add to the flour. Run machine at moderate speed, pushing fat and flour into the blades with a rubber spatula, until mixture looks like very coarse meal.

Beat the ice water, egg, sugar, and salt in your measuring cup to blend. Pour into the flour and butter, and mix at moderate speed for a few seconds until dough clogs in the blender.

Turn out onto a board and press dough into a rough mass. By 2-tablespoon bits, push the dough out and away from you with the heel of your hand in quick, rough 6-inch smears. This constitutes final blending of fat and flour, and incorporates any too-large bits of fat. Scrape dough into a ball, dust lightly with flour, and wrap in waxed paper. Refrigerate for 2 hours or overnight: flour needs rehydrating and butter needs chilling before dough can be rolled easily. (Dough may be frozen.)

UPSIDE-DOWN PASTRY SHELLS

(Preheat oven to 425 degrees.)

You can mold and bake pastry shells of almost any size and shape by forming the dough on almost any upside-down fireproof object, such as a cake or pie pan, a bread tin, a baking dish, a ring mold, or muffin cups. To do so, butter the outside of the mold lightly, roll the dough between ⅛ and ³⁄₁₆ inch thick, and press snugly onto the bottom of the mold. Even off edges with a ravioli wheel or knife to make the shell about 1 inch deep. To prevent dough from puffing in oven, prick all over at ¼-inch intervals with a sharp-pronged table fork. To minimize shrinkage during baking, refrigerate for an hour: this will relax the gluten in the dough.

To bake, place dough-covered mold, still upside down, on a baking sheet and set in middle level of oven for 6 to 8 minutes, until shell has just started to color and to separate slightly from the mold. Remove, let cool 5 minutes, and unmold on a rack. Baked shells may be frozen.

RULE FOR QUICHE FILLINGS

To measure the capacity of an upside-down shell, mark where the edge of the shell reaches on your mold, turn mold right side up, and fill with water up to your mark. Pour water into a measuring cup: you will need almost as much filling as you have water in the cup. The general proportion for *quiche* fillings is that each cup of filling includes 2 eggs; thus about ⅓ of your filling is egg, and ⅔ is liquid and flavoring. The flavoring may be almost anything from bacon or cheese to cooked chopped spinach, asparagus, mushrooms, chicken livers, or shellfish. Here are three classic examples, each for an 8-x-1-inch or 2-cup shell serving 4 to 6 people.

Whatever method you use for producing a partially baked shell, be sure the sides are sturdy. If necessary, patch any thin areas or cracks with raw dough before filling. If you have a long rectangular shape, brace the sides with bread tins during baking. And be sure to butter your baking sheet lightly, so the baked *quiche* will slide off easily onto your serving dish.

QUICHE LORRAINE
(Cream and Bacon Quiche)
For 4 to 6 servings

6 to 8 pieces thick-sliced bacon	**An 8-inch partially cooked pastry shell placed on a buttered baking sheet**

3 eggs (U. S. graded "large")	¼ tsp salt
	Pinch of pepper and nutmeg
1¼ to 1½ cups heavy cream	1 to 2 Tb butter

(Preheat oven to 375 degrees.)

Slice bacon into ¼-inch pieces and brown lightly in a frying pan; drain and spread in bottom of pastry shell. Beat eggs, cream, and seasonings in a bowl to blend. Just before baking, pour cream mixture into the shell, filling to within ⅛ inch of the top. Cut butter into bits and distribute over the cream. Bake in upper third of oven for 25 to 30 minutes, until *quiche* has puffed and browned, and a small knife, plunged into custard, comes out clean. Serve hot, warm, or cold; *quiche* will sink slightly as it cools.

QUICHE AU FROMAGE
(*Cheese Quiche*)
For 4 to 6 servings

1 cup grated Swiss cheese	3 eggs
An 8-inch partially cooked pastry shell placed on a buttered baking sheet	½ tsp salt
	Pinch each of pepper and nutmeg
1¼ to 1½ cups milk	1 to 2 Tb butter

(Preheat oven to 375 degrees.)

Spread ¾ of the cheese in the bottom of the shell. Beat milk, eggs, and seasonings in a bowl to blend. Just before baking, pour in the liquid to fill the shell to within ⅛ inch of the top. Sprinkle on the remaining cheese and the butter, cut into dots. Bake for 25 to 30 minutes.

QUICHE AUX CREVETTES
(*Shrimp Quiche*)

1 cup cooked and shelled shrimp	Salt and pepper
2 Tb butter	Pinch tarragon or oregano
	⅓ cup dry white vermouth

An 8-inch cooked pastry shell placed on a buttered baking sheet
1 Tb tomato paste
¼ cup grated Swiss cheese

(Preheat oven to 375 degrees.)

Toss the shrimp for 2 minutes in hot butter over moderately high heat. Season lightly with salt, pepper, and herbs, add the vermouth, and boil rapidly until liquid has almost entirely evaporated. Spread shrimp in the bottom of your pastry shell. Beat together the same amount of milk, eggs, and seasonings as in the cheese *quiche* recipe, add the tomato paste, and pour over the shrimp. Spread the grated cheese on top, and dot with the butter. Bake 25 to 30 minutes.

The Eighty-eighth Show

FISH DINNER FOR FOUR IN HALF AN HOUR

MENU:

Petites Caisses au Fromage
(Cheese and Artichoke Appetizers)
Tranches de Poisson à la Barbouille
(Fish Steaks with Eggplant and Tomato Sauce)
Noodle Shells *Rosé Wine*
Fantaisie Bourbonnaise (Baked Apricot)

Here is a three-course fish dinner that you can prepare any time in the day you have a spare half hour, and then finish off in one oven at your leisure. If you are really pressed for time, assemble all the ingredients before you start in cooking, and plan to carry on several operations simultaneously. Here is a suggested order of procedure.

1) *La Barbouille*
(*Ragoût of Eggplant, Onions, Peppers, and Tomatoes*)
For about 4 cups

To be served as a vegetable or as a thick sauce.

PREPARING THE EGGPLANT, PEPPERS, AND ONIONS

About 1½ lbs. eggplant   **1½ tsp salt**

Peel the eggplant and cut into ½-inch cubes: you should have 4 to 5 cups. Place in a colander, toss with the salt, and set aside. (Salt draws out excess vegetable water and removes puckery taste. A 10-minute steeping will do: 20 to 30 minutes are ideal. Eggplant will be dried and sautéed later.)

1 large green pepper   **2 Tb olive oil or cooking oil**
1 large yellow onion   **A 10-inch skillet**

Halve the pepper, remove stem and seeds, and cut pepper into ¼-inch crosswise slices. Peel, halve, and cut the onion into ¼-inch lengthwise slices. Cook onion and pepper slowly with the oil in the skillet for several minutes, until vegetables are tender. Meanwhile, prepare the dessert, and if you are cooking and serving immediately, set 6 quarts of water to boil for the noodles.

2) *Fantaisie Bourbonnaise*
(*Baked Apricot Dessert*)

A baking dish approximately 9 inches in diameter and 1½ inches deep
3 Tb butter
⅓ cup "granular" brown sugar
⅓ cup chopped peanuts

A 1-lb. can apricot halves, drained
1 large banana, peeled and sliced
1 lemon
¼ cup bourbon whisky

(Preheat oven to 375 degrees.)

Smear half the butter in the baking dish; sprinkle in half the brown sugar and half the peanuts. Arrange the apricot halves around the outside of the dish, and the banana slices in the center. Grate the rind of the lemon over the fruit, then squeeze on the juice; pour over the bourbon. Sprinkle on the rest of the sugar and peanuts, and dot with the remaining butter.

Cover and set aside until you are ready to bake, then place in upper third of oven for 50 to 60 minutes. Dessert is done when top is very lightly browned and when liquid has reduced to a thick syrup. Serve hot, warm, or cold, with heavy cream.

3) The Noodles

If you are cooking and serving immediately, start the noodles now. Two cups of 1½-inch shell-shaped noodles dropped into 6 quarts of boiling salted water take 12 to 15 minutes.

4) La Barbouille Again
(Sautéing the Eggplant)

Drain the salted eggplant, spread on several thicknesses of paper toweling, and pat dry. Remove the cooked peppers and onions to a side dish, leaving oil in skillet; add more oil if necessary to film pan by 1/16 inch. Raise heat to moderately high; when very hot, add the dried eggplant. Toss frequently for several minutes until eggplant is lightly browned. (While sautéing, start in on the fish, and carry on both operations together; you should be able to work in the first course as well.)

5) Les Tranches de Poisson
(The Fish Steaks)

About 1½ lbs. skinless fish steaks or fillets (cusk, halibut, cod, hake, or swordfish), ¾ inch thick and cut into 4 serving pieces

Salt, pepper, lemon juice, and flour
Olive oil or cooking oil
A fireproof serving platter

Season fish lightly with salt, pepper, and lemon juice. Just before sautéing, dredge in flour and shake off excess. Pour a ¹⁄₁₆-inch layer of oil into a heavy skillet; when very hot, sauté the fish. If you are serving immediately, sauté 4 to 5 minutes on each side; fish is done when a fork pierces flesh easily. If you are precooking, brown fish lightly on each side for a minute or so only. Arrange fish on platter.

6) *Finishing the Sauce and Assembling the Main Course*

1 cup tomato sauce or	½ bay leaf
marinara sauce	¼ tsp thyme
⅓ cup dry white vermouth	Salt and pepper
1 clove mashed garlic	1 Tb butter

Add the cooked onions and peppers to the sautéed eggplant; add the tomato, wine, garlic, and herbs. Boil slowly for several minutes to make a very thick sauce. Correct seasoning, and pour over the fish.

For immediate serving: Drain noodles, toss with salt, pepper, and butter; arrange around the fish.

For later serving: Omit noodles until serving time. Cover platter closely with aluminum foil and refrigerate. About 30 minutes before serving, set foil-covered platter in middle level of a preheated 375-degree oven to finish cooking fish; surround with buttered noodles and serve.

7) *Petites Caisses au Fromage*
(*Cheese and Artichoke Appetizers*)

4 baked pastry shells (fresh or frozen) about 3 x 1½ inches	2 Tb softened butter
	1 egg
	3 drops Tabasco sauce
2 packages (6 ounces) cream cheese with chives (remove from refrigerator 20 minutes before using, for easy mixing)	6 drops Worcestershire sauce
	4 canned artichoke hearts (or frozen hearts, cooked)

(Preheat oven to 475 degrees.)

Place patty shells on a fireproof serving dish. Beat the cream cheese with the egg and seasonings. Just before baking, place a spoonful of cheese in each shell, set an artichoke heart in the center, and cover with remaining cheese. Bake for about 30 minutes in the upper third of oven, until cheese filling has puffed slightly and browned on top.

The Eighty-ninth Show

FRENCH VEAL STEW

This most famous of all French veal stews is simply veal simmered in a lightly seasoned stock, then served in a sauce made from the cooking liquid, and garnished with small white onions and mushrooms. It is a perfect dish for informal entertaining because, like all stews, it may be cooked well ahead of serving time, and reheated. But the beauty of the *blanquette* lies entirely in the quality of its ingredients: choose veal of the palest pink color, the freshest mushrooms, the firmest onions.

VEAL CUTS FOR STEWING. The most interesting stews are made from a combination of veal cuts, so that you have bones for flavor and cartilage for sauce consistency, as well as plain meaty chunks. A recommended selection is neck and shank for meat and bones, breast for cartilage, and undercut of chuck (meaty strip on either side of upper backbone) for solid chunks. You will need 3 to 4 pounds of veal for 6 people, depending on bones and appetites.

BLANQUETTE DE VEAU
(*Veal Stew with Onions and Mushrooms*)
For 6 people

PRELIMINARY BLANCHING—FOR EASY REMOVAL OF SCUM

3 to 4 lbs. veal stew meat
  cut into 2-inch pieces
1 to 2 cups sawed veal bones
  (for extra flavor)

A heavy 4-quart kettle or
  casserole

Place veal and bones in the kettle or casserole, cover by 1 inch with cold water, and bring rapidly to the simmer. Simmer for 2 or 3 minutes, until heavy scum has ceased to rise. Drain through a colander into the sink, wash out the kettle, and wash scum deposit off meat and bones. Return to kettle.

SIMMERING THE VEAL

2½ cups veal or chicken
  stock or canned chicken
  broth
1 large onion stuck with 1
  whole clove
1 large carrot, scrubbed

1 medium celery stalk,
  washed
A medium herb bouquet: 4
  parsley sprigs, ½ bay leaf,
  and ½ tsp thyme tied in
  washed cheesecloth
Salt

Add the chicken stock or broth, the vegetables, and herb bouquet to the veal. Pour in enough cold water to cover ingredients by half an inch. Bring to the simmer, skimming off any additional scum for a few minutes. Salt lightly to taste. Simmer slowly, partially covered, for about 1½ hours, or until meat is tender when pierced with a fork. Let stand, uncovered, for half an hour or more, so veal will pick up flavor from cooking liquid. Then drain through a colander set over a large saucepan. Wash out kettle, and return meat to kettle, removing any loose bones. (Prepare vegetable garnish while veal is simmering.)

THE ONIONS

18 to 24 white onions about
  1 inch in diameter
½ cup stock dipped from
  veal-cooking liquid

¼ tsp salt
1 Tb butter
A wide saucepan or
  enameled skillet

To peel the onions, drop them into a large saucepan of rapidly boiling water, bring back to the boil, and boil 30 seconds. Drain. Shave off the two ends with a sharp knife, and slip off the peel with knife or fingers. To help keep onions from bursting while cooking, pierce a cross about ¼ inch deep in the root ends. To cook, arrange in one layer in the saucepan or skillet, add the stock, salt, and butter. Cover and simmer very slowly for about 30 minutes, or until onions are tender when pierced with a knife. Set aside until needed.

THE MUSHROOMS

About ½ lb. fresh mush-
  rooms
An enameled saucepan
¼ cup stock dipped from
  veal-cooking liquid

¼ tsp salt
½ Tb lemon juice
½ Tb butter

Trim and wash the mushrooms. Leave whole if very small; halve or quarter if large. Place in a saucepan with the stock, salt, lemon juice, and butter; toss to cover mushrooms with liquid. Cover and simmer for 5 minutes. Set aside until needed.

SAUCE AND FINAL ASSEMBLY

4 Tb butter
5 Tb flour
Salt, white pepper, lemon
  juice

2 to 3 egg yolks
About ½ cup heavy cream
A heavy-bottomed 2½-quart
  enameled saucepan

Make a *sauce velouté* as follows: Melt the butter in the saucepan, stir in the flour with a wooden spoon, and cook slowly until flour and butter froth together for 2 minutes without coloring. Remove from heat, let cool for a moment, then vigorously beat in a ladleful of hot veal-cooking liquid with a wire whip. Set over heat, stirring with wire whip and adding driblets of veal-cooking liquid to thin out the sauce; it should coat a spoon fairly heavily. Drain in the cooking liquids from the onions and the mushrooms (you will have added about 3 cups of liquids in all). Simmer for 10 minutes, stirring occasionally, and skimming as necessary. Taste carefully for seasoning, adding salt, white pepper, and drops of lemon juice as you feel them necessary.

Add the onions and mushrooms to the veal and pour the sauce over. (You may finish the cooking later: film top of sauce with a spoonful or two of veal liquid, set aside uncovered until cool, then cover and refrigerate.)

Shortly before serving, cover the veal and bring slowly to the simmer for 2 to 3 minutes. Blend the egg yolks and cream in a mixing bowl; gradually beat in a few spoonfuls of hot sauce to warm the egg yolks. Remove veal kettle from heat, pour in egg-yolk mixture, then return kettle over moderate heat gently shaking and swirling until egg yolks have thickened slightly in sauce.

SERVING SUGGESTIONS

Serve the *blanquette* on a hot platter, surrounded with steamed or boiled rice and decorated with parsley sprigs. No other vegetables are necessary, but you may wish buttered peas, asparagus tips, or braised cucumbers. Wine choices are red Bordeaux-Médoc, *rosé*, or a full-bodied white such as a Graves or Burgundy.

The Ninetieth Show

IMPROVISATION
⋅⋖⋅⋗⋅
(Molded Instant Potatoes and Ragoût)

You need never be at a loss for the makings of a good meal if you always keep your emergency stockpile filled. With eggs, butter, cream, cheese, and salad makings ever in the refrigerator, garlic and onions in the larder, and a choice selection of vegetables, broths, fruits, fish, meats, and condiments on the shelf and in the freezer, you have the fundamentals at hand for improvising a delicious meal. Here, for example, is a spur-of-the-moment main course that turns instant mashed potatoes into a handsome molded edifice, surrounded by a winy *ragoût* made from yesterday's roast.

TAMBOUR PARMENTIER
(Mold of Instant Mashed Potatoes)
For 6 to 8 people

This is instant mashed potatoes mixed with egg yolks, cream, and cheese, baked in a cylindrical dish, and unmolded for serving.

PREPARING THE MOLD

1 Tb soft butter	Waxed paper
A 6-cup cylindrical mold or baking dish	3 to 4 Tb fine dry white bread crumbs

(Preheat oven to 375 degrees.)

Butter the mold or dish heavily. Cut a round of waxed paper and fit it into the bottom of the mold. Butter the paper, then roll crumbs around in mold to cover bottom and sides; knock out excess crumbs.

THE MASHED POTATOES

1½ packages (or 12 "servings") instant mashed potatoes
¾ the total minimum amount of liquid specified
1½ tsp salt (or per package specifications)

6 Tb butter (or per package specifications)
3 egg yolks
⅛ tsp pepper
Big pinch nutmeg
¾ cup grated Swiss cheese
½ cup heavy cream

Prepare the mashed potatoes as directed on package, using only three fourths of the total minimum amount of liquid specified, to make a rather firm mixture. Then vigorously beat in the egg yolks one by one, the pepper, nutmeg, cheese, and cream. Taste carefully and correct seasoning. Pack into prepared mold.

BAKING AND SERVING

When ready to bake, set in middle level of preheated oven for about an hour. Potatoes are done when they have risen an inch or more and have browned nicely. (Be sure sides are brown, guaranteeing they will not collapse later.)

Unmold by running a small knife between potatoes and edge of mold. Turn a lightly buttered serving dish upside down over mold; reverse the two, giving a small downward jerk. Peel paper off top of potatoes if it has adhered. If top has not browned, sprinkle with a spoonful of grated cheese and run under a hot broiler for a minute or two. Keep hot if not served immediately.

Bring to table as a separate vegetable, or surround with meat and vegetables.

RAGOÛT A L'IMPROVISTE
(Leftover Roast Meat Simmered with Red Wine and Vegetables)
For 6 people

A slow simmer with wine, herbs, and aromatic vegetables can transform yesterday's roast into a first-class stew, or *ragoût*. You will find that whether or not the roast was tender, it will need about an hour's further cooking in flavored liquid for it to take on the texture and flavor that characterizes the proper stew. The following recipe is just a suggestion for the *improvisatore*, who will naturally change ingredients and proportions according to his larder and his temperament.

1 to 2 cups sliced onions
Optional: 1 cup sliced green
   peppers
2 Tb butter
A covered casserole
Cooking oil
A heavy skillet
About 3 cups cooked beef,
   veal, pork, or lamb, cut
   into 1½-inch cubes
Salt and pepper
3 Tb flour
1½ cups red wine such as
   Mountain Red or Chianti

1 or more cans beef bouillon
Optional: miscellaneous
   vegetable juices; gravy
   from the roast
1 to 2 cloves mashed garlic
2 Tb tomato paste
1 bay leaf
½ tsp thyme, savory, or
   rosemary
Optional for flavor: 1 to 2
   Tb Smithfield-ham spread
Optional vegetable garnish:
   1 to 2 cans whole baby
   carrots and chopped
   mushrooms

Cook the sliced onions and optional peppers in butter, in the casserole, letting vegetables soften and brown very lightly.

Meanwhile, film a heavy skillet with ¹⁄₁₆ inch cooking oil; heat to almost smoking. Add the meat, tossing and turning it for several minutes until very lightly browned. Season with salt and pepper, then toss with the flour; lower heat slightly and toss for 2 or 3 minutes to brown flour lightly. Remove from heat and swirl in the red wine, scraping up coagulated meat-browning juices. Scrape meat and wine into casserole of onions and peppers. Add enough liquid barely to cover the meat: bouillon, optional vegetable juices (from mushrooms, carrots, etc.), and any leftover meat gravy. Stir in garlic, tomato paste, herbs, and optional Smithfield-ham flavoring. Bring to the simmer, cover the casserole, and simmer slowly until meat is tender when pierced with a fork; this will take about an hour. Skim off fat. Cooking liquid should have boiled down and thickened slightly; if not thick enough to enrobe meat, blend a half tablespoon of cornstarch with a tablespoon of water, remove *ragoût* from heat, and stir in the starch. Boil a minute or two to thicken sauce. Carefully correct seasoning.

While meat is stewing, sauté optional drained carrots in hot butter, salt, and pepper to brown very lightly. Add optional mushrooms and sauté a moment more. Fold into *ragoût* when meat is tender. If you are not serving immediately, set aside uncovered. Cover and reheat for a few minutes before serving, to blend flavors.

Serve from casserole, or arrange the *ragoût* in a ring of steamed rice or buttered noodles, or around the preceding mold of mashed potatoes. Accompany with a green salad and the same red wine you used in the cooking.

The Ninety-first Show

THE EMPRESS'S RICE

ᴀ§ · §ᴀ

RIZ A L'IMPÉRATRICE
(*Molded Bavarian Cream with Rice, Fruits, and Kirsch*)
For 8 to 10 people

This is rice pudding in fancy dress, one of the grand old standbys of French family gatherings. The ingredients are simple: rice simmered in milk, vanilla, and sugar, a custard sauce flavored with glacéed fruits and kirsch, just enough gelatin for the dessert to be molded, and lightly whipped cream for delicacy. Here is an opportunity for you to use that fancy fluted antique mold you picked up in your wanderings. The proportions are for a 6-cup mold or dish.

FRUIT FLAVORING AND GELATIN

¾ cup (4 ounces) finely   ¼ cup kirsch or cognac
  diced glacéed fruits of   1½ envelopes (1½ Tb) un-
  various colors (can be   flavored powdered gelatin
  bought in jars)

Mix the fruits in a small bowl with the kirsch or cognac. Stir
in the gelatin and set aside.

COOKING THE RICE

½ cup plain raw white rice   2 Tb butter
4 quarts boiling water   A vanilla bean or 1 tsp
A flameproof 6-cup casserole   vanilla extract
1⅔ cups milk   A round of waxed paper
⅓ cup granulated sugar

(Preheat oven to 300 degrees.)
Sprinkle the rice into the boiling water, stir up once, and boil
rapidly uncovered for 5 minutes; drain immediately. (This pre-
cooking or blanching allows the rice to absorb the milk easily.)
Place drained rice in casserole, add milk, sugar, butter, and
vanilla bean or extract. Bring to the simmer, place waxed paper
on top (to prevent rice from browning in oven), set a tight-
fitting cover on the casserole, and bake in middle level of oven.
Rice is done in 30 to 40 minutes, when it has absorbed all the
milk and is very tender; it should not color at all. Set aside.

THE CUSTARD SAUCE

A heavy-bottomed 3-quart   1½ cups hot milk
  enameled or stainless-steel   3 Tb apricot jam forced
  saucepan   through a sieve
5 egg yolks   1 tsp vanilla extract if
¾ cup granulated sugar   needed
1 tsp cornstarch

While rice is cooking, make the custard sauce as follows.
Place the egg yolks in saucepan. Using a wire whip, gradually
beat in the sugar; continue beating for a minute or two until
yolks and sugar are thick and pale yellow. Beat in the cornstarch.

Then, by driblets so that the egg yolks will warm gradually, beat in the hot milk.

Set saucepan over moderate heat and stir rather slowly with a wooden spoon, reaching all over bottom of pan. Object is to warm the mixture gradually and allow the egg yolks to thicken without scrambling. As sauce heats, foam rises to the surface. Indications that sauce is about to thicken are a steamy vapor and a slow decrease in foam; the sauce is also too hot for your finger. At about 170 degrees, the sauce will have thickened enough to coat the spoon with a creamy layer. Note that sauce does not come near the simmer, but you must have the courage to heat it until it thickens.

Immediately remove from heat, stirring rapidly to cool very slightly. Scrape in the fruit and gelatin mixture, rinsing bowl in sauce to dislodge all gelatin. Stir sauce for a moment to be sure gelatin has completely dissolved. Stir in the strained apricot jam. Stir the rice into the custard, a spoonful at a time if rice is hot. Taste, and add a little vanilla if you feel it necessary.

Chill, stirring occasionally, until custard is cold but not quite set. Custard must be cold before whipped cream goes in, as a hot custard would liquefy the cream; custard must be almost set before molding, so that rice grains will not sink to bottom of mold.

THE WHIPPED CREAM AND THE MOLD

1 cup chilled heavy cream	aspic mold, ring mold,
A chilled mixing bowl and	spongecake tin, bread tin,
a large, chilled whip	or individual tins or cups
A 6-cup metal mold: fluted	

Beat the chilled cream in the chilled bowl with the chilled whip for several minutes until cream thickens enough to leave light traces on the surface; this is lightly beaten cream, or *crème chantilly*. (In very hot weather, set beating bowl over cracked ice.) Delicately fold the cream into the cold and almost-set custard and rice.

Rinse the mold or molds in cold water, and fill with custard. Cover with waxed paper or plastic wrap and chill for 4 to 6 hours, until fully set. Dessert may remain in refrigerator for 2 or 3 days before serving.

To unmold, run a sharp knife between dessert and edge of mold. Dip mold in very hot water for about 5 seconds. Turn a chilled serving platter upside down over mold; reverse the two, giving a sharp downward jerk to dislodge dessert. Repeat, if necessary. Chill for 10 minutes or so, to set dribble of cream on the platter. Cover with a bowl, if left in refrigerator for any length of time. Surround the Empress's rice with the following fruit sauce, and send a separate bowl of sauce to the table.

Sauce aux Fraises; Sauce aux Framboises

(Fresh Strawberry or Raspberry Sauce)

Either:	Or:
1 quart fresh strawberries or raspberries, hulled and sieved	Two 10-ounce packages frozen berries, thawed and drained *and*
About 1 cup instant or very finely granulated sugar	2 to 3 Tb kirsch, cognac, or lemon juice

Whip fresh berry pulp in a blender with the sugar, or beat in an electric mixer until sugar has completely dissolved. Sieve thawed berries and beat in some of the syrup to thin the purée. Flavor to taste with liqueur or lemon juice.

The Ninety-second Show

COQUILLES SAINT-JACQUES
❧ · ☙
(Sea Scallops)

The scallop is a mollusk, a bivalve, a creature of the sea that keeps house between two pink shells hinged at the bottom and lined in pearly white. There are bay scallops with 2- to 3-inch shells, and deep-sea scallops that can be as much as 8 inches across. One third of the scallop is a large white lump, the muscle, which opens and closes the shell. When scallops are dredged up from the bottom of the sea, scallop fishermen open the shell, disengage the muscle, and throw everything else overboard; thus it is only the muscle that we see in the market. But there are other edible portions of the scallop, the most important of which is the roe. This is a tongue-shaped piece nestling around the muscle; it is delicate in texture, and either bright coral or pearly gray in color. In most other parts of the scallop-eating world, the roe is considered the most delicious portion of the shellfish; it is cooked along with the muscle, and furnishes a decorative touch to the finished dish.

PREPARATION OF SCALLOPS FOR COOKING. Whether fresh or frozen, scallops should have a pleasant, sweet, fresh smell; they are very perishable. They should be kept under refrigeration and cooked as soon as possible. Wash and drain fresh scallops just before cooking; thaw frozen scallops in a sinkful of cold water. Large scallops may be left whole for broiling or deep frying. Cut them into half-inch pieces for sautéing; you may wish to slice them for poaching in white wine. Scallop roes are left whole. One pound or about 2 cups of scallops serve 4 as a first course, 2 as a main course.

COQUILLES SAINT-JACQUES
SAUTÉES A LA PROVENÇALE
(Scallops Sautéed with Garlic and Herbs)
For 4 to 6 people

Sautéed scallops should be crisp light brown outside and moistly tender inside. Keys to success are: have your sautéing oil very hot before the scallops go in, and have no more than one layer of scallops in the pan. Otherwise the scallops will steam, exude moisture, and will not brown. You may find, in using frozen scallops, that they will start out nicely, then suddenly release juices in the pan; to avoid this, blanch them before cooking by dropping them in a large pan of rapidly boiling water and bringing quickly back to the boil, then drain immediately, dry them, and proceed with the recipe.

1 lb. or about 2 cups scallops cut into ½-inch pieces	(preferably a no-stick pan)
Lemon juice, salt, and pepper	2 Tb minced shallots or scallions
About ½ cup flour	1 clove mashed garlic
Olive oil or cooking oil	2 Tb butter
A 10-inch frying pan	2 Tb minced fresh parsley

Dry the scallops in paper towels, then place on a large double sheet of waxed paper. Sprinkle with drops of lemon juice, then with salt and pepper. The moment before sautéing, dredge with flour and shake in a sieve to dislodge excess flour.

Film the frying pan with a 1/16-inch layer of oil. When almost smoking, add the scallops. Toss for 4 to 5 minutes until scallops are lightly browned. Then toss for a moment with the shallots or scallions, and garlic; finally toss with the butter and parsley, and serve.

SUGGESTED ACCOMPANIMENTS

If the scallops are a first course, accompany with French bread. For a main course, accompany with broiled tomatoes and green beans. A *rosé* wine would go nicely.

VARIATIONS &

Coquilles Saint-Jacques Gratinées à la Provençale
For 6 scallop shells

The preceding recipe may be served in little shells or dishes, with a light sauce and a sprinkling of cheese. Brown the scallops very lightly, for only a minute or two. Then toss with the garlic and double the amount of shallots or scallions, and pour in about ½ cup dry white wine or vermouth. Cover the pan and simmer for 2 minutes; uncover and boil for a moment until liquid has thickened lightly. Spoon the scallops and sauce into buttered shells or small shallow dishes, sprinkle each with a teaspoon of grated Swiss cheese and a few drops of melted butter. Reheat and brown under a moderately hot broiler just before serving.

Coquilles Saint-Jacques à la Parisienne
(*Scallops and Mushrooms in White Wine Sauce*)
For 6 scallop shells, or a 3-cup shallow baking dish serving 4 to 6 people

1 lb. or 2 cups sliced scallops	½ tsp salt
¾ cup dry white vermouth	White pepper
A stainless-steel or enameled	½ bay leaf
saucepan	2 Tb minced shallots or
2 cups sliced fresh mush-	scallions
rooms	

Place the scallops in the saucepan with the vermouth, mushrooms, seasonings, and herbs. Add water, if necessary, almost to cover ingredients. Bring to the simmer, cover the pan, and simmer very slowly for 5 minutes. Remove scallops and mushrooms to a bowl; rapidly boil down cooking liquid until reduced to 1 cup.

3 Tb butter	The 1 cup of hot scallop
A heavy-bottomed stainless-	liquid
steel or enameled pan	About ¾ cup milk
4 Tb flour	2 egg yolks

About ½ cup heavy cream   3 Tb grated Swiss cheese
Salt, white pepper, lemon   1 Tb melted butter
   juice

Melt the butter in the pan, stir in the flour, and cook slowly for 2 minutes without browning. Remove from heat and beat in the scallop liquid. Stir with a wire whip over moderately high heat until sauce thickens; thin out with milk. Blend egg yolks in a bowl with half the cream; beat in the hot sauce by driblets. Return to pan and stir over moderately high heat until sauce comes to the boil; thin out as necessary with more cream or milk. Carefully correct seasoning, adding lemon juice if needed.

Fold two thirds of the sauce into the scallops and mushrooms, and spoon into lightly buttered shells or baking dish. Spoon on the remaining sauce; sprinkle with cheese and butter. Refrigerate if not to be served immediately. Then reheat to bubbling and brown under a moderately hot broiler.

SUGGESTED ACCOMPANIMENTS

Accompany with French bread as a first course, or with rice and buttered peas or asparagus as a main course. Serve a white Graves or Burgundy wine.

The Ninety-third Show

MORE ABOUT STEAKS
৽ঌ · ঌ৽
(Baked Steak; Steak au Poivre)

The more you know about steak cuts and where they come from on the beast, the more you can fit steaks into your budget. Sirloins, porterhouses, and *châteaubriands* are all very well, but good steaks also come from other parts of the animal. Next time you are shopping for beef, try a steak from the arm, the part of the beef corresponding to your upper arm; or the blade, corresponding to your shoulder blade; or the undercut or inside of the chuck, meaty strips on either side of the upper backbone; or the flank, sometimes called London broil, a lean, flat, rectangular piece from inside the belly opposite the small of the back. When these less expensive cuts are taken from top-quality aged beef, prime or choice, they have excellent texture and a fine beefy flavor.

A RECOMMENDED REFERENCE BOOKLET. *Lessons on Meat,* 86 pages of text and illustrations on locating and recognizing meat cuts, and the buying, storing, freezing, and cooking of beef, veal, lamb, pork, variety meats, and sausages. Send 50 cents for each postpaid copy to: Consumer Communications Dept., National Livestock and Meat Board, 36 South Wabash Avenue, Chicago, Illinois 60603.

AMOUNT OF STEAK TO BUY. Depending on menu and appetites, 1 pound of boneless steak serves 2 to 3 people; for bone-in steak, such as sirloin or porterhouse, ¾ pound per person is usually required.

STEAK AU FOUR
(Steak Baked with Herbs)
For 6 people

This is an easy and succulent method for steak more than 1½ inches thick, and for frozen steaks more than an inch thick. The steak is browned in a skillet on top of the stove, then baked in the oven with herbs and seasonings to finish its cooking. If you are using frozen steak, let it thaw at room temperature for about an hour, or until the outside has softened slightly. Here is an example using a thick beef steak from the upper arm.

3 lbs. prime or choice boneless arm steak 2½ inches thick, excess fat removed
Olive oil or cooking oil

An iron skillet or shallow flameproof baking dish
1 Tb butter

½ Tb coarse salt
½ tsp dried herbs, such as
   thyme or "Italian seasoning"
4 cloves garlic, unpeeled

A meat thermometer
½ cup beef bouillon, red
   wine, or dry white
   vermouth
1 Tb butter

(Preheat oven to 375 degrees.)

Dry steak thoroughly on paper towels and rub lightly with oil. Film bottom of skillet or baking dish with a ⅟₁₆-inch layer of oil and heat on top of stove until oil is almost smoking. Brown steak for a minute or two on each side. Pour out cooking oil.

Spread the tablespoon of butter over the steak and sprinkle on the salt and herbs. Place the unpeeled garlic cloves around the meat and insert thermometer through side of steak, being sure point is buried halfway between top and bottom and as close to center of meat as possible. (If steak is frozen, insert thermometer when steak has thawed in oven.)

Bake steak in upper third of oven for 15 to 20 minutes (about 30 minutes if steak is frozen). Meat is medium-rare at 130 degrees, when red juices just begin to pearl up at surface. Remove thermometer and set steak on a hot platter.

Spoon out excess fat, add bouillon or wine, and set skillet or baking dish over high heat. Mash garlic into juices, discard peel, and boil down until liquid is slightly syrupy. Remove from heat, swirl in the butter a half tablespoon at a time until absorbed. Pour the sauce over the steak and serve.

STEAK AU POIVRE

(Steak Sautéed with Crushed Peppercorns)
For 4 people

This famous dish usually calls for individual tenderloin or loin strip steaks, but other cuts may be used if they are of top quality and tender.

4 boneless individual steaks
   cut ¾ inch thick, trimmed
   of fat and gristle
About 4 tsp peppercorns, a
   mixture of varieties if

possible (or 1 Tb cracked
   pepper)
1 Tb oil for rubbing steaks
1 Tb oil and 2 Tb butter for
   sautéing

Dry steaks thoroughly on paper towels, then rub with a light film of oil. Crush the peppercorns roughly in a bowl with a pestle or wooden spoon (or use bottled cracked pepper); press about ½ teaspoon into each side of steaks with heel of hand. Let steaks stand for an hour or two if possible, so pepper flavor will penetrate the meat.

Sauté steaks on each side in hot butter and oil; they are done to a medium rare when they feel slightly resistant to your finger, and when you see a faint pearling of red juices appear at the surface. Remove steaks to a hot serving platter. (Scrape off pepper, if you wish: this is a matter of personal taste.)

THE SAUCE

2 Tb minced shallots or scallions	1 tsp cornstarch blended with ¼ cup beef bouillon
½ cup dry white vermouth	2 Tb butter

Spoon out excess fat from skillet, add minced shallots or scallions, wine, and bouillon. Simmer, scraping up coagulated sauté juices with a wooden spoon, until sauce has thickened. Remove from heat, swirl in the butter, and pour the sauce over the steaks.

OPTIONAL FLAMBÉ

If you wish to flambé the steaks in cognac, sauté them to very rare, as they will continue cooking when flambéed. Place sautéed steaks in a chafing dish and pour the sauce over them. Set over flame and pour in ½ cup cognac. When bubbling hot, ignite with a match. Spoon flaming sauce over steaks until fire dies down; serve on very hot plates.

SUGGESTED ACCOMPANIMENTS

Broiled stuffed mushrooms and sautéed or French-fried potatoes garnished with watercress; French bread and a red Bordeaux-Saint-Emilion or Burgundy wine.

The Ninety-fourth Show

TO POACH A SALMON

꽃 • 꽃

How glorious is the sight of a whole cooked salmon, lying luxuriously on the buffet table. And there is no trick at all to cooking a 10-pound fish: all it does is sit quietly in liquid that never quite reaches the simmer; when the fish is done, out it comes, ready to be eaten. Your only problem, as a 10-pound salmon measures some 30 inches from nose to tail, is to find something around the house that will hold the fish. Failing a special fish poacher with removable rack, or a jumbo wash boiler, you can resort to the drastic step of cutting the fish into halves or thirds, poaching it in a turkey roaster, and using your decorative genius to disguise the surgery afterward. Count on ½ to ¾ pound cleaned raw salmon per person.

SAUMON POCHÉ
(Poached Whole Salmon)

A cleaned raw salmon weighing between 5 and 10 lbs. (if frozen, thaw in a sinkful of cold water before cooking)
A large piece of washed damp cheesecloth
A double length of heavy-duty aluminum foil
A collapsible meat-roasting rack

Cold water
Red or white wine vinegar
Salt
Any immersible type of thermometer that will register up to 200 degrees
A platter, tray, or foil-covered board to serve the salmon on

Have fish cleaned but not scaled, have fins left on, and if you want to cook and serve the salmon with its head on, have the gills removed. To keep fish in shape during cooking, wrap in several layers of damp cheesecloth. If you are not using a fish poacher with removable rack, lay fish on double length of foil and arrange on roasting rack: this will allow you to lift and drain the fish after cooking. Place the salmon in your fish poacher, boiler, or whatever you have chosen (if fish is a few inches too long, curl it around the inside of the poacher). Set on top of the stove, covering several burners.

Measuring in quarts, pour in enough cold water to cover fish by 2 inches. For each 2 quarts of water, add 1½ tablespoons wine vinegar and 1 tablespoon salt. Hang thermometer in kettle, being sure bulb is covered with water.

The fish will take about 2½ hours to cook; you may leave it as is until you are ready to go. Then regulate surface burners so that water temperature gradually reaches 185 degrees in approximately 45 minutes. Maintain water temperature at around 185 degrees for 45 minutes. (Note that the salmon never reaches the simmer; water moves slightly but does not bubble. This low, slow cooking keeps the flesh tender and prevents it from flaking.) Finally lower heat and allow water gradually to sink down to 140 degrees in 45 minutes. (Note that timing is the same whether fish is 5 or 10 pounds: decrease the 3 forty-five-minute periods slightly for smaller fish, increase them slightly for larger fish.)

Salmon is now cooked, and may be served hot or cold. If to be served hot, it may remain at 140 degrees for 20 to 30 minutes before you remove it; if to be served cold, let it cool for several hours in the liquid, then remove it. In any case, it should be peeled before serving.

TO PEEL A COOKED SALMON

Remove salmon from cooking liquid, drain, and place on a tray. Cut the cheesecloth and draw it gently out from under the fish. With a sharp knife and your fingers, remove fins and any small bones protruding from fins into flesh, particularly at top edge of fish. Remove jawbones attached to body at neck end on each side of fish. Peel off skin with knife and fingers (one side only if fish is to be served flat), and gently scrape off soft brown flesh on side of salmon to expose the pink meat underneath. Carefully slide salmon onto your serving platter, tray, or board.

SERVING SUGGESTIONS

HOT POACHED SALMON Decorate top of hot peeled salmon with paper-thin slices of cucumber or lemon, overlapping to suggest scales; or sprinkle heavily with chopped fresh parsley or dill; or coat with whatever sauce you are serving. Decorate with sprigs of fresh parsley. Accompany the salmon with melted butter, lemon or white butter sauce, or *hollandaise*, boiled new potatoes, sliced fresh cucumbers and/or fresh buttered peas, and a fairly full-bodied dry white wine such as Meursault or Gewürztraminer.

COLD DECORATED SALMON Cover the peeled salmon with plastic wrap and chill for several hours or overnight. You may decorate very simply with sliced cucumbers or lemon and parsley or watercress, or be more dressy with a *chaud-froid* sauce and aspic as follows.

3 envelopes (3 Tb) un-
   flavored powdered gelatin
4 cups clear chicken broth

2 cups chilled sour cream
Various cooked vegetables
   for decoration

Dissolve gelatin in the broth. Reserve 2 cups for the final aspic glaze. Beat 2 cups of chilled sour cream into the remaining broth and stir over cracked ice until liquid begins to thicken slightly. Meanwhile remove plastic covering and slip pieces of waxed paper under edges of fish on all sides, to catch decorating dribbles. Spoon the sauce over the chilled fish; you may need two coats to cover the fish nicely.

Before sauce has set, decorate the salmon in any way you choose. An easy and amusing design is to caricature a fishy look with various cooked vegetables. You can make a mouth with strips of canned red pimento, and teeth with diced black olives. An egg slice topped with a round of olive and ringed with thin strips of cooked green beans can be the eye. Make a nose out of a piece of cooked carrot and sprinkle the snout with dried dill weed. Strips of cooked green beans formed into touching semicircles can simulate scales, and taper off toward the tail in rounds of sliced cooked carrots. Strips of bean make the tailpiece, and a line of sliced pitted black olives can outline the sides of the fish. Spoon your reserved and almost-set gelatined broth over the decorations to keep them fresh and make them glisten. Remove waxed paper at the sides by slipping pieces of foil under it and pulling the paper over the foil. Chill the salmon until serving time. (You have wisely made sure your platter will fit into the refrigerator before you started in on all of this.)

At the last moment, tuck sprigs of parsley or watercress around the mouth and sides of the salmon. Serve with a dill-flavored mayonnaise-and-sour-cream sauce, cucumber salad, cold asparagus, French bread, and a Riesling, Traminer, or Meursault wine.

HOW TO SERVE A SALMON The central bone structure is flat, running the length of the salmon parallel to the flat sides. To serve, cut portions from top side down to bone. When entire bone is exposed, take salmon out to kitchen and remove the bone; then serve the bottom side of the salmon.

The Ninety-fifth Show

INVITATION TO LUNCH
ৼঌ · ঌ৵
(Ramequin; Glazed Oranges)

Guests for lunch are no problem when you have a few nice little main courses in your repertoire, and some decorative ideas for dessert. Here is a menu in which you can prepare everything ahead of time, leaving just the final touches before serving.

RAMEQUIN FORESTIÈRE
(Cheese and Mushroom Entrée)
For 4 to 6 people

The *ramequin* is a cross between a soufflé and a *quiche*; it is a mixture of thick sauce, eggs, and cheese that is poured into a dish and baked in the oven until it puffs up and browns. Very fast to assemble, it can be readied hours in advance of cooking. The filling is optional, and can be anything you choose, from sautéed chicken livers or shellfish to cooked chopped asparagus, spinach, or artichoke hearts. Here it is mushrooms.

THE FILLING

About 1 cup finely minced
    fresh mushrooms
1 Tb butter and 1 tsp
    cooking oil

1 Tb minced shallots or
    scallions
1 Tb flour
About 4 Tb heavy cream
Salt and pepper

Sauté the mushrooms in hot butter and oil with the shallots or scallions for about 5 minutes, stirring frequently, until mushroom pieces begin to separate from each other and to brown.

Lower heat to moderate, sprinkle in the flour, and stir for a minute to cook the flour. Remove from heat, pour in the cream, then stir over moderate heat until cream has thickened. Season with salt and pepper, and set aside.

THE RAMEQUIN MIXTURE

A heavy-bottomed 2½-quart saucepan
½ cup granular "instant-blending" flour (or regular flour)
2 cups cold milk
3½ Tb butter
½ tsp salt
⅛ tsp pepper

Speck of nutmeg
4 eggs
1⅓ cups coarsely grated Swiss cheese
A lightly buttered baking-and-serving dish, approximately 9 x 1½ inches
1 Tb butter

Place the flour in the saucepan and gradually beat in the milk with a wire whip. Stir slowly and constantly over moderately high heat until mixture comes to the boil and thickens. Remove from heat; beat in the butter, seasonings, and, one by one, the eggs. Then beat in 1 cup of the cheese.

Turn half the mixture into the buttered dish, spread the mushrooms on top, and cover with the rest of the mixture. Sprinkle on the remaining ⅓ cup of cheese, and distribute the tablespoon of butter over the cheese. (Set aside or refrigerate until you are ready to bake.)

BAKING AND SERVING

(Preheat oven to 400 degrees.)

Bake in upper third of oven for about 25 minutes (5 to 10 minutes longer if *ramequin* has been refrigerated). The *ramequin* is done when it has puffed to double in height and is beautifully browned. Serve immediately; it will gradually sink as it cools. Accompany with a green or mixed salad, French bread, and dry white wine such as a Riesling or Traminer.

LES ORANGES GLACÉES
(Fresh Oranges Glazed with Orange Peel)
For 4 people

Glazed fresh orange peel dresses up an otherwise simple dessert of sliced oranges or fruit mixtures. The peel is cut into julienne, blanched in simmering water until tender, then boiled up in sugar syrup to form a glaze for the fruit.

6 large, firm, bright navel oranges	and 1 cup granulated sugar
For the syrup: ⅓ cup water	For testing: a metal spoon and a cup of cold water

Cut off the orange part of the peel with a vegetable peeler, taking with it as little of the white as possible. Cut the peel into julienne, matchstick strips about 2 inches long and 1/16 inch wide. Put in a saucepan with a quart of water and simmer for 12 to 15 minutes, until peel is tender. Drain in a sieve, run cold water over the peel, and drain again thoroughly. (Blanched peel may be frozen.)

The peel is now ready to be cooked in a sugar syrup boiled to the firm-ball stage. To make the syrup, place the water and sugar in a small saucepan and set over high heat, gently swirling the pan until sugar comes to the boil and liquid is clear and unclouded. (It is essential that liquid clears, indicating sugar has dissolved completely; otherwise sugar will crystallize.) Cover the pan and boil for a minute or two; condensing steam will wash sugar crystals off sides of pan. Uncover pan and continue boiling rapidly for a few seconds until you observe the bubbles begin to thicken. Then dip your spoon into the liquid and pour a few droplets into the cup of cold water; syrup is at the soft-ball stage when you can gather it into a mass with your fingers. Immediately drop a bit more into the water; when the syrup makes a firmer ball that holds its shape softly, it is done. Remove from heat. (Note that as soon as syrup holds at all in the water, you must test rapidly or it will cook down too much. If you are making syrup for the first time, remove from heat before each test, then continue boiling until you have arrived at the firm-ball stage. This is 244 degrees on a candy thermometer.)

Immediately turn the blanched orange peel into the syrup and boil for a minute or two; syrup will be diluted by the peel and should be boiled until it has thickened slightly.

ASSEMBLING THE FRUIT

Cut off the white peel from the oranges, and cut oranges either into thin slices or skinless segments. Arrange in a serving dish. Spoon the peel and syrup over the oranges. Chill for an hour or two before serving.

VARIATION ॐ

Glace aux Ananas aux Oranges Glacées

Pack pineapple sherbet into a stainless-steel bowl or decorative mold. Cover with plastic or waxed paper and freeze for an hour. Dip into very hot water for a few seconds and unmold on a serving platter. Cover sherbet with plastic wrap and freeze. Just before serving, scrape dribbles off platter, and arrange the glazed oranges around the sherbet, decorating top of sherbet with a bit of the glazed orange peel.

The Ninety-sixth Show

BOEUF BOURGUIGNON—
BEEF IN RED WINE
ॐ · ॐ

When beef stew is in the oven, all's right with the world, and beef Bourguignon is the best beef stew known to man. Like most stews, this one may be prepared ahead at almost every step of the way. The beef is browned, then simmered in red wine, beef stock, herbs, and bits of bacon; the sauce is thickened lightly, and the stew is garnished with sautéed mushrooms and small cooked onions. You can cook the garniture the day before at any free moment, brown the meat, complete the stewing, or complete the whole dish and refrigerate or freeze it. *Boeuf bourguignon* actually seems to gain in flavor when made in advance; the meat and the sauce blend into even more glorious harmony.

BEEF CUTS.   You may use any stewing cuts of beef for this, but you will have more attractive servings with lean, boneless chunks from the round (hind leg) or rump, or from the chuck (shoulder). Two recommended cuts from the chuck are the "tender," a cone-shaped muscle about 12 inches long that lies along the ridge of the shoulder blade opposite the blade steak, and the "flanken," or boned chuck rib meat. (To learn more about meat cuts, send 50 cents for *Lessons on Meat* to: Consumer Communications Department, National Livestock and Meat Board, 36 South Wabash Avenue, Chicago, Illinois 60603.)

BOEUF BOURGUIGNON
(*Beef Stewed in Red Wine*)
For 6 people

A 6-ounce chunk of un-smoked, unsalted lean pork belly (fresh bacon), or fat and lean pork butt, or salt pork, or lean bacon (pork or bacon is traditional, but may be omitted)
Olive oil or cooking oil
A large skillet
3 lbs. lean stewing beef cut into 2- to 3-inch chunks and dried on paper towels

A 4-quart flameproof casserole or baking dish
3 cups full-bodied, young red wine such as Mâcon, Burgundy, or Mountain Red
About 2 cups beef bouillon
1 Tb tomato paste
2 to 3 cloves mashed garlic
½ tsp thyme
1 bay leaf
Salt as necessary

(Preheat oven to 325 degrees.)

Cut the bacon or pork into 1 x ¼-inch sticks; these are called *lardons*. If you are using smoked bacon or salt pork, place in a saucepan with 2 quarts of cold water, simmer for 10 minutes, rinse in cold water, drain and dry; this is to remove the smoky taste from bacon or the salt from salt pork. You will have about ¾ cup. Brown the *lardons* lightly in a frying pan with a little oil, to render out the fat; this you will use for browning the beef.

Pour the rendered fat into a large skillet, adding a little oil if necessary, to film pan by 1/16 inch. Set over moderately high heat. When almost smoking, brown the beef, a few pieces at a time so as not to crowd the pan; turn beef frequently to brown all sides. Place the beef, as it is browned, in casserole or baking dish.

Pour browning fat out of skillet, pour in the red wine and scrape up into it all the flavorful brown bits, then pour wine into casserole. Add the browned *lardons* to the casserole, and enough beef bouillon almost to cover the meat; stir in the rest of the ingredients and bring casserole to simmer on top of the stove. Cover the casserole and set in lower third of oven. Regulate heat so liquid simmers slowly for 2½ to 3 hours, or longer, until beef is tender when pierced with a fork. (You may simmer the stew on top of the stove if you wish, or use an electric skillet or kettle.)

THE ONION AND MUSHROOM GARNITURE

Do these while the beef is simmering, or at any convenient time.

About 1 lb. fresh mushrooms	**18 to 24 small white onions**
½ Tb oil	**(1-inch diameter)**
1½ Tb butter	**1 Tb butter**
¼ tsp salt	**½ tsp salt**
	Water

Trim mushroom stems, drop mushrooms in a large basin of cold water, swish about for a moment, lift out into a colander, and dry on a towel. Cut the caps into quarters, and the stems on the bias. Heat oil and butter in a skillet until butter foam begins to subside, add the mushrooms, and toss over high heat for 3 or 4 minutes to brown the mushrooms very lightly. Remove to a side dish until needed, then toss with the salt.

Drop the onions into boiling water, bring rapidly back to the boil for several seconds to loosen the skins. Drain. Peel carefully so as not to disturb the onion layers; to prevent onions from bursting while cooking, pierce a cross ¼ inch deep in the root ends. Place in one layer in a heavy saucepan; add the butter and salt and enough water to come halfway up. Cover and simmer very slowly for 20 to 30 minutes, or until onions are tender. Set aside, saving cooking liquid.

SAUCE AND SERVING

3 Tb softened butter   **3 Tb flour**

When the beef is done, set cover askew and drain the cooking liquid into a saucepan. You should have about 2½ cups; if liquid has boiled down too much, add a little beef bouillon. Skim off fat, bring liquid to the simmer, and taste very carefully for seasoning, adding salt and pepper as necessary. Cream the butter and flour in a small bowl with a rubber spatula, to make a smooth paste. Pour in several spoonfuls of beef-cooking liquid and blend with a wire whip, then pour this mixture into the beef liquid. Pour in the onion-cooking juices and bring liquid to the simmer, stirring. This is now your sauce.

Add the mushrooms and onions to the beef, pour on the sauce, cover and simmer slowly for 5 minutes to blend flavors, swirling casserole to baste meat and vegetables with sauce. The dish is now done. (If you are not serving immediately, uncover casserole; when cool, cover, refrigerate, and reheat later.)

Serve the *boeuf bourguignon* in its casserole, or arrange on a hot platter surrounded, if you wish, with boiled potatoes, noodles, or rice, and decorated with parsley. Accompany with hot French bread, buttered peas or a tossed salad, and the same red wine you used for the cooking.

The Ninety-seventh Show

YOUR OWN FRENCH ONION SOUP
ᴇᵉᵍ • ᵍᵉᵥ

Soupe à l'oignon, a large bowl of it bubbling under a brown crust of cheese, is practically a meal in itself. Serve it after a football game, at a Sunday-night supper, or as a midnight snack. Its rich aroma, its wonderful flavor and savor, have made French onion soup a world favorite. Here are directions for brewing your own, and for giving your personal touches to canned and dehydrated onion soups.

SOUPE A L'OIGNON, MAISON
(*Homemade French Onion Soup*)
For 6 to 8 servings

Onion soup is simply a large quantity of sliced onions slowly cooked and browned in butter, then simmered in beef bouillon. To achieve the true homemade taste, you'll need a homemade bouillon—beef bones and shank meat simmered for several hours with the usual carrots, onions, celery, seasonings, and herbs. If your own bouillon is lacking, substitute canned beef bouillon.

A heavy 4-quart saucepan or casserole
3 Tb butter
1 Tb olive oil or cooking oil
About 1½ lbs. or 5 to 6 cups thinly sliced yellow onions
1 tsp salt
½ tsp sugar

3 Tb flour
2 quarts hot beef bouillon (you may dilute canned bouillon with 2 cups of water)
1 cup red or white wine
1 bay leaf
½ tsp sage
Salt and pepper to taste

Melt the butter with the oil in the saucepan or casserole; add the sliced onions and stir up to coat with the butter. Cover the pan and cook over moderately low heat for 15 to 20 minutes, stirring occasionally, until onions are tender and translucent. Then uncover the pan, raise heat to moderately high, and stir in the salt and sugar. (Sugar, by caramelizing, helps onions to brown.) Cook for about 30 minutes, stirring frequently, until onions have turned an even deep golden brown.

Then lower heat to moderate, stir in the flour, and add a bit more butter if flour does not absorb into a paste with the onions. Cook slowly, stirring continually, for about 2 minutes to brown the flour lightly. Remove from heat.

Pour in about a cup of the hot bouillon, stirring with a wire whip to blend flour and bouillon. Add the rest of the bouillon and the wine, bay, and sage, and bring to the simmer. Simmer slowly for 30 to 40 minutes, season to taste with salt and pepper, and the soup is done. If you are not serving immediately, let cool uncovered, then cover and refrigerate.

Serve with French bread and grated Parmesan cheese, or bake with cheese as follows.

VARIATIONS ⮞

Soupe à l'Oignon Gratinée
(Onion Soup Gratinéed with Cheese)

This turns onion soup into a hearty main course; all you need to complete the meal is a bottle of red wine, perhaps a green salad, and fresh fruit. You may prepare all the elements for this ahead of time, but once the soup is assembled in its casserole, you should proceed with the recipe or the bread may sink to the bottom of the dish. (*Note:* You will need a chewy homemade type of bread; the light flimsy kind usually disintegrates in the soup.)

A loaf of French bread	A peeled 2-inch raw onion
Olive oil or melted butter	A 2-ounce piece Swiss cheese
The preceding soup, brought to the simmer	1½ cups grated Swiss and Parmesan cheese, mixed
Optional: ¼ cup cognac	

Cut the bread into slices 1 inch thick, paint lightly with oil or butter, and arrange in one layer on a baking sheet. Place in middle level of a preheated 325-degree oven for 15 to 20 minutes until beginning to brown lightly; turn and brown lightly for 15 to 20 minutes on the other side. These are called *croûtes*.

Pour the hot soup into a serving casserole or baking dish. Pour in the optional cognac, grate in the onion, and shave the piece of cheese into fine slivers and strew over the soup. Place a closely packed layer of *croûtes* over the top of the soup and spread on the grated cheese, covering the *croûtes* completely. Sprinkle a tablespoon of oil or butter over the cheese, and set the soup in the middle level of a preheated 350-degree oven. Bake for about 30 minutes, or until soup is bubbling slowly and cheese has melted.

Meanwhile, heat your broiler to red hot; just before serving, run the soup under the hot broiler for a moment to brown the cheese lightly. Pass remaining *croûtes* in a bread tray along with the soup.

Your Own Dehydrated or Canned Onion Soup

Reconstitute the soup as directed on the package or can. Then add a cup of red or white wine, a bay leaf, and a half teaspoon of sage or thyme (for 7 to 8 cups of soup); simmer the soup for 20 minutes. If consistency seems too thin, you can thicken it by creaming a tablespoon or two of flour and butter together in a small bowl, beating in a bit of hot soup, then pouring this back into the soup and simmering for a few minutes. Serve the soup as is, or substitute it for the homemade soup in the preceding recipe.

The Ninety-eighth Show

HOLLANDAISE AND BÉARNAISE
ⅇ⅊ · ⅊ⅇ

That buttery, lemony ambrosia known as *hollandaise* is the most famous in all the French sauce repertoire. It is also the most dreaded, as it can refuse to thicken; it can curdle; it can scramble. These dismal phenomena occur because one is dealing with egg yolks. Balky and recalcitrant when abused, egg yolks are graciously amenable when treated with tender understanding, for *hollandaise* is nothing but egg yolks and lemon warmed into a cream into which butter is beaten. You will never have trouble with egg yolks and *hollandaise* if you always keep the following in mind:

HEAT. Egg yolks will thicken into a smooth cream if you warm them gently and gradually. Too sudden heat turns them granular; too much heat scrambles them. Granular or scrambled yolks cannot absorb butter and turn into a sauce.

BUTTER PROPORTIONS. Egg yolks will readily absorb butter when it is fed to them slowly, giving them time to digest each addition before another is presented. But egg yolks will only absorb a certain amount of butter—3 ounces or ¾ stick per yolk; if you go beyond this proportion, the yolk's absorption powers break down and the sauce thins out.

HAND-MADE HOLLANDAISE SAUCE
For 1 to 1½ cups serving 4 to 6 people

A 6-cup medium-weight stainless-steel or enameled saucepan

A wire whip
A pan of cold water (to cool yolks)

A wet pot holder (to steady
pan while beating in the
butter)
3 egg yolks
1 Tb lemon juice
1 Tb water

¼ tsp salt
Pinch of white pepper
1 Tb cold butter
1½ to 2 sticks (6 to 8
ounces) softened or
melted butter

Your first step: always to beat the egg yolks in the saucepan with a wire whip for a minute or two, to thicken them slightly and prepare them for what is to come. Then beat in the lemon juice, water, salt, and pepper; continue beating for a moment. Add the tablespoon of cold butter; this will melt slowly as you heat the egg yolks, and provide a little anti-scramble insurance.

Finally place saucepan over low heat and stir the egg yolks at moderate speed with your wire whip, removing pan from heat now and then to be sure egg yolks are not cooking too fast. If they seem to be lumping at all, plunge bottom of pan in cold water, beating to cool them. Then continue beating over heat. The yolks are beginning to cream as soon as you notice a steamy vapor rising from the pan; in a few seconds they should be thick enough so you can see the bottom of the pan between strokes. When they form a creamy layer over the wires of the whip, they are done; you are ready to beat in the butter.

Immediately remove pan from heat and, beating continually, start adding the butter by quarter teaspoons or driblets at first, beating sauce to absorb each addition before you add the next. When sauce thickens into a heavy cream, you may beat in the butter by half tablespoons. Correct seasoning, and the sauce is ready to serve.

KEEPING THE SAUCE WARM

Hollandaise is served warm, not hot; if kept too warm, it will thin out or curdle. When made ahead, set pan over faint heat on top of stove, over a pilot light or near a burner. Or set in a pan of lukewarm water. Or use the minimum amount of butter; just before serving, heat the rest of the butter to bubbling, and beat it by driblets into the sauce.

REMEDY FOR THINNED, CURDLED, OR SEPARATED SAUCE. If you have beaten in your butter too quickly and the sauce thins or curdles, or if completed sauce separates, it is easily remedied. Put a teaspoon of lemon juice and a teaspoon of sauce in a mixing bowl, beat with a wire whip until sauce smooths into a cream. Then beat in the rest of the sauce half a tablespoon at a time, beating until each addition has creamed in the sauce before adding more.

ELECTRIC-BLENDER HOLLANDAISE SAUCE
For about ¾ cup serving 4 people

3 egg yolks
2 Tb lemon juice
¼ tsp salt
Pinch of white pepper

1 stick (4 ounces) butter, heated to bubbling hot in a small pan

Place egg yolks, lemon juice, salt, and pepper in jar of blender. Cover and blend at high speed for 30 seconds. Uncover, and still blending at high speed, start pouring in the hot butter by droplets. The heat of the butter warms the egg yolks, and by pouring very slowly you are giving the yolks time to absorb the butter. When about two thirds of the butter has gone in, sauce should be a thick cream and you can pour a little more quickly.

FOR MORE SAUCE

You cannot add more butter to the blender as the machine clogs after 1 stick has gone in, but the 3 egg yolks are capable of absorbing 1 stick more. To do this, scrape sauce out of blender jar into a bowl, and beat up to 1 stick more melted butter into sauce with a wire whip.

DISASTER REMEDIES.   If the sauce refuses to thicken, or if completed sauce curdles, remove it from the blender jar. Then, blending at high speed, pour it back in again by driblets. Or use the remedy suggested for hand-made *hollandaise*.

SAUCE BÉARNAISE

For about 1 cup

¼ cup wine vinegar
¼ cup dry white wine or
  vermouth
1 Tb minced shallots or
  scallions
½ tsp dried tarragon

¼ tsp salt
⅛ tsp pepper
3 egg yolks
1 to 1½ sticks (4 to 6
  ounces) butter

Boil the vinegar, wine and herbs, and seasonings in a small saucepan until liquid has reduced to about 2 tablespoons. Let cool, then proceed as for *hollandaise* sauce, making the *béarnaise* either by hand or in the blender; the vinegar mixture takes the place of the lemon flavoring. *Béarnaise* usually has less butter than *hollandaise*, but you may add ½ stick more if you wish.

SERVE HOLLANDAISE SAUCE WITH Asparagus, cauliflower, broccoli, boiled fish, egg dishes.

SERVE BÉARNAISE SAUCE WITH Steaks, broiled fish, broiled chicken, egg dishes.

The Ninety-ninth Show

CHICKEN EN COCOTTE

୶ঌ · ঌ౿

(*Casserole-roasted Chicken*)

Whole chicken roasted in a covered casserole, in a buttery steam of herbs and aromatic vegetables, has a very special tenderness and flavor. Hot, served simply with the juices it has produced in its casserole, or cold on the buffet table or picnic, *poulet en cocotte* is one of the great French contributions to the art of chicken cookery. Except for the browning of the chicken on top of the stove before roasting, which is for the sake of appearances, this is a practically effortless cooking method.

CHICKEN TALK AND ROASTING TIMETABLE. Broilers are too young for casserole roasting; they tend to break apart. Roasters and large capons are best, but you can use large fryers. Any roasting time table is only an estimate, and larger chickens require fewer cooking minutes per pound than smaller chickens. A useful guide to follow is: a basic 45 minutes for any size of chicken, plus 7 minutes for each pound. Thus a 1-pound oven-ready chicken requires 45 minutes plus 7, and a 5-pound bird requires 45 minutes plus 35. This is for unchilled, unstuffed chickens; add about 10 minutes to the total estimate for chilled chicken, and 15 to 20 to the total for stuffed chicken.

HOW TO TELL WHEN A CHICKEN IS DONE. A chicken is done when the flesh is cooked through so that its juices, when the meat is pricked deeply with a fork, run clear yellow with no trace of rosy color; prick the chicken at the fattest part of the drumstick. Another indication is that the drumsticks move easily in their sockets; their flesh is tender when pressed. Finally when the chicken is drained, the last juices from the vent run clear yellow with no rosy traces.

STUFFINGS. More often than not, the French roast their chickens with a simple flavoring in the cavity, no stuffing.

POULET EN COCOTTE
(Whole Chicken Roasted in a Casserole)
For 4 to 6 people

PREPARING THE CHICKEN FOR BROWNING

A 4½- to 5-lb. oven-ready
roasting chicken with
giblets
½ tsp salt

½ tsp dried tarragon or 3
or 4 sprigs of fresh
tarragon

3 Tb celery tops	and carrots, previously
3 Tb each of minced onions	cooked in 1 Tb butter
	2 Tb softened butter

Remove giblet package and all excess fat from chicken cavity. Look over chicken and remove any hairs, feather follicles, and feathers. Cut the protruding knobs off each elbow and, if you wish easier carving, remove the wishbone. Skewer, tie, or truss the wings and neck skin to the body. Sprinkle salt and tarragon in the cavity, add the vegetables and 1 tablespoon of the butter. Tuck the liver into the cavity if you wish; it will cook, and can be served along with the chicken. Skewer, tie, or truss the drumsticks and tail piece together, to close the ventral cavity. Dry the chicken thoroughly, and massage the skin with the remaining tablespoon of butter.

BROWNING THE CHICKEN

A large skillet	¼ cup each of sliced onions,
Olive oil or cooking oil	celery stalk, and carrots
A heavy flameproof casserole	The chicken giblets
just large enough to hold	½ tsp coarse salt or regular
chicken comfortably	salt
3 Tb softened butter	1 tsp dried tarragon or 3 or
	4 sprigs of fresh tarragon

(Preheat oven to 325 degrees for next step.)

Film skillet with a ¹⁄₁₆-inch layer of oil and set over moderately high heat until oil is almost smoking. Then lay in the chicken, breast down, and brown for a minute or two; turn the chicken on its side and brown, and continue turning until chicken is a nice golden color almost all over, particularly on the breast and legs. Use 2 rubber spatulas or a towel, if necessary, for turning, so as not to break the chicken skin. This will take about 10 minutes. While you are browning, cook the vegetables as follows:

To the casserole add 2 tablespoons of the butter, melt over moderate heat, and stir in the vegetables and giblets. Cover and cook slowly until vegetables are tender.

When chicken is browned, spread vegetables and giblets to

the sides of the casserole, and put in the chicken, breast up. Spread remaining tablespoon of butter over the chicken, and sprinkle with the salt. Strew the tarragon over the vegetables and giblets.

(You may brown the chicken, let it cool uncovered, then cover and refrigerate. Heat casserole on top of stove before proceeding.)

ROASTING THE CHICKEN

Place a piece of aluminum foil or buttered brown paper over the chicken, place a heavy cover on the casserole, and set in lower third of preheated oven. Regulate heat so chicken is making quiet cooking noises in casserole throughout the cooking; chicken should be done in about 1 hour and 20 to 30 minutes. If you are not serving immediately, set cover askew and leave casserole in turned-off oven, or in warming oven at 140 degrees; chicken can be kept warm for 30 to 40 minutes.

SAUCE AND SERVING

¼ cup port

When you are ready to serve, remove chicken from casserole. Remove vegetables and giblets with a slotted spoon, and skim fat off cooking juices. If you wish, pour in about ¼ cup port wine and boil for a few minutes until juices are lightly syrupy. If chicken is carved in the kitchen and arranged on a platter, pour the juices over the chicken. If carving is at the table, pass juices in a hot gravy bowl.

SUGGESTED ACCOMPANIMENTS

Stuffed mushrooms, glazed carrots, and onions; or scalloped potatoes and green peas or beans; or broiled tomatoes, buttered beans or peas, and sautéed potatoes; or *ratatouille* (eggplant casserole) and sautéed potatoes; and hot French bread and a light red wine, such as a Bordeaux.

The Hundredth Show

QUEEN OF SHEBA—REINE DE SABA
~§·§~
(Chocolate, Rum, and Almond Cake)

This is a very special cake of rum, almonds, butter, and chocolate; it is somewhat moist in the center, and literally melts in the mouth. Like most French cakes, this one is only an inch and a half high, which makes it easy to cut, serve, and eat. The Queen of Sheba is a dessert in itself, or can be the main attraction at a tea, coffee, or champagne party.

You will note that as usual the batter contains no baking powder: the cake rises because of its beaten egg whites. These must be whipped until they form peaks but are not dry and grainy, and they must be folded into the batter so swiftly and delicately that they retain their airy volume. Another important key to success is the melted chocolate. This must be smooth and softly liquid; if it is stiff and granular it will harden the batter and make folding the egg whites so difficult that they will deflate. Finally, you must watch the baking: several minutes too long in the oven and the cake will be dry rather than moist, and lose its special character.

REINE DE SABA
(Chocolate, Rum, and Almond Cake)
For an 8-inch cake serving 6 to 8 people

PRELIMINARIES

A round one-piece cake pan 8 inches in diameter and 1½ inches deep	½ tsp softened butter 3 Tb flour

⅔ cup semisweet chocolate
  morsels or 4 ounces (4
  squares) semisweet bak-
  ing chocolate broken into
  small pieces

2 Tb dark rum, or 1 Tb
  instant coffee dissolved in
  2 Tb boiling water

(Preheat oven to 350 degrees.)

Set rack in middle level of oven. (If you are not sure of your thermostat, check temperature with an oven thermometer.) Prepare the pan for the cake by rubbing inside of pan with softened butter, then roll the flour around so that entire bottom and sides are covered with a thin layer; knock out excess flour.

To melt the chocolate, place it with the rum or coffee in a small lightweight saucepan. Fill another and slightly larger saucepan with water; bring to the simmer and remove from heat. Set the chocolate pan in the hot water and stir with a rubber spatula until chocolate begins to melt, then set aside; it will be almost melted and smooth when you return to it later.

Measure out all the rest of the ingredients listed in the next step before you start preparing the batter.

THE CAKE BATTER

A 2½-quart mixing bowl
  with a wooden spoon, or
  an electric mixer and its
  large bowl
1 stick (4 ounces) unsalted
  butter, soft if possible
⅔ cup granulated sugar
3 eggs (U. S. graded
  "large"), separated
A scant ¼ tsp cream of
  tartar
Pinch of salt

2 Tb granulated sugar
⅓ cup pulverized blanched
  almonds (skinless al-
  monds put through a
  cheese grater or electric
  blender)
¼ tsp almond extract
¾ cup plain bleached cake
  flour (measure by sifting
  directly into ½- and ¼-
  cup measures, and sweeping off excess flour)

Either by hand or in your electric mixer, cream the butter and sugar together until soft and fluffy. Beat in the yolks of the 3 eggs.

You may prepare the batter in advance to this point, beating before you proceed, so mixture is again soft and fluffy. From now on, you must complete the batter and get the cake into the oven; this is so that the batter will remain soft enough for easy folding in of the beaten egg whites.

To whip the whites of the 3 eggs, place them in a very clean dry beating bowl and with a very clean dry beater start whipping them at low speed for a moment or two until the egg whites begin to foam. Then add the cream of tartar and salt, and gradually increase beating speed to fast. As soon as the egg whites hold their shape in a soft mass, beat in the two spoonfuls of sugar and continue beating for a moment. The egg whites are done when you can lift a bit in a rubber spatula and they hold their shape, dropping off into a little point with curling tip. The texture should be smooth and shiny: do not overbeat. Set aside.

Stir up the chocolate, to make a perfectly smooth soft cream. (You may have to reheat the water, if chocolate has cooled too much; if by any chance it has turned granular, beat in a few drops of warm water.) Stir the chocolate into the butter, sugar, and yolk mixture. Stir in the almonds, almond extract, and flour.

With a rubber spatula, stir in one fourth of the beaten egg whites to soften the batter, then scoop the rest of the egg whites on top of the batter. Still using a rubber spatula, rapidly and delicately fold the egg whites in by cutting straight down through them to the bottom of the bowl, drawing scraper quickly toward you against edge of bowl, turning, and lifting it out; you thus bring a bit of the batter up over the egg whites each time. Continue rapidly, revolving the bowl as you go, until egg whites and batter are blended. The whole process should not take more than a minute.

Turn the batter into the prepared cake pan, tilting pan in all directions to run batter up to rim of pan so cake will bake evenly and not hump in the center.

BAKING

(Oven has been preheated to 350 degrees.)

Set cake in middle level of preheated oven and bake for about 25 minutes. Cake is done when it has puffed to top of pan, and 2½ to 3 inches around the circumference are set so that a toothpick plunged into that area comes out clean. The center should move slightly when pan is shaken. If not quite done, bake a few minutes more. Then remove from oven and cool in pan for 10 minutes. Run a knife around the edge of the pan, turn a rack upside down over cake, and reverse the two to unmold cake on rack. Remove pan, and let cake cool for 2 hours before icing. (Cooled cake may be wrapped and frozen.)

Glaçage au Chocolat
(Chocolate-Butter Icing)
For an 8-inch cake

½ cup semisweet chocolate morsels or 3 ounces (3 squares) semisweet baking chocolate

1½ Tb dark rum or strong coffee
6 Tb softened unsalted butter

Melt the chocolate in the rum or coffee. A tablespoon at a time, beat in the butter, beating until perfectly smooth. Then beat over cold water, if necessary, until icing is of spreading consistency.

Ice the cake, and decorate with blanched or slivered almonds. (Cake may be frozen: refrigerate first, to set icing, then wrap and freeze.)

The Hundred and First Show

TO POACH SOLE FILLETS
⋖৯ • ৯⋗
(Sole in White Wine)

The French are marvelous with fillets of sole. Delicately cooked, served in velvety sauces, and titled with fanciful names such as *andalouse, bonne femme, normande, mornay*, these beautiful dishes seem beyond the reach of mortal cooks. Happily for us all, however, they each stem from one recipe, fish fillets poached in white wine, and from one sauce, that ubiquitous old friend, the *velouté*. The names of the various sole dishes change according to the decorations or garnitures accompanying them. *Sole andalouse* is sole poached in wine with peppers and tomatoes; *sole bonne femme* has mushrooms; *normande* includes oysters; *mornay*, cheese; and so forth. Thus when you have made any one of these dishes, you can make all of them.

FISH TALK. Choose lean-fish fillets, such as sole, flounder, dab, whiting, ocean perch, pollack, baby halibut, or freshwater trout. Whether fresh or frozen, be sure the fish smells fresh and appetizing. Before cooking frozen fish, defrost it in a basin of cold water.

FISH STOCK. The beautiful flavor of French fish sauces is due in large part to their having been made with fish stock, which is simply the boiling up of the fish bones and trimmings with aromatic vegetables, herbs, and water. The stock is then used for poaching the fish, and the poaching liquid is turned into a sauce. If fish trimmings are not available, buy a little extra fish, substitute clam juice as indicated in the following recipe, or just do without.

Simple Fish Stock
For about 2 cups

4 to 6 cups trimmings from
the fish fillets (heads,
bones, skin), or 1 to 2
cups lean fish, or 1½ cups
bottled clam juice
⅓ cup thinly sliced onions
¼ cup thinly sliced carrots
Optional: ⅓ cup chopped
mushroom stems

½ bay leaf
6 to 8 parsley stems
¼ tsp salt (no salt if you are
using clam juice)
An enameled or stainless-
steel saucepan
Water

Place all ingredients in the saucepan. If you are using fish trimmings, add enough water to cover ingredients; add 3 cups water if you are using fish; 1 cup water if you are using clam juice. Simmer uncovered for 30 minutes, letting liquid boil down to about 2 cups. Strain through a fine-meshed sieve, and correct seasoning. (Fish stock may be refrigerated for a day, or frozen for several weeks.)

FILETS DE POISSONS POCHÉS AU VIN BLANC
(Fish Fillets Poached in White Wine)
For 6 people as a main course

1½ Tb softened butter
A flameproof baking-serving
dish about 12 inches long
and 1½ inches deep
2 Tb finely minced
shallots or scallions
2½ lbs. lean fish fillets, one

of the types mentioned in
the introductory remarks
Salt and white pepper
⅔ cup dry white vermouth
or dry white wine
Cool fish stock or water

(Preheat oven to 350 degrees.)

Smear half the butter in the dish and sprinkle in half the shallots or onions. Dry the fish fillets on paper towels. Lightly score (draw a sharp knife across, barely cutting flesh) the milky side of the fillets, which lay next to the skin; this is to keep fillets from curling. Sprinkle lightly on both sides with salt and white pepper. If fillets are thin, less than ¼ inch, fold them in half end to end. Arrange fillets, slightly overlapping, in one layer in the baking dish. Sprinkle on the remaining shallots or scallions. Pour in the wine, enough fish stock or water almost to cover the fish, and distribute the remaining butter over the top. Cut or tear a piece of waxed paper to the size of the baking dish and lay it over the fish. (Refrigerate if fish is not to be poached at this point.)

POACHING THE FISH

Set baking dish on top of the stove over moderate heat, using a flame tamer if necessary. Bring barely to the simmer— water is barely bubbling. Then place dish on bottom rack of preheated oven for 8 to 10 minutes. The fish is done when it has turned milky white and it slightly resilient rather than squashy when you press it with your finger. Do not overcook; the fish should not be dry and flaky.

Place a cover over the dish and drain out all the cooking liquid into an enameled or stainless-steel saucepan. Fish is now ready for saucing; it may be covered and kept warm for a few minutes over hot but not simmering water. Or set it aside, covered with its piece of paper, and reheat later for a few minutes over simmering water. Before saucing the fish, drain off any liquid which may have accumulated in the dish.

Sauce Velouté
(Basic White-wine Fish Sauce)
For about 2 cups

The fish-poaching liquid	or stainless-steel sauce-
3 Tb butter	pan
A heavy-bottomed enameled	4 Tb flour
	About 1 cup milk

Rapidly boil down the fish-poaching liquid until it has reduced to about 1 cup. Meanwhile melt the butter, blend in the flour with a wooden spoon, and cook slowly until butter and flour have foamed together without coloring for 2 minutes. Remove from heat, pour in the hot fish-poaching liquid, and immediately blend vigorously with a wire whip. Set over moderate heat and bring to the simmer, stirring, and thinning out sauce with dollops of milk. Sauce should be thick enough to coat a spoon fairly heavily.

This is now *sauce velouté*; it may be enriched with cream, egg yolks, butter, truffle juices, or whatever your recipe may call for. In the following, it is turned into a *sauce Mornay*, with cheese and cream.

VARIATION ?❧

Filets de Poisson Mornay
(*Fish Fillets Gratinéed with Cheese*)
For 6 people as a main course

2 cups *sauce velouté*	About ½ cup grated Swiss
4 to 5 Tb heavy cream	cheese
Salt, white pepper, and	1 Tb butter
lemon juice	

(Preheat oven to 400 degrees.)

Bring the *sauce velouté* to the simmer; stir in the heavy cream. Taste carefully for seasoning, adding salt, white pepper, and drops of lemon juice as you feel them necessary. Remove from heat and stir in about ¼ cup grated Swiss cheese. Pour the sauce over the hot fish, spread 3 to 4 tablespoons grated cheese over top of sauce, and dot with a tablespoon of butter cut into bits. If you are serving immediately, run under a hot broiler for a moment to brown the top of the sauce lightly; or refrigerate, then set in upper third of a preheated oven for about 25 minutes, until bubbling hot and top has browned lightly.

Serve with chopped buttered spinach, boiled potatoes, French bread, and a full-bodied dry white wine such as Graves, Burgundy, or Traminer.

The Hundred and Second Show

CHOP DINNER FOR FOUR
IN HALF AN HOUR

◀§ · ℥▶

Here is another menu to add to your repertoire of little three-course dinners which can be assembled and cooked in about half an hour.

MENU:

Consommé Madrilène
Casserole of Veal or Pork Chops with Vegetables
Red Médoc or Rosé Wine
Chocolate Pots de Crème

While the main course is cooking, fix the rest of the menu. If you are doing everything in advance, the soup and dessert may be chilled, otherwise you will serve them hot. Start in with the chops, as they take the longest to cook.

1) Côtelettes à la Nivernaise
(*Casserole of Veal or Pork Chops Baked with Carrots,
Potatoes, and Artichoke Hearts*)

BROWNING THE CHOPS

A heavy fireproof casserole
or an electric skillet about
12 inches in diameter

Cooking oil
4 veal or pork loin chops
about 1¼ inches thick

Film the casserole or skillet with ¹⁄₁₆ inch of cooking oil and heat until almost smoking. Dry chops on paper towels, and brown for 2 or 3 minutes on each side. Meanwhile, prepare the vegetables as follows:

THE VEGETABLE GARNISH

4 to 5 large carrots	A large saucepan with boil-
4 to 6 large "boiling"	ing salted water
potatoes	Useful: a wire salad basket
1 package frozen artichoke	or a vegetable steamer
hearts	

Peel the carrots and potatoes, and cut them into quarters about 2½ inches long; round the edges to make rough olive shapes if you have time. Drop them into boiling water and bring rapidly back to the boil for 2 minutes; drain. Then, if artichoke hearts are solidly frozen, drop them also into the boiling water for a moment so they will come apart. Drain.

FINAL COOKING

Salt and pepper	¼ cup chopped shallots or
½ tsp dried thyme, tar-	scallions
ragon, or herb mixture	1 to 2 Tb softened butter

(Preheat oven to 325 degrees.)

When the chops are browned, remove them to a side dish leaving fat in pan. Add the drained carrots and potatoes and toss in the fat for a minute or two to dry them off so they will not stick to the pan later. Drain out fat. Push vegetables to sides of pan, return chops to pan, and season with salt, pepper, and herbs. Strew the shallots or scallions on top. Dot with the butter. Cover pan and cook over moderately low heat or in the lower third of preheated oven for about 20 minutes, basting meat and vegetables with the juices in the pan 2 or 3 times during cooking. Add artichoke hearts the last 10 minutes of cooking, salting lightly and basting with pan juices. The chops are done when meat juices run clear yellow if meat is pricked with a fork. Do not overcook. (If you wish to bake the dish in advance of serving, remove from heat when almost done and let cool uncovered. Then refrigerate and complete the cooking later.)

Serve from the casserole or skillet, or arrange on a hot platter and pour the cooking juices over the chops and vegetables.

2) *Petits Pots de Crème au Chocolat*
(*Chocolate Cream Custards*)

⅔ cup semisweet chocolate
   bits or 4 ounces (4
   squares) semisweet baking chocolate
About 1 cup all-purpose or
   medium cream
Optional: 2 to 3 Tb sugar

1 whole egg plus 2 egg yolks
   (U. S. graded "large")
1½ Tb dark Jamaican rum
4 ramekins or chocolate pots,
   ½-cup capacity
A baking dish to hold them

(Preheat oven to 350 degrees.)

Place chocolate in a quart measure and add enough cream to come to the 1½-cup mark. Pour into a saucepan and set over low heat, stirring occasionally until chocolate has melted completely. Stir in sugar to taste. Blend egg and yolks in a bowl just enough to mix them; stirring the eggs, gradually pour on the hot chocolate mixture in a thin stream. Stir in the rum, then strain through a fine-meshed sieve back into the quart measure. Remove all foam with a spoon: foam will make holes in top of custards.

Pour into the ramekins, and again remove all foam and bubbles. Set ramekins in baking dish and add boiling water to two thirds the height of the ramekins. Cover baking dish loosely with aluminum foil, to prevent tops of custards from crusting.

Bake in lower third of preheated oven for about 20 minutes, regulating heat so that water in baking dish never quite simmers. Timing and temperature are important here, as too much heat makes custard granular and too long cooking makes it separate when it cools. Custards are done when they have puffed into a slight dome but still tremble gently.

Serve hot, warm, or chilled, with lightly sweetened whipped cream. (You may form whipped cream into fancy shapes with a pastry bag on waxed paper, and freeze; these decorations are then available any time you need them.)

3) Consommé Madrilène
(Consommé with Fresh Tomato and Herbs)

About 1½ cups excellent beef consommé, fresh or canned	2 Tb finely chopped parsley or a mixture of fresh herbs, such as parsley,
2 large, ripe, firm tomatoes	tarragon, chives
Salt and pepper	2 to 3 Tb port wine

Bring the consommé to the simmer in a saucepan. Drop the tomatoes into boiling water and leave for 10 seconds. Remove stem and peel and add to consommé; halve the tomatoes and gently squeeze seeds and juice into consommé. Mince the pulp very fine and set aside. After it has simmered 5 minutes, strain the consommé into another saucepan and add the minced tomato pulp. Heat for a moment or two without simmering, to cook the tomato pulp. Add salt and pepper to taste, stir in the herbs and wine.

Serve hot with Melba toast or crackers, or chill.

The Hundred and Third Show

FILET OF BEEF WELLINGTON

FILET OF BEEF WELLINGTON
(Whole Tenderloin of Beef Baked in Pastry)
For 8 people

Take a tenderloin of beef, marinate it in herbs and wine, cover it with a rich cloak of mushrooms, bake it in decorated pastry, and you have *filet* of beef Wellington. This is a splendid dish when you want to make a vast impression on your guests, and if you have prepared all the various elements a day ahead of time the assembling and cooking are easy indeed.

THE BEEF

Order a whole loin tenderloin (*filet*) of beef. Have the out-side membrane and all excess fat removed, but have the suet (fat covering) saved. Have the tail or small end turned back over the meat to make an even cylinder about 12 inches long, and have the meat tied at 1-inch intervals around the circumference.

OPTIONAL MARINADE   Although the tenderloin is the most ex-pensive part of the beef, it has the least flavor. A 24-hour mari-nade will give it more character, and you can use the marinade again, for making the sauce.

⅓ cup light olive oil or   3 allspice berries or cloves
  cooking oil   6 peppercorns
A small heavy saucepan   An oval casserole or baking
½ cup each of sliced onions,   dish 12 inches long
  carrots, and celery stalks 1 tsp salt
¼ tsp each of dried thyme   1 cup dry white vermouth
  and sage   ⅓ cup cognac
1 bay leaf

Place the oil in the saucepan and add the vegetables and herbs; cover the pan and cook slowly until vegetables are tender —about 10 minutes. Place the tenderloin in casserole or baking dish, sprinkle with salt, cover with the cooked vegetable mixture, and pour on the wine and cognac. Cover and refrigerate. Turn and baste the meat every several hours for at least 24 hours. Just before the next step, scrape off marinade and dry meat in paper towels.

PRELIMINARY BAKING

Before it is cooked in pastry, the tenderloin has a preliminary baking to stiffen it, so it will hold its shape in the crust.

1 Tb cooking oil   Suet or oil
A shallow roasting pan

(Preheat oven to 425 degrees.)
Rub the meat with the oil and place in roasting pan. If you

have saved the suet, place it over the beef to protect and baste it during roasting. (Lacking suet, you will have to baste the meat with oil every 5 minutes during roasting.) Set in upper third of oven and roast for 25 minutes, turning and basting the meat once with the fat in the pan. Remove from oven and let cool for 30 minutes or longer. If you are doing this ahead of time, wrap and refrigerate the meat when it is cold; bring to room temperature before final cooking.

THE MUSHROOM FLAVORING

This is a mushroom *duxelles* with wine and *foie gras*, which bakes around the meat.

2 lbs. mushrooms	½ cup dry Sercial Madeira
2 Tb butter	Salt and pepper
4 Tb minced shallots or scallions	4 to 5 Tb *mousse de foie* or *foie gras*

Trim, wash, and dry the mushrooms; chop them into small pieces less than ⅛ inch in size. You will have about 6 cups of minced mushrooms; so that they will cook dry, which is necessary for this recipe, twist them, a handful at a time, in the corner of a towel to extract as much juice as possible. Save juice for the sauce. Then sauté the mushrooms for 7 to 8 minutes in the butter with the shallots or scallions; when mushroom pieces begin to separate from each other, add the Madeira and boil rapidly until liquid has evaporated. Season to taste with salt and pepper, and beat in the *mousse de foie* or *foie gras*. Refrigerate in a covered bowl; beat to soften just before using.

THE PASTRY

The beef is baked and served *en croûte* or in a pie-crust dough. Use the following proportions:

3 cups all-purpose flour (scoop cup into bag, level off with straight-edged knife)	1¾ sticks (7 ounces) chilled butter
	4 Tb chilled shortening
	2 tsp salt
	¾ cup iced water

Blend together all the ingredients listed and chill for 2 hours before using. So that the crust will be crisp when served, it is done in two parts: a cooked bottom case to hold the beef, and a flaky dough topping.

THE BOTTOM PASTRY CASE Butter the outside of a loaf-shaped tin approximately 12 by 3¼ inches bottom diameter, and 3 inches deep. Roll about three fifths of the chilled pastry into a rectangle 16 by 7 inches, and ⅛ inch thick. Lay pastry on upside-down tin, press in place, and trim so pastry forms a case 1½ inches deep. With the tines of a table fork prick sides and bottom of dough at ¼-inch intervals to keep it from puffing in the oven, and chill at least half an hour to relax the dough. Bake until very lightly browned in middle level of a preheated 425-degree oven for 12 to 15 minutes. Let cool 10 minutes on tin, then unmold. (Case may be refrigerated or frozen.)

THE PASTRY TOPPING Roll remaining dough into a 16x7-inch rectangle, spread bottom half with 1½ tablespoons cold but soft butter and fold in half to enclose butter. Repeat with another 1½ tablespoons butter. Roll again into a rectangle and fold in thirds, as though folding a business letter. This is now mock puff pastry, with layers of butter between layers of dough; it will be light and flaky when baked. Chill for 2 hours, then roll into a 16x10-inch rectangle. Cut a 3-inch strip from the long end and reserve for decorations; lay large rectangle flat on a baking sheet lined with waxed paper; cover with waxed paper and a damp towel, and refrigerate.

THE DECORATIONS Cut strips, circles, diamonds, or leaf shapes from the 3-inch strip and chill with the pastry topping.

ASSEMBLING AND BAKING THE BEEF WELLINGTON

The beef takes about 45 minutes to bake, and should rest for 20 minutes before carving and serving. It is assembled just before baking.

ASSEMBLING Place the baked pastry case on a baking and serving platter or a buttered baking sheet and spread half of the mushroom mixture in the bottom of the case. Remove trussing strings and set the beef in the case, covering the meat with the remaining mushrooms. Paint sides of case with egg glaze (1 egg beaten with ½ teaspoon water), lay pastry topping over meat allowing edges to fall down about 1 inch on sides of case; press pastry onto sides of case. Paint pastry topping with glaze, affix decorations, and paint again with glaze. Make cross-hatch markings over glaze with a knife, to give texture to the glaze when baked. Make three ⅛-inch vent holes centered about 3 inches apart in top of pastry and insert paper or foil funnels for escaping steam. Plunge a meat thermometer through central hole and into center of meat.

BAKING   Bake for 20 to 25 minutes in middle level of a preheated 425-degree oven or until pastry has started to brown. Then lower thermostat to 375 degrees and bake 20 to 25 minutes more, or to a meat thermometer reading of 137 degrees for rare beef. Let rest at a temperature of not more than 120 degrees for at least 20 minutes before serving, so juices will retreat back into meat tissues before carving. (To serve, carve as though cutting a sausage into 1½-inch slices. Pastry will crumble slightly as you carve the beef; a very sharp serrated knife will minimize this.)

SAUCE SUGGESTIONS

SAUCE MADÈRE.   Simmer marinade ingredients and mushroom juices with 2 cups beef bouillon and 1 tablespoon tomato paste for 1 hour; when reduced to 2 cups, strain, degrease, season, and thicken with 2 tablespoons of cornstarch beaten with ¼ cup of Madeira.

SAUCE PÉRIGUEUX.   Simmer 1 or 2 minced canned truffles and their juice for a moment in the *sauce madère.*

SAUCE COLBERT.   Just before serving, beat 1 cup of *sauce béarnaise* gradually into 2 cups of *sauce madère.*

VEGETABLE AND WINE SUGGESTIONS

Accompany Beef Wellington with braised lettuce, endive, or celery and broiled tomatoes, or a vegetable salad, and an excellent red Bordeaux-Médoc or Graves.

The Hundred and Fourth Show

APPLE CHARLOTTE

CHARLOTTE AUX POMMES

(*Molded Apple Dessert*)

For 6 to 8 people

This extremely good dessert is a thick rum-and-apricot-flavored marmalade of apples piled into a cylindrical baking dish which has been lined with butter-soaked strips of white bread. It is baked in a hot oven until the bread is golden brown, and is then unmolded. For the sake of drama, choose a baking dish 3½ to 4 inches deep, and be sure your apple mixture is very thick indeed or the dessert will not hold its shape when unmolded.

FOR THE APPLE MARMALADE

About 8 lbs. firm eating or cooking apples
A heavy-bottomed enameled pan about 12 inches in diameter and at least 5 inches deep
½ cup apricot jam forced through a sieve
About 1 cup granulated sugar
2 tsp vanilla extract
¼ cup dark Jamaican rum
3 Tb butter

Quarter, peel, and core the apples; cut into rough ½-inch slices. You should have about 6 quarts. Place in pan, cover, and cook over low heat, stirring occasionally, for 20 minutes or until the apples are tender.

Uncover the pan and beat in the apricot jam, sugar, vanilla, rum, and butter. Raise heat and boil, stirring almost continuously for 15 to 20 minutes until the water content of the apples has evaporated and the apples have turned into a very thick marmalade which holds itself in a solid mass in the spoon. The success of this dish depends entirely on how compact a mass your apples have cooked down to. If the apples form a stiff paste, your charlotte will keep its shape nicely when unmolded, but you may find the eating consistency too firm. A softer apple mixture will spread out slightly after you unmold the dish. In any case, make a very thick paste the first time you try the dessert, so you will be sure of successful unmolding.

The apple marmalade may be cooked several days in advance and kept in a covered bowl in the refrigerator.

ASSEMBLING AND BAKING

12 to 14 slices of homemade-
   type white bread, 4 inches
   square and ¼ inch thick
A fireproof 6-cup cylindrical

baking dish 3½ to 4
inches deep
About 1 cup (½ lb.) melted
butter

(Preheat oven to 425 degrees.)

Remove crusts from bread. To line the bottom of the dish, arrange 4 pieces of bread in a square, with inside edges closely fitting. Place baking dish on top of square, centering it carefully. Cut bread around bottom of dish, to make 4 pie-shaped pieces. Cut a 1½- to 2-inch circle out of one of the bread scraps. Heat ⅛ inch of clear melted butter in a skillet and sauté the pie-shaped pieces of bread and the circle to a light golden brown on each side. Fit the pie-shaped pieces into the bottom of the dish; reserve the circle for final decoration later.

Cut the rest of the bread into strips about 1¼ inches wide. Dip in clear melted butter; fit them upright and slightly overlapping each other around the inner circumference of the dish.

Pack the apple marmalade into the dish, adding layers of butter-dipped bread, if you have any left over, and filling the dish so that it humps into a dome ¾ inch high in the center. Cover with 4 or 5 butter-dipped bread strips. Cut off any protruding bread ends, and pour remaining clear butter (do not add milky residue at bottom of pan) over the bread strips around the dish.

Place a large pie plate on the bottom rack of the preheated

oven to catch melted butter drippings, and set the charlotte on the rack just above. Bake for about 30 minutes; charlotte is done when you can slip a knife between bread and sides of dish and see that bread strips are nicely browned.

Remove from oven and let cool for 15 to 20 minutes. To unmold, run a knife between edge of dish and bread strips; turn a serving plate upside down over the charlotte and reverse onto the serving plate. Then lift baking dish up a few inches to be sure charlotte has set; if there is any suggestion of collapse, lower the dish again and wait 5 to 10 minutes more. Then remove the dish. (The charlotte may spread, and look more like a cone than a cylinder; this depends upon the stiffness of your initial apple mixture.)

FINAL DECORATION AND SERVING

½ cup apricot jam forced
    through a sieve
2 Tb granulated sugar
Optional: 3 Tb dark rum

Custard sauce, lightly
    whipped cream, or heavy
    cream

Boil the apricot jam, sugar, and optional rum in a small saucepan until mixture is thick and sticky. Paint it over the charlotte. Place the reserved sautéed bread circle on top, and paint with apricot.

Serve the charlotte warm or cold, accompanied with custard sauce (*crème anglaise*), whipped cream, or heavy cream.

The Hundred and Fifth Show

MORE GREAT BEGINNINGS
❧ • ☙
(Crab Appetizers)

There is nothing more appetizing than to start out a dinner with
an attractive little first course. It sets the stage, it turns an otherwise simple meal into a party, and it shows your guests that you
honor them. Shellfish is almost universally popular and has a
luxurious air; here are two ideas for crab, one hot and one cold.

CRAB TALK.   Both recipes use cooked crab, either fresh, frozen,
or canned. You can buy frozen crab in the shell, such as Alas-
kan crab legs, or frozen cooked crab meat in the package:
thaw just before using in a big basin of cold water, then rinse
meat well in cold water to remove the saline preservative usually present. Drain canned crab meat, rinse in cold water to remove preserving juices, and drain. Be sure to break up and pick
over your crab meat, and remove all bits of hard tendon and
shell.

PETITS GRATINS DE CRABE AU VIN BLANC
(Ramekins of Crab Meat in White-Wine Sauce)
For 4 people as a hot first course

PRELIMINARY FLAVORING

2 Tb butter
An 8-inch enameled or no-
  stick skillet
2 Tb minced shallots or
  scallions

Salt and pepper
½ lb. (about 1 packed cup)
  crab meat
¼ tsp dried tarragon
⅓ cup dry white vermouth

Melt the butter over moderate heat; stir in the minced shallots or scallions, and cook for a moment. Then stir in the crab; sprinkle lightly with salt and pepper, and the tarragon. Cook, stirring, for a minute or two, then pour in the wine. Raise heat and boil, stirring, until liquid has almost evaporated. Remove from heat.

SAUCE

1 Tb cornstarch	½ tsp tomato paste
A small mixing bowl	Salt, white pepper, and
About ¾ cup heavy cream	lemon juice as needed

Place cornstarch in mixing bowl and beat in 2 or 3 tablespoons of the cream to make a smooth paste. Gradually beat in 4 tablespoons more cream, and the tomato paste. Stir the mixture into the crab and set over moderate heat, stirring. Simmer, stirring, for 2 to 3 minutes to cook the starch. Crab mixture should be fairly thick; thin out, if necessary, with spoonfuls of cream. Taste carefully for seasoning, adding salt, pepper, and lemon juice if you feel them necessary.

ASSEMBLING, BAKING, AND SERVING

4 lightly buttered ramekins, shells, or other individual fireproof containers of about ½-cup capacity	2 Tb finely grated Swiss cheese About 1 Tb melted butter

Spoon the crab into the ramekins and sprinkle with grated cheese and melted butter. Refrigerate if not to be baked now.

To heat and brown the cheese, either set in upper third of a preheated 400-degree oven for about 15 minutes or under a moderately low broiler for 5 to 7 minutes. Serve with hot French bread and a moderately full, dry white wine, such as a Graves, Traminer, or Pouilly Fuissé.

MAYONNAISE DE CRABE

(*Cold Crab Appetizer*)
For 4 people as a first course

PRELIMINARY FLAVORING

½ lb. (1 packed cup) crab
meat
A mixing bowl
About ½ Tb lemon juice
2 Tb light olive oil
Salt and either white pepper
or Tabasco

1 Tb finely minced shallots
or scallions
2 to 3 Tb fresh minced
herbs, such as parsley, or
parsley and tarragon,
chervil, basil, or chives

Place the crab meat in mixing bowl. Season to taste with lemon juice, oil, salt, pepper or Tabasco, and herbs. Toss lightly and let stand at least 20 minutes (or several hours in the refrigerator) to absorb the flavor of the seasonings.

ASSEMBLING AND SERVING

About ½ cup mayonnaise
(homemade if possible)
Optional: cooked crab legs,

tomatoes, hard-boiled egg
slices, capers, anchovies,
parsley sprigs

Shortly before serving, drain the crab if there is more than a tablespoon of liquid in the bottom of the bowl. Toss with just enough mayonnaise to enrobe the crab. Taste again for seasoning.

Serve on individual plates lined with shredded lettuce, or in shells or ramekins. Top each serving with a spoonful of mayonnaise. Decorate with crab legs, tomatoes, hard-boiled egg slices, capers, anchovies, parsley sprigs, or other appropriate items.

Accompany with French bread and a fairly dry white wine, such as a Riesling or Chablis.

The Hundred and Sixth Show

ROAST SUCKLING PIG

From the apple in its mouth to its crackling brown skin, its wonderful aroma, and its promise of glory, nothing equals the drama of a roast suckling pig. But when you want to have one for a feast, be sure to put in your order well in advance. Specify a genuine, milk-fed suckling pig weighing, if possible, 12 pounds, 14 pounds maximum; heavier pigs, being older, have developed more fat, tougher skin, and may well be too big for your oven. A 12-pound pig measures about 20 inches from snout to tail and takes approximately 3 hours to roast; it will suit itself nicely to your schedule as you can make it ready for the oven the day before the banquet, and once it is roasted you may keep it warm for an hour or more before carving.

PRELIMINARIES. To prepare the pig for roasting, soak it for 2 to 3 hours in cold water with ¼ cup of vinegar and 2 tablespoons of salt per each 4 quarts. (If your pig is frozen, it will defrost at the same time.) Clean inside the ears, nostrils, and mouth, and scrub the feet. Remove the lungs, heart, liver, and kidneys from inside the main cavity: these you may chop, sauté, and add to a stuffing or save for a meat *pâté* or pie. Go over the pig thoroughly to remove any hairs that may have been missed. You should also remove the eyeballs, as they burst during roasting: use a grapefruit knife and scissors. Dry the pig thoroughly inside and out.

STUFFING VERSUS FLAVORING. Although you may use 10 cups of any stuffing suitable for turkey or goose, such as sausages and apples, prunes or chestnuts, or onions and bread crumbs, a simple herb and vegetable flavoring allows you to prepare the pig in advance, cuts down on roasting time, and makes serving easier. The following recipe is for a flavoring rather than a stuffing.

ROAST SUCKLING PIG
For 8 to 12 people

SEASONING AND TRUSSING

A 12- to 14-lb. suckling pig, cleaned, dried, and ready to roast
1 Tb salt
½ tsp each of sage and thyme
6 allspice berries or cloves
6 peppercorns
2 cups each of chopped

celery and onions, previously cooked in 4 Tb butter and ½ tsp salt, then cooled
6 to 8 skewers or finishing nails 3 inches long
White butcher's twine
Aluminum foil

Sprinkle the salt, sage, thyme, allspice or cloves, and peppercorns inside the main cavity of the pig, and spread in the cooked celery and onions. Close the cavity with skewers or nails, and string. If there is a slit under the pig's chin, simply sprinkle inside with salt and pepper; the slit need not be closed. Brace the mouth open with a 2-inch ball of aluminum foil.

INTO THE ROASTING PAN

A shallow roasting pan at least 20 inches long, with rack
About ½ cup light olive oil

or cooking oil, for preliminary basting
Aluminum foil
A meat thermometer

Place the pig in the pan in the position you want to present and carve it; ideally it is roasted with back legs folded under rump and head resting between the extended front legs. Unless you have a restaurant-sized pan and oven, you will have to arrange the pig diagonally, extend the hind legs under the belly, or even curl the rump and legs in the angle of the pan. Tie or skewer front and back legs in place. Rub the surface of the pig with 2 tablespoons of the oil. Make tents of aluminum foil to protect the ears, and tuck tail into the hole under the end of the rump. To prevent roasting juices from dropping into your oven, it may be necessary to slip a double fold of foil between pig and pan at the rump and snout ends, letting foil stick 2 inches above rim of pan. Insert a meat thermometer into the thigh.

You may do all this the day before roasting; cover the pig with plastic wrap and refrigerate, but remove it 2 to 3 hours before roasting so pig will come to room temperature for accurate timing. (*Note:* If you are using a regular stuffing rather than a flavoring, do not fill the pig in advance, and be sure both pig and stuffing are at room temperature when you stuff the pig. Spoiled or inadequately cooked stuffings have caused many a case of food poisoning!)

ROASTING

A basting brush
For the roasting pan: 1 cup
   each of sliced carrots and
   onions; 2 whole garlic
   cloves

Basting glaze: ¼ cup each
   of dry mustard, soy sauce,
   and honey and 3 Tb water
   beaten in a bowl with
   2 Tb Worcestershire

(Preheat oven to 450 degrees.)

Count on about 3 hours in all for a 12- to 14-pound pig; this includes 2 to 2½ hours of roasting, and a rest of 30 minutes or more in a warm oven so juices will retreat back into meat tissues before carving.

Roast for 30 minutes at 450 degrees, brushing the pig with oil after 15 minutes.

Turn oven down to 350 degrees, baste again with oil, and baste again in 15 minutes.

When the pig has been in for 1 hour, strew the sliced carrots and onions, and garlic in the pan, and baste both pig and vegetables with oil. Baste again in 15 minutes. Then baste every 15 minutes with the glaze: at first it will not adhere to the skin but will gradually build up into a beautiful brown as you continue basting. If mixture seems too thick, beat in a spoonful or so of water. If vegetables and juices begin to blacken in the pan, lower oven thermostat to 325 degrees.

As soon as meat thermometer reaches 185 degrees, in a little over 2 hours, the pig is done: the thigh meat is tender when pressed, and the legs move in their sockets. Turn oven down to 140 degrees (or turn it off), and let pig remain warm until you are ready to carve. Then remove strings and skewers, drain the pig, and place on your serving platter or board.

THE SAUCE

2 cups beef bouillon	wine, or dry white
Remains of basting glaze	vermouth
Optional: 1 cup port, red	

Remove rack. Spoon fat out of roasting pan; pour in the bouillon, the remains of the basting glaze, and, if you wish, a cup of wine. Bring to the simmer, scraping up coagulated roasting juices into the liquid; simmer 5 to 10 minutes while the pig is being carved. Strain into a warm sauce bowl for serving.

DECORATIONS

Decorate the platter with leaves and flowers or fruit, place a garland of leaves or flowers around the pig's neck, stick leaves or flowers in the eyes, replace the ball of foil in its mouth with a shining red apple, and bring your roast suckling pig triumphantly to the table.

CARVING

To carve, slit the skin on either side of the backbone. Start on one side, removing the front leg and shoulder, and the back leg; cut the meat from each into serving pieces. Slice parallel to the backbone to remove side meat. Repeat on the other side. Scrape off any adhering fat, and cut the crisp brown skin in squares to accompany each serving of meat. (An electric carving knife is useful to make initial cuts, and poultry shears are handy for skin squares.)

SUGGESTED ACCOMPANIMENTS

Peeled apple quarters basted with melted butter, lemon juice, and sugar, baked in the oven; Brussels sprouts or broccoli; roast potatoes; a light red wine such as a Bordeaux from the Graves district.

The Hundred and Seventh Show

MORE ABOUT POTATOES
ఇక్ష్ • ఇ఼

Here are two more recipes for that versatile vegetable the potato. First is *pommes duchesse*, for mashed-potato borders and decorations to garnish the meat platter, the fish dish, or the sauced leftovers. Second is *pommes Anna*, a handsome cake of sliced potatoes to serve with chops, steaks, sausages, and chicken.

POMMES DE TERRE DUCHESSE
(Mashed-potato Mixture for Borders and Other Decorations)

This is simply a mixture of mashed potatoes and egg yolks, formed into decorations and browned in the oven. Although you can shape them with a spoon and fork, they look far more stylish when squeezed through a pastry bag.

THE MASHED POTATOES

Use home-made or instant mashed potatoes for this recipe; they must be warm when you mix and form them.

HOMEMADE Use "baking" potatoes or old floury potatoes. Peel, quarter, and boil in salted water to cover, until potatoes are just tender. Drain immediately and put through a ricer or beat in an electric mixer. To dry them out, stir in a heavy saucepan over moderate heat for a minute or two until the potatoes begin to film on the bottom of the pan.

INSTANT MASHED   Here the potato mixture must be fairly firm, so use 2 or 3 tablespoons less than the amount of boiling salted water called for on the package, and omit the butter and milk.

THE DUCHESSE MIXTURE   (For each 2 cups of plain, hot mashed potatoes)

3 egg yolks (U. S. graded	2 to 3 Tb heavy cream
"large")	Salt, pepper, and nutmeg
3 Tb butter	

Beat the egg yolks one by one into the hot mashed potatoes, then the butter. Gradually beat in the cream, being sure that you do not soften the potatoes too much: they should hold their shape when lifted in a spoon. If too soft, they sag and lose their shape when baked. Season to taste with salt, pepper, and a speck of nutmeg. Set uncovered in a pan of hot water, and use while still warm.

SERVING

FLUTED BORDERS   (For meat platters, or dishes to be filled with creamed mixtures)   Butter the inside edge of the baking-and-serving platter. Choose a pastry bag with ¾-inch cannelated (toothed) tube opening, and fill with the warm *duchesse* mixture. Squeeze out a decorative design around the inside of the platter. Sprinkle with finely grated Swiss cheese and a little melted butter. Set aside or refrigerate until ready to bake.

Bake in upper third of a preheated 400-degree oven for about 30 minutes, until potatoes are lightly browned. If not served immediately, keep warm; the potatoes lose their light and delicious quality if cooled and reheated.

INDIVIDUAL SERVINGS   (To place around the meat platter) Lightly butter a baking sheet and dust with flour. Squeeze out rosettes, mounds, or other shapes; or form mounds of the *duchesse* mixture with a spoon; or flour your hands and roll the potatoes into balls or cylinders. Sprinkle with cheese and melted butter, and bake as for fluted borders.

POMMES DE TERRE ANNA
(Mold of Sliced Potatoes Baked in Butter)
For 4 to 6 people

When you bake sliced potatoes with butter in a very heavy dish in a very hot oven, you can turn them out onto a platter and they form a cake that is crisp and brown on the outside, tender and buttery inside. The only trick to this recipe is that the potatoes must crust on the outside and not stick to the dish. Essentials for success are a very heavy heat-conducting container, dry potato slices, clarified butter and, finally, as learned from sad experience, completing the cooking once you have started, so that the potatoes will not exude any moisture which will make them stick to the bottom of the dish.

ASSEMBLING AND BAKING

A heavy cast-iron frying pan about 8 inches at the top, 6 inches at the bottom, and 2 inches deep; or any round, straight-sided, heavy flameproof dish of copper, ceramic, or cast aluminum of approximately the same dimensions

½ lb. (2 sticks) butter
About 2 lbs. "boiling" potatoes (about 6 to 7 cups when sliced)
Salt and pepper
A close-fitting cover for the frying pan or baking dish
A large pie plate or pan to set under the potatoes in the oven

(Preheat oven to 450 degrees.)

Set one rack in the very bottom level of the oven and another just above it. Melt the butter, skim off the foam, and pour out the clear yellow liquid into a small saucepan, leaving the milky residue at the bottom. The clear liquid is non-sticking clarified butter.

Peel the potatoes and trim into cylinders about 1¼ inches in diameter. Slice into even rounds between $\frac{1}{16}$ and $\frac{1}{8}$ inch thick. Dry very thoroughly in a double thickness of toweling.

The potato slices are now to be arranged in even layers, so that when they are unmolded for serving the sides and bottom present an attractive design. Pour $\frac{1}{4}$ inch of the clarified butter into your frying pan or baking dish and set over moderately high heat. As soon as the butter is hot, place one potato slice in the center of the pan, and arrange an overlapping circle of potatoes around it; arrange a second overlapping circle around the first, and another if necessary, to rim the edge of the pan. Arrange a second layer of potatoes over the first and pour on a spoonful of butter.

You now have to decide about the edging. The easiest method is simply to build it neatly with layers of potatoes. A more decorative system is to place overlapping upright slices around the edge of the pan, bracing them into place with successive flat layers of potatoes as you fill the pan.

Whatever method you choose, continue rapidly arranging layers of potatoes, basting each with a spoonful of butter. Starting with the third layer, add a sprinkling of salt and pepper; these final layers are arranged less carefully except at the sides of the pan where they must form a solid support. Shake the pan gently now and then to be sure the potatoes are not sticking. Fill the pan completely, allowing potatoes to hump up into a $\frac{1}{4}$-inch dome in the center. You should have added enough butter so that you can see it bubbling up the sides of the pan.

Press the potatoes down, using the bottom of a heavy saucepan, and set on the cover. Immediately place on the upper of the two racks in the preheated oven, and set a pan on the lower rack to catch butter drippings. Bake for 20 minutes, then uncover, press down the potatoes again, and bake uncovered for 20 minutes more.

Place a cover on the pan, tip gently, and drain out excess butter, which can be used again. Run a knife around the edge of the potatoes, and if you are using a frying pan, reverse them onto a buttered baking sheet before sliding them onto a hot dish or platter. If not served immediately, keep warm in a turned-off oven.

The Hundred and Eighth Show

STEAK DINNER FOR FOUR
IN HALF AN HOUR
ఆర్ • ৡ৵
(Garlic Soup; Flank Steak; Ice-Cream Mold)

MENU:

Aïgo Bouïdo (Provençal Garlic Soup)
Broiled Flank Steak with Brussels Sprouts
and Baked Whole Tomatoes
Hot French Bread   Beaujolais or Mountain Red Wine
Temple de Glace à la Martiniquaise
(Mold of Ice Cream with Rum and Chocolate)

Any time you produce a fast and successful meal, keep notes, list your shopping requirements, and put down the order in which you did things; with your plans ready made, half the work is done. This three-course dinner can be assembled early in the day, or the night before. At serving time, the dessert is ready, the soup just needs its final fillip; you can broil the steak and finish the vegetables between courses while your guests are smacking their lips over the memory of that Aïgo Bouïdo and wondering what in the world it was. Here is a suggested schedule of events.

1) *Preparing the Flank Steak*
    (Cooking time: about 6 minutes)
    Flank steak is a paddle-shaped piece of meat with fibers running lengthwise. One flank lies inside each half of the beef belly opposite the loin or small of the back. To be tender and juicy, flank steaks should come from aged prime or choice beef car-

casses; a ready-to-broil flank, trimmed of covering membrane and fat, should weigh 2 pounds or slightly more, be about 14 inches long, 1 inch thick, and 6 inches at the widest part. Store the steak tightly rolled up in plastic wrap, to keep the meat from drying out. Just before proceeding with any recipe, score the meat on each side to prevent it from curling while broiling. A preliminary marinade will give the meat added flavor and tenderness.

THE MARINADE

3 Tb minced scallions or shallots	Big pinch pepper or drops of Tabasco
1½ Tb soy sauce	The juice of ½ lemon
2 Tb olive oil	A broiling pan
½ tsp thyme or "Italian seasoning"	

Mix the marinade ingredients in a bowl. Lay the flank steak flat in the bottom of your broiling pan and spread on half the marinade. Turn the steak and spread with the rest of the marinade. Cover with waxed paper, and leave for at least 20 minutes, or refrigerate for several hours or a day or two. (While the steak is marinating, start in on your soup.)

2) Aïgo Bouïdo—Provençal Garlic Soup

THE SOUP BASE

2 large heads garlic	¼ tsp sage
2 quarts boiling water	1 bay leaf
2 tsp salt	2 whole cloves
¼ tsp thyme	Pinch saffron flowers

Remove loose outside skin from garlic heads, chop heads roughly, and add to the boiling water. Stir in the salt, herbs, cloves, and saffron; boil slowly, uncovered, for 20 to 30 minutes or until the garlic is very soft. Strain, pressing juices out of garlic, return soup to pan, carefully correct seasoning, and set aside until you are ready to serve. Make the following *liaison* whenever you have a free moment.

THE LIAISON

A small mixing bowl   A wire whip
3 egg yolks   ¼ cup fruity olive oil

Beat the egg yolks until they are thick and sticky. Then beat
in the oil by droplets to make a thick sauce like mayonnaise.
Cover the bowl and set aside.

SERVING

A soup tureen   1 cup grated Parmesan
Fresh chopped parsley   cheese
Rounds of toasted French
  bread

Whenever you are ready to serve, bring the soup base to the
boil and scrape the *liaison* into your soup tureen. Beating the
liaison with a wire whip, dribble on the hot soup until at least
a cup has gone in, then stir in the rest of the soup. Decorate
with a sprinkling of parsley, and serve immediately, accompanied by French bread and grated Parmesan cheese.

3) *Temple de Glace à la Martiniquaise—Mold of Ice Cream
   with Rum and Chocolate*

1 cup semisweet chocolate   20 or more ladyfingers, or
  bits melted with ¼ cup   strips of stale spongecake
  water   1 quart vanilla ice cream
¼ cup dark rum, orange   (removed from freezer so
  liqueur, or other flavoring   it will soften slightly)

(To speed things up, you could start melting the chocolate
before you marinate the steak, and finish the dessert while the
soup is cooking.) Choose a straight-sided, cylindrical dish or
mold 3 to 4 inches high; line bottom with a round of waxed
paper. Place the rum or other flavoring in a soup plate, and
dilute with water to make about 1 cup of liquid; sweeten to
taste with sugar. One by one, dip ladyfingers or cake strips into
liquid, and line bottom and sides of dish. Pour in 2 to 3 spoonfuls of chocolate. Beat ice cream in a bowl, if necessary to soften
it; spoon it into the dish, filling dish by one third. Press several

dipped ladyfingers over the ice cream, spoon on more chocolate, and continue in layers until mold is filled. Cover with plastic wrap and freeze at least an hour.

SERVING

When ready to serve, unmold onto a chilled plate; decorate top with melted chocolate. Pass bowl of chocolate at the table, if you wish. (If you are not serving immediately, cover with a large pan or bowl and return dessert to freezer.)

4) The Vegetables

As soon as these are prepared for cooking, your large chores are done.

THE BRUSSELS SPROUTS

Trim a quart of Brussels sprouts and pierce a cross ¼ inch deep at base of stems (for quick cooking); wash rapidly in cold water, and place in a wire salad basket. Have a deep kettle with 6 to 8 quarts of salted water boiling by the time you are ready to broil the steak, drop in the basket of sprouts and let them boil rapidly, uncovered, for about 7 minutes or until just tender and the steak is carved. Drain and arrange about the platter, sprinkled with salt, pepper, and melted butter.

THE TOMATOES

Choose large cherry tomatoes or 2-inch regular tomatoes and place in a shallow baking dish. Pour on a spoonful or so of olive oil, rolling the tomatoes around to cover them with the oil; sprinkle with salt and pepper. Have your oven preheated to 425 degrees or more by the time you are ready to broil the steak, set the tomatoes in the middle level and bake 5 or 6 minutes, just until the skins split.

5) Broiling the Steak

This will take only 5 to 6 minutes in all; let your broiler heat to red-hot while you are having the soup course. When cleaning up between courses, set the steak, just as it is, as close as possible under hot broiler and leave for 3 minutes. Then turn the steak with tongs and broil the other side for 2 to 3 minutes. Steak should be rosy rare.

CARVING AND SERVING

Flank steaks must be carved in very thin slices across the grain of the meat, to make tender eating. Lay steak on carving board. Starting 3 inches from one end of steak, hold a very sharp, long knife at a 10-degree angle and make a slice ⅛ inch thick toward the end of the meat. Continue carving in wide thin slices, your knife always angled almost flat to the board. Arrange the slices on a warm platter; pour carving juices and pan juices over the meat. Decorate with parsley sprigs and the vegetables; serve immediately.

The Hundred and Ninth Show

THE ENDIVE SHOW
◈ · ◈

Chicory, succory, witloof, or *Cichorium intybus Linn*—whatever you call it, endive is a beautiful vegetable. Neatly boxed, the pale pointed heads lying in serried rows between layers of blue paper, endives look expensive—and they are. Although endive can be grown anywhere, the Belgians have made a specialty of its cultivation, and almost all that we buy is imported. Endive is a member of the chicory, or frizzy-lettuce family; it is grown in special trenches, and covered with light soil until the heads swell into their characteristic spike-formed shape. Entirely deprived of light, endives remain white except for the palest greenish-yellow at their tips.

Endive is familiar in salads, either alone or combined with watercress or other greens, but it is delicious as a cooked vegetable when you want something new and unusual. Serve cooked endive with roasts, steaks, and chops; it goes particularly well with veal and chicken.

BUYING AND STORING ENDIVE. This is a winter vegetable; the season is from late October through March. Select firm, white heads all of the same size (4 to 5 inches long), and be sure that each is tightly closed into a point at the tip. The tips of poor, old, stale, or end-of-season endives are open, and show traces of yellowish-green rather than of pale greenish-yellow. Endives will keep a week or more, wrapped in slightly dampened paper towels and placed in a plastic bag in the refrigerator. For cooked endives, count on 2 to 3 per person.

TRIMMING AND WASHING. With a small knife, shave any discolored bits off the root end of each endive, being careful not to loosen outside leaves. Endive has a slightly bitter taste which is presumably concentrated in the root: you may core a cone-shaped piece out of the root if you wish. Run cold water over the endives, drain, and they are ready to cook.

BLANCHING, OR PRECOOKING. Again, because of the slightly bitter taste, some cooks like to blanch endives for 10 minutes in boiling salted water before proceeding to any recipe. This can be useful with end-of-season endives, and can speed up the cooking process if you are in a hurry, such as for the following recipe.

ENDIVES À LA MEUNIÈRE
(Sautéed Endives with Black Butter Sauce)
For 6 people

12 endives
A 3-quart saucepan with
    boiling salted water
About 1 stick (¼ lb.) butter,
    previously melted
A 10- to 12-inch no-stick,

enameled, or stainless-
    steel skillet with cover
½ Tb lemon juice
Salt and pepper
3 Tb minced fresh parsley

Trim and wash the endives. Drop into the boiling water, bring to the boil again, and boil slowly, uncovered, for 10 minutes. Drain and, when cool enough to handle, gently squeeze each endive to remove as much water as possible.

Skim off any surface foam, and pour 3 tablespoons of clear melted butter into the skillet. Set over moderately high heat, and when butter is almost beginning to brown, add the endives in one layer. Sauté, turning the endives, until lightly browned. Add the lemon juice, a sprinkling of salt and pepper, cover the skillet and cook slowly for 30 minutes, until endives are very tender. (If you have time, another 20 to 30 minutes of slow cooking will only improve the flavor; the endives may be cooked ahead and reheated later.)

Just before serving, transfer the endives to a hot dish; spoon 4 to 5 tablespoons of clear melted butter into the skillet. Heat until butter is nut-brown, and pour over the endives. Sprinkle with fresh parsley.

ENDIVES BRAISÉES A LA FLAMANDE
(Endives Braised in Butter)
For 6 people

12 endives, trimmed and washed	½ cup water
A flameproof casserole with cover (if possible, large enough to hold endives in one layer)	1 Tb lemon juice
	4 Tb butter
	A round of waxed paper

(Preheat oven to 325 degrees.)

Arrange the endives in the casserole; they will cook more evenly if they are in one layer, but you may use two if necessary. Add the salt, water, lemon juice, and butter. Spread the waxed paper over, to keep the endives moist, and to prevent them from burning in the oven. Cover the casserole and boil slowly on top of the stove for about 20 minutes, or until endives are fairly tender and liquid has reduced to half. Bake in the lower middle of a preheated oven for about 1½ hours, until the endives have turned a pale golden color and almost all liquid has evaporated. They will smell deliciously of endive, butter, and lemon. (May be cooked ahead and reheated.)

Arrange on a hot serving dish or around your meat platter, and sprinkle with parsley. Or dress them up in one of the following ways:

VARIATIONS ❧

Endives à la Normande
(Braised Endives Simmered in Cream)
For 6 people

12 endives butter-braised as in preceding recipe	Salt, white pepper, and lemon juice
A wide, heavy enameled saucepan or skillet	1 Tb softened butter
About ½ cup heavy cream	Chopped parsley

Arrange the braised endives in the saucepan or skillet; pour on enough heavy cream almost to cover them. Simmer slowly, uncovered, for 10 to 15 minutes, basting with the cream occasionally, until cream has reduced by at least half: it will look slightly curdled.

Remove the endives to a hot serving dish. Stir 3 to 4 tablespoons more cream into pan and heat to smooth out the sauce. Season to taste with salt, white pepper, and drops of lemon juice. Remove from heat and swirl the tablespoon of butter into the sauce; pour over the endives and decorate with chopped parsley.

Endives Braisées au Madère
(Endives with Madeira and a Brunoise of Vegetables)
For 6 people

12 braised endives	A small saucepan
A shallow baking dish	¾ cup of good beef bouillon
3 Tb each of very finely diced boiled ham, carrots, and onions	3 to 4 Tb Madeira
	Any endive-braising juices
1 Tb butter	Parsley sprigs

(Preheat oven to 325 degrees.)

Arrange the braised endives in the baking dish. Place the ham, diced vegetables, and butter in saucepan, and cook slowly until vegetables are tender. Add the beef bouillon, the Madeira, and any endive-braising juices; boil until liquid has reduced by half. Spoon the sauce and vegetables over the endives, cover, and bake for about 30 minutes; this allows the endives to absorb the flavor of the sauce. (May be baked ahead and reheated.) Serve decorated with parsley sprigs.

Endives et Jambon, Mornay

(Endives and Ham, Baked in Cheese Sauce)

For 6 people

12 braised endives	hot milk, salt, pepper,
12 slices boiled ham	pinch of nutmeg, and ¼
A buttered baking dish	cup grated Swiss cheese)
2 cups *sauce mornay* (4 Tb	Grated Swiss cheese
butter, 5 Tb flour, 2 cups	Melted butter

(Preheat oven to 375 degrees.)

This makes an attractive main-course luncheon or supper dish. Wrap each braised endive in a thin slice of boiled ham. Arrange in baking dish, cover with *sauce mornay*, sprinkle with grated Swiss cheese and melted butter. About 30 minutes before serving, bake in the upper third of preheated oven until endives are bubbling and sauce has browned nicely on top.

The Hundred and Tenth Show

SADDLE OF LAMB

✧ • ✧

Roast saddle of lamb has a wonderfully luxurious sound: it speaks of good restaurants and great feasts in English country houses. Oddly enough, the saddle is rarely thought of by most home cooks, yet it is far easier to roast and carve than a leg of lamb, takes half as long to cook, and is the perfect small roast for that elegant little dinner party of six people.

BUYING A SADDLE OF LAMB. In culinary language, the saddle is the backbone section between the hip bone and the ribs; in other words, it is a giant loin chop with 2 loin strips of meat on top, and 2 *filets* or tenderloin strips underneath. Tell your butcher that you want the double or kidney loin (the loin contains the kidneys), and point it out to him on yourself; it is the small of your back on both sides, from the top of your hip up to and including your thirteenth or floating bottom ribs, and following around to your front (or flank, in butcher language).

Ask that the papery outside covering be removed, as this can be difficult. The rest is easy to do at home, or give the following instructions: Remove kidneys and as much interior fat as possible, including the inside strip of fat running parallel to the *filets* and partially hidden by the flanks. Remove the remaining ribs. Cut off all but a 3-inch strip of the flanks, leaving just enough so the two ends of flank meet at the underside of the backbone. Shave off all but a ⅛-inch layer of covering fat, and score lightly at ½-inch intervals.

The best or choicest quality saddles come from so-called spring lambs weighing up to 45 pounds. A trimmed saddle will weigh about 3½ pounds and serves 4 to 6; if you want a bit extra, ask that the saddle be cut so as to include 3 or 4 extra ribs on each side, which will give you another pound or so. If the lamb has not been properly hung (aged), wrap the saddle tightly in plastic wrap and store for 2 days in the coldest part of the refrigerator; this will make the meat more tender.

SELLE D'AGNEAU RÔTIE PERSILLADE
(*Roast Saddle of Lamb with Parsley and Bread Crumbs*)
For 4 to 6 people

ROASTING TIME: About 45 minutes, to medium rare, 140 degrees.

¼ tsp salt
Pepper
¼ tsp rosemary
A trimmed 3½-lb. saddle of lamb (at room temperature)
White butcher's string
A heavy, shallow baking dish just large enough to hold saddle comfortably
A meat thermometer
Melted butter and a basting brush
½ cup each of sliced carrots and onions
1 or 2 large, unpeeled garlic cloves

(Preheat oven to 475 degrees.)

Sprinkle salt, pepper, and rosemary on the underside of the saddle. Fold the two flank ends against the underside of the *filets*, meeting under the backbone. Tie the circumference of the saddle in three or four places to keep flanks in place. Set the saddle top side up in the roasting pan and insert your meat thermometer at a long, slanting angle into the thickest part of one of the loin strips (top of meat); be sure the point of the thermometer reaches just to the middle of the meat and is not touching the backbone. Paint the two exposed ends of meat with melted butter. (May be done ahead and refrigerated; leave for 30 minutes at room temperature before roasting.)

ROASTING START. Set lamb in upper-middle of preheated oven and roast for 15 minutes.

15-MINUTE MARK. Turn thermostat down to 425 degrees, strew the vegetables around the meat, and baste meat with melted butter.

22-MINUTE MARK. Baste again, with the fat in the pan, basting the vegetables also.

30-MINUTE MARK. Baste again rapidly; if vegetables are blackening, turn heat down to 400 degrees.

37-MINUTE MARK. Baste again. Meat thermometer should be almost at 130 degrees.

45-MINUTE MARK. Meat thermometer should be at 140 degrees, medium rare; if not, roast a few minutes longer. (A 4½-pound saddle will take about 10 minutes longer.)

When lamb is done, turn off oven, pull rack to front, and leave oven door open. The meat should rest for 15 minutes before carving, so the juices will retreat back into the tissues.

While the lamb is roasting, or at any convenient time beforehand, prepare the *persillade*.

THE PERSILLADE

3 Tb finely minced shallots or scallions	1 cup fine white bread crumbs
4 Tb butter	Salt and pepper
An 8-inch frying pan	⅓ cup finely minced fresh parsley

Cook the shallots or scallions in butter for 1 minute, then stir in the bread crumbs. Stir and toss over moderately high heat for several minutes until crumbs are golden brown. Remove from heat, season to taste with salt and pepper. Just before serving, mix in the minced parsley.

THE SAUCE

¼ cup dry vermouth	1 tsp tomato paste
1 cup beef bouillon	

After removing the saddle from the roasting pan, spoon all but a tablespoon of fat out of the pan; pour in the vermouth, bouillon, and tomato paste. Scrape up coagulated roasting juices and mash vegetables into liquid with a wooden spoon; boil rapidly until liquid has reduced by about half. Strain into a warm sauce bowl.

CARVING AND SERVING

You may carve the saddle at the table, or carve in the kitchen and reassemble it, sprinkled with the *persillade*.

To carve in the kitchen, preheat oven to 475 degrees—you may need to reheat the roast before serving. Turn the saddle upside down and cut off the flanks. Then, cutting parallel to the backbone on either side, remove the two *filet* strips and cut them into crosswise slices about ¾ inch thick; set aside. Turn the saddle right side up.

If you want long slices of meat, shave off outside fat with a long slice parallel to the backbone on one side. Then starting at the outside, make long thin slices parallel to the backbone, piling up the slices in the order in which you cut them. Repeat on the other side.

If you want crosswise slices of meat, cut down one side of backbone at the top of the meat; following the angle of the bone outward, remove the loin strip, and cut into crosswise slices an inch thick. Repeat on the other side.

Place the flanks lengthwise on your hot platter and set the saddle bone securely on top. Replace the slices of loin strip, and pile the pieces of *filet* at either end. Baste with several spoonfuls of sauce, and sprinkle the saddle with the *persillade*. (If necessary to reheat, set platter in oven for 2 minutes.) Serve immediately, accompanied by the sauce.

VEGETABLE AND WINE SUGGESTIONS

Potatoes Anna, braised endive or lettuce, and broiled or baked tomatoes; or a beautifully arranged platter of mixed vegetables, such as braised carrots, onions, and turnips, or buttered peas, beans, and cauliflower, and sautéed or boiled potatoes.

Serve your best château-bottled red Bordeaux wine, from the Médoc or Graves district.

The Hundred and Eleventh Show

NAPOLEONS—MILLEFEUILLES
ఆ§ · ೯ిఴ
(French Puff Pastry—Pâte Feuilletée)

Some of the handsomest items on the pastry tray in a good restaurant or bake shop are the rectangular Napoleons, their white toppings covered with decorative lines of dark chocolate. When you cut into one, you find layers of kirsch-flavored cream sandwiched between layers of light, buttery pastry. They are a treat for dessert, for a snack at the coffee break, and look beautiful on a buffet or tea table.

To form Napoleons, you bake a large, thin sheet of French puff pastry, cut it into 3 four-inch strips, mount the strips on top of each other with filling in between, then decorate the top, and cut the three-tiered strip into 2-inch pieces. The filling for Napoleons is either pastry cream or whipped cream, and the white topping may be either white fondant frosting or a thick layer of powdered sugar.

FLOUR NOTE: Since this book was first published, we have found that a combination of 1 part plain bleached cake flour to every 3 parts all-purpose flour makes an excellent formula for puff pastry.

PÂTE FEUILLETÉE
(French Puff Pastry)

THE DÉTREMPE

4 cups or 18 ounces flour—
1 cup plain bleached cake
flour and 3 cups all-
purpose flour (measure
by scooping dry-measure
cups into container and
leveling off excess with
straight edge of knife)

A large mixing bowl
¾ stick (3 ounces) chilled
butter
2 tsp salt dissolved in 1 cup
cold water
3 sticks (¾ lb.) additional
chilled butter

(*Note*: Puff pastry is easiest to make when everything is cold: if you have a pastry marble, chill it in the refrigerator; if your pastry softens while you are rolling, chill it immediately for 15 minutes, then continue.)

Place flour in a large mixing bowl. Cut the ¾ stick chilled butter into ¼-inch pieces, and rub flour and butter rapidly together between the tips of your fingers, or work with a pastry blender, until mixture resembles coarse meal. Rapidly blend in the water, at first with a rubber spatula, then with the slightly cupped fingers of one hand, pressing mixture together to make a firm but pliable dough. (Work in a few drops more water if necessary.) Knead briefly into a rough ball; wrap in waxed paper and chill for 30 to 40 minutes. Then roll out into a 10-inch circle. (Dough should look rough; it will smooth out later.)

THE PACKAGE

Beat and knead the 3 additional sticks of chilled butter until smooth, free from lumps, malleable, yet still cold. Shape into a 5-inch square, and place in middle of dough circle. Bring edges of dough up over butter to enclose it completely, sealing top edges together with your fingers.

TURNS 1 AND 2

Lightly flour the package, and roll the dough into an even rectangle about 16 by 8 inches. Your object is to spread the butter layer evenly between the dough layers, the length and width of the rectangle. Then, as though folding a letter, bring bottom edge of dough up to the middle, and the top edge down to cover it, making three even layers. This is called a "turn." Rotate pastry so top edge is to your right, roll dough again into a rectangle, fold in three, then wrap in waxed paper and a dampened towel. Chill 45 to 60 minutes.

TURNS 3 AND 4; 5 AND 6

Repeat with two more rolls and folds; chill again 45 minutes, then complete the final two rolls and folds, making six turns in all. Chill again for 45 to 60 minutes (2 hours if you are using instant-blending flour), and the dough is ready for shaping and baking. (Note: The first four turns should be completed within an hour; after the fourth turn, you may leave the pastry overnight, or freeze it.)

Napoleons—Millefeuilles

For 16 pieces

ROLLING OUT AND BAKING THE PASTRY

The preceding puff pastry	4 baking sheets, 12 by 18
1 Tb softened butter	inches

(Preheat oven to 450 degrees.)

Roll the chilled pastry again into a rectangle; cut in half and chill one piece. Roll the remaining piece rapidly into a 13-by-19-inch rectangle ⅛ inch thick. Run cold water over a baking sheet, roll up pastry on your pin, and unroll over the baking sheet. With a knife or pastry wheel, cut off ½ inch of dough all around. To keep pastry from rising when baked, prick all over at ⅛-inch intervals with two forks or a rotary pastry pricker. Chill for 30 minutes to relax dough. Repeat with the second half of the pastry.

Lightly butter undersides of other baking sheets and lay one over each sheet of dough. Set in upper- and lower-middle racks of oven and bake for 5 minutes. Lift covering sheets, prick pastry again, and replace covering sheets, pressing down on pastry. Bake 5 minutes more, then remove covering sheets to let pastry brown; if pastry begins to rise more than ¼ inch, or starts to curl, replace coverings. Bake 18 to 20 minutes in all, or until pastry is nicely browned. Cool 5 minutes, with covering sheets, then unmold and cool on racks. (Cooled baked pastry may be frozen.)

FORMING AND CUTTING THE NAPOLEONS

1 cup apricot jam forced through a sieve and boiled to 128 degrees with 2 Tb sugar

2 cups pastry cream (see The Eighty-third Show) or stiffly beaten whipped cream, sweetened and flavored with kirsch

1 cup white fondant icing (see The Hundred and Nineteenth Show) or powdered sugar in a sieve

1 cup melted chocolate

A paper decorating cone (see The Hundred and Nineteenth Show)

Cut the baked pastry into even strips 4 inches wide. Paint the top of each with warm apricot, and spread about ¼ inch of pastry cream or whipped cream on two strips; mount one on top of the other, and cover with the third. Repeat with the other three strips. Spread melted fondant icing or a ⅛-inch coating of powdered sugar on top of each. Make a cone of heavy freezer paper or foil, cut the point to make a ⅛-inch opening, and fill cone with melted chocolate. Squeeze crosswise lines of chocolate over the top of each strip, spacing lines about ⅜ inch apart. Draw the dull edge of a knife down the middle of each strip, then draw another line in the opposite direction on each side, to pull the chocolate into a decorative pattern.

Let chocolate set for a few minutes, then cut the strips into crosswise pieces 2 inches wide, using a very sharp knife held upright; cut with an up-and-down sawing motion.

SERVING

Arrange the Napoleons on a serving tray and chill an hour. Remove from refrigerator 20 minutes before serving, so that chocolate (and fondant) will regain their bloom. Napoleons are at their best when freshly made, though you may keep them several days under refrigeration or you may freeze them.

The Hundred and Twelfth Show

PAËLLA A L'AMÉRICAINE

ఆఙ · ఙ

A whole rice dinner in one pot, Spanish style—that's the *paëlla*, and a hearty, savory party dish it is too. *Paëlla* also makes a lively conversation piece: you will never find agreement on what besides rice should go into it. It appears that each region and each cook in Spain has a personal recipe and technique. You will hear emphatic pronouncements that the one and only true *paëlla* contains rice, chicken, and rabbit. Aficionados of another persuasion insist that there is no *paëlla* without a squid or two, or some snails, or lobsters and mussels, or those red Spanish sausages called *chorizos*. Whatever in the end goes into a *paëlla*, all the various ingredients cook together with the rice, producing a glorious mixture of taste.

A NOTE ON THE RICE. Rice is the key to a successful *paëlla*: it must be perfectly cooked, with the grains separate and slightly *al dente*. The type of rice used in Spain is rather short, grayish, and cooks perfectly in an uncovered pan in 12 to 14 minutes; if you can find this in a Spanish neighborhood grocery store where you live, you will have no problems. The short, fat imported Italian rice, which is sold in white cotton bags in many Italian neighborhoods, is equally good. Long-grain Carolina rice, unless very carefully handled, turns gummy in a *paëlla*. The best alternative to Spanish or Italian rice is the patented specially treated packaged rice with "parboiled" on the label; you can find it in any market, but do not confuse the parboiled type with the pre-cooked instant rice. Parboiled rice does not become gummy and despite directions on the box it will cook, uncovered, in about 15 minutes.

PAËLLA A L'AMÉRICAINE
For 8 people

You can put anything into a *paëlla* you want, as long as you also have rice, saffron, garlic, and paprika. The object is that all the ingredients cook with the rice, giving off their individual flavors. As the rice takes about 15 minutes to cook, you precook some ingredients and add others near the end, timing each so that everything is done when the rice is tender. The following recipe is for a *paëlla* featuring chicken, shrimps, sausages, and other delicacies amassed from the copious shelves of an American supermarket.

PRELIMINARIES WITH CHICKEN AND SAUSAGES

A 10-inch skillet
½ lb. (1 cup) fresh pork butt, lean bacon, or lightly smoked ham
1 lb. fresh *chorizos* or Italian pork sausages simmered 10 minutes in water and roughly diced; or cooked pork sausages, such as Polish or *chourico*, diced
2 Tb olive oil
A 6-quart flameproof *paëlla* pan, casserole, or electric skillet, and a cover
1 cup sliced yellow onions
1 cup sliced green or red bell peppers

8 chicken thighs or drumsticks (frying chicken)
½ cup dry white wine or vermouth
4½ cups brown chicken stock, or half canned chicken broth and half beef bouillon
½ tsp saffron flowers
1 tsp paprika
¼ tsp ground coriander
1 bay leaf
½ tsp each of dried thyme and oregano
2 to 3 cloves garlic, minced
Salt and pepper

Sauté the diced pork, bacon, or ham and the sausages in olive oil until lightly browned; pour rendered fat from skillet into *paëlla* pan. Add the onions and peppers to the pork and sausages, cover skillet, and cook slowly until vegetables are tender—about 10 minutes.

Meanwhile dry the chicken pieces thoroughly, heat the pork fat in the *paëlla* pan, then brown the chicken nicely on all sides. Pour excess fat out of *paëlla* pan, and add the cooked vegetable mixture from the skillet. Pour in the wine and stock, add the saffron and other flavorings, and season to taste with salt and pepper. Cover the pan and simmer slowly for 20 minutes. Chicken should be about two thirds cooked; it will finish later with the rice. You may complete this preliminary ahead of time: when cold, cover and refrigerate; bring to the boil before proceeding.

THE SHRIMPS AND OTHER GARNISHINGS

1 lb. boiled shrimps, shelled
and deveined
1 Tb lemon juice
¼ tsp dried oregano
2 Tb olive oil
Salt and pepper
4 quarts boiling salted water
2 to 3 medium tomatoes

1 to 2 cups shelled green
peas and/or diced green
beans
1 cup canned chick-peas
(*garbanzos*), drained
Optional: 24 fresh mussels
and/or clams

Place the shrimps in a bowl and toss with the lemon juice, oregano, oil, and seasonings; refrigerate until ready to use. Drop tomatoes into the boiling water for 10 seconds, peel, halve, squeeze out juice and seeds, and chop roughly; set aside. Drop the peas and/or beans into the boiling water, bring to the boil, and boil uncovered for 5 minutes, or until almost tender; drain, refresh in cold water, drain again and set aside. Scrub the optional shellfish and let stand in several changes of cold water for about an hour so they will render their sand; lift out into a colander when ready to use.

FINAL COOKING OF THE PAËLLA

(15 to 20 Minutes)

2 cups imported Spanish or Italian rice or packaged "parboiled" rice (see page 332)	2 lemons, quartered 2 to 3 Tb fresh chopped parsley

Bring the contents of the *paëlla* pan to a rapid boil on top of the stove. Sprinkle in the rice, mixing it down into the liquid with a spoon. Let boil rapidly for 5 to 6 minutes; do not cover the pan and do not stir the rice. When rice has begun to swell, and has absorbed enough liquid so that it has risen to the surface, strew on the shrimps, peas and/or beans, chick-peas, and tomatoes. Again do not stir, simply push them down into the rice with a spoon. With liquid still boiling, insert the optional shellfish, hinged end down, into the rice.

Reduce heat and let *paëlla* simmer for another 7 to 8 minutes, or until rice is just tender—it should be slightly *al dente*. It is important that you never stir the contents of the pan, or the rice will become gummy. At the end of the cooking, all liquid should have been absorbed. (It is best not to cover the pan, but if you feel the rice is not cooking properly, you may cover it for a few minutes, sprinkling on a few tablespoons of stock or water, then uncover to finish the cooking. This is a matter of your eye, taste, and judgment, and of trying out a *paëlla* once or twice in the same pan.)

Decorate the *paëlla* with lemon quarters and parsley, and serve as soon as possible. Accompany with a salad of lettuce, tomatoes, anchovies, capers and black olives, French bread, and a dry white, young red, or *rosé* wine.

The Hundred and Thirteenth Show

DINNER PARTY: FIRST COURSE
⋅⋅⋅
(*Scallops à la Créole*)

Every once in a while it is good for the soul to give a very formal, carefully planned, and beautifully appointed dinner, with the finest food and wines that one can muster. Such an affair keeps the chef in fighting trim! When you are doing all the cooking and serving yourself, you have to arrange a menu which will not only be nicely balanced but which will suit your time schedule—in other words, the main cooking is finished well before your guests arrive. Your first course, which is the pace setter, must be light and savory if it precedes a rich main course but can be rich and creamy if it is followed by a roast. Here is an unusual recipe for scallops in white wine sauce, a beautiful opening to a main course of roast beef or lamb. The scallops, sauce base, and trimmings are prepared in advance, and the final details are finished a few minutes before serving.

COQUILLES SAINT-JACQUES A LA CRÉOLE
(*Scallops in Wine Sauce Garnished with Tomato Fondue*)
For 8 to 10 people

In this recipe, the scallops are simmered in a highly spiced white-wine *court-bouillon* which is then boiled down, forming the base for an egg yolk and butter sauce, like a *hollandaise*. Scallops and tomato flavoring are folded into the sauce, and the finished dish is decorated with truffles and puff-pastry *fleurons*, or with toast points and parsley.

THE COURT-BOUILLON AND SCALLOPS

1 cup full-bodied dry white
 wine or ¾ cup dry white
 vermouth
1 cup water
1 medium onion, finely
 sliced
6 to 8 parsley stems
¼ tsp salt
4 peppercorns
1 bay leaf
4 allspice berries or cloves

4 shakes hot pepper sauce or
 a big pinch of cayenne
 pepper
2 cloves garlic, mashed
A 2½- to 3-quart stainless-
 steel or enameled
 saucepan
1½ lbs. (3 cups) scallops,
 washed and cut into ½-
 inch pieces

Place all ingredients except the scallops in the saucepan; cover and simmer slowly for 20 minutes. Strain, pressing juices out of ingredients, and return the liquid to the pan. This is now a *court-bouillon*; let cool to tepid.

Add the scallops to the *court-bouillon* and, if necessary, enough cold water to just cover them. Bring to the simmer, cover the pan, and cook at a slow boil for about 3 minutes. The scallops are done when springy rather than squashy to the touch; do not overcook them. Let cool for 10 minutes in the *court-bouillon* so they will pick up its flavor; strain into a bowl. Return the *court-bouillon* to the pan and boil it down rapidly until reduced to about ½ cup; it will be almost syrupy—keep your eye on the liquid during the last minutes; it burns easily. Let cool to tepid. Meanwhile prepare the tomatoes as follows:

FONDUE DE TOMATES—COOKED TOMATO PULP

2 to 3 medium tomatoes
1½ Tb butter
An enameled saucepan or
 skillet

1 Tb minced shallots or
 scallions
Salt and pepper

Drop the tomatoes in boiling water for 10 seconds; remove stem ends and peel, halve tomatoes crosswise, and squeeze out juice and seeds. Cut pulp into ¼-inch dice. Heat the butter, stir in the minced shallots or scallions, cook slowly for 1 minute, then stir in the tomatoes. Sauté over moderate heat, tossing and swirling the pan occasionally, until tomatoes have rendered their juice, and juice has almost entirely boiled away (5 minutes or so). Season lightly with salt and pepper; set aside.

SAUCE VIN BLANC À LA CRÉOLE—FINAL ASSEMBLY AND SERVING

¼ cup heavy cream
4 egg yolks
1 tsp cornstarch
1 to 1½ sticks (4 to 6 ounces) melted butter
Salt, white pepper, and lemon juice

12 to 18 puff-pastry *fleurons* (see end of recipe) or triangles of white bread sautéed in clear melted butter
A chopped truffle or parsley sprigs

Pour the cream into the reduced *court-bouillon*. Beat in the egg yolks and cornstarch; beat for a minute to thicken the yolks slightly. Then set pan over moderate heat and stir with a wire whip until liquid thickens into a cream which coats the wires of the whip. (Be careful not to overheat the yolks and scramble them: they should thicken gradually, and are almost done when you see a light steam rising. You must heat them enough so they do thicken properly, or your final sauce will not be thick enough.) Remove sauce base from heat.

You may complete the recipe to this point, and refrigerate both scallops and sauce base. Just before serving, reheat scallops in a double boiler, stir sauce base over gentle heat until tepid, heat melted butter to almost bubbling, lightly butter and warm your serving platter, and proceed to the final step.

Set pan with sauce base on a wet potholder. By driblets, beat in the melted butter with a wire whip, exactly as though you were making a *hollandaise* sauce. When you have beaten in as much butter as you wish, taste the sauce very carefully for seasoning, beating in salt, white pepper, and drops of lemon juice as needed. Fold the tomato fondue and hot scallops into the sauce, and turn out onto the warm platter. Decorate with *fleurons* or sautéed bread triangles, and chopped truffle or parsley. Serve immediately.

FLEURONS—PUFF-PASTRY DECORATIONS

A 6x4x2-inch piece of   A 3-inch fluted cutter
French puff pastry (*pâte*   1 egg beaten with 1 tsp
feuilletée)   water

(Preheat oven to 450 degrees.)
Roll out the puff pastry to a thickness of ⅛ inch. Cut into ovals or crescents. Run cold water over a baking sheet, arrange the decorations on the sheet, and prick them all over at ¼-inch intervals with a fork. Paint with beaten egg, so they will glaze when baked. Bake in middle level of preheated oven 12 to 15 minutes, until puffed and nicely browned. Cool on a rack. (To reheat, preheat oven to 350 degrees, set the *fleurons* in the oven and immediately turn it off; leave about 5 minutes.)

WINE SUGGESTIONS

An excellent white Graves, white Burgundy, or Traminer.

A NOTE ON WINEGLASSES. The perfect all-purpose wineglass contains 8 ounces and has a tulip-shaped bowl; it is filled only by half. A large, partially filled glass allows the bouquet of the wine to develop, and inward slanting sides concentrate the aroma in the glass. You can serve white wine, red wine, or champagne in this type of glass; it is always correct.

The Hundred and Fourteenth Show

DINNER PARTY: MAIN COURSE

∾ᴓ • ᴕ∾

(*Casserole Roast of Beef; Braised Carrot Slices*)

A beautiful, juicy roast of beef surrounded by fresh vegetables is always a hit at any dinner party, even the most formal one. Here is a change from the usual roasting method; this recipe calls for a boneless roast which is browned, then baked in a covered casserole with herbs and aromatic vegetable flavorings. It makes its own sauce as it bakes, and you can add potatoes to cook along with the beef and pick up its delicious aromas. All you need to complete the main course is a fresh vegetable or two, such as braised carrots, green beans, or peas, and a fine red wine.

BUYING THE BEEF. The ideal as well as the most expensive cut is the loin strip, sometimes called the top loin or shell; this is a long, solid, lean piece lying along the small of the back or loin. When cut into steaks, the loin gives porterhouses and T-bones; when the loin is boned, it furnishes the tenderloin and the loin strip. In French the loin strip is called *faux-filet* or *contre-filet*. Alternate cuts are a roast from the sirloin (hip or rump), the eye of the rib, or its less expensive continuation into the chuck, sometimes called the undercut chuck. Order your roast in advance, specifying a well-aged, top-quality cut of beef that has been boned, trimmed of all outside fat and gristle, and tied into a cylindrical shape about 5 inches in diameter. A 4½-pound roast will be 8 to 9 inches long and serve 8 to 10 people. Ask also for a piece of suet (beef fat) or a strip of fresh pork fat the length and width of the roast; this you can lay over the meat and it will act as an automatic baster.

TIMING. Any cylindrical, lean roast of beef about 5 inches in diameter will take approximately an hour to cook to an internal temperature of 130 degrees (medium rare) in a 350-degree oven. It is the diameter of the meat, not its weight or length, that determines the timing. If the roast is 6 inches long, it will take a few minutes less, and if it is 12 inches long it will take a few minutes more than an hour. You should allow 10 minutes for browning the beef, which you can do several hours before roasting, and 15 to 20 minutes of rest after roasting, to allow the juices to retreat back into the meat before carving. If you have a well-regulated oven, you can leave the roasted meat at 120 degrees for an hour or more, and have no fears about overcooking.

ᐳ

RÔTI DE BOEUF POÊLÉ A LA MATIGNON

(*Casserole Roast of Beef with Aromatic Vegetables and Potatoes*)
For 8 to 10 people

PRELIMINARIES AND ROASTING

A 4½-lb. boned and trimmed roast of beef tied into a cylinder about 5 inches in diameter

A heavy oval or rectangular casserole or roaster just large enough to hold beef and potatoes (13x10x5 inches, for example)

Salt

Cooking oil

1 cup cooked *mirepoix* (⅔ cup each of finely diced celery, carrots, and onions, and ¼ cup diced boiled ham, all cooked together in 2 Tb butter until very lightly browned)

16 or more "boiling" potatoes trimmed into 3 by 1½-inch ovals

½ tsp dried thyme

A meat thermometer

A 10x6x¼-inch piece of beef suet or fresh pork fat

A cover for the casserole or roaster

(Preheat oven to 350 degrees.)

Dry the beef thoroughly on paper towels. Film the bottom of the casserole with ⅛-inch layer of oil and set over moderately high heat. When oil is almost smoking, brown the beef on all sides and on the two ends—8 to 10 minutes. Remove the beef. Dry the potatoes in a towel, and brown them in the hot fat in the casserole; drain the fat out of the casserole, salt the potatoes, and push them to the sides. Salt the meat and return it to the casserole. Sprinkle the thyme over the meat, and spread on the cooked *mirepoix*; cover the meat with the suet or pork fat. Insert meat thermometer, being sure its point reaches the center of the meat, and that it is angled so that the casserole cover will not disturb it. (You may complete all of this step in advance of roasting, except for the browning of the potatoes; reheat casserole to sizzling before you proceed. Note that if the browned beef has been chilled, you should add about 10 minutes more to the roasting time.)

Cover the hot casserole and set in lower-middle level of pre-heated oven. Roast for about an hour, basting potatoes twice with the juices in the casserole. As soon as meat thermometer reaches 120 degrees, watch out: temperature rises very quickly from this point on. Immediately when meat thermometer registers 130 degrees for medium rare (125 for rare), remove casserole from oven and take beef out of casserole, discarding suet or pork fat, and scraping *mirepoix* back into casserole. You will note that temperature on meat thermometer will continue to rise a few degrees; if meat remains in hot casserole it may overcook. Discard beef-trussing strings but leave thermometer in place unless you are serving shortly. Test potatoes with a knife: if not done, cover casserole and return to oven for an additional few minutes.

THE SAUCE

1 to 2 cups beef bouillon or stock	1 Tb tomato paste
	Salt and pepper

Remove potatoes to a side dish. Skim fat off cooking juices and set casserole over high heat. Stir in the stock or bouillon and the tomato paste, and boil rapidly for a few minutes to concentrate flavor, adding salt and pepper if necessary. The *mirepoix* vegetables remain in the sauce.

IF NOT SERVING IMMEDIATELY

If you are not serving immediately, return beef and potatoes to casserole. Cover and set in turned-off oven, or in warming oven at not more than 120 degrees. When the beef has cooled slightly, and when oven temperature is no more than 120 degrees, the meat may safely remain for an hour or more before carving and serving.

SERVING

Carve the beef and arrange the slices on a warm platter, surrounded by the potatoes and whatever other vegetables you have chosen. Spoon the sauce with its *mirepoix* over the meat, and serve immediately.

An excellent, fairly full-bodied red, such as a Bordeaux-Saint-Emilion, or one of the lighter red Burgundies.

Carottes en Feuilles, Braisées au Beurre
(*Carrot Slivers Braised in Butter*)

2 lbs. carrots	½ tsp salt
A 10- to 12-inch skillet	¼ tsp sugar
2 Tb butter	⅔ cup water

Peel the carrots; cut into 2-inch crosswise pieces, then into lengthwise slices less than ⅛ inch thick—use a special slicing machine, or the slicing side of a grater for this. Place the carrot slivers in skillet with the butter, salt, sugar, and water. Cover and cook at a slow boil for about 20 minutes or until liquid has evaporated and carrots are tender. Then uncover and toss over moderately high heat for several minutes to brown very lightly. Season to taste. (May be cooked in advance and re-heated.)

The Hundred and Fifteenth Show

DINNER PARTY:
MERINGUE DESSERT
(*Le Vacherin*)

Beat egg whites and sugar to snowy peaks, and you can build yourself one of the most stunning desserts imaginable: a meringue case, the *vacherin*, an edible dish to hold the main body of your final course. It is a beautiful sight to see and to eat, and amusing to construct.

The *vacherin* is made of ordinary meringue mixture, and consists of a large flat circle 7 to 8 inches in diameter, 3 large rings, and various small decorative shapes. After these different elements have been baked, the rings are mounted on the circle to form a cylinder, the sides are spread with uncooked meringue, and the decorations are pressed on. The case is then baked again until the meringue has set.

BAKING TALK. Like ordinary meringues or kisses, the *vacherin* does not actually bake: it dries out slowly in the oven, and should not color any more than a pale ivory. It is therefore imperative that you regulate your oven so that the heat does not go over 200 degrees. If your oven is unreliable, turn it on for 10 minutes, turn it off for 20 minutes, and keep turning it on and off to maintain the heat at not more than 200 degrees (and have a good oven thermometer). The first part of the cooking takes 1 to 1½ hours; the final assembled masterpiece, about an hour or more.

THE TOOLS OF THE TRADE. You will need an electric mixer to beat the meringue, and the easiest way to form the meringue shapes is with an old-fashioned pliable canvas pastry bag. You will need one bag 14 inches long and another 12 inches long; one metal tube with a round ½-inch opening and another with a ¼-inch opening. If you have trouble finding pastry bag sets, look in the classified directory under hotel and restaurant supplies or bakery supplies; this is standard professional equipment.

LE VACHERIN

(Meringue Case for Dessert Creams, Ice Cream,
or Fruit and Berry Mixtures)
For a 7- to 8-inch vacherin about 4 inches high

THE MERINGUE MIXTURE

Note that proportions are ⅓ cup sugar per egg white: ½ of the sugar is beaten in, the other half is folded in. One "large" egg white is 2 tablespoons.

6 egg whites (¾ cup), at
room temperature
An electric mixer and mixer
bowl
¼ tsp cream of tartar
¼ tsp salt

1 cup granulated sugar
("instant" very fine if
possible)
2 tsp vanilla extract
1 additional cup granulated
sugar

Be sure egg whites are at room temperature, and that mixer bowl and beater are absolutely dry and free of grease, otherwise the egg whites will not mount properly.

Start beating the egg whites at moderately slow speed until they foam but are still soft and shapeless. Then beat in the cream of tartar and salt. Gradually increase speed to moderately fast. As soon as the egg whites hold their shape softly (in about a minute), beat in ¼ cup of the sugar. Beat for 30 seconds, add another ¼ cup sugar, beat for 30 seconds, and continue thus until the first cup of sugar has been added. Beat in the vanilla. Increase beating speed to fast and beat for 2 to 3 minutes, until the sugar has completely dissolved (you can feel no sugar granules on your tongue), and the mixture forms very stiff upstanding peaks when a bit is lifted on a spatula. Draw the spatula through the egg whites, scraping the bottom of the bowl: the spatula path remains; the walls do not tumble down. It is important that the meringue be stiff, so you can form it into the shapes you wish.

Remove beater bowl from stand and immediately sprinkle ¼ of the additional cup of sugar over the meringue mixture, rapidly fold in with a rubber spatula, and continue rapidly folding in the sugar by ¼-cup sprinkles. You are now ready to form the *vacherin* elements.

FORMING THE VACHERIN ELEMENTS

2 baking sheets at least
15½x11½ inches ("no-
stick" if possible)
1 Tb butter
All-purpose flour

2 canvas pastry bags, 14 and
12 inches long, and metal
tubes with round ½- and
¼-inch openings

(Preheat oven to 250 degrees.)

Lightly butter the entire top surface of each baking sheet; roll flour around to cover entire top surface with a thin film and knock off excess flour. Mark two circles 7 to 8 inches in diameter on each baking sheet—making four circles in all— drawing around any convenient object such as a cake pan or soufflé mold. These are to guide you in forming the meringues. Fit the 14-inch bag with a ½-inch tube, and fill with the meringue mixture.

THE BOTTOM CIRCLE Starting at the inside rim of one circle mark, squeeze out a line of meringue the width of your thumb, going round and round in a diminishing spiral until you have filled in the circle. Smooth out the meringue with a spatula. The circle should be about ⅜ inch high.

THE THREE RINGS These form the sides of the cylinder. Squeeze out three rings of meringue about 1 inch wide and ½ inch high in the three other circle marks. Smooth with a spatula.

DECORATIONS Squeeze your decorations into the empty spaces in and around the three circles and around the ring. For example, make a dozen round meringues about 1¼ inches in diameter and 1 inch high. Place your filled pastry bag in the spare bag fitted with a ¼-inch tube, and make twenty little meringues ¼ inch in size; make four to six "V" shapes 3 inches long to stick on the sides of the *vacherin*.

You will have about 2 cups of meringue mixture left; save this for final assembly.

BAKING

Set the baking sheets on the upper-middle and lower-middle racks of your preheated 250-degree oven; immediately turn heat down to 200 degrees. Bake for an hour or more, regulating oven heat so that meringues are not coloring. Meringues are done when you can gently push them loose from the baking sheets.

ASSEMBLING AND FINAL BAKING

The uncooked meringue mixture should still be stiff enough

for spreading; if it has softened, beat it for a moment at high speed until it again forms peaks.

Mount the meringue rings on the circle, holding them in place with uncooked meringue. If they break, cement them together with uncooked meringue; the breaks will not show when all is assembled.

Smooth a ¼-inch coating of uncooked meringue around the sides and top of the case, using a flexible spatula. Press your decorative elements onto the top and sides.

Return the *vacherin* to a 200-degree oven for about an hour, or until the uncooked meringue has dried to the touch. (You can set the *vacherin* on a heatproof serving dish for this final baking.)

Keep *vacherin* in turned-off oven until serving time. If weather is humid, you may have to keep heat on low (100 degrees), or reheat again before serving. A baked *vacherin* may be frozen; dry it out in a 200-degree oven before serving.

FILLING SUGGESTIONS (To Be Spooned into the Vacherin Just Before Serving)

Fresh fruit macerated in liqueur and sugar, and folded into whipped cream or pastry cream (*crème pâtissière*); or ice cream or sherbet decorated with fruits; or fresh berries macerated in liqueur and sugar, and whipped cream passed separately.

The Hundred and Sixteenth Show

SOUPS

ও§ • ইৣ

(Provençal Vegetable Soup; Cream of
Cucumber Soup)

Soup as a main course, soup to begin the meal—and when it is homemade, it is soup to nourish the soul. Here are two unusual recipes, one a hearty and fragrant main-course soup from Provence, and the other a cucumber soup which you can serve either hot or cold.

SOUPE AU PISTOU
(Provençal Vegetable Soup with Garlic, Basil, and Cheese)
For 6 people

Early summer is the Mediterranean season for *soupe au pistou*, when fresh basil, fresh white beans, and broad *mange-tout* beans are all suddenly available, and the marketwomen shout in the streets, "Mesdames, faites le bon piste, faites le pistou!" The word *pistou*, like the Italian *pesta*, means a sauce of garlic, basil, tomato, and cheese into which the hot soup is stirred just before serving. The soup always contains potatoes, carrots, leeks or onions, dried beans, and a handful of *pasta*, but you can enrich the brew with other vegetables in season, such as fresh peas, zucchini, green or red peppers. The soup base of root vegetables can be boiled up several hours in advance, and this is quickly done in a pressure cooker; the green vegetables are boiled in the soup only shortly before serving, so they will retain their fresh color.

THE SOUP BASE

For a pressure cooker: 2
quarts water

For an open 4-quart kettle:
3 quarts water

2 Tb salt
2 cups each of diced carrots,
diced "boiling" potatoes,
and diced white of leeks
or yellow onions

Optional: 2 cups fresh white
beans or cranberry or
horticultural beans

Place all ingredients in the pressure cooker or kettle. Either cook for exactly 5 minutes under 15 pounds pressure and release pressure under cold water, or simmer uncovered for 40 minutes. If you are cooking the base in advance, set aside uncovered until 20 minutes before you wish to serve the soup, then bring to the boil and proceed with the recipe.

ADDITIONAL VEGETABLES AND FLAVORINGS

(To Be Added 15 Minutes Before Serving)

2 cups diced fresh green
beans
⅓ cup small *pasta* or
spaghetti broken into ½-
inch pieces
1 slice stale white bread,
crumbled
If you have not used fresh
white beans: 1 cup canned

cannellini, navy, or kidney
beans, drained
Large pinch saffron flowers
Large pinch pepper
Optional: 1 to 2 cups or a
mixture of diced fresh
zucchini, green peas, red
or green bell peppers
Boiling water if necessary

Add the additional vegetables and flavorings to the boiling soup base and boil slowly, uncovered, until green vegetables are tender. Add boiling water if soup seems too thick. Carefully correct seasoning, and soup is ready for the *pistou* flavoring and serving.

PISTOU FLAVORING, AND SERVING

A soup tureen or serving
casserole
4 cloves garlic
4 Tb tomato paste
¼ cup fresh basil leaves,

chopped; or 1½ Tb dried
basil
½ cup grated Parmesan
cheese
½ cup olive oil
3 to 4 Tb fresh parsley,
chopped

While the soup is boiling prepare the *pistou* flavoring in a soup tureen or serving casserole. Put the garlic cloves through a press; stir in the tomato paste, basil, and cheese. Then, with a wire whip, gradually beat in the oil by droplets to make a thick paste.

Just before serving, dribble several ladlefuls of hot soup into the *pistou*, stirring constantly; gradually stir in the rest of the soup. Stir in the parsley, and serve at once accompanied by hot French bread.

POTAGE AUX CONCOMBRES
(Cream of Cucumber Soup, Hot or Cold)
For 4 to 6 people

This delicious soup has a surprise thickening: *semoule de blé*, or farina, which turns out to be baby's breakfast cereal. Serve the soup hot as a first course, or chill it for a hot summer day.

2 eight-inch cucumbers (1 lb.)	3 Tb quick-cooking farina breakfast cereal
2 Tb butter	A food mill with medium disk, or a coarse sieve and wooden spoon
A heavy 3-quart saucepan	
¼ cup chopped shallots or scallions	
4 cups clear chicken broth	Milk or more chicken broth if needed
1 tsp wine vinegar	Salt and pepper
½ tsp dried dillweed or tarragon	About 1 cup sour cream
	1 Tb dillweed or chopped parsley

Peel the cucumbers. Cut 12 to 18 paper-thin slices and reserve in a bowl for later. Chop the rest of the cucumbers into ½-inch chunks: you will have about 3 cups.

Melt the butter in the saucepan, stir in the shallots or scallions, and cook over moderate heat for 1 minute, then add the cucumber chunks, chicken broth, vinegar, and dill or tarragon. Bring to the boil, then stir in the farina. Simmer uncovered for 20 minutes, or until farina is very tender. Purée through food mill or sieve, and return the soup to the pan. It should be the consistency of *vichyssoise;* thin out with spoonfuls of milk or chicken broth if necessary. Season to taste with salt and white pepper; if soup is to be served cold, oversalt slightly.

SERVING

To serve hot, bring soup to simmer just before serving and beat in ½ cup of sour cream. Ladle into soup bowls; place a dollop of sour cream in each bowl, float slices of cucumber on top, and decorate with a sprinkling of dill or parsley.

To serve cold, beat in ½ cup of sour cream and allow soup to cool, stirring occasionally to prevent a skin from forming on top; cover and chill. Ladle into chilled soup cups, adding a spoonful of sour cream and a topping of cucumber slices and dill or parsley to each cup.

The Hundred and Seventeenth Show

QUENELLES

One of France's great contributions to the art of fish cookery is the *quenelle,* a purée of fish bound together with a very thick sauce, eggs, and cream which is then formed into 3-inch cylinders or ovals. These are poached in seasoned liquid until they swell almost double in size, and can then be served with any of the lovely sauces and garnitures you would use for fillets of sole. Serve *quenelles* as a first course, or with a fresh green vegetable or salad and chilled bottle of white wine for luncheon or supper.

CHOICE OF FISH. The type of fish to use for *quenelles* is one with lean, close-grained flesh of a slightly gelatinous quality which will combine solidly enough with the rest of the ingredients so that a good amount of cream can be beaten in; the more cream the paste will absorb, the more delicate and delicious the *quenelle*. In France, pike (*brochet*) is traditional. Although perfect in texture, pike is so webbed with tiny bones that you must shred or pound the fish and purée it through a sieve or food mill to extract them. Boneless and skinless fish fillets can simply be put through a meat grinder. Recommended choices are halibut, particularly baby halibut; cusk; conger or sea eel; silver hake; green or ocean cod; or one of the firmer-fleshed flounder or soles, such as gray sole or dab. You may also use lean fresh salmon.

QUENELLES DE POISSON

(Fish Quenelles)
For about 16 three-inch pieces serving 8 people

THE PÂTE À CHOUX, PANADE, OR THICK SAUCE BASE

1 cup water	(measure by sifting di-
½ stick (2 ounces) butter	rectly into dry-measure
cut into ½-inch pieces	cup; sweep off excess with
2 tsp salt	straight edge of knife)
A heavy-bottomed 3-quart	2 eggs (U. S. graded
saucepan	"large")
1 cup all-purpose flour	2 egg whites (¼ cup)

Bring water, butter, and salt to the simmer. As soon as butter has melted, remove saucepan from heat, pour in all the flour at once, and beat vigorously with a wooden spoon until thoroughly blended. Return saucepan over moderately high heat and continue beating with a wooden spoon for a minute or so, until mixture forms a ball which leaves the sides of the pan, leaves the spoon clean, and finally begins to film the bottom of the pan: this is to evaporate all excess moisture.

Again remove saucepan from heat. Make a depression in the center of the hot paste with your spoon, break an egg into the depression, and beat vigorously until the egg is absorbed into the paste—about a minute. Repeat with the second egg, then with one egg white (2 tablespoons), and the final egg white. Spread the paste in a flat, lightly buttered dish, cover with lightly buttered paper, and chill thoroughly—30 minutes in the freezer if you are in a hurry.

PÂTE À QUENELLES—THE QUENELLE PASTE

2 cups (1 lb.) finely ground   Pinch of nutmeg
   lean raw fish fillets, chilled   Salt and white pepper
2 to 8 Tb heavy cream,
   chilled

Place the chilled ground fish in the large bowl of an electric mixer, or a large mixing bowl. Measure out 2 cups of the chilled *pâte à choux*, add to the fish, and beat vigorously for several minutes until paste is thick, glutinous, and holds its shape in a quite solid mass.

Then start beating in the chilled cream, 2 tablespoons at a time, and beating a good minute before the next addition. The object here is to beat in as much cream as possible, but still to retain enough body so that the paste can be shaped and poached without disintegrating. This you will have to judge by eye and feel, and by test: drop a spoonful into not-quite-simmering water and poach for several minutes; beat another spoonful or two of cream into the paste if the test sample seems too dry. Finally beat in a pinch of nutmeg, and salt and white pepper to taste.

SHAPING AND POACHING THE QUENELLES

Fill a 12-inch skillet or saucepan with 2 inches of water, salt to taste, and bring to the simmer.

For cylindrical shapes, take dessertspoon bits of the *quenelle* paste and roll with the palm of one hand on a lightly floured board, making sausage shapes about 3 inches long and 1 inch in diameter. Slip into the salted water.

For spoon shapes, dip a dessertspoon into cold water, gather up a rounded mass of the paste, and transfer spoon to your left hand. Dip a second spoon into cold water, invert the bowl over the paste to smooth the top, then rotate the spoon around under the paste and dislodge it into the water. Rapidly form *quenelles* with the rest of the paste in the same manner.

Let the *quenelles* poach uncovered for 12 to 15 minutes, maintaining water not quite at the simmer. They will swell almost double, and roll over easily. Remove with a slotted spoon and drain on paper towels. They should be very delicate in texture, and must be handled gently.

If the *quenelles* are not to be served immediately, arrange in a lightly buttered baking dish, brush with melted butter, cover with waxed paper. They will keep a day or two in the refrigerator, or may be frozen.

SERVING SUGGESTIONS

Quenelles Gratinées au Fromage. Sprinkle the *quenelles* liberally with grated Swiss cheese and melted butter. Bake in upper third of a preheated 375-degree oven for about 25 minutes, until cheese has browned nicely.

Quenelles Gratinées à la Florentine. Arrange the *quenelles* on a bed of chopped cooked spinach, cover with cheese sauce, grated cheese, and melted butter; bake as in the preceding suggestion.

Quenelles à la Parisienne. Cover the *quenelles* and bake in the middle level of a 350-degree oven for 20 minutes, or until thoroughly heated. Garnish with hot poached oysters and cooked shrimp or lobster meat. Top with an excellent white-wine fish *velouté* or *hollandaise* sauce, and decorate with fluted mushrooms and chopped truffles.

The Hundred and Eighteenth Show

GÉNOISE CAKE

✧ · ✧

(French Butter Cream with Sugar Syrup)

When you are in the mood for a great layer cake, a wedding cake, or *petits fours*, the *génoise* is the one cake to bake. In contrast to spongecakes or *biscuits* which have beaten egg whites folded into the batter and, as the name implies, are rather spongy and soft in texture, the *génoise* is a firmer and drier cake: this makes it ideal for splitting into layers or for cutting into *petits fours*. Made in an entirely different manner than spongecakes, the *génoise* consists of whole eggs and sugar beaten over hot water until warm and foamy, then beaten at room temperature until cool and thick before flour and tepid melted butter are folded in. As there is long beating involved, an electric mixer is useful, and when you come to the final phase of the batter, be sure your butter is barely tepid and that you fold both butter and flour rapidly into the eggs, then bake immediately. If the butter is warm, it may deflate the eggs, and if you dally before baking, the butter may sink to the bottom of the cake pan.

GÉNOISE CAKE

For about a 9-inch cake serving 6 to 8 people

PRELIMINARIES

4 Tb (2 ounces) butter
1 tsp softened butter (for pan and paper)
A 6-cup round (9x1½ inches) or square (8x 8x2 inches) cake pan
Waxed paper cut to fit bottom of pan exactly
¼ cup all-purpose flour

(Preheat oven to 325 degrees.)

Melt the butter and set somewhere on top of the stove so it will stay melted; it must be barely tepid when you use it later. Smear butter over the entire surface of the cake pan and fit the waxed paper in the bottom. Butter the paper. Roll flour inside of pan to cover it completely; knock out excess flour. Set rack in middle of oven.

BEATING THE EGGS AND SUGAR

4 eggs (U. S. graded "large")
The large bowl of your electric mixer or a copper or stainless-steel mixing bowl
⅔ cup granulated sugar

2 tsp vanilla extract
The grated rind of 1 lemon or orange
A large pan of almost-simmering water
A very large wire whip

Break the eggs into the mixing bowl, add the sugar, vanilla, and lemon or orange rind. Set bowl over pan of almost-simmering water and beat with your large wire whip, using an up-and-down circular motion, 2 strokes per second. Beat until mixture is foaming, has almost doubled in volume, and is warm to your finger—5 minutes or more.

Remove bowl from hot water, set on mixer stand (or in cold water), and beat at a moderately fast speed for 5 minutes or more until cool. The egg mixture should be thick and creamy; when you lift a bit with a rubber spatula or whip, it will drop back onto the surface forming a slowly dissolving ribbon.

FOLDING IN THE FLOUR AND BUTTER, AND BAKING

1½ cups plain bleached cake flour

A rubber spatula
4 Tb melted butter, barely tepid

Measure the flour by sifting directly into 1- and ½-cup dry measures, sweep off excess with straight edge of knife, and return flour to sifter. When the egg mixture is cool and thick, you are ready to fold in the flour and the barely tepid butter; this is to be done in alternating bits, and as rapidly as possible.

Set the egg-mixture bowl on a wet potholder or in a heavy casserole to hold it steady. With one hand, sift on one fourth of the flour and rapidly fold it with the rubber spatula held in the other hand. When almost incorporated, fold in a tablespoon of the barely tepid butter, then one third of the remaining flour, then another tablespoon butter. Continue rapidly with half the remaining flour, another tablespoon of butter, and finally the last of the flour and a fourth tablespoon of butter (be sure not to add the milky residue at the bottom of the butter pan, as this tends to deflate the batter).

Immediately turn batter into prepared cake pan, tipping pan in all directions to run batter up sides, so cake will not puff in the middle; bang pan lightly on table to settle the batter. Pan will be filled by about two thirds.

Set at once in middle level of preheated oven and bake for 35 to 40 minutes. Cake is done when it has risen to the rim of the pan, is springy when pressed, and has begun to show a very faint line of shrinkage from the edge of the pan. Remove from oven and let cool for 10 minutes, then reverse onto a cake rack, peel off paper, and let cake cool completely. (If not to be iced when cold, wrap in a plastic bag and refrigerate or freeze; cake will dry out if not covered air-tight.)

FILLING AND FROSTING

Split cool cake in half horizontally and separate the two halves, their insides facing up. If you are using liqueur in your filling, sprinkle each half of the cake with a few drops. Spread a ¼-inch layer of filling on top half, and re-form the cake which will now be upside down, as bottom face is the smoothest. Spread frosting over cake, and smooth with a metal spatula dipped in water. Decorate with lines of melted chocolate pushed through a paper cone, with rosettes, or with whatever else may strike your fancy. (Following is a recipe for French butter cream which may be used for both filling and frosting.)

Crème au Beurre, au Sucre Cuit
(French Butter Cream Made with Sugar Syrup)
For about 2 cups

1 egg plus 3 egg yolks
The large bowl of your
    electric mixer or a 2½-
    quart copper or stainless-
    steel mixing bowl
⅔ cup granulated sugar
3 Tb water
A small heavy saucepan
A pan of almost-simmering
    water

2 sticks (½ lb.) softened
    unsalted butter
Flavoring choices: 2 to 3 Tb
    kirsch, rum, orange
    liqueur, or strong coffee;
    or 1 Tb vanilla extract; or
    2 to 3 ounces melted
    chocolate

Break eggs into the bowl. Place the sugar and water in sauce-pan and swirl over high heat until sugar has melted and liquid is clear; boil rapidly to the soft-ball stage (238 degrees). Then, beating the eggs with a wire whip, pour the hot sugar syrup by droplets onto the eggs. Set bowl over pan of almost-simmering water and beat with a wire whip until mixture is very hot to your finger, and when a bit is lifted it drops back onto the surface forming a slowly dissolving ribbon. Set bowl in mixer stand (or over cold water) and beat until cool—5 minutes.

Beat in the softened butter by tablespoonfuls, then beat in the flavoring. If cream separates a bit after you have added the flavoring, simply beat in more softened butter by spoonfuls until cream is again smooth and velvety. (If too soft for spreading, chill until firm enough to handle easily. Butter cream will keep for 4 to 5 days under refrigeration, or may be frozen—let soften at room temperature before using, and beat to smooth and cream it. You may have to add a bit more butter if it appears grainy.)

The New Year Show

CROQUEMBOUCHE

᪥ • ᪥

CROQUEMBOUCHE

Here is a splendid edible centerpiece for your New Year's table, the *croquembouche*—row upon row of tiny cream puffs mounted into a conical tower and glittering with caramel. It's fun to assemble and is guaranteed to bring gasps of delight from your guests.

Les Choux

(The Cream Puffs)

For about 70 puffs, for a croquembouche 16 inches high

THE PÂTE À CHOUX—CREAM-PUFF PASTRY

1½ cups water
9 Tb (1 stick plus 1 Tb)
    butter
¼ tsp salt
2 tsp sugar
A heavy 3-quart saucepan
1½ cups all-purpose flour

(measure by sifting directly into 1- and ½-cup dry measures; sweep off excess flour)
5 to 6 eggs (U. S. graded "large")

Place water, butter, salt, and sugar in saucepan and bring to the boil. When butter has melted and water is bubbling, remove saucepan from heat; immediately pour in all the flour and beat with a wooden spoon to blend thoroughly. Set over moderate heat and beat with wooden spoon for a minute or two, until mixture leaves sides of pan clean, leaves spoon clean, and begins to film on the bottom of the pan; this is to evaporate all excess moisture. In culinary language, you now have a *panade*.

Make a depression in the center of the hot *panade* with your spoon, break an egg into it, and beat thoroughly until the egg is absorbed. Continue with four more eggs one at a time, and beating in each until thoroughly absorbed. (You may use an electric mixer for adding the eggs; if the mixture clogs the beaters, you'll have to resort again to the spoon.)

Whether or not to add all or part of the sixth egg depends on the consistency of the pastry: if it is too soft, it will spread out when formed. Test by lifting up a mass of the paste in your spoon: it should hold its shape; plop a bit on a plate: it should hold its shape. If it seems too stiff, beat the sixth egg in a small bowl, then beat a tablespoon into the pastry; test again, adding more egg if you think it necessary.

This is now *pâte à choux*; use it while still warm, or it becomes too stiff.

FORMING THE PUFFS

2 large baking sheets
   (14x18 inches is a good
   size)

Egg glaze (1 egg beaten.
   with ½ tsp cold water)

(Preheat oven to 425 degrees.)

Lightly butter the two largest baking sheets that will fit into your oven. Either with a soup spoon or with a pastry bag and ½-inch tube, form circular blobs of *pâte à choux* 1 inch in diameter and 1 inch high, spaced 1½ inches apart on the sheets. With leftover pastry, make a decoration for the top of the *croquembouche*, such as a 4x2½-inch oval ¼ inch thick, continuing one end of the oval into a 2-inch stem. (You may have to put this on a separate sheet and bake it later.)

Paint the tops of the puffs with egg glaze, pushing them into shape if necessary with the flat of your brush. Be careful not to let glaze dribble down the sides of the puffs onto the baking sheet; this will prevent puffs from rising.

BAKING

Place the filled baking sheets in the upper- and lower-middle levels of the preheated oven and bake for about 20 minutes, or until puffs are a nice golden brown and crisp to the touch;

they should double in size. Turn oven down to 350 degrees and bake 10 minutes more, then turn oven off, leave door ajar, and let puffs cool. They must be thoroughly dried out and crisp for the *croquembouche*. (Baked and cooled puffs may be frozen.)

FILLING SUGGESTIONS

If you wish to mount the *croquembouche* hours ahead of time, it is best to use unfilled puffs. Filled puffs may become soggy in 2 hours.

As you can easily transform *pâte à choux* into a pastry-cream filling, you could make a little extra *pâte à choux* to begin with, by adding to the original proportions: ½ cup water, 3 tablespoons butter, ½ cup flour, and 1 egg. When you have finished forming your 70 puffs and the decoration, beat the extra pastry with 2 to 3 tablespoons of milk in a heavy saucepan over moderate heat. When mixture is simmering, thin out to desired consistency with dribbles of milk, and sweeten to taste with several tablespoons of sugar. Flavor to taste with vanilla and kirsch, rum, or coffee. The easiest way to fill the puffs is with a pastry bag and a ¼-inch tube, plunged into the bottom or sides of the puffs.

MOUNTING THE CROQUEMBOUCHE

When you are ready to assemble, find any type of slant-sided container that is about 8 inches at the top, 7 inches at the bottom, and 4 or more inches deep (a flowerpot lined with heavy aluminum foil would do). Smear the entire interior with tasteless salad oil. You will line this container with caramel-dipped puffs to form the base of the *croquembouche*; because the container is oiled, you can slip the base out of it.

THE CARAMEL

2 cups granulated sugar	2 Tb corn syrup
⅔ cup water	A heavy saucepan

Bring the sugar, water, and corn syrup to the boil over high heat, swirling pan until sugar has completely dissolved and liquid is clear and limpid. Cover pan closely: rising steam will condense on cover, drop down sides of pan, and wash off sugar crystals. Remove cover in 3 to 4 minutes, when bubbles have become large and liquid is a thick syrup. Continue boiling several minutes more until syrup turns amber. Swirl pan slowly as syrup darkens into a golden caramel brown; remove pan from heat just before it is quite as dark as you wish it to be, as the heat of the pan will deepen the color. To prevent caramel from hardening, either set pan in another pan of simmering water, or place it on 2 or 3 asbestos mats over very low heat.

BUILDING

Spearing puffs with a small knife, dip them one by one into the caramel and make a ring of upside-down puffs around the inside of the container, being sure each puff is glued to its neighbor with caramel. Build another ring on top of the first, and continue until the sides of the mold are covered. Let cool 5 minutes, then run a thin knife between puffs and edge of container to loosen the base; unmold onto an upturned cake tin. Build four or more rows of right-side-up caramel-dipped puffs on top of the base, slanting each row slightly inward to make a conical shape. Dip stem of decoration into caramel and set into the center of the top row.

FINAL DECORATION

Dip a spoon into the caramel and dribble lines over the entire *croquembouche*, then dip a fork into the caramel and wave it around and around the *croquembouche* to surround it with threads of spun caramel. Set on a serving platter.

Tuck sprigs of holly around the base, and decorate with any other items that will make for a HAPPY NEW YEAR!

The Hundred and Nineteenth Show

PETITS FOURS
ఆ§ • ?ఎ
(*Fondant Icing*)

Petits fours are little filled cakes about 2 inches in diameter, covered with sugar frosting called fondant, and topped with such decorative items as candied violets, sugar flowers, nuts, or chocolate. The cake for *petits fours* can be plain spongecake, but the *génoise* is easier to handle because it is firmer and drier. The filling can be anything you wish; French butter cream is particularly good. Fondant frosting is sugar syrup boiled to the soft-ball stage, then kneaded until the syrup miraculously turns snowy white. To use fondant, you simply soften it over heat with a little liqueur or other flavoring. It is always useful to have fondant on hand, as it keeps for months, and is ever ready to become a smooth, fine icing for cakes, cookies, glacéed fruits, or nuts.

FONDANT
(*Sugar Frosting for Cakes, Petits Fours*)
For about 2 cups

BOILING THE SUGAR SYRUP

3 Tb white corn syrup (or ¼ tsp cream of tartar)
1 cup water
A heavy-bottomed 2-quart saucepan

3 cups (about 20 ounces) granulated sugar
A candy thermometer and/ or a quart measure with 3 cups water, and a metal spoon

Dissolve the corn syrup or cream of tartar with a bit of the water in the saucepan; pour in the rest of the water, and the sugar. Set over high heat, swirling pan gently as liquid comes to the boil and until sugar has completely dissolved and liquid is clear. (You should never stir the syrup, and swirl the pan only as much as necessary to dissolve the sugar: stirring may cause sugar crystals to form on sides of pan.) As soon as syrup is clear, cover pan and boil rapidly for 3 minutes; steam condensing on pan cover washes crystals down sides of pan. Then remove cover, insert candy thermometer if you are using one, and continue boiling for a few minutes to the soft-ball stage: 238 degrees on a candy thermometer, or if you drop a bit of syrup into cold water it holds its shape softly when you pick it up in your fingers, and relaxes as soon as pressure is released. (*Note:* If you do not boil the syrup to the soft-ball stage, your finished fondant will be too soft; if you go beyond it, the fondant will be hard to knead and difficult to melt.)

COOLING THE SYRUP

Pour the syrup onto a marble surface at least 18 by 24 inches, or into a jelly-roll pan or large metal tray, bracing edge of pan or tray against a wall. Let syrup cool about 10 minutes, until barely tepid to the touch: when you press it, the surface will wrinkle.

KNEADING

With a pastry scraper, a painter's spatula, or a short and stout metal turner, start kneading the syrup by pushing it up into a mass, spreading it out, and repeating this movement for 5 minutes or more. After several minutes of kneading, the syrup will

begin to whiten; as you continue kneading, it will gradually turn snow white, and finally stiffen so that you can no longer knead it—it is now fondant. (Do not be discouraged if the syrup takes more than 5, or 8, or 10 minutes to turn; this sometimes happens. It will eventually turn. If you happen to have leftover fondant, work 3 spoonfuls into the syrup after 2 or 3 minutes of kneading: this will make the turn more rapid.)

CURING

Although you can use the fondant immediately, it will have better texture and sheen if you let it rest for at least 12 hours. Pack it into a jar or bowl, top with several thicknesses of well washed, damp cheesecloth, then cover air-tight. As long as the top is damp, fondant will keep for months in the refrigerator.

HOW TO USE FONDANT

2 cups fondant
A heavy saucepan
A wooden spoon
1 or more Tb kirsch, rum,

orange liqueur, or strong
coffee; or 1 tsp vanilla
and 2 or more tsp water

Place the fondant in the saucepan with a tablespoon of liquid and set over very low heat or barely simmering water; stir thoroughly as fondant slowly softens into a very smooth cream which naps the spoon fairly heavily. Add more liquid by droplets if necessary, and heat only enough to soften and smooth the fondant. Use immediately, either pouring the fondant directly over a cake set on a rack over a tray, or spreading it rapidly on cookies, or dipping into it nuts, fruits, or *petits fours*. It sets rapidly, so you must work quickly to obtain a smooth surface.

FOR COLORED FONDANT Use strong coffee for mocha or tan, ½ cup or more of melted chocolate stirred into the melted fondant for chocolate or brown, and drops of food coloring for pastel shades.

STORING MELTED FONDANT See directions for fresh fondant; combine with several spoonfuls of fresh fondant before using again.

PETITS FOURS
For 9 pieces

A filled 8- to 9-inch *génoise*
or spongecake, 1½ inches
high
1 cup apricot glaze (1 cup
apricot jam forced
through a sieve, and
boiled to 128 degrees with
2 Tb sugar)
2 cups fondant

2 sharp-pronged kitchen
forks
A cake rack set over a tray
Decorative suggestions:
walnut or pecan halves,
candied violets or rose
petals, melted chocolate
Paper cones or cake-decorat-
ing tubes

Cut the cake into squares, rectangles, triangles, diamonds, or wedges about 2 inches in diameter. Paint tops and sides with warm apricot glaze.

Melt the fondant with whatever flavorings you have chosen and set in a pan of hot water. Pierce one of the cake pieces with a fork, entering one side of the bottom at an angle; tip fondant pan, and rotate cake in fondant to cover top and sides. Place cake on rack and dislodge it with second fork; excess fondant will drip onto tray and may be added to fondant pan later. Continue rapidly with the rest of the cakes; after dipping two or three you will begin to get the feel and to judge the correct thickness for the fondant.

Press nuts, leaves, etc., onto the *petits fours* (you may have to glue them with melted fondant), or decorate with lines or rosettes of melted chocolate pushed through a paper cone or decorating tube. If you are making chocolate *petits fours*, you may decorate them with white fondant pushed through a tube. After frosting has set, arrange the *petits fours* on a serving tray or in paper cups.

STORING PETITS FOURS

Petits fours may be refrigerated in a covered container, or frozen. Let them come to room temperature before serving, or even leave them for a moment on the open door of a warm oven, so the fondant will regain its sheen.

HOW TO MAKE A PAPER DECORATING CONE. Cut heavy freezer paper into a right-angle triangle whose short sides are 15 and 12 inches. Hold the longest or hypotenuse side of the triangle with your left hand, thumb on top, and opposite the right angle. With your right hand, curl the longer end of the hypotenuse bringing its underside around so that its point lies against the top side of the right angle. Curl the other end of the hypotenuse around the outside, its point reaching the right angle, and you have your cone shape. Secure the ends with a straight pin, and cut the point of the cone to make any size of opening you need.

The Hundred and Twentieth Show

THE MAYONNAISE SHOW

The only trouble with homemade mayonnaise is that once you've eaten your own you will never again be satisfied with anything else. It makes such a difference when you have fresh eggs, the best oil, and your own flavorings; you can then season your mayonnaise to suit the food it accompanies. Contrary to mysterious rumors perpetually circulating about the difficulties of making this famous sauce, it is extremely easy to whip up in the blender, the mixer, or by hand. Mayonnaise is nothing but egg yolks, flavorings, and oil beaten into a thick creamy sauce. As soon as you understand how the egg yolk works, you will never ever have any failures.

UNDERSTANDING THE EGG YOLK. Egg yolks are delighted to absorb oil and turn it into an emulsion—meaning a thick sauce— under the following conditions:

1. They prefer to be at room temperature.

2. They must be beaten first until they are thick and lemon-colored; this prepares them to receive the oil.

3. The oil must be fed to them in droplets at first, until the emulsion process begins; then the oil can go in more rapidly.

4. Egg yolks can only absorb a certain amount of oil; if they receive more than they can digest, the emulsion relaxes and the sauce thins out. Oil proportions are a maximum of ¾ cup per egg yolk. Thus 3 yolks can take 2½ cups, making about 2½ cups of sauce; 5 yolks can take 3¾ cups of oil, making about a quart of sauce. You can add less oil than the maximum, but never more.

HAND-MADE MAYONNAISE

For about 2½ cups of sauce

The best way to see, feel, and understand the egg yolk is to make mayonnaise by hand; after you have done it two or three times, you will find you can easily beat up a quart of sauce in less than 10 minutes.

THICKENING THE EGG YOLKS

A heavy round-bottomed 3-quart mixing bowl set upon a wet potholder or in a heavy casserole

3 egg yolks (U. S. graded "large" or larger)
A large wire whip

Warm the bowl in hot water and dry it. Add the egg yolks and beat for 1 to 2 minutes, until the yolks are thick and lemon-colored.

THE FLAVORING

½ Tb wine vinegar or lemon juice

½ tsp salt
¼ tsp dry mustard

Add the vinegar or lemon juice, salt, and mustard; beat again for 1 minute.

ADDING THE OIL

1½ to 2¼ cups of excellent olive oil, salad oil, or a mixture of each	Drops of vinegar or lemon juice Salt and white pepper

Note: The egg yolks are now ready to receive the oil, and while it goes in, drop by drop at first, you must not stop beating until the sauce has thickened; this will be after about ½ cup of oil has gone in. A beating speed of 2 strokes per second is fast enough. You can switch hands or switch directions; it makes no difference as long as you keep beating during this initial period. Keep your eye on the oil as you pour, not on the sauce; stop pouring oil occasionally and beat the sauce for several seconds to be sure all oil is being absorbed, then continue with the oil. Now to begin the sauce:

Beating the yolks continually, start adding the oil by droplets either from a spoon or from the bottle. Beat without stopping until about ½ cup of has gone in, the sauce has thickened into a heavy cream, and looks like mayonnaise. As soon as this has happened, you can relax, stop beating for a moment, and then continue. Now you may add the oil by tablespoon dollops, beating for several seconds after each addition. When sauce thickens too much, thin out with drops of vinegar or lemon juice. When you have added as much oil as you wish, up to the maximum 2½ cups, season to taste.

If you are not serving the mayonnaise immediately, scrape into a bowl or jar and cover closely to prevent a skin from forming on the surface. Store in the refrigerator; it is best not to keep mayonnaise for more than a week.

REMEDY FOR TURNED OR THINNED MAYONNAISE. A mayonnaise has turned when it refuses to thicken, or when a finished mayonnaise thins out. The remedy is simple:

Warm a mixing bowl in hot water, dry it, and add a teaspoon of prepared mustard (Dijon-type strong mustard, preferably). Add a tablespoon of the thinned sauce and beat with a wire whip for several seconds until mustard and sauce cream together; beat in the rest of the sauce by teaspoons, thickening each addition before adding the next. This always works.

MAYONNAISE IN THE ELECTRIC MIXER

This is exactly the same as hand-made mayonnaise, but you are using electricity instead of elbow grease.

MAYONNAISE IN THE ELECTRIC BLENDER

For this you must use a whole egg rather than egg yolks, and you can only make about 1¼ cups of sauce.

1 whole egg	1 Tb lemon juice or wine
¼ tsp dry mustard	vinegar
½ tsp salt	1 cup oil

Break the egg into the blender jar; cover and blend at top speed for 30 seconds. Add the mustard, salt, lemon juice or vinegar, and blend 15 seconds. Uncover jar, and blending at high speed, pour the oil into the center of the egg mixture in a very thin stream of droplets. The sauce will begin to thicken after about ½ cup of oil has gone in, and the machine clogs when you have reached about 1 cup.

VARIATION ⏀

Mayonnaise Verte (Green Mayonnaise)

This is mayonnaise with a purée of green herbs and leaves, to be served with cold egg dishes, salads, fish and shellfish, or anything you think green mayonnaise would go with. For 2½ cups of plain mayonnaise, you should have about 1 packed cup of greenery such as watercress, spinach, green peppers, scallions, and fresh herbs such as parsley, basil, chervil, tarragon. Chop roughly and add the tougher items, like scallions and peppers, to a large saucepan of boiling water. When barely soft, add the tender leaves like spinach, cress, and herbs. Boil uncovered 30 to 40 seconds, then drain and run cold water over them. Purée in the blender, drain through a sieve, and press all the water out. Beat the purée into finished mayonnaise, or add to blender while making blender mayonnaise.

The Hundred and Twenty-first Show

SWORDFISH DINNER FOR FOUR
IN HALF AN HOUR
&ᴄ § · ᶾ ∍
(Tapénade, Green Beans, Bananas Flambée)

Rule number one for quick dinners: they must never taste hasty. Success, however, depends on careful plotting of your time if you want to get everything done in one fell swoop. Here is an unusual menu to cook and serve in about 30 minutes, or to prepare in advance.

MENU:

Tapénade (Provençal Hors d'Oeuvre of Olives,
Anchovies, and Capers)
Poisson d'Épée au Four (Swordfish Steaks Baked
with Herbs and Wine)
Dés de Haricots Verts au Beurre
(Diced Green Beans in Butter)
Hot French Bread   Riesling or Pinot Blanc Wine
Bananes Flambées
(Baked Bananas, Flambée)

1) **Sautéing the Fish** (The fish is first sautéed, then baked; while it is sautéing, you can prepare the bananas.)

1½ to 2 lbs. swordfish, 1 to 1¼ inches thick, cut into steaks
Waxed paper
Salt and pepper
½ cup all-purpose flour
Olive oil or cooking oil
A flameproof baking dish just large enough to hold fish in one layer; or a skillet for sautéing, and a baking dish
A kettle with 5 to 6 quarts salted water, set to boil for the beans

Cut surrounding skin off the swordfish, wash steaks in cold water, dry on paper towels, and place on waxed paper. Salt and pepper both sides of steaks, roll in flour, and shake off excess. Pour a ⅛-inch layer of oil into baking dish or skillet and set over moderately high heat; when almost smoking, brown fish lightly for 2 to 3 minutes on each side. (Transfer from skillet to baking dish if you are not sautéing in a flameproof dish.) The swordfish is now ready for the oven.

2) *The Bananas*   (These may be prepared at any convenient time, and baked later; here they are made ready while the fish is being sautéed.)

4 Tb softened butter
A baking-serving dish just
   large enough to hold
   bananas in one layer
8 small or 4 large bananas
¼ to ½ cup dry white

vermouth, dry white wine,
   or cider
⅓ to ½ cup honey
1 Tb lemon juice
½ tsp cinnamon

Smear 2 tablespoons of the butter in the baking dish. Peel the bananas and arrange in the dish; pour on the wine or cider, honey, and lemon juice. Sprinkle with cinnamon and dot with the remaining butter. (May be prepared in advance.)

BAKING

The bananas will take about 15 minutes in the middle level of a preheated 400-degree oven, or 20 to 25 minutes in a 375-degree oven (with the fish). Baste about every 5 minutes with the liquid in the dish until bananas are soft and liquid is syrupy. You may bake ahead, and reheat; you may serve them plain or flambéed.

TO FLAME THE BANANAS

1 Tb granulated sugar   ⅓ to ½ cup cognac

Be sure that bananas are bubbling hot. Sprinkle on the table-spoon of granulated sugar, then pour the cognac around them (warm the cognac in a pan if you are not using a chafing dish). Averting your face, ignite the cognac with a lighted match and spoon it over the bananas until the flames die down. Serve on hot plates.

3.) *Baking and Serving the Fish* (Fish and bananas may bake at the same time; while they are in the oven, prepare the beans and the first course.)

½ tsp oregano	½ cup fresh white bread
¼ cup chopped shallots or	crumbs
scallions	About ½ cup dry white
	vermouth

(Preheat oven to 375 degrees.)

Sprinkle the herbs and shallots or scallions over the fish and cover with a ⅛-inch layer of bread crumbs. Baste with the sautéing oil (if burned, baste with fresh oil or with melted butter). Pour the vermouth around the fish; it should came about halfway up. (May be prepared in advance to this point.)

Bake for 20 to 25 minutes in upper third of a preheated oven, basting several times with the liquid in the dish. The steaks are done when a fork pierces them easily; do not overcook or the fish will be dry. (You may bake in advance and reheat the fish if you are very careful not to overcook it.)

Either serve the fish from the baking dish or transfer it to a hot platter and surround with the cooked green beans. If you have more time, you might add buttered noodles tossed with fresh cream and Parmesan cheese; if not, plenty of hot French bread will suffice.

4) *The Fresh Green Beans* (Tip and dice these at any spare moment, complete the preparation when the fish is in the oven, then boil them. Refreshed in cold water in the French manner, the beans may be cooked in advance and finished off hours later with no loss of color, flavor, or texture.)

1½ to 2 lbs. fresh green	A kettle of boiling salted
beans	water

A large enameled saucepan	Optional: 1 tsp lemon juice
or skillet	and 2 Tb minced fresh
3 to 4 Tb butter	parsley

Snap off the two ends of the beans and discard. Line up the beans, a small handful at a time, and cut into crosswise pieces about ½ inch long. Drop into the kettle of boiling salted water and boil rapidly, uncovered, for 5 to 6 minutes, or until just tender when you sample one. Drain, run cold water over the beans for 2 to 3 minutes, and drain again. (Refrigerate until ready to use.)

SERVING

Three minutes or so before serving, toss the beans briefly over moderately high heat in saucepan or skillet to evaporate moisture, then toss with butter and salt and pepper to taste. When thoroughly heated through, season with optional lemon juice, more butter, and the optional parsley. Serve immediately.

5) *Tapénade* (You can make this while the beans are boiling. Proportions are variable: as long as you have black olives, anchovies, and capers, the rest is up to you.)

½ cup dry "oil cured"	1 or more cloves peeled
Mediterranean or Greek	garlic
olives, pitted	¼ tsp each of ground bay
¼ cup drained capers in	and thyme
vinegar	½ Tb Dijon-type mustard
5 or more anchovy fillets in	Drops of cognac and lemon
olive oil	juice
⅓ cup canned tuna	Freshly ground pepper
	3 Tb minced parsley

Tapénade is traditionally made in a large marble mortar and all ingredients are pounded into a purée, but the electric blender works nicely too. Purée the pitted black olives, then add and purée the capers, anchovies, tuna, garlic, and herbs. Scrape into a bowl, season to taste with cognac, lemon juice, and pepper, and stir in the parsley.

SERVING

Optional for decoration: hard-boiled eggs, and
  lettuce leaves or water-   homemade mayonnaise
  cress, quartered tomatoes,

Serve in a bowl, or arrange on a small platter and decorate with lettuce or cress, tomatoes, eggs, and mayonnaise. *Tapénade* may also be used as a spread or dip for appetizers.

The Hundred and Twenty-second Show

OSSOBUCO

❧ · ☙

(*Braised Veal Shanks*)

Ossobuco sounds like an exotic dish, but it is actually just a particularly succulent brown veal stew of Italian origin. What makes it unusual is that it is made of veal shanks, and its pungent brown sauce is deliciously flavored with orange and lemon peel. Like all stews, you can get the cooking done way in advance, and it is easy on your budget. Served with rice, noodles or boiled potatoes, a fresh green vegetable or tossed salad, and a simple red wine or *rosé, ossobuco* is a perfect dish to delight your family or to have at an informal dinner.

THE VEAL. *Ossobuco* means marrow bone, or the hind shank of veal; that is, the marrow bone and surrounding meat of the back leg from below the knee to above the ankle. In French, this is called the *jarret de derrière*. Because some butchers include the shank as part of a roast leg of veal, you may have difficulty in finding hind shanks and will probably have to order them. A prime or large shank weighs about 2 pounds; you will need three to four for 4 people.

If you cannot get hind shanks, you may use foreshanks. The foreshank is larger and its bone is bigger in circumference; while its meat contains more separations and tendons than the hind shank, it is also more gelatinous, meaning it will give you a richer sauce. A prime foreshank usually includes the knuckle, and weighs around 4½ pounds; two will serve 4 people.

Have the shanks sawed into crosswise pieces 1½ to 2 inches thick; each piece will contain a round piece of marrow bone in the center. Cuts from the foreshank will not have as neat an appearance, and some pieces will have very little meat; simmer the meatless pieces and knuckles for 3 to 4 hours in water to cover, with onions, carrots, celery, and herbs, and use the resulting rich broth as a braising stock for the *ossobuco*.

OSSOBUCO

*(Veal Shanks Braised with Wine and Herbs
and Flavored with Lemon and Orange)*
For 4 people

BROWNING THE VEAL

3 to 4 veal hind shanks (6 to 8 lbs.), or 2 foreshanks (9 lbs. including knuckles), sawed into crosswise pieces 1½ to 2 inches thick
Salt and pepper
1 cup all-purpose flour

Olive oil or cooking oil
1 or 2 heavy skillets
A heavy casserole just large enough, if possible, to hold meat in one layer
½ cup each of sliced carrots and onions
A cover for the casserole

Lay the meat on a tray or a large sheet of waxed paper. Salt and pepper all sides, dredge in flour, and shake off excess. Pour a ⅛-inch layer of oil into the skillet or skillets and set over moderately high heat. When oil is almost smoking, brown the meat on all sides. (Do not crowd the meat or it will not brown properly; you may have to brown in several batches.)

While meat is browning, pour 2 tablespoons of oil into the casserole, stir in the sliced carrots and onions, cover, and cook over moderate heat for 5 to 6 minutes, until vegetables are tender.

ADDING THE BRAISING INGREDIENTS

1 cup dry white wine or ¾
cup dry white vermouth
About 2 cups excellent veal
stock, or half-and-half
canned chicken broth and
canned beef bouillon

2 to 3 firm, ripe red tomatoes
1 to 2 cloves garlic, crushed
1 tsp basil
1 orange
1 lemon

When the meat is brown, arrange it in the casserole with the cooked carrots and onions; the meat should fit in one layer, but this is not always possible, especially with foreshanks. Pour browning oil out of skillets and deglaze by pouring in the wine, setting over heat, and scraping coagulated juices into wine with a wooden spoon; pour the wine over the meat. Add stock, or broth and bouillon, to come halfway up the meat.

Drop the tomatoes for 10 seconds in boiling water, cut out stems, and peel. Cut tomatoes in half crosswise, squeeze out juice and seeds, chop the pulp roughly, and add to the casserole. Stir in the garlic and basil. Cut the colored part of the peel off the orange and lemon, then cut peel into very fine julienne strips ⅟₁₆ inch wide. To remove bitterness from peel, simmer for 10 minutes in 1 quart of water, drain, and add to casserole. (Recipe may be prepared ahead to this point; bring to simmer before proceeding.)

BRAISING

Cover the casserole and either simmer over low heat on top of the stove, or set in lower middle of a preheated 325-degree oven. (Oven is preferable because of its more even heat.) Maintain liquid at a slow simmer for about 1¼ hours (usually 1½ hours for foreshanks), or until meat is tender when pierced with a fork. Do not overcook; the meat should not fall from the bone.

FINISHING THE SAUCE

When meat is tender, remove it from the casserole to a side dish. Tip casserole and skim off cooking fat. Set casserole over high heat and boil down braising liquid rapidly to concentrate its flavor and to thicken it slightly; you should end up with about 2 cups. Taste carefully for seasoning, adding salt and pepper if necessary. If you are not serving immediately, return meat to casserole and set aside, uncovered. To reheat, cover and simmer for 3 or 4 minutes.

SERVING

Either serve from casserole or arrange the meat on a hot platter surrounded by rice, noodles, or boiled potatoes. Pour the sauce over the meat and decorate platter with parsley sprigs.

The Hundred and Twenty-third Show

BRAINS AND SWEETBREADS

ᵔᵏᵎᵎ · ᵎᵏᵔ

When you find you are in a menu quandary, and want a change from roasts, steaks, hamburgers, and fish, give sweetbreads and brains a try. They have a deliciously delicate quality, and can be served in a variety of ways. Though both are much the same in texture and taste, and the cooking processes are similar, brains are the more delicate of the two. Whether or not they have been soaked and cleaned before you buy them, brains and sweetbreads always need several hours of further soaking in cold water to whiten them before cooking, and as they are very perishable, you should prepare them as soon as possible.

CERVELLES
(Brains)

Calf's brains, cervelles de veau, are the best known to most people, but you can also use beef brains, which are larger, or lamb or pork brains, which are smaller. One pound of brains will serve 2 to 3 people. Calf's brains usually come in pairs; 1 set is an ample serving for 1 person. Brains must be handled carefully or they will fall apart.

SOAKING

Wash the brains in cold water, delicately pull away the thin membrane covering any dark spots, then place the brains in a large bowl of cold water. Change water several times, or set bowl under a dripping tap. In about an hour, delicately pull off as much more membrane as you easily can, being careful not to tear the flesh. Soak again for 1½ to 2 hours, this time in several changes of cold water containing 1 tablespoon each of vinegar and salt for each quart of water. Finally peel off as much more membrane as you can, trim off opaque white bits at base of the brains, and you are ready to cook them.

BLANCHING, OR PRELIMINARY COOKING

If brains are to be braised, they need not be blanched; you can also omit blanching if you plan to sauté or deep-fry them. Blanching firms the brains so they are easier to slice; it also preserves them for a day or two if you are not serving them immediately.

To blanch them, place the soaked and trimmed brains in an enameled or stainless-steel saucepan just large enough to hold them. Cover by 2 inches with boiling water and add 1½ teaspoons of salt and 1 tablespoon of lemon juice per quart of water. Heat to just below the simmer and maintain water at a not-quite-simmering temperature for 20 minutes (15 minutes for lamb and small pork brains; 30 minutes for beef brains). Let cool for 20 minutes in cooking liquid.

To firm them more and to make them easier to slice, drain the cooked brains and set on a plate; weight down with a heavy dinner plate for 2 hours or more in the refrigerator.

Cervelles au Beurre Noir
(*Sautéed Brains in Brown Butter Sauce*)
For 6 people as a main course

This delicious preparation is often served as a separate course, but if you wish it as a main course, accompany with parsley potatoes, buttered peas or spinach, and a light red Bordeaux, a *rosé*, or a white Burgundy wine.

2 lbs. brains, previously soaked, trimmed, and blanched	1 or 2 large skillets
	About 1 cup (½ lb.) melted butter
Salt and pepper	3 to 4 Tb drained capers
1 cup all-purpose flour	3 Tb minced fresh parsley

Cut the brains into slices ½ inch thick. Just before sautéing, season, roll in flour, shake off excess. Heat a ⅛-inch layer of clear melted butter in the skillet or skillets; when almost beginning to brown, add the brains in one layer and sauté for 2 to 3 minutes on each side, until nicely browned. Remove to a hot serving dish and immediately pour about ½ cup of clear melted butter into one skillet, being careful not to include the milky residue at bottom of butter pan; it burns and speckles. Set over high heat, swirling pan, until butter has browned lightly. Add the capers and parsley and swish over heat for a few seconds; pour over the brains and serve immediately.

RIS DE VEAU
(*Calf's Sweetbreads*)

A whole sweetbread, which is the thymus gland of a calf and usually weighs about 1 pound, consists of two lobes connected by a soft white tube. The smoother, rounder, and more solid of the lobes is the kernel, heart, or *noix*, and the choicest piece. The second lobe, called the throat or "gorge," is more uneven, broken by veins, and often slit. Your butcher has usually separated the lobes and discarded the tubes.

SOAKING AND TRIMMING

Wash, soak, and peel sweetbreads following directions for brains. Pull or cut off any bits of tube; trimmings may be saved for the stock pot.

BLANCHING

Blanching is optional, and sweetbreads are far better when braised. If you wish to blanch, follow directions for brains, but start the sweetbreads in cold water and cook at below the simmer for 15 minutes; drain immediately and plunge into cold water to firm them.

Ris de Veau Braisés

(*Braised Sweetbreads*)

For 6 people

Whether you are going to sauté sweetbreads, serve them hot in a sauce or cold in a salad, braising is the most succulent way to cook them.

4 Tb butter
A flameproof casserole just large enough to hold the sweetbreads in one layer
½ cup each of finely diced celery, onions, and carrots
Optional: ¼ cup diced ham
2 lbs. sweetbreads, previously soaked and trimmed

A medium herb bouquet: 4 sprigs parsley, ½ bay leaf, and ¼ tsp thyme tied in washed cheesecloth
Salt and pepper
¼ cup dry white vermouth
About 1 cup excellent meat or chicken stock or canned beef bouillon

(Preheat oven to 325 degrees.)

Melt butter in casserole, stir in diced vegetables and optional ham, cover casserole, and cook slowly for about 10 minutes, until vegetables are tender but not browned. Season sweetbreads with salt and pepper and arrange over vegetables, basting with juices in casserole. Bury the herb bouquet among the sweetbreads, cover casserole, and cook slowly 5 minutes; turn sweetbreads on other side, baste, cover, and cook 5 minutes more. (If more than ¼ cup of juice exudes in casserole, drain it out, boil down rapidly to 2 tablespoons, and pour back over the sweetbreads.)

Pour in wine and enough stock or bouillon barely to cover. Bring to the simmer, cover the casserole and bake in lower middle of preheated oven for 45 minutes. Let sweetbreads cool in cooking liquid until you are ready to use them; to reheat, cover and simmer a few minutes until hot through.

VARIATION ❧

Ris de Veau à la Crème
(Braised Sweetbreads in Cream)

Remove hot sweetbreads to a hot serving dish. Rapidly boil down cooking liquid until almost syrupy; pour in ⅔ to 1 cup heavy cream. Simmer a few minutes until lightly thickened, correct seasoning adding a bit of lemon juice if necessary. Pour sauce and its vegetables over sweetbreads, decorate with parsley, and serve accompanied by steamed rice, buttered peas or spinach, and a fine white Burgundy wine.

The Hundred and Twenty-fourth Show

ASPARAGUS FROM TIP TO BUTT
❧ • ❧
(Sauce Maltaise—Hollandaise with Orange)

A great platter of freshly cooked green asparagus is a splendid way to begin any meal, or makes a handsome interlude instead of the salad course. If you want to enjoy fresh asparagus to the full, buy it carefully, store it properly, and cook it the French way so that it is just tender, not limp, and retains all of its fresh color, texture, and taste.

CHOOSING ASPARAGUS. Pick spears that are firm, unwrinkled, bright green; the scales at the tips should lie flat and be tightly closed into a point; the moister the butt ends, the fresher the asparagus. If your market takes asparagus seriously, they will keep it cool, and stand the spears upright so the butts are on dampened absorbent paper or in half an inch of water. Fat spears are just as tender as thin ones; for 10-inch spears ¾ to 1 inch in diameter, count on at least 6 per person, 8 to 10 if the asparagus is to be a separate course.

STORING FRESH ASPARAGUS. If you are not preparing the asparagus immediately, shave ¼ to ½ inch off the butts, or until you reach the moist flesh. Set the asparagus upright in half an inch of water and cover loosely with a plastic bag, or wrap in dampened paper towels and plastic; refrigerate until you are ready to prepare the asparagus for cooking.

PREPARING FRESH ASPARAGUS FOR COOKING. The French method of cooking asparagus is to peel it, tie it in bundles, and plunge it into a very large kettle of rapidly boiling water. Peeled asparagus cooks more quickly than unpeeled asparagus, retains its maximum color and texture, and can be eaten all the way down to the butt. The object in peeling is not just to remove the skin, but to shave off enough of the tough outer part at the lower end so that the moist flesh is exposed, and the whole spear is tender from tip to butt. Peeling adds considerably to preparation time, but you will find the results spectacularly successful not only gastronomically but visually, as whole long spears are wonderfully dramatic on a platter.

Peeling. Although you may use a vegetable peeler or cheese slicer, a small very sharp paring knife is easiest to control. Hold an asparagus spear with its butt end up in the tips of your fingers, resting the spear against the palm of your hand. Shave across the butt until the flesh is moist, then start peeling down from the butt, going deep enough to expose the moist flesh and gradually making the cut shallower as you come to the tender green portion near the tip. Continue all around the asparagus. Run several inches of cold water in the sink, swish the peeled spears around for a moment, and drain.

Tying. Divide the asparagus into groups about 3½ inches in diameter. Leave one spear loose, for a cooking test later. Line up the tips of each group and make one tie with heavy, soft white string about 2 inches below the tips, and another tie about 2 inches from the butt ends. Cut off any protruding butts, to make all spears the same length. If you are not cooking immediately, wrap the bundles in damp paper towels and plastic, and refrigerate.

LES ASPERGES EN BRANCHES
(Whole Boiled Asparagus)

The French method for boiling fresh asparagus is to plunge it into a very large quantity of rapidly boiling water; the more water you have, the more rapidly will it come back again to the boil, sealing in the vegetable juices so the asparagus will retain its maximum color, texture, and taste.

4 to 6 bundles and 1 loose spear of peeled asparagus
A large kettle or oval casserole or roaster containing 7 to 8 quarts of rapidly boiling water

1½ tsp salt per quart of water
A serving platter with perforated inset, or lined with a folded white napkin to absorb the asparagus liquid

Lay the asparagus bundles and the loose spear in the rapidly boiling water; add the salt. When boil is reached again, in 3 to 4 minutes, boil slowly, uncovered, for 6 minutes or longer (depending on asparagus quality). Start testing after 5 to 6 minutes: a knife should pierce the butts easily. Insert a fork under each tie of string and lift a bundle: the spears should bend slightly—if they droop limply, you have overcooked. As a final test, eat the loose spear: it should be just tender, with the slightest suggestion of crunch.

As soon as the asparagus is done, lift out the bundles one by one with two forks: hold each up for a few seconds to drain, place carefully on the platter, cut and draw off the strings, and proceed quickly to the next bundle.

If you cannot serve the asparagus immediately, set the platter over the hot water and cover the asparagus with a folded napkin. The asparagus will soften somewhat as it waits, and exude some of its water; the sooner you can serve it, the better.

Sauce Maltaise
(*Orange-flavored Hollandaise for Asparagus and Broccoli*)
For about 1¼ cups serving 6 people

1 orange	1 lemon
A grater	¼ tsp salt
A 1½-quart stainless-steel	1 cup (¼ lb.) melted butter
or enameled saucepan	A Tb for adding the butter
3 egg yolks	A wet potholder for steady-
A wire whip	ing the pan

Grate the rind of the orange into the saucepan, add the 3 egg yolks and beat vigorously with your wire whip for about a minute, until yolks are thick and sticky. Squeeze the juices of the orange and lemon into a bowl; beat 2 tablespoons into the yolks along with the ¼ teaspoon of salt.

Set pan over moderate heat and beat with wire whip, reaching all over bottom of pan, until mixture gradually turns into a smooth cream which coats the wires of the whip—be careful not to heat the yolks too quickly or they will scramble.

Immediately remove from heat and beat in the butter by droplets at first (until sauce is very thick), then by teaspoons. Thin out, if necessary, with drops of orange and lemon juice; taste for seasoning. Keep over lukewarm water or on warm top of stove until ready to use.

Other Sauces for Hot Asparagus

Lemon juice and salt, for dieters
Melted butter or lemon butter
Mock *hollandaise,* or cream sauce with lemon flavoring
Plain *hollandaise,* or *hollandaise* with whipped cream or beaten egg whites
A mixture of bread crumbs sautéed in butter, chopped parsley, and chopped hard-boiled egg

The Hundred and Twenty-fifth Show

OPERATION CHICKEN
⊷⋅⊶

Take a fine fat roasting chicken, remove the breast works, and you have a boat-shaped cavity with leg and wing appendages. Mound a savory stuffing in the cavity, cover it with the breast meat, fold the skin over, and you have a rebuilt bird that cooks like any ordinary roaster but is easy to carve and serve and even more delicious to eat. This simple operation, though it is described here for chicken, may be performed in the same way on any poultry from chicken to turkey, from squab to duck.

POULARDE DEMI-DÉSOSSÉE
(Half-boned Chicken)
For 6 people

A 4- to 4½-lb. roasting chicken	A very sharp small knife
2½ to 3 cups of any appropriate stuffing	Heavy shears

PRELIMINARIES

Remove giblets: liver, heart, gizzard, neck pieces, fat. Cut the pointed elbow flaps off the two wings. Be sure fat glands have been removed: these are two yellowish lozenge-shaped fatty deposits under the skin at the back of the tail piece; they have a strong taste. Check chicken all over, pulling out any hairs, feathers, feather follicles. Cut off the neck, if necessary, so that it does not protrude beyond the shoulders. Remove the wishbone by slitting the flesh at either side of each prong, cutting through the flesh at the prong ends, then twisting the prongs to release the V-shaped tip of the wishbone at the top of the breast opening.

REMOVING THE BREAST MEAT

Place the chicken on its back. Slit the breast skin lengthwise from neck to tail. With your fingers, peel the skin away to expose the entire expanse of meat on each side of the breast down to the shoulders and second joints.

Starting on one side of the ridge of the breastbone, cut down its length to release the flesh on that side. Then scrape down against the carcass from one end of the bone to the other, pulling the flesh away with your fingers as you cut. Continue down the side of the bone and the rib cage until you have released the whole layer of white meat; detach it from the shoulder end where it joins the ball joint of the wing. Be careful not to slit the skin at the sides of the breast; it must remain intact when the chicken is re-formed. Remove the meat on the other side in the same manner.

You now have two boneless and skinless breast-meat pieces; these are called *suprêmes*. Each *suprême* is composed of two layers; the large piece is the *filet*, and the small layer underneath it is the *filet mignon*. On the underside of each *filet mignon* is a small white cord or tendon which is tough and should be removed: grasp the end of it in a towel, slit the flesh on either side, and scraping against it with your knife, gently pull the tendon out.

Cut the breast meat into lengthwise strips about ⅜ inch wide. Salt lightly and, if you wish, sprinkle with a few drops of cognac.

REMOVING THE BREASTBONE STRUCTURE

The breastbone structure consists of the ridged bone itself and the top ribs which are its continuation. The backward-slanting top ribs join the forward-slanting bottom ribs at an angle point midway down each side of the carcass. With heavy shears, cut between top and bottom ribs at this point the length of the carcass on each side. Cut through each end of the V-shaped bone at the neck end, and the breastbone is freed. You now have a breastless chicken with a boat-shaped cavity.

STUFFING THE CHICKEN

Salt   The 2 to 2½ cups stuffing
Optional: a few drops of   An 8- to 10-inch skewer or
  cognac   knitting needle

Salt the cavity lightly and, if you wish, sprinkle in a few drops
of cognac. Fill with the stuffing, building it into a dome at the
front end to simulate a full breast. Raise the legs upright, push
the knees against the armpits, and run a skewer through the carcass under the knees; this will hold the legs in place for the rest
of the operation. Lay the strips of breast meat lengthwise over
the stuffing to cover it completely. Fold the two flaps of breast
skin over the stuffing; the skin must completely enclose the
white meat with an overlap of about ¼ inch, thus you may have
to remove a bit of stuffing.

TRUSSING

An 8- to 10-inch trussing   with hole bored in one
  needle or topless pointed   end
  plastic knitting needle   White string

Thread the needle with the white string.

THE BREAST SKIN Starting at the tail end, but not going
through the tail piece, stitch a straight line up the breast skin
to the neck. Turn the chicken over and secure the neck skin to
the back, completely enclosing the stuffing at the neck end.
Leave about 4 inches of loose string at either end, for easy removal after cooking.

TRUSSING LEGS AND WINGS The legs and wings are to be attached to the body with one tie. Place chicken on its back and
fold wings akimbo, so tips are caught under shoulders. Remove
drumstick skewer and push threaded needle through carcass
under knee on one side; come out at corresponding point under
knee on other side. Turn chicken over and, on the same side as
you came out from under the knee, go through one wing, catch
a piece of the backbone at the neck, and come out through the
wing on the other side. You now have the two string-ends on the

same side, one at the wing and one at the knee; draw tightly, tie, and cut the string.

TRUSSING TAIL AND DRUMSTICKS   Draw threaded needle through the underside of the tail piece, then through the skin on tops of the drumstick ends. Draw tightly, tie, and cut the string. Drumstick ends and tail have now closed the vent opening, the stuffing is contained, and the chicken is trussed.

AHEAD-OF-TIME NOTES

If your chicken is fresh and your stuffing is cold, you may bone, stuff, and truss the chicken the day before cooking; pack in cracked ice and refrigerate, loosely covered. Drain, dry, and leave at room temperature for at least an hour before cooking, so that you may time accurately.

COOKING METHODS

Poularde demi-désossée may be cooked like any ordinary chicken—roasted, casserole-roasted, or poached.

The Hundred and Twenty-sixth Show

TO POACH A CHICKEN
⋇ᵇ • ᵇᵉ
(*Rice Stuffing, Albuféra*)

One of the most attractive French ways to do a whole roasting chicken is to poach it, which means to place it in a covered casserole with herbs, white wine, and chicken broth to come halfway up, then to let it cook quietly in the oven. The dark meat simmers, the white meat steams, and you end up with a wonderfully juicy bird plus a delicious cooking broth which you can turn into a sauce.

BUYING THE CHICKEN. You will need a true roaster chicken; this means a bird 5½ to 9 months old weighing 4 pounds or more ready-to-cook. If the chicken is too young its juvenile flesh may fall apart when cooked this way.

PREPARING THE CHICKEN FOR POACHING. You may poach the chicken stuffed or unstuffed, whole and trussed in the usual way, or partially boned as specified for the following recipe. To bone it, slit the breast skin lengthwise from neck to tail, remove the white meat and cut into ⅜-inch lengthwise strips; cut out the breastbone and upper half of the ribs, and mound the stuffing in the cavity, covering it with strips of breast meat; fold the skin over, sew it together, and truss the legs and wings to the body, enclosing the stuffing. (See preceding show.)

STUFFING. Use about ¾ cup of any appropriate stuffing for each pound of chicken. The following recipe is for a rice stuffing.

Farce Évocation Albuféra
(*Rice, Mushroom, and Chicken-Liver Stuffing*)
For about 3 cups

1 Tb butter
A small skillet or heavy
 saucepan
1 Tb minced shallots or
 scallions
1 cup quartered mushrooms,
 stewed or canned, and
 drained
1 or 2 chicken livers cut into
 ¼-inch dice

Salt and pepper
2 to 3 Tb Madeira or port
A mixing bowl
1½ cups previously boiled
 white rice (about ½ cup
 raw rice)
1 egg
¼ tsp oregano

Melt the butter, stir in the minced shallots or scallions, then the mushrooms and diced liver. Season lightly with salt and pepper, stirring and tossing; pour in the wine. Boil for about 2 minutes, or until wine has almost entirely evaporated. Scrape into the mixing bowl and stir in the rice. Beat the egg in a bowl with a fork; stir into the rice along with the oregano. Taste, and correct seasoning.

POULARDE DEMI-DÉSOSSÉE, ÉVOCATION ALBUFÉRA

(*Partially Boned Chicken Poached in White Wine; Rice, Mushroom, and Chicken-Liver Stuffing; Curried Sauce Suprême*)
For 6 people

POACHING THE CHICKEN

2 Tb butter

A heavy flameproof 6- to 8-quart casserole, preferably oval

½ cup each of sliced carrots, onions or leeks, and celery

1 Tb softened butter

3 or more cups clear chicken broth

½ tsp oregano

½ tsp salt

The chicken giblets (heart, gizzard, neck piece)

1 cup dry white wine or ¾ cup dry white vermouth

A 4½-lb. roaster chicken, partially boned, stuffed, trussed

A strip of fresh pork fat or suet, approximately 4x8x ⅛ inches

Waxed paper, size of casserole top

Casserole cover

(Preheat oven to 325 degrees.)

Melt the butter in the casserole, stir in the sliced vegetables, and cook slowly, covered, for about 8 minutes or until vegetables are tender but not brown.

Massage the tablespoon of softened butter into the chicken skin; place chicken breast up in casserole over the vegetables. Strew the giblets around the chicken; pour in the wine and enough chicken broth to come halfway up the chicken. Add the oregano. Sprinkle chicken with salt and lay the fat or suet over the breast and legs. Bring just to the simmer on top of the stove. Lay the waxed paper over the chicken, cover the casserole, and set in lower third of a preheated oven.

Liquid in casserole should barely simmer; if it really boils the chicken skin will burst—it should remain whole and handsome. Check cooking in about 20 minutes: liquid should be bubbling quietly. You will probably have to turn oven down to around 300 degrees. No basting is necessary.

Chicken should be done in about 1 hour and 45 minutes: the drumsticks are tender when pressed, they move in their sockets, and if you prick the flesh deeply with a fork, the juices run clear yellow with no trace of rosy color.

Remove chicken to a hot platter; cut and discard trussing strings.

THE SAUCE—SAUCE SUPRÊME AU CARI   (For about 2½ cups)

4 Tb butter	chicken-cooking broth,
1 tsp curry powder	degreased
5 Tb flour	Salt and pepper
About 2 cups hot strained	About ½ cup heavy cream

Melt the butter in a heavy-bottomed 2-quart saucepan over moderate heat; stir in the curry powder and cook for a moment, then stir in the flour. Cook for 2 minutes, stirring continually, then remove pan from heat. This is now a *roux*; when it has stopped bubbling, pour in 2 cups of the hot chicken-cooking broth and beat vigorously with a wire whip to blend. Simmer, stirring, for 2 minutes. Thin out with spoonfuls of cream; sauce should coat a spoon nicely—meaning it will cover the chicken with a decorative coating. Correct seasoning.

Pour several spoonfuls over the chicken to mask it attractively. Thin out the remaining sauce with spoonfuls of cream if it seems too thick, and pour into a warm sauceboat.

PRESENTATION AND SERVING

Decorate the platter with watercress or parsley sprigs. Accompany the chicken with buttered fresh peas, green beans, or asparagus tips, hot French bread, and a chilled full-bodied dry white wine, such as a Burgundy or Pinot Blanc.

CARVING

Remove the legs and wings in the usual manner. You may cut the breast in outward-slanting slices, and spoon out the stuffing; a neater method is to make a lengthwise cut down the middle of the breast, cut one slice from the center, then remove meat and stuffing with serving spoon and fork. Give each guest both dark- and white-meat slices and stuffing, and spoon some of the sauce over each serving.

The Hundred and Twenty-seventh Show

MOUSSES, BOMBES, AND PARFAITS
⊰ · ⊱
(*Walnut Pralin or Brittle*)

Frozen mousses, stately parfaits, and decorated molds of ice cream—you can make them all in your freezer or ice-tray compartment, and all three come from one basic mixture; what you serve it in determines the name of the frozen dessert. In French cooking there are two types of frozen mousses, one with sugar syrup and cream, and the other with custard and cream. This recipe is of the second type, and features a *pralin* of caramelized walnuts which is unusual, delicious, and useful to have on hand for decorating other desserts or for sprinkling on ice cream.

Pralin aux Noix

(Caramelized Walnuts, or Walnut Brittle)

For 2¾ cups

1⅓ cups granulated sugar	A heavy 2-quart saucepan
½ cup water	with cover
2 cups or 8 ounces shelled	A lightly buttered baking
walnuts (reserve 6 to 8	sheet
whole halves for decorations)	

Boil the sugar and water in the saucepan over high heat, swirling pan by handle gently as liquid begins bubbling, to be sure that sugar dissolves completely and liquid is perfectly clear. Then cover pan and boil rapidly for 2 minutes: condensing water on cover will wash sugar crystals down sides of pan. Uncover when syrup is thick; boil, swirling occasionally, until syrup gradually turns a nice caramel brown, a little darker than the walnut skins.

Immediately remove pan from heat and add the reserved walnut halves; rapidly dip them out one by one with a fork and place at one end of buttered baking sheet. If necessary, reheat caramel again to liquefy; remove from heat and pour in the rest of the walnuts, stirring with metal spoon to cover with caramel. Turn them out onto the baking sheet. (To clean the caramel pan, fill with water, add dipping fork and metal spoon; simmer 5 minutes to melt caramel, then wash as usual.)

POUNDING UP THE PRALIN

When caramel has hardened, in about 30 minutes, break up the mass into 1-inch pieces. Pound in a heavy bowl, about ½ cup at a time, or grind in an electric blender, flicking switch on and off rapidly. Do not grind the *pralin* too fine: some pieces should be almost ⅛ inch in diameter to give texture and interest.

STORING PRALIN

Store ground *pralin* in an airtight container; it keeps best in the freezer, where you can leave it for several months.

MOUSSE GLACÉE, PRALINÉE AUX NOIX, OU APPAREIL A BOMBE

(Basic Mixture for Frozen Mousses, Bombes, and Parfaits)
For 4 to 5 cups serving 8 to 10

You will note that the mousse is beaten until thick, heavy, and thoroughly chilled before freezing. Although you can beat by hand, it is infinitely easier by machine; choose a bowl, preferably of stainless steel, which will fit surrounded by ice in the large bowl of your mixer.

A 2-quart bowl which will fit into large bowl of an electric mixer
4 egg yolks
½ cup milk
A wide saucepan containing 2 inches almost-simmering water
2 cups ground *pralin* (see previous recipe)

An electric mixer with large bowl to hold ice
1 to 2 trays ice cubes
¼ cup salt
1 cup heavy cream, chilled
¾ cup additional ground *pralin* (you may reserve 3 Tb for decorations)
3 Tb kirsch or light rum, or 1 Tb vanilla extract

Beat the egg yolks in the bowl for a moment or two until pale, thick, and sticky, then beat in the milk and set in pan of almost-simmering water over moderately low heat. Beat slowly for several minutes until mixture gradually thickens enough to coat the spoon with a creamy layer; indications of thickening are that the surface foam begins to subside, a slight steam vapor rises, and the mixture is very hot to your finger. Do not over-heat and scramble the yolks, but you must thicken them.

Remove from heat and beat a few seconds to stop the cooking, then beat in the 2 cups of *pralin*. Continue beating for several minutes to dissolve part of the caramel and sweeten the custard. Fill large bowl with ice, salt, and enough water to cover ice cubes; set custard bowl into the ice and beat until mixture is thoroughly chilled and forms a thick ribbon when a bit is dropped from beater back onto surface. This will take 4 to 5 minutes.

Add the chilled cream and beat until mixture again forms a thick ribbon and holds its shape softly in a spoon. Do not overbeat, or the cream will turn into butter. Beat in the kirsch, rum, or vanilla extract, and the additional ¾ cup of *pralin* which does not melt in the chilled mousse, but retains its texture. The mousse is now ready for freezing.

FREEZING TALK. The mousse must be frozen at zero degrees or less, or it will not take properly; sufficiently frozen, it will hold its shape, and will cut like cream cheese. Two to 4 hours are sufficient for individual servings or parfaits; you will need at least 6 hours for large bowls or an ice-cream mold—overnight to be on the safe side. You may hold a mousse at zero degrees for several weeks at least.

SERVING SUGGESTIONS

MOUSSE GLACÉE   Pile the chilled mousse into a decorative bowl or into individual serving dishes; cover with plastic wrap and freeze. Decorate with caramelized walnuts or ground *pralin*.

SOUFFLÉ GLACÉ   Pin a double strip of foil or waxed paper around a soufflé dish, making a collar which sticks 1 inch above the rim and all around. Pile the chilled mousse into dish, letting mousse rise about ½ inch up the collar. Lay waxed paper or foil over the top, and freeze at least 6 hours. Remove collar just before serving; decorate with caramelized walnuts or *pralin*.

PARFAITS   Fill parfait glasses or stemmed wineglasses to within ¼ inch of top. Cover each glass with foil or plastic wrap and freeze 2 to 3 hours. Decorate each with whipped cream swirls and/or a caramelized walnut.

BOMBE GLACÉE OR ICE-CREAM MOLD   Allow 1 quart of vanilla ice cream to soften just enough so that you can spread it around the inside of a chilled 2-quart metal mold or bowl; cover and freeze for 30 minutes or until hardened. Fill with chilled mousse and freeze at least 6 hours or overnight. To unmold, run a knife around inside rim, hold mold for several seconds in a basin of cold water, and unmold on a chilled serving dish. Decorate with caramelized walnuts and/or ground *pralin*. If not served immediately, cover with a bowl and keep in freezer.

The Hundred and Twenty-eighth Show

BOURRIDE AND AÏOLI
❧ • ☙
(*Provençal Fish Stew; Garlic Mayonnaise*)

Here is a marvelous fish dinner from Provence, an unusual fish stew called the *bourride*. This ancient recipe goes back more than two thousand years, and it is said the Phoenicians used to sup upon it when they stopped by the port of Marseille in their wanderings about the Mediterranean. The *bourride* is big chunks of fish cooked in a pungent broth; the fish is served on a platter and the broth is enriched with a thick garlic mayonnaise called *aïoli*. It is such a fulsome dish that you need serve nothing else for the meal except a sturdy dry white wine, a green salad, and fresh fruit.

CHOICE OF FISH. You need lean, white, firm-fleshed fish for this stew, as the fish should hold its shape during cooking. A combination of two or three different kinds will make for more interesting texture and flavor . . . and be sure your fish smells deliciously fresh and appetizing.

On the Mediterranean, one uses fish native to those waters, such as *baudroie* (goose or angler fish), *loup* (Mediterranean bass), *merlan* (whiting or silver hake), *congre* or *fiélas* (conger eel).

Among American choices are hake, cod, cusk, halibut, whiting or silver hake, ocean perch, sea trout or weakfish, conger eel, monk or goosefish (*Lophius americanus*), ocean whitefish, catfish or wolf fish (*Anarhichas lupus*). Scallops, though hardly Mediterranean, are excellent in a *bourride*.

Cut the fish into fillets or into steaks 1 to 1½ inches thick, and then into serving chunks 2½ to 3 inches in diameter. The skin and bones may be left on or removed, whichever you wish. Leave scallops whole. Count on about ½ pound of trimmed fish per person.

If you have bones and trimmings, cover them with cold water, simmer 40 minutes, strain, and use this fish stock in your cooking broth; it will make your *bourride* even better.

BOURRIDE
(*Provençal Fish Stew with Garlic Mayonnaise*)
For 6 people

THE FISH

3 to 4 lbs. assorted lean, firm-fleshed white fish cut	into 3-inch chunks 1 to 1½ inches thick

Prepare, wash, and refrigerate the fish until you are ready to cook it.

THE VEGETABLES FOR THE COOKING BROTH

1 large onion	3 Tb strong olive oil
1 medium carrot	A 7- to 8-quart flameproof
1 large leek, or another onion	casserole or a heavy-bottomed kettle

Peel and slice the onion and carrot. Cut off the root, quarter the leek lengthwise, then wash thoroughly under running water and slice. Pour the oil into the casserole, add the sliced vegetables, cover, and cook over low heat for 8 to 10 minutes, or until vegetables are tender but not browned.

COMPLETING THE COOKING BROTH

1 to 2 tomatoes	1 cup dry white wine or dry
3 quarts fish stock or water	white vermouth

1 bay leaf
¼ tsp thyme
2 cloves garlic, halved
¼ tsp fennel seeds or
　flowers

2-inch strips dried orange
　peel or ¼ tsp bottled
　orange peel
2 pinches saffron flowers
1½ Tb salt

Chop the tomato roughly, add to the vegetables, and cook 2 minutes. Then add the liquids and flavorings. Simmer 10 to 15 minutes to blend flavors; correct seasoning. (May be prepared in advance.)

THE AÏOLI, OR GARLIC MAYONNAISE

⅓ cup stale white bread
　crumbs
1 to 2 Tb wine vinegar or
　cooking broth
A heavy 2½-quart mixing
　bowl or mortar
A rounded wooden pestle,
　masher, or heavy ladle
　(for pounding)
4 to 8 cloves garlic

A garlic press
¼ tsp salt
2 egg yolks
1½ to 2 cups strong olive oil
Wine vinegar
A large wire whip
White pepper or cayenne
　pepper
4 additional egg yolks

Moisten the bread crumbs with vinegar or cooking broth in the mixing bowl and pound to a dampish paste. Add the garlic and pound for several minutes until garlic and bread make an absolutely smooth purée. Then add the salt and 2 egg yolks; pound and stir for a minute or two until very sticky.

By droplets, start pounding and stirring in the olive oil; when sauce is very thick and heavy, thin out with drops of vinegar. Then beat in the oil by teaspoon additions, using a wire whip. Sauce should be thicker and heavier than ordinary mayonnaise, and should hold its shape in a spoon. Season to taste with salt and pepper.

Scrape half the sauce into a serving bowl and set aside for the dining room. Beat the 4 additional yolks into the remaining *aïoli*; this is to be combined with the soup later. (May be prepared in advance.)

COOKING THE FISH

The cooking broth	A soup tureen
The prepared fish	A small serving bowl
A warm serving platter and	The *aïoli* with egg yolks
cover	A large sieve, ladle, wire
2 Tb minced fresh parsley	whip, and wooden spoon

About 15 minutes before serving, bring the cooking broth to a rolling boil and add the prepared fish. If necessary, add boiling water to cover the fish. Boil slowly, uncovered, for about 10 minutes; fish is done when it feels firm rather than squashy—do not overcook. As soon as the fish is done, arrange it on the platter and decorate with parsley; cover and set in a warming oven, on a hotplate, or over a pan of hot water.

Strain cooking broth into tureen and correct seasoning. Reserve a cupful in the small serving bowl. Then, beating the *aïoli* in the mixing bowl with a wire whip, dribble on several ladlesful of hot broth. Pour back into casserole, pour in the remaining broth, and stir with a wooden spoon over moderate heat until soup slowly thickens enough to coat the spoon—4 to 5 minutes—and do not let the soup come to the simmer and scramble the egg yolks. Pour the soup into the tureen and you are ready to serve.

SERVING

For each serving place 2 slices of French bread, ¾ inch thick, in a wide soup plate. Moisten bread with a spoonful of the reserved broth, arrange chunks of fish over the bread, and ladle on the soup. Each guest adds a spoonful of *aïoli* sauce, and eats the *bourride* with soup spoon and fork.

The Hundred and Twenty-ninth Show

TO POACH AN EGG
◈ • ◈
(*Spinach Soufflé Florentine*)

The egg is one of our most protean ovoids, gastronomically speaking, and a poached egg is the most versatile of its forms. The French, who never eat an egg for breakfast, dress a poached egg in aspic, pose it in a tartlet shell, decorate it with sauces and garnitures, or tuck it into a soufflé and serve it proudly as a hot first course or the mainstay for a light meal.

EGGS FOR POACHING. Poached in the French manner the egg is dropped from its shell into a pan of barely simmering water where it sits quietly for 4 minutes, until the white is set but the yolk remains liquid. The perfect specimen is a graceful free-form oval; the white masks the yolk completely. To achieve this attractive result, you must have very fresh eggs. To tell if an egg is fresh, break one into a saucer: the yolk stands high and the white clings to it, only a small amount of watery liquid falls away from the main body of the white. A stale egg cannot be poached in the free-form manner because its relaxed and watery white trails off in the poaching liquid, leaving the yolk exposed. Therefore, test an egg from your supply before you poach them this way.

OEUFS POCHÉS
(*How to Poach Eggs in the French Manner*)

White vinegar	containing 2 inches sim-
A wide saucepan or skillet	mering water
8 to 10 inches in diameter,	Very fresh eggs

PRELIMINARIES

Vinegar helps the egg white to coagulate around the yolk; add 1 tablespoon for each quart of simmering water. Add no salt, as salt tends to have the opposite effect. Again, to help the white coagulate and to achieve an oval shape, place the whole eggs, two at a time, in the simmering water for 8 to 10 seconds and then remove them.

POACHING

A slotted spoon   A kitchen timer
A wooden or rubber spatula

Break one of the eggs on the side of the pan, giving it a sharp crack for a clean break. Holding it as closely over the surface of the water as possible, open the shell wide and let the egg fall in. If white does not closely surround yolk, immediately rotate the egg gently against the side of the pan with your spatula. Set timer for 3½ minutes—you will probably have spent 30 seconds fussing with the egg, and each should poach 4 minutes. Continue with 3 more eggs in the same manner, breaking them around the edge of the pan clockwise. Throughout the poaching, maintain water at barest simmer.

REMOVING AND KEEPING

A large bowl of cold water   A clean, folded towel

When timer goes off remove first egg and place it in the bowl of cold water; this stops the cooking and washes off the vinegar. Remove rest of eggs as they are done, and poach others in the same water if you are doing more. If you are not using the eggs immediately, set the uncovered bowl in the refrigerator where the eggs will keep perfectly for 2 to 3 days. If you wish to serve them hot, drain the eggs and place for about a minute in very hot salted water to heat through without overcooking. Remove one at a time with a slotted spoon, and drain by rolling back and forth over folded towel.

Oeufs Pochés en Soufflé à la Florentine

(*Soufflé of Poached Eggs on a Bed of Creamed Spinach*)

For 6 people

Who would expect to cut into the puff of an innocently fragrant cheese soufflé and find a warm soft poached egg on a bed of spinach? That's drama, and it is even more intriguing because the soufflé is baked on a flat dish.

THE CREAMED SPINACH

1½ Tb butter	1½ cups previously cooked
A heavy-bottomed stainless-	spinach, squeezed dry,
steel or enameled sauce-	and chopped
pan	1 Tb flour
1 Tb minced shallots or	Salt, pepper, and nutmeg
scallions	About 1 cup heavy cream

Melt the butter in the saucepan, stir in the shallots or scallions, then the spinach. Stir to impregnate spinach with butter, then sprinkle in the flour, stirring and cooking slowly for 2 minutes over moderate heat. Add salt and pepper to taste, and a pinch of nutmeg. Stir in half the cream, cover pan, and cook slowly stirring frequently for 5 to 6 minutes or until spinach is tender; add more cream by spoonfuls if spinach is becoming too thick. It should hold in a mass in a spoon. Correct seasoning.

BAKING AND SERVING—Baking time: 25 minutes

The creamed spinach	¼ cup all-purpose flour
6 *croûtons* (3-inch rounds	(measure by dipping ¼-
of white bread previously	cup dry measure into flour
sautéed in clear melted	and leveling off with a
butter)	knife)
A lightly buttered fireproof	A heavy 3-quart saucepan
serving dish	¾ to 1 cup milk
6 previously poached eggs,	Salt, pepper, and nutmeg
cold (see preceding rec-	4 egg yolks
ipe)	

5 egg whites (⅔ cup) at
   room temperature
A pinch of salt
¼ tsp cream of tartar

½ cup coarsely grated Swiss
   cheese (save 2 Tb for
   decoration)

(Preheat oven to 375 degrees.)

Mound 2 to 3 spoonfuls of creamed spinach on each *croûton*, arrange on serving dish, and top each with a poached egg.

Place the flour in saucepan and gradually beat in ¾ cup of the milk with a wire whip. Beat over high heat until sauce thickens and comes to the boil. It should be very thick but not stiff: thin out if necessary with spoonfuls of milk. Beat in the 4 egg yolks, and salt, pepper, and nutmeg to taste.

Beat the egg whites slowly in a clean dry bowl until they begin to foam, then beat in the salt and cream of tartar (no tartar is necessary if you are using an unlined copper bowl). Gradually increase speed until stiff peaks are formed.

Stir one fourth of the egg whites into the sauce base; delicately fold in the rest along with three fourths of the grated cheese. Mound soufflé mixture over each egg and top with a big pinch of the reserved grated cheese. Set immediately in upper third of preheated oven and bake for about 25 minutes, until soufflé has puffed and browned.

Serve at once; if soufflé waits in oven the poached eggs will overcook. Accompany, if you wish, with a light *hollandaise* sauce, French bread, and a dry white wine of medium strength, such as a Pouilly Fumé or Fuissé, or Traminer, or a *rosé*.

The Hundred and Thirtieth Show

ROAST LEG OF LAMB

◄ঃ • ঃ►

(Boned, Stuffed, with Mustard Coating)

One of the greatest pleasures of life is having a roast of meat carved at the table, but it takes an expert to deal with a whole leg of lamb in public. After the first few slices he runs into the big leg bone, and then he has to struggle with that complex knife-stopper, the hip. But if these offending structures are removed before the lamb is roasted, anyone can carve like an expert. In the following recipe, only the shank bone is left in the lamb, a stuffing replaces the leg bone, and the meat is roasted with an herbal mustard coating.

BONING THE LAMB. Ask your butcher to remove the fell (outside membrane) and all fat from a whole 6½-pound leg of lamb. He will willingly remove the hip and tail assembly at the large end of the meat, but may balk at taking out the leg bone (knee to hip) from inside the meat. If you have to do this yourself, locate the ball-jointed end of the leg bone buried in the thick end of the meat. Cut around it to loosen the flesh, then scrape the flesh away down the length of the bone until you come to its opposite ball joint inside the meat at the knee. Now comes the most difficult part of the operation: releasing the bone from the tendons attaching it to the knee or shank. Being very careful not to pierce through the knee flesh, as you want no holes in the main body of the roast, cut all around the ball joint from inside the meat. As you gradually free the joint you can begin to twist the bone, get your knife through the tendons, and pull the bone out.

The meat that formerly surrounded the hip bone at the

large end is called the sirloin; it forms two flaps. Leave the thin straggly flap on the meat; it will help hold in your stuffing. Cut off the thick side; reserve the best part to cook as a steak at another meal, and grind the rest (about 8 ounces or 1 cup) for your stuffing.

Lamb and Rosemary Stuffing
For 1½ to 2 cups

¾ cup fresh bread crumbs
A mixing bowl
2 to 3 Tb milk
2 Tb minced shallots or
    scallions
2 Tb butter
1 cup (8 ounces) lean raw

lamb ground with ¼ cup
    (2 ounces) pork fat or
    suet
1 clove mashed garlic
¼ tsp ground rosemary
¼ tsp salt
A big pinch of pepper

Place bread crumbs in a mixing bowl and moisten with the milk, squashing into a paste with a rubber spatula. Sauté shallots or scallions for a moment in butter to soften. Press crumbs with spatula and pour out any excess liquid. Beat in the sautéed shallots and the rest of the ingredients.

Herb and Mustard Coating for Roast Lamb
For about 1 cup

½ tsp ground rosemary
1 clove mashed garlic
1 Tb soy sauce

½ cup strong Dijon-type
    prepared mustard
4 Tb olive or cooking oil

Mix rosemary, garlic, soy sauce, and mustard in a small bowl with a wire whip, then beat in the oil by droplets to make a thick mayonnaise-like sauce.

GIGOT FARCI, RÔTI A LA MOUTARDE
(Partially Boned and Stuffed Leg of Lamb Roasted
with a Mustard Coating)
For 8 people

Timing Note: The lamb will take about 1½ hours to roast, and needs 20 minutes out of the oven before carving. To be on

the safe side, put the roast in the oven 2½ hours before you
intend to serve.

STUFFING AND SKEWERING THE LAMB

A 6½-lb. whole leg of lamb
trimmed and boned as
described (makes about
4 lbs.)
1½ cups lamb and rosemary

stuffing (see preceding
recipe)
3-inch skewers
White string

Locate the hole in the large end of the meat from which
the leg bone was removed; push the stuffing down into it. (Note
location of thickest part of solid meat, for later insertion of meat
thermometer.) If outside skin has been pierced through at the
knee, close with a skewer. Skewer meat at large end to hold in
the stuffing, and lace with string.

MUSTARD COATING AND FINAL MANEUVERS

A roasting pan with rack
1 cup herb and mustard
coating (see preceding
recipe)

A meat thermometer
Pan vegetables: ½ cup each
of sliced carrots and
onions and 2 cloves garlic

Lay lamb on rack in roasting pan, with its less presentable
side up; paint this side with mustard coating, turn lamb, and
paint coating over the rest of the lamb. Reserve 2 to 3 tablespoons of the mustard mixture to flavor your sauce after roasting. Insert meat thermometer, its point reaching the thickest
part of solid meat. Strew the pan vegetables around the meat.
(May be done hours in advance and refrigerated, but for accurate timing leave lamb out at room temperature for at least 2
hours before roasting.)

ROASTING THE LAMB

(Preheat oven to 350 degrees.)
Roast lamb in lower middle level of oven for about 1 hour
and 30 minutes, or to a meat thermometer reading of 140 degrees for medium rare, pink and juicy. No basting or turning are
necessary. A sure indication of medium rare is that meat juices

just begin to fall into the pan; if you prick the meat with a fork, the juices run rosy red.

Immediately remove lamb from oven and place on a hot platter; remove skewers and string, but leave thermometer in until just before serving. Let rest at room temperature for 20 minutes before carving; this allows juices to retreat back into tissues and assures juicy slices of meat.

You can hold the roast perfectly for an hour or more as follows: turn off oven and open door, to cool oven; in 20 minutes, reset to 120 degrees, return lamb to oven, and close oven door. (Or regulate oven by turning it on and off at intervals, but never let oven temperature go over 120 degrees.)

SAUCE

2 cups brown lamb stock or beef bouillon	2 to 3 Tb reserved mustard coating

Spoon fat out of roasting pan. Pour in stock or bouillon and boil rapidly for several minutes, scraping up coagulated juices and mashing vegetables into liquid with a wooden spoon. Remove from heat, stir in reserved mustard, and strain sauce into a warm bowl.

CARVING AND SERVING

Carve from the large end, making several bias slices first on half of one side, then on the other; when you reach the thinner portion near the shank, you may cut straight across. Serve each guest both meat and stuffing, basted with a spoonful of the sauce. An attractive accompaniment is a mixture of green beans and white beans, broiled tomatoes, and a medium full red wine such as a Bordeaux-Saint-Emilion or Côtes-du-Rhône.

The Hundred and Thirty-first Show

LOBSTER THERMIDOR

᠂᠊ᢄᡐ᠂ᢄᡐ᠊

Lobster Thermidor was allegedly created on January 24, 1894, Chez Maire, a Paris restaurant on Les Grands Boulevards, to celebrate the opening of Victorien Sardou's play *Thermidor*. The play survived only its first night, but the recipe has continued to make the lobster famous. Diced cooked lobster meat warmed in butter and wine, folded into a rich sauce, then piled back into the shells, lobster Thermidor is a delicious and sumptuous dish. You may use any size of lobster from the 1-pounder, for modest servings, up to a 7½-pound giant, which will do nicely for six. You may also adapt the recipe for canned or frozen cooked lobster meat, which you can serve in individual shells or a baking dish.

TO REMOVE THE MEAT FROM A BOILED LOBSTER. The object here is to keep the whole hard top of the shell intact so that you can use it as a baking dish; sharp-pointed lobster or kitchen shears are your best tools. Turn the lobster on its back, its legs in the air. Cut off claw joints and legs close to the body. Starting at the tail end, cut around the under part of the shell where it attaches itself to the top shell at each side; lift up under-shell from tail end, and cut straight across where it joins the chest. Lift up tail meat from tail end, and being careful not to detach the tail and chest parts of the hard shell, gently pull tail meat out from chest cavity.

The chest structure is lightly attached to the hard shell near the tail joint; cut it loose, then lift it at right angles toward the head until the whole structure breaks free from the chest shell.

Lodged at the head end of the shell is the greenish stomach

sack, about ¾ inch long and ½ inch in diameter; remove and discard it. Also in the shell is a soft green mass known as the tomalley. If it tastes as it should, deliciously fresh and richly lobstery, scoop it out into a sieve set over a bowl; add any pink coral that you may find in the shell or attached to the tail meat; add also any coagulated white matter clinging to the shell. Push this all through the sieve with a wooden spoon, and reserve for later enrichment of your *sauce Thermidor*.

To remove claw meat, slowly bend the lower and smaller section of the claw at right angles and backward to break it off, drawing out at the same time the cartilage lodged in the meat of the large claw section. Dig the meat out of the small claw part; cut around the lower sides of the large claw shell, and draw out the meat. Cut the claw joints at each side and remove meat. Reserve legs for stock or decoration.

The chest contains very little meat, but what is there is delicious. To get at it, pull off and discard the gills, soft feathery strands attached to either side of the structure. Break the chest in half lengthwise and dig out the small bits of meat between the cartilaginous interstices.

Slit the tail meat lengthwise down the center of its outward curve. Spread the flesh apart to expose the intestinal tube; remove and discard the tube. Cut the tail meat in half lengthwise, then into ½-inch pieces.

Set all the meat aside in a bowl. Arrange the hard top-shells in a baking dish or broiling pan. Reserve shell trimmings and debris for lobster stock.

Lobster Stock
For about 1 cup

The lobster shell trimmings and debris	1 cup dry white wine or ¾ cup dry white vermouth
A stainless-steel or enameled pan	1 bay leaf
⅓ cup each of chopped celery, onions, and carrots	6 sprigs parsley
	½ tsp dried tarragon

To make the best possible *sauce Thermidor*, you will need

a white-wine fish stock, made from the lobster-shell discards. Chop the shell debris into 2-inch pieces and place in pan. Add the vegetables, wine, herbs, and water to cover. Boil slowly for 40 minutes, strain, then boil down until liquid has reduced to about 1 cup.

HOMARD THERMIDOR
(*Lobster Thermidor*)
For 4 people

4 boiled lobsters, about 1½ lbs. each
3 Tb butter
A large heavy-bottomed enameled or stainless-steel skillet
2 Tb minced shallots or scallions
¼ tsp dried tarragon
Salt and white pepper
¼ cup cognac

½ lb. fresh mushrooms, trimmed, washed, and quartered (about 2 cups)
A medium-sized enameled or stainless-steel saucepan and a cover
1 Tb lemon juice
¼ tsp salt
3 Tb water
1 Tb butter

Remove the lobster meat as described in the introductory section; you will have 5 to 6 cups. Melt the butter in skillet; stir in the shallots or scallions, then the lobster meat. Cook over moderately high heat, folding gently with a spatula or spoon, until the lobster meat turns pinkish—3 to 4 minutes. Season lightly with salt and white pepper, sprinkle on the tarragon, and pour in the cognac. Boil slowly, uncovered, for several minutes until liquid has almost entirely evaporated.

Toss the mushrooms in the saucepan with the lemon juice, salt, and water. Add the butter, cover the pan, and simmer 5 to 6 minutes. Strain juices into lobster stock (next step); add mushrooms to lobster meat.

THE SAUCE THERMIDOR AND SERVING

4 Tb butter
A 1½-quart heavy-bottomed enameled or stainless-steel saucepan
A wooden spoon

¼ cup regular all-purpose flour (measure by scooping dry measure into flour and leveling off)

2 cups hot liquid: the preceding lobster stock and
mushroom juice plus milk
Optional but desirable: the
sieved lobster tomalley
2 egg yolks
1 Tb dry mustard
Big pinch of cayenne pepper

or several drops hot
pepper sauce
¼ to ½ cup heavy cream
Salt, white pepper, and
lemon juice as necessary
¼ cup grated Parmesan
cheese
2 Tb melted butter

Melt the butter in the saucepan, stir in the flour with a wooden spoon and cook slowly without coloring for 2 minutes. Remove from heat, let cool for a moment, then pour in the hot liquid and blend vigorously with a wire whip. Bring to the boil, stirring; simmer and stir for 1 minute. Remove from heat.

Beat the egg yolks, mustard, cayenne or pepper sauce, and ¼ cup of cream together with the optional tomalley. Gradually beat in half of the hot sauce; pour the mixture back into the remaining sauce in the pan. Set over moderately high heat and stir with a wooden spoon, reaching all over bottom of pan, until sauce comes to the boil. Boil and stir for 1 minute. Sauce should coat a spoon quite heavily; thin out with additional spoonfuls of cream if necessary. Correct seasoning.

Fold two thirds of the sauce into the lobster and mushrooms and spoon into the lobster shells. Spoon the remaining sauce over the lobster; spread on the grated cheese and sprinkle with melted butter. Refrigerate if not to be baked at this point.

About 20 minutes before serving, place in upper third of a preheated 425-degree oven and bake until lobster is bubbling and cheese has browned nicely. Serve as soon as possible, accompanied with hot French bread and an excellent white Burgundy or Graves.

Lobster Thermidor is a rich dish and is best as a separate course. You could precede it with a clear soup, follow it with a salad, cold artichokes, or asparagus, and end the meal with a fruit dessert.

The Hundred and Thirty-second Show

SPEAKING OF TONGUES
꣬ ꣬

Speaking of delicious, dressy, but inexpensive meat dishes, don't neglect beef tongue. Half the price of beef itself, it's all solid meat. While plain boiled fresh tongue is on the dull side, tongue braised in an aromatic sauce smells, looks, and tastes so good you need have no hesitation at all in serving it to company. And as it is one of those nice recipes that can be prepared even a day or two in advance, it is a treasure to add to your repertory.

TONGUE TALK. You may buy beef tongue fresh, pickled, or smoked. We are concerned here with fresh tongue. Best-quality beef tongues weigh 3½ to 5 pounds fully trimmed. Trimming means that the pound or more of extraneous matter attached to the underneath and to the large end of the tongue has been removed. Except for the nubbly skin covering, which will be peeled off after cooking, and a few bits underneath, the trimmed tongue is solid eating meat. Fresh tongue is perishable; give it the attention it needs within a day of bringing it home.

Soaking. To freshen the tongue, to dissolve any clinging saliva, and to remove all blood, first scrub the tongue with a vegetable brush under warm running water, then let it soak for 2 to 3 hours in a sinkful of cold water. Drain.

Optional Salting. To improve flavor and tenderness as well as to preserve the tongue for several days, you can salt it. To do so, choose an enameled bowl or oval casserole, spread a ¼-inch layer of coarse (Kosher) salt in the bottom, lay the tongue over the salt, and spread a layer of salt all over it. Place waxed paper on top, and a plate and a 5-pound weight (meat grinder parts, for instance). Refrigerate for at least overnight; 2 to 3 days preferably. Wash off the salt when you are ready to cook the tongue.

Frozen Fresh Beef Tongue. Remove wrapper and thaw the tongue in a sinkful of cold water. Trim as necessary, and follow the preceding directions.

LANGUE DE BOEUF BRAISÉE AU MADÈRE

(Fresh Beef Tongue Braised in Madeira Sauce)
For 6 to 8 people

In most classical French recipes, the tongue is boiled for 2 hours, or until two thirds cooked, then it is peeled, trimmed, and braised whole. In this recipe it is boiled and peeled but is sliced before braising—this makes serving much easier, and the braising sauce penetrates the sliced meat far more succulently.

BOILING THE TONGUE

A fully trimmed fresh beef   A large kettle
tongue weighing 3½ to
4 lbs.

Prepare the tongue for cooking as described in the introductory section. Place the tongue in the kettle, cover by 5 inches with water, and bring to the slow boil. Skim off grayish scum for several minutes, until it ceases to rise. If you have not salted the tongue, add to the kettle 1½ teaspoons salt for each quart of water. Boil slowly for 2 hours, uncovered or partially covered. The tongue is now about two thirds cooked and still quite firm. (Note that the resulting tongue-cooking water will have little flavor; you may use the liquid as a base for boiled dinner or meat stock, or if you already have one of these in process, the tongue could have cooked along with it.)

PEELING

Remove tongue from kettle and plunge for a moment in cold water. As soon as it is cool enough to handle, slit the skin all around the top edge and peel the top surface of the tongue using your fingers, and a knife if necessary. The skin will come quite easily off the top; underneath you will have to slit the skin in lengthwise strips and remove it with a knife. Trim fatty parts and loose meaty bits off the thick part of the tongue underneath, and remove any bones lodged in the flesh at the large end.

SLICING

The object here is to make slices about ⅜ inch thick and as uniform in diameter as possible; if you manage to slice up the whole tongue from one end to the other and have no too large and no too small pieces, you have won. The plan of attack is to cut several vertical slices at the thick end, and then begin to slice on a bias, slanting toward the thick end as you come off the hump, slanting more and more until your knife is almost horizontal with the cutting board as you reach the tip.

THE MADEIRA SAUCE

2 Tb butter
A heavy-bottomed 2-quart saucepan
½ cup each of finely diced carrots, onions, and celery
¼ cup finely diced boiled ham
3 cups brown beef stock or canned beef bouillon

1 Tb tomato paste
½ tsp thyme
1 bay leaf
2 Tb powdered arrowroot (if not available at your grocery, try a pharmacy)
¼ cup dry Sercial Madeira or a dry sherry
Salt and pepper

Melt the butter in the saucepan, stir in the diced vegetables and ham, cover the pan, and cook slowly for about 10 minutes, stirring occasionally, until vegetables are tender and very lightly browned. Add the stock or bouillon, tomato paste, thyme, and bay leaf; simmer 30 minutes, then remove from heat. Stir the arrowroot in a small bowl, adding enough wine to make a smooth paste; stir in the rest of the wine, then beat the mixture into the hot liquid. Bring to the simmer for about 2 minutes, until sauce has thickened and cleared. Carefully correct seasoning. (May be done in advance; set aside or refrigerate until ready to use.)

BRAISING THE TONGUE

A heavy-bottomed 10- to   casserole, or electric
12-inch chicken fryer,   skillet

Arrange the sliced tongue in the casserole or skillet, pour on
the sauce with its vegetables, cover, and simmer slowly for 30
to 40 minutes, or until tongue can be pierced easily with a
fork. (May be braised in advance, and reheated just before
serving.)

SERVING SUGGESTIONS

Lightly butter a hot serving platter and mound hot mashed
potatoes or buttered noodles in the center. Arrange upright
slices of tongue against the mound and spoon a bit of the
sauce over each slice. Surround the tongue with braised carrots
and onions, or with buttered green peas. Pour the rest of the
sauce into a warm gravy bowl. Accompany with hot French
bread and a red Bordeaux wine.

The Hundred and Thirty-third Show

PIPÉRADE FOR LUNCH
◆§ • §◆
(*Strawberry Sherbet; Cooky Cups*)

MENU:

Omelette Pipérade   (Open-faced Omelette with Basque Garnish)
A Salad of Tossed Greens, or Cold Vegetables Vinaigrette
French Bread   Rosé Wine
Mousse de Fraises en Coupelles
(Strawberry Sherbet Served in Cooky Cups)

Here is an attractive but informal menu for lunch or supper, most of which you can prepare days in advance. The dessert is stored in the freezer, the *pipérade* garnish can be refrigerated, and on the day of the event you have only the salad to fix, a few strawberries to hull for decoration, and the omelette to make. Let us start with the dessert and work backward, with no recipe at all for the salad.

COUPELLES EN PÂTE A LANGUES DE CHAT
(*Cooky Cups*)
For 8 cooky cups 3½ inches in diameter

This rapidly made "cat's tongue" cooky batter is spread in 5- to 6-inch circles, baked, then pressed while still hot and pliable into a teacup so that each cooky crisps into shape.

PRELIMINARIES AND BATTER

½ stick (2 ounces) softened butter
2 baking sheets approximately 14x18 inches in diameter
⅓ cup granulated sugar
The grated rind of 1 lemon
¼ cup egg whites
A mixing bowl
⅓ cup regular all-purpose flour (measure by scooping dry-measure cup into flour; level off with straight-edged knife)

(Preheat oven to 425 degrees.)
Lightly butter the 2 baking sheets; dust with flour and knock off excess. Mark 4 circles about 5½ inches in diameter on each sheet, using a saucer or other round object. Lightly oil 2 large teacups or small bowls about 4 inches in diameter at the top, 2 inches at the bottom, and 2½ inches deep. Provide yourself with a flexible-blade spatula for removing cookies from baking sheet.

Beat the butter, sugar, and lemon rind in a mixing bowl with a wooden spoon, or in an electric mixer. When pale and fluffy, pour in the egg whites and mix just enough to blend. Place the flour in a sifter or sieve, gradually stir it in. Place a tablespoon of the batter in the center of each circle on one of the baking sheets; spread out to a thickness of about $\frac{1}{16}$ inch with the back of a spoon, or with a spatula. (Form cookies on second sheet while first is baking.)

BAKING AND MOLDING

Bake in middle level of preheated oven for about 5 minutes, or until cookies have browned lightly to within about an inch of the center. Set baking sheet on open oven door; immediately remove a cooky with blade spatula and turn upside down over one of the oiled teacups, pressing cooky into cup with your fingers. Press another cooky into second cup. Remove first cooky, which will have crisped into shape, and proceed in the same manner with third and fourth cookies. Close oven door and wait until temperature has again reached 425 degrees before baking second sheet. (Note that you must work quickly; if cookies cool, you cannot mold them.)

STORING

Cookies will stay crisp for several days in an airtight container unless weather is humid; if you wish to keep them longer, or if weather is damp, freeze them.

MOUSSE GLACÉE AUX FRAISES
(Fresh Strawberry Sherbet)
For about 1½ quarts

You can make this deliciously fresh sherbet right in your freezer or ice-cube compartment. Made of sieved fruit, sugar, lemon juice, and a bit of egg white, it needs just a short beating after it has begun to set, and that is all there is to it.

THE MIXTURE

2 quarts fresh strawberries, or 4 ten-ounce packages frozen strawberries, thawed and drained, and no sugar
A mixing bowl

1½ cups "instant superfine" sugar
¼ cup lemon juice
2 egg whites
Optional: 1 cup chilled heavy cream

Hull and wash the strawberries; purée through a food mill or sieve set over a mixing bowl. Add the sugar and lemon juice; beat for a minute or two until sugar has completely dissolved—you can feel no granules on your tongue. Beat the egg whites in a separate bowl until they form soft peaks, then beat into the strawberry purée—egg whites discourage large ice crystals from forming.

FREEZING

Set freezer to zero degrees, or ice compartment to coldest temperature. Cover and freeze for several hours or until purée has almost set. Beat vigorously with a wire whip for several minutes to break up ice crystals and to lighten the texture; if you want cream, add it at this point and beat just enough so that the mixture holds its shape in a spoon. Cover and return to freezer until sherbet has fully set. (*Note:* First freezing takes 4 to 5 hours; if it has hardened too much for beating, let it thaw until softened; second freezing takes 3 to 4 hours or leave overnight. If you wish to speed things up, freeze in a shallow pan or in ice-cube trays.)

SERVING

Serve the sherbet in a decorative bowl, individual dishes, or cooky cups. Decorate with whole or sliced strawberries.

OMELETTE PIPÉRADE
(Open-faced Omelette Garnished with Tomatoes,
Peppers, Onions, and Ham)
For 4 to 6 people

THE PIPÉRADE MIXTURE

Olive oil or cooking oil	1 small clove of garlic
1 to 2 cups each of thinly sliced onions and bell peppers	4 medium-sized tomatoes, peeled and juiced, pulp cut into ¼-inch strips
An enameled or no-stick skillet with cover	Salt and pepper
	¼ tsp dried basil or oregano

4 to 6 strips boiled ham ¼
inch thick, 2 by 4 inches
in diameter

Cook the sliced onions and peppers in oil in covered skillet for 8 to 10 minutes, or until tender but not browned. Purée the garlic and stir into the vegetables, lay the tomato strips over, and season with salt, pepper, and herbs. Cover and cook slowly 5 minutes; uncover, raise heat, and cook, shaking pan occasionally, until juices have almost entirely evaporated. Set aside or refrigerate. Brown ham strips lightly in oil in a separate pan; set aside.

COOKING THE OMELETTE

8 to 10 eggs
¼ tsp salt
Big pinch pepper
2 Tb oil or butter

2 Tb chopped fresh parsley
An 11- to 12-inch shallow
flameproof serving dish or
fancy skillet

Reheat *pipérade* mixture and ham. Beat the eggs, salt, and pepper in a bowl until thoroughly mixed. Heat butter or oil in serving dish or skillet. When hot, pour in the eggs and stir rapidly with a large fork until eggs have just set into a creamy mass. Remove from heat and spread over them the hot *pipérade*, scumbling a bit of it delicately into the eggs. Lay the ham over the *pipérade*, sprinkle with parsley, and serve immediately.

The Hundred and Thirty-fourth Show

TURBAN OF SOLE

◆ · ◆

(Fish Mousse)

TURBAN DE FILETS DE SOLE
(Mousse Baked in a Ring of Fish Fillets)
For a 7- to 8-cup mold serving 6 to 8 people

This is a ring mold lined with fillets of sole, then filled with a delicate fish mousse; when baked and unmolded, the fillets form a handsome crown on the serving platter. Sauced and decorated to suit your mood and your menu, this can be the fish course for an elaborate dinner, or the main course for a luncheon. Although it appears complicated, this dish is relatively quick to assemble and can be made ready for the oven several hours before baking.

WHITE-WINE FISH STOCK

3 to 4 cups or more of fish
  trimmings (heads, bones,
  skin of the sole fillets; or
  2 cups sole, whiting, or
  halibut meat)
1 cup dry white vermouth
1 sliced onion

1 sliced carrot
8 to 10 parsley stems
½ bay leaf
½ tsp salt
An enameled or stainless-
  steel saucepan

Place all ingredients in saucepan and add cold water to cover. Bring to simmer, skim, and simmer uncovered for 40 minutes. Strain, then boil down rapidly until you have 1½ cups. Measure out ½ cup and set aside for fish mousse; continue boiling down remainder until you have ½ cup, which will be used in final sauce.

FISH MOUSSE

The reserved ½ cup fish
stock
½ cup water
4 Tb butter
1 tsp salt
A heavy-bottomed enameled
or stainless-steel saucepan

¾ cup all-purpose flour (to
measure, dip dry-measure
cup into flour sack and
level off excess with
straight-edged knife)
2 eggs and 2 egg whites
(U. S. graded "large")

Bring the fish stock, water, butter, and salt to the boil in saucepan. As soon as butter has melted, remove pan from heat and pour in all the flour at once. Beat vigorously with a wooden spoon to blend, then beat over moderate heat for a minute or two with a wooden spoon until mixture leaves sides of pan and begins to film bottom of pan. Remove from heat, make a well in the center with your spoon, and break in 1 egg; beat vigorously to blend. Repeat with the second egg, then 1 egg white, and finally the last egg white. This is now a *panade*. Let cool, or chill.

¾ lb. (1¾ cups) skinless
and boneless sole, whit-
ing, or halibut
A large mixing bowl

Salt, white pepper, and
nutmeg
½ to ⅔ cup chilled heavy
cream

Put the fish through the finest blade of your meat grinder and pack into a 2-cup measure; you should have about 1½ cups of purée. Place in large mixing bowl and measure out 1½ cups (or an equal amount) of *panade*. Beat vigorously together for several minutes until mixture has enough body to hold its shape in a spoon. Beat in seasonings to taste, then start beating in the cream by spoonfuls. Beat well after each addition, being sure mixture still holds its shape in a mass.

FILLING THE MOLD

1 Tb butter
A 7- to 8-cup ring mold

8 or more skinless and boneless sole fillets
Salt and white pepper

(Preheat oven to 375 degrees for next step.)

Butter the inside of the mold. Season fish fillets lightly with salt and white pepper, and score the less presentable sides (those which were next to the skin); this keeps fillets in shape during baking. Lay the fillets crosswise, scored side up, in the mold, like the spokes of a wheel. Pack the mousse mixture into the mold, filling it to about ¼ inch of the top. Fold dangling ends of fillets on top of the mousse. (If not to be baked immediately, cover with buttered waxed paper and refrigerate.)

BAKING

(About 1 hour; make the sauce while the mousse is in the oven.)

Set mold in a pan of boiling water, pour boiling water around outside of mold to come ⅔ the way up, and place in lower third of preheated oven. Bake for about an hour, or until mousse has swelled about ¼ inch over the top of the mold. (If not served immediately, keep in hot water in turned-off oven; mousse will sink slightly as it cools. Drain out accumulated liquid before unmolding.)

SAUCE SUPRÊME   (For about 2½ cups)

4 Tb butter	¾ cup heavy cream
A heavy-bottomed enameled	Optional for color: 1 Tb
or stainless-steel saucepan	tomato paste
5 Tb flour	Salt, white pepper, and
1¼ cups hot milk	lemon juice
The second ½ cup fish stock	4 to 8 Tb butter

Heat butter in saucepan; blend in flour and cook slowly, stirring with a wooden spoon, for 2 minutes without browning. Remove from heat and let cool a moment, then pour in all the hot milk at once, beating vigorously with a wire whip to blend. Beat in the fish stock, half the cream, and the optional tomato paste. Boil, stirring, for 1 minute. (If made ahead, clean off sides of pan with a rubber scraper and float 2 tablespoons of cream on top of sauce to prevent a skin from forming; reheat to simmer before proceeding.) Slowly simmering sauce, thin out with more cream added by spoonfuls; sauce should be thick enough to coat a spoon fairly heavily. Season carefully with salt, pepper, and lemon juice. Remove from heat just before serving, and beat in the enrichment butter by spoonfuls. (Do not reheat after butter has been added or sauce will thin out.)

SERVING

Unmold mousse onto a hot, buttered serving dish; fill center with creamed shellfish or mushrooms, or buttered asparagus tips or broccoli. Spoon a bit of the sauce over the mousse and send rest to table in a hot sauceboat. A rather full-bodied white wine would go best with this dish—a Burgundy or Graves.

Index

About the Author

Julia Child fell in love with France and French cooking literally after the first bite, and as soon as her husband Paul Child was assigned to the American embassy in Paris, she enrolled in the Cordon Bleu. Through mutual friends Julia met Simone Beck, who introduced her to Louisette Bertholle. The three women eventually opened their own cooking school in Paris, L'Ecole des Trois Gourmandes — the school of the three hearty eaters.

Mastering the Art of French Cooking, Volume I, by Child, Beck, and Bertholle was published in 1961 and transformed the way Americans cook. Also in 1961, Paul and Julia settled in Cambridge, Massachusetts. Julia was invited to appear on the WGBH program "I've Been Reading," and during the interview she made an omelet and beat up egg whites in her large copper bowl with her large balloon whip. WGBH then suggested a cooking series, and on February 11, 1963, Julia Child and "The French Chef" went on the air. Her cooking shows have been aired and repeated ever since.

Additional television series with Julia Child include "Julia Child & Company," "Julia Child & More Company," "Dinner at Julia's," "Cooking with Master Chefs," "In Julia's Kitchen with Master Chefs," and "Baking with Julia." She has published numerous books as well, including *Mastering the Art of French Cooking,* Volume II (with Simone Beck), *From Julia Child's Kitchen, Julia Child's Menu Cookbook,* and *The Way to Cook,* among others.

Julia Child is very committed not only to the furthering of gastronomy as a recognized discipline, but to the encouragement of young people to enter the profession. To this end she is a sponsor of the International Culinary Fellowship administered by the Boston Foundation. She is also a member of the International Association of Cooking Professionals, the Women's Culinary Guild of Boston, the Culinary Historians of Boston, the James Beard Foundation, and the Chefs Association of Santa Barbara County. She is also a founder and honorary chairman, with Robert Mondavi, of the American Institute of Wine and Food. She lives in Cambridge, Massachusetts.